23

Robert Emmet
A Life

Robert Emmet
A Life

Patrick M. Geoghegan

Gill & Macmillan

Gill & Macmillan Ltd
Hume Avenue
Park West
Dublin 12
with associated companies throughout the world
www.gillmacmillan.ie

© Patrick M. Geoghegan, 2002
0 7171 3387 7
Index compiled by Helen Litton
Design and print origination by Carole Lynch
Printed by MPG Books Ltd, Cornwall

*The paper used in this book comes from the wood pulp of
managed forests. For every tree felled, at least one tree
is planted, thereby renewing natural resources.*

A catalogue record is available for this book
from the British Library.

1 3 5 4 2

Frontispiece
*James's Street, Thomas Street and the surrounding districts: from
John Rocque's map of Dublin (1756)*

Contents

List of illustrations

A pencil sketch of Robert Emmet made in 1802 (courtesy of the National Library of Ireland, not yet catalogued).

The west front of Trinity College in the late eighteenth century (courtesy of the National Library of Ireland, library ref. no. PD 3181 TX 49).

A nineteenth-century remembrance of the patriots of 1798, showing Wolfe Tone in the centre and Emmet at top left. The others shown (in clockwise order) are Michael Dwyer, Lord Edward Fitzgerald, Henry Joy McCracken and James Napper Tandy (courtesy of the National Library of Ireland, library ref. no. PD HP (1798) 1).

The long room of Trinity College Library as it was in Emmet's day. The ceiling shown here was replaced in the mid nineteenth century by the more dramatic barrel vault that one can see today (courtesy of the National Library of Ireland, library ref. no. PD 3818 TX 55).

Thomas Addis Emmet (courtesy of the National Gallery of Ireland, catalogue no. 211).

A nineteenth-century view of the Upper Castle Yard in Dublin Castle (courtesy of the National Library of Ireland, library ref. no. 1963 (TX) 25(B)).

John Philpot Curran (courtesy of the National Library of Ireland, library ref. no. 2115 (TX) 79).

College Green showing Daly's Club, left foreground, the Parliament House, left background, the statue of King William III in the centre and the front of Trinity College in the background (courtesy of the National Library of Ireland, library ref. no. 452 TB).

A view of the Wicklow Hills, where Emmet and his small band of followers fled after the failed rebellion in a desperate attempt to elude capture (courtesy of the National Library of Ireland, library ref. no. 2091 (TX) 34).

Peter Burrowes (1753–1841), Counsel for Robert Emmet at his trial and friend of Thomas Addis Emmet (courtesy of the National Library of Ireland, library ref. no. BURR-PE (1) EP).

Robert Emmet in the dock (courtesy of the National Library of Ireland, library ref. no. 3002 (TX).

Illustration from a broadside showing Emmet speaking at his trial (courtesy of the National Library of Ireland, library ref. no. 2129 TX 9).

A highly stylised nineteenth-century view of Emmet's speech (courtesy of the National Library of Ireland, library ref. no. EP EMME-RO (19) IV).

Robert Emmet's execution (courtesy of the National Library of Ireland, library ref. no. PD HP (1803) 4).

Preface

In the pantheon of Irish national heroes Robert Emmet occupies a central place. Although his life was short and his attempt to lead a rebellion was unsuccessful, he none the less managed to achieve in death a victory which transcended the failure of his rebellion on the night of 23 July 1803. From the unravelling of his conspiracy came the weaving of a powerful nationalist myth which elevated him to the first rank of Irish patriots. His youthful idealism became an inspiration to future generations and the romance and tragedy of his life created an enduring legend in which he was honoured as a noble martyr in the cause of Ireland. This was recognised by W. B. Yeats in a famous address in New York in 1904, when he noted that 'Ireland has placed him foremost among her saints of nationality' and 'honours him most, of all those who have laid down their lives to serve her.'[1]

Contributing to the deification of Emmet was the brilliance of his speech from the dock, which is considered to be one of the greatest courtroom orations in history. This speech was rewritten, revised and reimagined in the years after its delivery until finally there was no consensus about what had actually been said. Even the famous last words have been disputed as scholars challenged the authenticity of Emmet's poignant plea for his epitaph to remain unwritten until Ireland has taken her place among the nations of the earth. But the controversy has failed to shake the essential truth of his life and it is this which captured the popular imagination and became engraved on the national consciousness. The story of Robert Emmet has all the ingredients of a tragic myth: a young hero attempting to free his country, a failed rebellion, a doomed romance, a defiant courtroom performance and the courageous spirit with which he faced death on the scaffold. It was a story that lent itself well to myth-making, containing many of the archetypes identified by Joseph Campbell in his seminal study, *The hero with a thousand faces*.[2] There was the hero as warrior, the hero as lover, the hero as redeemer, and finally the hero as saint. Even Emmet's remarkable bravery at the scaffold contributed, for as Campbell noted,

> The last act in the biography of the hero is that of the death or departure. Here the whole sense of his life is epitomised. Needless to say, the hero would be no hero if death held for him any terror: the first condition is reconciliation to the grave.[3]

By attempting to lead a rebellion and, ironically, by failing, Emmet had performed the modern hero-task. He had chosen not to be guided by society but to do precisely the reverse. 'The supreme ideal' of a modern hero lies not in 'the bright moments of his tribe's victories, but in the silence of his personal despair.'[4]

Three years after Robert's death, his brother Thomas Addis Emmet reflected from New York on whether he would ever return to Ireland. He confessed to Peter Burrowes, his friend who had defended Robert in court, that he could not bear 'to tread on Irish ground' and walk over 'the graves of my nearest relatives and dearest friends'.[5] Nor did he have any desire to see his children return to his homeland and he admitted that he would prefer to see his estates pass into the hands of his 'greatest enemy' rather than have his eldest son travel to Ireland to sell it. Embittered by the suffering which his family had endured over the previous eight years, he closed the letter with the poignant comment: 'There is not now in Ireland an individual that bears the name of Emmet — I do not wish that there ever should, while it is connected with England.' However, he ended with a cautious prediction about the family name which proved to be prophetic: 'and yet it will perhaps be remembered in its history'.

When writing his masterful biography of Robert Emmet in the mid-nineteenth century Richard R. Madden observed: 'There have been among the United Irishmen persons of greater intellectual powers than Robert Emmet — better qualified, certainly, to carry into successful execution very great designs.'[6] But Madden was perhaps a little harsh. There was a genius to Emmet and he displayed it in his spectacular oratory, his precocious insights into military strategy and weaponry and his astonishing inspirational powers. His tragedy was that it was a flawed genius and his youthful idealism was unable to compensate for his failings as a leader in the field of battle and his sometimes spectacular lapses of judgment. Yeats was correct when he made his throwaway comment that Emmet 'had indeed mastered everything but human nature'.[7] Perhaps in time he would have matured into a successful revolutionary leader — after all he was only twenty-five when he died — but his capture and execution brought an end to his dreams of liberating Ireland. The character of Robert Emmet was more complex and less quixotic than some of his supporters have claimed. The challenge for his biographer is to separate the myth from the reality. This difficulty was recognised by Madden when he warned:

> It is no part of the duty of the biographer of Robert Emmet to set him forth as a hero of romance, or a man of a matured judgement and master mind, in whose great intellectual powers, duly developed, were reunited all the vigorous qualities that are essential to the character of an individual capable of concocting, guiding, and achieving a revolution.[8]

Rather, Madden recognised: 'It is the duty of the biographer of Robert Emmet to set him forth in his true proportions, to abstain from all exaggeration of them, to represent the man fairly, as one like Robert Emmet would desire to be dealt with.'

Unfortunately for Emmet his true character was obscured in the nineteenth and twentieth centuries as zealous defenders of his reputation attempted to deify his life. Hagiographers sacrificed the complexity for a more simple interpretation which was at once easier to grasp but also far less compelling than the truth. Emmet's childhood friend, the poet Thomas Moore, contributed to the mythologising with his romantic verses on the death of Sarah Curran, 'She is far from the land'. Cleverly circumventing Emmet's request for his epitaph to remain unwritten, he also wrote emotionally charged verses about the uninscribed tomb of his friend:

Oh! breathe not his name, let it sleep in the shade,
Where cold and unhonour'd his relics are laid.

As Norman Vance has correctly identified, the name of Emmet had been 'absorbed into and slightly irradiated by unvoiced national sentiment'.[9] His body became holy 'relics' as befitted a saint and he himself had been transfigured into a martyr awaiting resurrection. Moore referred to 'the night-dew that falls', employing the biblical idiom of dew as a 'symbol and instrument of divine grace and renewal for God's people'. Emmet had become the successor and representative of all the heroes of 1798 and Vance recognised that 'by extension he could become the type of all Irish national heroes'.

With deliberate intent Emmet's life was recast in the nineteenth century in explicit Christian iconography. The unreliable testimony of Brother Luke Cullen, who claimed to have accurate transcripts of conversations provided by Anne Devlin, was rich in religious imagery which contributed to the deification of Emmet. This was done for a particular agenda and continued the process which Moore had begun of retelling his story with added Christ-like resonances. The gospel story of the disciple's three denials was reworked with Anne Devlin as a resolute St Peter and Robert Emmet as both tempter and saviour. Similarly, when reviewing Madden's ground-breaking work on the United Irishmen, the *Nation*, the newspaper of the Young Ireland movement, declared that 'The history of every land is a history of its great men, or of its revolutions . . . the biographies of the former are the narratives of the latter.'[10] Reflecting on the attempt to unite all Irishmen and win independence between 1798 and 1803, it concluded that this 'grandest effort' had Wolfe Tone as its soul and Robert Emmet as its epitaph.

A year after the centenary of Robert Emmet's death, W. B. Yeats delivered his lecture at the Academy of Music in Brooklyn, New York. John Devoy's newspaper, the *Gaelic American*, reported that it was attended by 4,000 people, 'the cream of the Irish race', who were packed into the hall despite the heavy rain that had fallen all day.[11] Among this number were three direct descendants of Thomas Addis Emmet, the son of John Mitchel and O'Donovan Rossa. Yeats spoke a little unwillingly, masking the private doubts and ambiguities he harboured, but the spirited lecture nevertheless offered many important insights into Emmet's character.[12] The speech was later published in the *Gaelic American* with the grandiloquent title of 'Emmet the apostle of Irish liberty'. Yeats discussed the criticisms of Emmet and ably refuted the charge that he was nothing more than 'a wild, hair-brained, vain young man'.[13] Employing the methodology of the Roman Catholic Church, he investigated the 'curious ceremony which precedes the canonisation of a saint'. This enabled him to explain how Emmet was now the leading 'saint of [Irish] nationality' whose picture hangs 'in thousands of Irish cottages beside the picture of St Patrick and the picture of the Mother of God'.[14]

The most important Irish revolutionary figure of the twentieth century, Patrick Pearse, delivered an even more powerful address at another Emmet commemoration, also at the Academy of Music in New York on 2 March 1914. In a fervent evangelical oration Pearse began by declaring that he was commemorating 'heroic faith and the splendour of death'.[15] Patriotism, he insisted, was 'at once a faith and a service'.[16] Reflecting on Emmet's life and the nature of heroism, he revealed his belief that,

> There are in every generation those who shrink from the ultimate sacrifice, but there are [also] in every generation those who make it with joy and laughter, and these are the salt of the generations, the heroes who stand midway between God and men.

At this time Yeats was highly suspicious of Pearse's character and motives and is reported to have dismissed him as 'half-cracked and wanting to be hanged'. He believed that Pearse had 'Emmet delusions same as other lunatics think they are Napoleon or God'.[17] There was some truth in this. Profoundly moved by Emmet's final sacrifice which seemed to exemplify so well his own eschatology, Pearse admitted that 'No failure, judged as the world judges these things, was ever more complete, more pathetic than Emmet's.' But, he explained, despite this failure Emmet 'has left us a prouder memory than the memory of Brian [Boru] victorious at Clontarf or of Owen Roe victorious at Benburb. It is the memory of a sacrifice Christ-like in its perfection.'[18] As Pearse moved inexorably towards his own martyrdom in 1916, he drew much comfort from Emmet's life and was reassured by the belief that he had achieved redemption for Ireland through his death. For him Emmet 'redeemed Ireland from acquiescence in the union. His attempt was not a failure, but a triumph for that deathless thing we call Irish nationality.'[19] Critical of the Dublin populace for standing by and watching Emmet's execution, Pearse promised that the capital would 'one day wash out in blood the shameful memory of that quiescence'. Emmet had been elevated from the first 'saint of Irish nationality' into a position as the saviour of Ireland whose death had opened the way for eventual freedom and independence. Through his speech from the dock, 'the most memorable words ever uttered by an Irish man', and his courageous acceptance of death, it was clear to Pearse that 'This man was faithful even unto the ignominy of the gallows, dying that his people might live, even as Christ died.' The deification of Emmet was complete.

Napoleon Bonaparte, whose military genius reshaped the European continent in the early nineteenth century, believed that to understand a man you had to know what was happening in the world when he was twenty. When Emmet turned twenty he was about to be expelled from Trinity College for his involvement in the United Irishmen on the eve of the 1798 Rebellion, an event which would transform Irish society and change dramatically the political structures of the country. Emmet would soon embark on his career as a committed revolutionary and within a few years would meet with Napoleon in Paris to discuss the future of Ireland. It is interesting that while Napoleon admired Emmet's youthful determination, he for his part had little time for the French general. He rejected the neo-imperialism of the French state and was repelled by its treatment of smaller countries in Europe. Given the traditional partnership between the United Irishmen and France this may seem surprising, but Emmet's idealistic nature was intolerant of any injustice and he was not prepared to purchase Irish freedom at the cost of fundamental principles. The genesis of Emmet's ideals came from the United States and he was profoundly influenced by the example of the American War of Independence. He studied it carefully from an early age and fixed his dreams on the images of the colonists fighting successfully against British rule. It was Emmet's intention to become an Irish George Washington, and while he was prepared to accept aid from France, it was on the explicit condition that Ireland's independence would never be compromised by French interference.

This study draws on new research from archives in Ireland, the United States, France and the United Kingdom. But, as significantly, it is a re-interpretation of Emmet's life based on a re-evaluation of material already known. It is perhaps tempting to suggest that Robert Emmet does not deserve a biography of this length. His life ended early and in apparent failure. He left no journal of his beliefs or ideas. He gave his name to a rebellion which degenerated into a drunken riot, little deserving of the name, and which he himself abandoned in disgust. And yet he became the symbol of Irish resistance to British rule and an inspiration to men like Patrick Pearse, who revered and venerated him over a century later. This was not just because of the mythologising which had taken place. The legend which was created reflected much of the truth of his life. Robert Emmet possessed extraordinary abilities: as a speaker, as a military theorist and as an innovative revolutionary. Even his most serious weakness, his over-eagerness to trust others, was a direct result of the absence of any artifice or cynicism in his character. W. B. Yeats would suggest in one of his greatest poems that Emmet had been affected by the 'delirium of the brave'. But perhaps it would be closer to the truth to suggest that he had been moved by a genuine love of his country to plan a daring attempt to win Irish independence, which was ingenious in its design and utterly disastrous in its execution. Defeated and demoralised, he won an unlikely victory in his final days through his spellbinding oratory and his courageous display of idealism, tolerance and heroism. Instead of being the liberator of his country, it was his destiny to become the spirit of it.

Acknowledgments

Robert Emmet is not only one of the founding fathers of the Irish Republic but also one of its favourite sons. I would like to thank Fergal Tobin of Gill & Macmillan for suggesting writing this biography, at a time when I was searching for a follow-up to my book on the Irish Act of Union. Initially reluctant, I soon came to realise that Emmet's short but eventful life demands a modern re-examination.

My first experience with Emmet, many years ago, did not end well. I was fourteen years old and speaking in a schools' semi-final proposing the motion 'That this house believes that Emmet's epitaph should now be written.' Appropriately enough the debate took place in the Edmund Burke Theatre of the College Historical Society in Trinity College Dublin, but of course the significance was lost on me. Sadly, I was unable to match my subject in youthful eloquence and lost the debate. I took no interest in Robert Emmet after that.

This book would not have been possible but for the help and support of a number of people. First, I would like to thank the various libraries and archives visited for their assistance and permission to quote from their papers. My thanks therefore to the directors and staff of the Manuscripts Department of Trinity College Dublin, the Royal Irish Academy, the National Library of Ireland, the National Archives of Ireland, the Public Record Office of Northern Ireland, the New York Public Library, the New York Historical Society, the Massachusetts Historical Society, the British Library, the Public Record Office (London), Cambridge University Library, the Archives Nationales, and the Ministère des Affairs Étrangères (Paris).

Nor would this have been possible but for the support of my family. I would like to record my debt of gratitude to my mother (who once again deserves much of the praise), my sister Rosena, my brother Tomás, my sister-in-law Jennifer and my Aunt Ro. But this book is also for all my relations and especially the Geoghegan, Londra, Colgan, Halpin, Lynskey, O'Connell and Mercogliano families. While researching in the United States I benefited enormously from the hospitality of my relatives, and for that I would like to thank Marge Halpin, Moira and Rory O'Connell, and my favourite football-loving cousins, Adrian and Benjamin. Because of them I discovered a new folder of Thomas Addis Emmet letters. I would also like to thank Mrs Mary Connellan for her continued support throughout the years, Fr Gerry Hipwell O. Carm. who was an excellent history teacher, and the late Fr David Conaghan for many things.

I worked on the Royal Irish Academy's *Dictionary of Irish Biography* for five enjoyable years, and it gave me invaluable experience in biographical research and the writing of history. I would like to thank everyone involved and wish them and the project every success in the future. In particular it was very rewarding to work alongside scholars like Dr Christopher Woods and Richard Hawkins, and I owe a special debt to Dr James Quinn who was always on hand with advice about Emmet and other things.

A number of people were kind enough to read and comment on early drafts of this work and I would like to thank them all for their assistance. I am greatly indebted to Dr James Kelly for his perceptive comments, and to Dr David Dickson for his insights and advice. Professor Marianne Elliot, whose ground-breaking scholarship on this period has been so important, was also kind enough to listen to my ideas about Emmet and discuss the subject on a number of occasions. I would also like to thank Dr Anthony Malcomson for his gener-ous hospitality whenever I was in Belfast, and also for his support throughout my career. It has been a great privilege and pleasure to lecture in the Department of Modern History in Trinity College Dublin and I would like to thank my colleagues for their encouragement and support. In particular I would like to thank Professor Aidan Clarke, Professor John Horne, Dr Helga Robinson-Hammerstein and Ms Louise Kidney for all their kindnesses. Professor Eunan O'Halpin also listened to my ramblings about Emmet and provided much useful advice along the way, while Dr Jim Livesey was very help-ful on the subject of France.

Dr Patrick Kelly very kindly allowed me to examine his microfilm of Robert Emmet's copy of John Locke's *Two treatises of government* which was greatly appreciated. I would also like to thank Dr Jim Smyth of the University of Notre Dame (where the copy of Locke is held) for generously sending me his un-published article on the subject. One of the great things about working in a university is being able to call upon experts in various different fields. For example, Dr Judith Mosssman of the Classics Department in Trinity provided some invaluable help on Latin translations. It was also a great pleasure discussing Emmet with Dr Kevin Rockett of the Drama Department, whose work on this area has been so important. In particular I am grateful to him for showing me an Emmet film from the 1910s and other important archival footage. The Provost, Professor John Hegarty, has also taken a great interest in Robert Emmet, and I would like to thank him for his support. I am also delighted by the interest of the Taoiseach, Mr Bertie Ahern, and his Department, in Robert Emmet and his bicentenary.

Once again it was a pleasure working with Gill & Macmillan and I would like to thank Deirdre Rennison Kunz and all the staff. I would also like to record my debt of gratitude to Mrs Patricia Hourican and her family for their many kind-nesses and support.

Very special thanks are due to Dr Ciaran Brady who has been an enormous support over the last few years. Many of our conversations began with a dis-cussion about his research on James Anthony Froude but quickly degenerated into discussions about this book, which were always thoroughly enjoyable and hugely influential. It has been a great honour to teach alongside him, and he has been both a friend and inspiration.

My friends were somewhat short-changed in the acknowledgments to my last book and so I am determined to rectify that neglect here. My thanks (in some sort of alphabetical order) must go to Alan Ford, Alastair McMenamin, Anna Bryson, Anne Fay, Brian Hanley, Caoilfhionn Gallagher, Carol Ballantine, Christopher Finlay, Claire Mitchell, Clare Bassett, Colin Walsh, David Murphy, Eithne MacDermott, Elizabethanne Boran, Eoin Lawlor, Erik Eastaugh, Gerry Cronin, Harrison O'Malley, Ivan McAvinchey, Jenifer Ní Grádaigh, Joanne Drum, Leona Walker, Lynne Roach, Marie Coleman, Mary Fay, Michael Brown, Paul O'Connor, Peter Martin, Rory Whelan, Rosemary Mallon, Sandra Hynes, Sarah Fennell, Stefanie Jones, Susan Murphy, Tom Kelley, Toni Melvin, Triona Walsh, Vivian Cooke and Yvonne Campbell. Four people deserve a special mention for their specialised help, and I must record my debt to Eoin Keehan, Bridget Hourican, Declan Lawlor and Paul Geaney.

Finally, this book is dedicated to Mr James McGuire who inspired me to become a historian.

The Emmet legend

In the final months of the American Civil War a powerful letter was sent to President Abraham Lincoln pleading for the life of a young Confederate spy who had been sentenced to death. This was the case of Lieutenant Samuel B. Davis, a distant relative of the Confederate president, who had made an heroic speech from the dock after being found guilty. Senator Willard Saulsbury, no friend of either Lincoln or his administration, begged him to study the speech carefully and 'compare it with the celebrated defence of Emmet' (7 February 1865, Abraham Lincoln papers at the Library of Congress, series 1). It was a shrewd gamble. Emmet's famous speech was required reading for aspiring orators in the United States in the nineteenth century and Lincoln had been so impressed that he memorised it in his youth. The evening before the execution Lincoln sent an executive order saving the life of Davis.

The dramatic story of Robert Emmet's life and death created a powerful legend. It also gave rise to its own folklore. One play, written at the beginning of the twentieth century, offered a bizarre explanation for why the rebellion failed. In this version a young woman got horribly drunk on the night of 23 July 1803 and made sexual advances on Emmet, who was so disturbed he took out his pistol and shot her dead. As a result, the rising was cancelled.

A few years later a touring acting company staged the trial of Robert Emmet in the Irish provinces. In one town the crowd were particularly nationalist and became increasingly hostile towards the actors who were playing the forces of the crown. As the evening went on the theatre company decided to put their own safety first. When the jury was asked to declare their verdict Robert Emmet was found not guilty.

PART I

~

INTRODUCTION

1

SACRIFICE AND CATHARSIS: 19–20 SEPTEMBER 1803

~

'He who has never failed somewhere, that man can not be great. Failure is the true test of greatness.'

(Herman Melville)

'Now the betrayer had arranged a signal with them, so when he arrived he went straight up to Jesus and said "Rabbi" and kissed him.'

(Gospel of St Mark 14: 43–5)

Robert Emmet greeted the news of his guilt with a callous indifference. It was the evening of Monday 19 September 1803, and the trial for high treason which carried the death penalty had lasted the entire day. For more than twelve hours the packed courthouse at Green Street in Dublin had heard clear evidence of Emmet's complicity in the insurrection of 23 July and there was never any doubt about the final outcome. The jury only needed a few minutes to reach its verdict and did not even retire from the box. Dressed all in black, with Hessian boots, and a silk stock around his neck, Emmet's self-confidence and defiant countenance unnerved some onlookers.[1] Defended by Peter Burrowes and Leonard MacNally, he had made no attempt to argue his case. Indeed he had actively discouraged his counsel from cross-examining witnesses, preferring to assume complete responsibility for the rebellion and its consequences. Sometimes he stopped Burrowes from rising to speak with a quiet command: 'Pray do not attempt to defend me — it is all in vain.'[2] The government was delighted with its good fortune. As the lord lieutenant, the earl of Hardwicke, boasted to his brother, 'It is universally admitted that a more complete case of treason was never stated in a court of justice. He produced no witnesses and made no defence.'[3]

All that remained was for the sentence to be passed. The clerk of the crown called Emmet to the bar but was interrupted by MacNally who made a motion for judgment to be deferred until the following day. The request was denied. Reading the indictment to the court, the clerk concluded with the routine question for the prisoner. Emmet had been found guilty of three counts of high treason and his fate was decided: 'What have you, therefore, now to say, why judgement of death and execution should not be awarded against you according to law?'[4] It was Emmet's first proper opportunity to address the court. One hostile onlooker, who had known him in university, remarked that at this point 'he seemed to consider himself as rising into a martyr'.[5] It was over five years since Emmet had addressed a similar public gathering and that had been the Historical Society in Trinity College Dublin. On that occasion he had failed. His oratory had attracted much praise when he was a student, but had also aroused some opposition. At his final debate the college authorities had brought in an outsider to answer his arguments. For the first time in his life Emmet was bested. Point by point he was challenged and attacked until in the end he 'broke down', much to the embarrassment of his debating friends who had idealised him as their 'chief champion and ornament'.[6]

Almost five feet seven inches in height, Emmet was described by one journalist present at his arraignment as being 'thin and alert' with 'short fair hair, [a] sharp visage and [an] expressive countenance'.[7] R. R. Madden has left a similar account based on the reports of people who knew him: 'His features were regular, his forehead high and firmly found; his eyes were small, bright and full of expression; his nose sharp, remarkably thin and straight.'[8] According to Madden, there was nothing in Emmet's appearance which made him remarkable, 'except when [he was] excited in conversation, and when he spoke in public on any subject that interested him'. On these occasions, and the trial was certainly one of them, 'his countenance then beamed with animation: he no longer seemed the same person, every feature became expressive of his emotions'.[9]

The trial for treason had begun at 9.30 in the morning and had continued without pause, interruption or break for food. Exhausted from standing all day, hungry, and aware that his death was fast approaching, Emmet began a speech that would transform the failed rebellion into a symbolic gesture of defiance which would survive long after his own death. The irony is that Emmet had offered to remain silent. Determined to protect the woman he loved, Sarah Curran, from prosecution, he had informed the government that he would not speak from the dock in exchange for a promise about her future. The Castle administration had unwisely refused to make a deal, even though it had never any intention of charging Sarah Curran. Underestimating the quality and possible consequences of Emmet's oratory, the government allowed him to speak, unafraid of anything he might have to say: it was a terrible miscalculation. Surrounded by a hostile judge and an unsympathetic court, Robert Emmet delivered a brilliant speech that both inspired future generations and ensured his own immortality. His life reached its apotheosis in the moment of his greatest crisis.

'My lords, as to why judgement of death and execution should not be passed upon me I have nothing to say; why the sentence which in the public mind is usually attached to that of the law, ought to be reversed, I have much to say.'[10] Robert Emmet began his famous oration without a prepared text or any kind of *aide-mémoire*. Even as a student he had a precious ability to speak without notes and did not require any at his trial. However, while completing his research on this subject in the nineteenth century, R. R. Madden became convinced he had discovered an original manuscript of the speech from the dock which had been prepared by Emmet in advance.[11] He subsequently realised that it was only a transcript.[12] Thomas Moore also believed he had discovered notes that Emmet had written, but he too was mistaken. There is no extant copy of Robert Emmet's draft speech, nor indeed is it likely that he prepared one. But he was clear about what he wanted to say, and had key concepts worked out in advance. Regularly interrupted by the judge, Lord Norbury, he never completed the speech he had intended, but he was able to present his themes and adjust his thoughts despite the intolerable pressure he was under.

Fighting not for his life which he knew was forfeit, but for his place in history, Robert Emmet delivered a spellbinding defence of his character. He knew he would change few opinions in the courtroom, so his impassioned oratory was aimed at a wider audience:

> I stand here a conspirator, as one engaged in a conspiracy for the overthrow of the British government in Ireland. For the fact of which I am to suffer by the law; for the motives of which I am to answer before God. I am ready to do both. Was it only the fact of treason, was it that naked fact alone with which I stood charged, was I to suffer no other punishment, than the death of the body, I would not obtrude on your attention, but having received the sentence, I would bow my neck in silence to the stroke. But, my lords, I well know, that when a man enters into a conspiracy, he not only has to combat against the difficulties of fortune, but to contend against the still more insurmountable obstacles of prejudice. And that if, in the end, fortune abandons him and delivers him over bound into the hands of the law, his character is previously loaded with calumny and misrepresentation. For what purpose, I know not, except, that the prisoner, thus weighed down in mind and body, may be delivered over a more unresisting victim to condemnation. It is well.

In a clever play on his status as a prisoner, Emmet then declared that he was now determined to 'unmanacle his reputation': 'Not, my lords, that I have much to demand from you. It is a claim on your memory, rather than on your candour, that I am making.'

It was powerful rhetoric and had a profound effect on those who listened. Even Henry Brereton Code, a government spy and informer, was moved by the oration. Later in the year he published, anonymously, an account of the rebellion at the request of Dublin Castle which was scathing in its attack on the nature of the rebellion and the character of Emmet. But in his preface Code did acknowledge that 'the warning voice of the unfortunate Emmet' had impressed him. It was a 'voice that spoke almost from the grave' and which seemed to possess 'the energy and inspiration of eternal truth'.[13] Projecting his voice with the assurance of an expert debater, Emmet's speech could be heard at the outer doors of the courthouse. But although his voice was loud, 'there was nothing boisterous in its delivery, or forced or affected in his manner; his accents and cadence of voice, on the contrary, were exquisitely modulated'.[14] Throughout the speech his hands were chained. Yet this did not interfere with his concentration or distract him from his objective. From his time in Trinity he had developed a habit of swaying his body when he spoke in public, and he seemed to use this as a metronome to modulate his style: 'his action was very remarkable; its greater or lesser vehemence corresponded with the rise and fall of his voice'.[15]

Addressing the accusations that had been made against him, Emmet turned these into a defence of his character:

> I do not ask you to believe implicitly what I say. I do not hope that you will let my vindication ride at anchor in your breasts. I only ask you, to let it float upon the surface of your recollection, till it comes to some more friendly port to receive it, and give it shelter against the heavy storms with which it is buffeted.

The word 'character' appears seven times in his speech and was the most important concept in his oration. Another crucial but secondary theme was the autonomy of the insurrection. He was keen to assert that he was not an agent of France; rather he had been acting independently to liberate his country from British rule. While he had been prepared to accept French aid, he rejected French authority and would not have swapped one imperial domination for another:

> I am charged with being an emissary of France, for the purpose of inciting insurrection in the country and then delivering it over to a foreign enemy. It is false! I did not wish to join this country with France. I did join, I did not create the rebellion, not for France, but for its liberty. It is true, there were communications between the United Irishmen and France; it is true, that by that, the war was no surprise upon us.

Robert's brother Thomas Addis was at that moment in Paris negotiating with the French and he revealed to the courtroom that the French would not be allowed to land unless certain assurances were received in advance. The American example during the War of Independence was being followed and he explained: 'Before any expedition sails, it is intended to have a treaty signed, as a guarantee, similar to that which [Benjamin] Franklin obtained for America.' This was an important point for Emmet and he was clear that,

> it never was the intention to form a permanent treaty with France, and in the treaty which they did make, they had the same guarantee which America had, that an independent government should be established in the country, before the French should come. God forbid that I should ever see my country under the hands of a foreign power.

He explained that he would not barter victory over the British for tyranny under the French:

> Small indeed would be our claim to patriotism and to sense, and palpable our affection of the love of liberty, if we were to sell our country to a people who are not only slaves themselves, but the unprincipled and abandoned instruments of imposing slavery on others.

The comments about the French caused outrage in Paris and were later deleted from some translations of the trial. There were even some French claims that the British government had added the paragraphs to discourage a foreign invasion of Ireland. But Emmet had spent much time on the continent and had been horrified at the treatment of small countries by Napoleon. The fact that he coldly and deliberately made these sentiments public at his trial was a clear indication that he was prepared to accept the consequences and alienate the French. He no longer wanted any kind of assistance from France and was not afraid to damage the connection for others; for him the rebellion was over.

One of the key charges made against Emmet's character before his trial, and indeed ever since, was that he was a vain young man who had foolishly engaged in a doomed conspiracy. But if Emmet suffered from an excess of anything then it was of youthful idealism and not arrogance. Even after he had been found guilty he did not attempt to claim credit for everything. Speaking for the historical record, and not his own reputation, he was prepared to admit that he was 'not the head and life's blood of this rebellion'. He had been willing to accept full responsibility during the trial to protect others from prosecution, but there was now nothing to be gained from such honesty. In fact there was much to lose, but he was not concerned with self-aggrandising myth-making: 'When I came to Ireland I found the business ripe for execution. I was asked to join in it. I took time to consider, and after mature deliberation I became one of the provisional government.' Returning to the theme of French involvement, he then admitted that a United Irishmen agent in Paris had negotiated with Napoleon about aid, but denied that this would have damaged Irish independence. Any attempts to establish French hegemony would have been met by force, and he was uncompromising that their invading army would have been repelled as surely as if they were British soldiers:

Connexion with France was indeed intended, but only as far as mutual interest would sanction or require. Were they to assume any authority inconsistent with the purest independence it would be the signal for their destruction. We sought aid and we sought it, as we had assurance we should obtain it, as auxiliaries in war and allies in peace.

In a fiery declamation which lasted almost an hour, it is significant that almost one-third of that time was spent attacking the French. Before Emmet could explain his motives he had to make it clear about what exactly the rebellion was *not*. He knew that it would be impossible to vindicate his character or justify his conduct as long as there was any suspicion that he had been a pawn of the French. Therefore it was necessary to reveal the extent of his hostility towards all forms of tyranny including the new imperialism on the continent. The French would either come as allies, with specific terms of reference, or else they would not be allowed to come at all. One of the most impassioned sections of the speech concerned the prospect of an unwelcome landing by the French. He struggled to contain his emotions as he imagined that possibility, in a passage which revealed conversely his vision of what real independence should mean for Ireland:

> If the French come as a foreign enemy, oh my countrymen, meet them on the shore with a torch in one hand — a sword in the other — receive them with all the destruction of war. Immolate them in their boats, before our native soil shall be polluted by a foreign foe. If they succeed in landing, fight them on the strand, burn every blade of grass before them, as they advance; raze every house. And if you are driven to the centre of your country, collect your provisions, your property, your wives and your daughters, form a circle around them, fight while two men are left, and when but one remains, let that man set fire to the pile, and release himself and the families of his fallen countrymen from the tyranny of France.

The behaviour of France towards smaller nations was abhorrent to Emmet:

> See how she has behaved to other countries, how she has behaved to Switzerland, to Holland, and to Italy. Could we expect better conduct towards us? No! Let not then any man calumniate my memory, by believing that I could have hoped for freedom from the government of France . . . by committing it to the power of her most determined foe.

He was adamant that he would not betray 'the sacred cause of liberty' by handing Ireland over to a new foreign power:

> Had I done so I had not deserved to live — and dying with such a weight upon my character, I had merited the honest execration of that country

which gave me birth, and to which I would give freedom. What has been the conduct of France towards other countries? They promised them liberty, and when they got them into their power they enslaved them.

Emmet cited the example of Switzerland, a country which the government had claimed he had visited. Dismayed at being dismissed in court as the 'emissary of French tyranny and French despotism', he was determined to correct that impression. He explained that:

> If I had been in Switzerland I would have fought against the French; for I believe the Swiss are hostile to the French. In the dignity of freedom, I would have expired on the frontiers of that country, and they should have entered it only by passing over my lifeless corpse. But if I thought the people were favourable to the French, I have seen so much what the consequences of the failure of revolutions are, the oppressions of the higher upon the lower orders of the people, I say, if I saw them disposed to admit the French, I would not join them, but I would put myself between the French and the people, not as a victim, but to protect them from subjugation, and endeavour to gain their confidence, by sharing in their danger.

Compared to the shame of the charge of having betrayed Ireland, the threat of imminent death held little power. This was the point of his long digression against the French: he conceded that he may have been a traitor to Britain, but he would never accept that he was a traitor to Ireland. The allegation of being a pawn of the French struck at the heart of his conception of what the rebellion had attempted, and therefore his entire character:

> My lords, it may be part of the system of angry justice to bow a man's mind to humiliation to meet the ignominy of the scaffold; but worse to me than the scaffold's shame or the scaffold's terrors would be the imputation of having been the agent of the despotism and ambition of France; and whilst I have breath I will call upon my countrymen not to believe me guilty of so foul a crime upon their liberties and against their happiness.

Everything Emmet had been arguing was building up to this point: his declaration of Irish independence. By showing what the rebellion had not been about, he now felt confident of proclaiming its purpose: 'So would I have done with the people of Ireland, and so would I do, if I was called upon tomorrow. Our object was to effect a separation from England.'

Lord Norbury was horrified by this pronouncement. Interrupting Emmet for the first time, he attempted to stop him from continuing with his treasonous oration. There had been little problem with the attacks on the French, but the judge was not prepared to sit idly by while his own government was assailed. Emmet, however, had come a long way from his days at Trinity, and was now more than capable of holding his own against an older voice. If he felt any nerves he did not show them and faced off to Norbury in an increasingly charged confrontation. Embracing the inevitability of his death, he turned his impending execution into a rallying cry for future generations:

> When my spirit shall have joined those bands of martyred heroes who have shed their blood on the scaffold and in the field in defence of their country, this is my hope, that my memory and name may serve to animate those who survive me.

Swept up by the passion of his own rhetoric, he launched into a savage critique of the British administration in Ireland. Repeating the word 'which' for dramatic emphasis, he declared that the government was one

> which displays its power over man as over the beasts of the field; which sets man upon his brother, and lifts his hands in religion's name against the throat of his fellow who believes a little more or less than the government standard; which reigns amidst the cries of the orphans and of the widows it has made . . .

Norbury could take no more and refused to allow Emmet to complete the sentence. Changing the subject, Emmet attempted to give a complete account of the rebellion's objectives and discuss whether it might have succeeded. Again Norbury interrupted him. Struggling to remain calm, Emmet delivered a stern rebuke which confirmed his confidence that he was addressing a wider audience than just the magistrates:

> What I have spoken was not intended for your lordships, whose situation I commiserate rather than envy; my expressions were for my countrymen. If there be a true Irishman present, let my last words cheer him in the hour of his affliction.

Angered by this comment, Norbury once more reminded the prisoner that it was not his place to speak subversion. Again Emmet ignored him and delivered a stringent attack on the people who would try to silence him. Chastened by this censure, Norbury remained silent.

> I have always understood it to be the duty of a judge, when a prisoner has been convicted, to pronounce the sentence of the law. I have also understood that judges sometimes think it their duty to hear with patience and to speak with humanity — to exhort the victims of the laws, and to offer with tender benignity his opinions of the motives by which he was actuated in the crime of which he was adjudged guilty. That a judge has thought it his duty so to have done I have no doubt; but where is the boasted freedom of your

institutions — where is the vaunted impartiality, clemency, and mildness of your courts of justice, if an unfortunate prisoner whom your policy, and *not justice*, is about to deliver into the hands of the executioner, is not suffered to explain his motives sincerely and truly, and to vindicate the principles by which he was actuated?

There had been many different things which Emmet had intended to say at his trial. Norbury's antipathy threw his carefully thought out structure into disarray and the remainder of his oration became a justification of his right to speak as much as a defence of his character. Unplanned and unscripted, it was all the more dazzling because of that. Found guilty of high treason and about to be sentenced to death, Emmet demonstrated a remarkable lack of nerves as he cut open the conduct of Lord Norbury for public examination:

My lords, it may be a part of the system of angry justice to bow a man's mind by humiliation to the purposed ignominy of the scaffold. But worse to me than the purposed shame of the scaffold's terrors would be the tame endurance of such foul and unfounded imputations as have been laid against me in this court. You, my lord, are a judge. I am the supposed culprit. I am a man — you are a man also. By a revolution of power we might change places, though we could never change characters.

It was a heartfelt outburst which stunned Norbury who listened in silence. Developing this theme as far as it could go, Emmet returned to the question of his treatment in the courtroom. All his repressed feelings from the past month burst forth, and his body language mirrored his inner turmoil. As one observer later remembered, when Emmet was 'enforcing his arguments against his accusers, his hand was stretched forward, and the two forefingers of the right hand were slowly laid on the open palm of the other'.[6] Rhythmically, he would gently tap his fingers on his palm for added emphasis during his speech. Building up to a sustained assault on Norbury's conduct at the trial, Emmet segued into a brilliant defence of his reputation: 'If I stand at the bar of this court and dare not vindicate my character, *what a farce is your justice!* If I stand at this bar and dare not vindicate my character, *how dare you calumniate it?*'[17]

Emmet admitted that he was concerned with how he would be perceived in the years ahead: he was 'a man to whom fame is dearer than life'. But while the executioner might be able to carry out the court's 'unhallowed policy' and 'condemn my tongue to silence', no hangman could prevent him from defending himself at his trial:

while I exist I shall not forbear to vindicate my character and motives from your aspersions . . . I will make the last use of that life in doing justice to that reputation which is to live after me, and which is the only legacy I can leave to those I honour and love, and for whom I am proud to perish.

Growing increasingly confident in his delivery, Emmet attempted to imagine the possible judgment of a more supreme court:

> As men, my lords, we must appear on the great day at one common tribunal, and it will then remain for the searcher of all hearts to show a collective universe, who was engaged in the most virtuous actions, or actuated by the purest motives: my country's oppressors or . . .

He was not allowed to complete the comparison. Once again he was interrupted, this time by the clerk of the crown, who reminded him that he was only there to say why sentence of death and execution should not be passed against him, not to attempt a personal vindication. Emmet refused to be stopped. He had been found guilty by the law, but was now demanding justice. With renewed vigour he continued his attack:

> My lords, will a dying man be denied the legal privilege of exculpating himself in the eyes of the community from a reproach thrown upon him during his trial, by charging him with ambition, and attempting to cast away for a paltry consideration the liberties of his country? Why then insult me, or rather why insult justice, in demanding why sentence of death should not be pronounced against me?

Turning the clerk's question to his advantage, Emmet poured scorn on the supposed fairness of his trial. Disputing that the verdict could have gone any other way, he mocked the court for pretending it was impartial:

> I know, my lords, that the form prescribes that you should put the question; the form also confers a right of answering. This, no doubt, may be dispensed with, and so might the whole ceremony of the trial, since sentence was already pronounced at the Castle before your jury was empanelled. Your lordships are but the priests of the oracle, and I submit, but I insist on the whole of the forms.

At this Emmet stopped speaking, waiting to see how the court would respond. Apparently moved by his oration, Norbury asked him to continue. Emmet returned to his role in the rebellion, modestly disavowing full responsibility for its leadership:

> I have been charged with that importance in the efforts to emancipate my country as to be considered the key-stone of the combination of Irishmen, or, as it has been expressed, 'the life and blood of the conspiracy'. You do me honour overmuch. You have given to the subaltern all the credit of the superior. There are men concerned in this conspiracy who are not only superior to me, but even to your own conceptions of yourself, my lord. Men,

before the splendour of whose genius and virtues I should bow with respectful deference, and who would not deign to call you friend; who would not disgrace themselves by shaking your bloodstained hand.

Upon hearing such provocative language, Norbury called Emmet to order. Restraining the vehemence of his comments, but only just, Emmet argued that he was not to be blamed for the violence of the rebellion:

What, my lord, shall you tell me on my passage to the scaffold — which that tyranny, of which you are only the intermediate minister, has erected for my death — that I am accountable for all the blood that has and will be shed in this struggle of the oppressed against the oppressor? Shall you tell me this, and must I be so very a slave as not to repel it?

The trial was rapidly degenerating into a private duel between Norbury and Emmet. Nevertheless Emmet was determined to fix the argument around the themes that mattered most: his character, the role of France, and his disavowal of responsibility for the bloodshed. Returning to religious imagery, he insisted that he feared nothing from a meeting with 'the omnipotent judge'. Why then, he asked, should he fear anything when standing before 'a mere remnant of mortality'? As he defended his reputation, he laid down a challenge to those who survived him:

Let no man dare, when I am dead, to charge me with dishonour; let no man attaint my memory by believing that I could have engaged in any cause but of my country's liberty and independence. The proclamation of the provisional government speaks my views: no inference can be tortured from it to countenance barbarity or debasement. I would not have submitted to a foreign oppression for the same reason that I would have resisted tyranny at home.[18]

It was a brilliant rhetorical construction: Emmet denied that even Dublin Castle could 'torture' any reference from his proclamation to infer that he was in favour of 'barbarity and debasement'.

Mindful of his legal responsibilities, once more Norbury interrupted the speaker. He wished to make it clear that Emmet was stretching the patience of the court and had no right to demand time to justify his actions.

Mr Emmet, you have been called upon to show cause, if any you have, why the judgement of the law should not be enforced against you. Instead of showing anything in point of law why judgement should not pass, you have proceeded in a manner the most unbecoming a person in your situation. You have avowed and endeavoured to vindicate principles totally subversive of the government, totally subversive of the tranquillity, well-being and happiness of that country which gave you birth, and you have broached treason the most abominable.

Norbury was perfectly correct in legal terms. Emmet had indeed furnished further proof of his guilt by his comments and had provided little reason why he should not be sentenced to death. But Norbury's next comments were destined to irritate rather than soothe Emmet's agitated feelings. Referring to Emmet's deceased father and brother in a patronising attempt to instil some guilt, Norbury only encouraged him to continue in his denunciations:

You, sir, had the honour to be a gentleman by birth, and your father filled a respectable station under the government. You had an eldest brother whom death snatched away, and who when living was one of the greatest ornaments of the bar. The laws of this country were the study of his youth, and the study of his maturer life was to cultivate and support them. He left you a proud example to follow, and if he had lived he would have given your talents the same virtuous direction as his own, and have taught you to admire and preserve that constitution, for the destruction of which you have conspired with the most profligate and abandoned.

There was a certain amount of snobbery in Norbury's well-meaning but condescending comments. He deigned to recognise that Emmet was born a gentleman but ended with a horrified admission that he had nevertheless 'associated' himself 'with hostlers, bakers, butchers, and such persons, whom you invited to council when you erected your provisional government'.

It was never an approach that was likely to work with Emmet. His late father, the state physician, had engendered him with patriotic ideals from an early age and would not have been as critical as Norbury imagined. Nor were the references to Christopher Temple Emmet, Robert's older brother, calculated to cool the rising temperatures in the courtroom. Enlisting the support of his dead father, Emmet made a poignant plea for understanding:

If the spirits of the illustrious dead participate in the concerns of those who were dear to them in this transitory scene, dear shade of my venerated father look down on your suffering son and see has he for one moment deviated from those moral and patriotic principles which you so early instilled into his youthful mind, and for which he now has to offer up his life.

Moving around the dock, Emmet's gestures became increasingly rapid and agitated. As he swayed in front of the railing at the dock, and then back again, his rhythmic motions had an almost hypnotic effect on those who watched. The tapping of his hand, the movement of his body and the careful modulation of his voice all combined to increase the power of his oration. The effect was 'as if his body, as well as his mind, were swelling beyond the measure of their chains'.[19]

Realising that he would not be able to deliver the speech he had intended, and recognising that further interruptions were inevitable, he decided to bring his remarks to a close. His peroration would echo for eternity. Some historians would later question whether he actually delivered the final lines, but they appear in many contemporary accounts of the trial and there is little reason to doubt their provenance.[20]

It was now almost 10.30 in the evening. The trial had lasted thirteen hours and no one was more exhausted than Emmet. Nevertheless, defiantly insisting that he felt no fear, he roused himself for one final attempt to defend his honour. It marked the culmination of his entire speech and many of the themes used to defend his character here reached their natural conclusion:

My lords, you are impatient for the sacrifice. The blood which you seek is not congealed by the artificial terrors which surround your victim. It circulates warmly and unruffled through its channels, and in a short time it will cry to heaven. Be yet patient! I have but a few words to say: my ministry is now ended. I am going to my cold and silent grave; my lamp of life is nearly extinguished.

Referring to everything he had sacrificed in his struggle, Emmet touched on the subject that pained him the most, Sarah Curran. This was the only farewell he could give her:

I have parted with everything that was dear to me in this life for my country's cause, and abandoned another idol I adored in my heart, the object of my affections. My race is run. The grave opens to receive me, and I sink into its bosom.

Moving to conclude his address, Emmet launched into the most famous and quoted passage of his entire speech:

I have not been allowed to vindicate my character. I have but one request to ask at my departure from this world: it is *the charity of its silence*. Let no man write my epitaph; for as no man who knows my motives dares now vindicate them, let not prejudice or ignorance asperse them. Let them rest in obscurity and peace: my memory be left in oblivion and my tomb remain uninscribed, until other times and other men can do justice to my character. When my country takes her place among the nations of the earth, then, and not till then, let my epitaph be written. I have done.

It was left to Lord Norbury to pronounce sentence: Emmet was to be hanged and beheaded the very next day at Thomas Street, the scene of part of the crime. Upon hearing the news, Robert Emmet's defence counsel, Leonard MacNally, leaned over and theatrically kissed him on the forehead.[21]

Removed to Newgate Prison at 11 o'clock at night, Emmet was brought to Kilmainham Jail two hours later. There he spent his final night, although he slept little, if at all. His thoughts were elsewhere and he wrote a number of letters to the people who were closest to him. Unable to write to Sarah Curran directly, he wrote about her and, he hoped, to her. One letter was to his brother Thomas Addis Emmet and his wife Jane. The pathos of this final communication with his closest surviving relatives could not have been more pronounced: 'My dearest Tom and Jane, I am just going to do my last duty to my country. It can be done as well on the scaffold as on the field.'[22] There was little sign in the letter that Emmet felt any fear about his fate; whatever he thought he kept it to himself and allowed no tremor of anxiety to seep into his writing. Instead he attempted to rally their spirits which he knew would be thrown by the news of his death:

> Do not give way to any weak feelings on my account, but rather encourage proud ones that I have possessed fortitude and tranquillity of mind to the last. God bless you and the young hopes that are growing up about you. May they be more fortunate than their uncle; but may they preserve as pure an attachment to their country as he has done.

Bequeathing his father's watch to his nephew, he hoped that 'little Robert' would 'not prize it the less for having been in the possession of two Roberts before him'.

Always his thoughts returned to Sarah Curran, and he implored his brother to act as her protector if she was abandoned. With a final solemnity he explained:

> I have one dying request to make to you. I was attached to Sarah Curran, the youngest daughter of your friend. I did hope to have had her as my companion for life. I did hope that she would not only have constituted my happiness but that her heart and understanding would have made her one of Jane's dearest friends.

He ended the letter with a tender appeal on her behalf:

> She is now with her father and brother, but if those protectors should fall off and that no other should replace them, take her as my wife and love her as a sister. God Almighty bless and preserve you all. Give my love to all my friends. Robert Emmet.

The letter never reached his brother. It was suppressed by the prison officials and sent straight to Dublin Castle.

Sarah Curran never escaped his thoughts. Writing to her brother Richard, Emmet attempted to express the guilt he felt for compromising her. His final anxiety was for Sarah's future, not his own impending death. Opening his heart to Richard, his letter was full of regret as he sought redemption for his actions:

> I find I have but a few hours to live, but if it was the last moment, and that the power of utterance was leaving me, I would thank you from the bottom of my heart for your generous expressions of affection and forgiveness to me. If there was any one in the world in whose breast my death might be supposed not to stifle every spark of resentment, it might be you. I have deeply injured you. I have injured the happiness of a sister that you love, and who was formed to give happiness to every one about her, instead of having her own mind a prey to affliction.[23]

Pleading for understanding, Emmet continued to beg for forgiveness. His relationship with Sarah had been a secret, even from Richard, and he apologised for any deception. It had not been safe to announce it publicly because of the planned insurrection. He hoped his friend would understand how much Sarah had genuinely meant to him:

> Oh Richard! I have no excuse to offer, but that I meant the reverse. I intended as much happiness for Sarah as the most ardent love could have given her. I never did tell you how much I idolised her. It was not with a wild or unfounded passion, but it was with an attachment increasing every hour, from an admiration of the purity of her mind and respect for her talents. I did dwell in secret upon the prospect of our union. I did hope that success, while it afforded an opportunity of our union, might be a means of confirming an attachment which misfortune had called forth.

Again his modesty was evident. He had not wanted public glory, but would have been satisfied with the love of his wife: 'I did not look to honours for myself; praise I would have asked from the lips of no man; but I would have wished to read in the glow of Sarah's countenance that her husband was respected.'

Although writing to Richard Curran, Robert hoped that he was also speaking to Sarah. By the end of the letter this thought had overpowered him and he addressed her directly: 'My love, Sarah!' In a paragraph rich with pathos he described his dreams of what their life together might have been like. But a 'rude blast' had destroyed them 'and they have fallen over a grave'.

Filled with remorse, Emmet revealed the extent of his suffering in prison. Addressing Richard in his final paragraph, he admitted that his guilt over Sarah had affected him more than anything else. But still he attempted to remain firm:

> This is no time for affliction. I have had public motives to sustain my mind, and I have not suffered it to sink; but there have been moments in my

imprisonment when my mind was so sunk by grief on her account, that death would have been a refuge. God bless you my dearest Richard, I am obliged to leave off immediately.

Desperate to discover Emmet's final thoughts, the government requested detailed reports of all his conversations in prison. Not all of these sources were reliable, so it is difficult to establish the truth of some of the different statements. For example, Emmet was apparently asked if he favoured a French invasion, to which he replied: 'I execrate the French, they are only actuated by a thirst of carnage and spoil, and I consider Bonaparte as the most savage tyrant.'[24]

Dr Thomas Gamble, the resident clergyman at Newgate Prison, visited him in his cell at Kilmainham before midday. He had attended to Emmet briefly the night before at Newgate and sought to give him spiritual support in his final moments. A detailed report of their conversation was sent to the home office in London that evening. Gamble was accompanied by the Rev. Mr Grant, a clergyman who lived at Island Bridge. They stayed with Emmet until his execution.

Expecting to find a heretic, or at the very least a deist, they were astonished to discover that Emmet had strong religious principles and was happy to describe himself as a Christian.[25] Some loyalist historians refused to accept this version of events and invented their own transcript. In his history of the rebellion, W. H. Maxwell wrote that Emmet argued with the clergymen all the way to the scaffold and rejected their ministering with a frank admission that he was an unbeliever: 'I appreciate your motives and I thank you for your kindness, but you merely disturb the last moments of a dying man unnecessarily. I am an infidel from conviction and no reasoning can shake my unbelief.'[26] This was partially based on some contemporary newspaper reports which claimed that the clergymen 'endeavoured to win him from his deistical opinions, but without effect'.[27] The story of the clergymen was quite different. Finding Emmet receptive to their enquiries, they discovered that he defined himself as 'a Christian in the true sense of the word, that he had received the sacrament, though not regularly and habitually, and that he wished to receive it then'.[28] Gamble believed that Emmet was a 'visionary enthusiast' and as he had confessed that he was 'conscious of sins, and wished to receive the sacraments', he was willing to perform his duties as a minister.

Concerned with saving Emmet's soul, as well as reporting to the Castle, the clergymen then attempted to persuade him to renounce the rebellion. Here they made no progress. Emmet refused to 'abjure those principles' which had led him to attempt the overthrow of the government, but he did clarify some points regarding it. As the report revealed: 'He disclaimed any intention of shedding blood, professed a total ignorance of the murder of Lord Kilwarden, before which he declared he had left Dublin, and also professed an aversion to the French.'[29] At 10 a.m. Leonard MacNally arrived to talk to Emmet and discovered him reading the litany of the service of the Church of England.[30]

Allowed into an adjoining room for some privacy, MacNally had his final conversation with his client.

A great friend of John Philpot Curran, MacNally was famous in radical circles for defending the United Irishmen. His unpopular stance had made him, according to Charles Philips, 'the man most obnoxious to the government of that day' after Curran, the figure 'who most hated them [the government], and was most hated by them'.[31] Side by side with his friend he had 'denounced oppression, defied power, and dared every danger', despite all risks to himself. Popular at both the English and Irish bars, MacNally was also a poet and playwright and had written a new version of *Robin Hood* which is credited with reviving interest in the story in Britain. Jonah Barrington, the acerbic diarist, revealed that he was 'one of the strangest fellows in the world'.[32] Short and stocky, MacNally had only one thumb, 'a face which no washing could clean', and legs of unequal length; he was forced to hobble wherever he went. As Barrington concluded, he was 'a good-natured, hospitable, talented, dirty fellow'. He was also a government spy.

Having betrayed the confidences of previous clients, and Emmet himself, MacNally now sought further information to report to the Castle. His version was published in *The London Chronicle* later in the month; a separate account was given by John Patten, Thomas Addis Emmet's brother-in-law, to R. R. Madden.[33] According to this second version, one of the first questions Emmet asked concerned the health of his mother. MacNally hesitated, not wishing to answer the question, but Emmet persisted. 'I know, Robert, you would like to see your mother' was all he would say, at which Emmet replied, 'Oh, what I would not give to see her!' Revelling in his role of trusted counsellor, MacNally raised his hand to heaven and smugly revealed, 'Then, Robert, you will see her this day.' Emmet's mother had died ten days previously. It is impossible to verify this transcript of events, but Emmet received very little information while in prison and his reactions have an air of authenticity. According to MacNally's account, Emmet 'exulted at the intelligence of his mother's death . . . and expressed a firm confidence of meeting with her in a state of eternal bliss, where no separation could take place'.[34] Patten's version was more plausible, with Emmet having a restrained and sensitive reaction. He made no reply to the news of his mother's death, but stood motionless before admitting, 'It is better so.' As Madden recorded, 'He was evidently struggling hard with his feelings and endeavouring to suppress them. He made no further allusion to the subject but by expressing a confident hope that he and his mother would meet in heaven.'[35]

At 1 p.m. the guards came to take Robert from his condemned cell. He seemed prepared for the journey to Thomas Street and descended the stairs calmly with the sheriff. Halfway down he remembered one final responsibility and asked permission to return to his room so 'that he might perform an essential duty which he had omitted'.[36] Generously the sheriff granted him this final request and Emmet climbed the stairs to his cell where he was supplied with pen, ink and paper.[37] Seemingly oblivious to the pressure he was under, he then wrote a letter to William Wickham, the chief secretary at Dublin Castle, 'in a strong firm hand, without blot, correction, or erasure'.[38] When it was finished he closed and sealed the letter before giving instructions for it to be sent to Dublin Castle, where it arrived at 4 o'clock. His last duty done, he was satisfied and announced, 'I am now quite prepared.'[39] It was a powerful letter which would have a profound effect on Wickham when he read it shortly after the execution. It would haunt him for the rest of his life.

The Rev. Gamble and the Rev. Grant accompanied Emmet on the journey from Kilmainham to Thomas Street, near the centre of the city. On the way they continued to debate the morality of the insurrection with him, hoping to make him recant before his execution. One question they put to him was whether he would still have attempted to overthrow the government if he could have 'foreseen the blood that had been spilt in consequence of his attempt'.[40] Emmet was bemused by their efforts, but refused to accept the implicit reproach. As he explained to them, 'no one went into battle without being prepared for similar events', arguing that his efforts were 'free from moral reproach in consequence of what he conceived to be the good of the motive that produced it'.[41]

A romantic idealist, Emmet wanted to wear his green rebel general's uniform at his execution. The request was refused and he wore the same clothes as at his trial: a simple black outfit with a dark stock around his neck, Hessian boots and a cloak.[42] Arriving at Thomas Street, he saw the scaffold assembled in front of St Catherine's Church. It was a temporary one and Madden explains that it was

> formed by laying boards across a number of empty barrels, that were placed for this purpose nearly in the middle of the street. Through this platform rose two posts, twelve or fifteen feet high, and a transverse beam was placed across them. Underneath this beam, about three feet from the platform, was a single narrow plank, supported on two slight ledges, on which the prisoner was to stand at the moment of being launched into eternity.[43]

The platform was almost six feet above the ground, with a ladder resting against it. Descending the carriage, his hands tied, Emmet was brought to the steps of the scaffold by the executioner. A secret government report ten days earlier had confidently predicted that he would 'wince' when about to 'experience the terror of execution'.[44] He displayed no such fear. Instead he requested permission to address the large crowd that had gathered to witness his death. This was refused. According to the clergymen present, he had intended to say that he had never taken any oath except that of the United Irishmen and that he was going to abide by it.[45] The officials were unwilling to take any chances, however, and feared that any address might produce 'tumult and bloodshed'. Emmet received the decision calmly and acquiesced, 'without appearing to be disturbed or agitated'.[46] Needing no encouragement to climb the ladder, he 'mounted quickly and with apparent alacrity'.[47]

Many of the people who had gathered to watch Emmet's execution were unsympathetic to his fate. Some journalists were disgusted by his conspicuous indifference and insisted that his *sang-froid* could only be explained as arrogance. *The London Chronicle* was particularly hostile:

> In short, he behaved without the least symptom of fear, and with all the effrontery and nonchalance which so much distinguished his conduct on his trial yesterday. He seemed to scoff at the dreadful circumstances attendant on him; at the same time, with all the coolness and complacency that can be possibly imagined.[48]

But the paper insisted that this composure could not be attributed to any religious strength: it was so 'utterly unlike the calmness of Christian fortitude'. Supporters of Robert Emmet would spend years exalting the courage he showed on the scaffold. But few would match this unintentional tribute from *The London Chronicle* journalist who despised him. Despite all his hostility, he could not help admitting: 'Even as it was, I never saw a man die like him; and God forbid I should see many with his principles.'

Another observer confirmed that Emmet 'boldly mounted the ladder'.[49] His hands were untied. There at the top of the platform he addressed the crowd with one final statement: 'My friends, I die in peace and with sentiments of universal love and kindness towards all men.'[50] The pro-government *Dublin Evening Post* newspaper reported a simpler sentence: 'I die at peace with mankind'; while another onlooker wrote that he said, 'My cause was a noble one and I die at peace with all the world.'[51] Shaking hands with some people on the scaffold, Emmet presented his watch to the executioner and removed his black stock. The hangman put the rope around his neck and drew a hood over his face. It seems Emmet wanted to remove the cover, but after a few words with the executioner it was fixed securely. With everything in place, a handkerchief was placed in Emmet's hand. This was the signal: when it fell the plank would be removed from under his feet and the grave would open beneath him.

'Are you ready, sir?' Having waited a few seconds, the hangman looked for the sign to execute the sentence of death. Robert Emmet replied in a firm voice, 'Not yet.' There was a short pause. Again the executioner asked, 'Are you ready, sir?' Still Emmet replied, 'Not yet.' We will never know who or what he was waiting for in the final moments of his life. The executioner put the question a third time, 'Are you ready, sir?' Requesting further time, Emmet began to say 'Not yet.' He never completed it. The impatient executioner had waited enough and tilted the plank off the ledge after hearing the first word. The noose tightened around Robert Emmet's neck as he fell to his death. It was noted that his 'life lasted much longer than is usual due to the lightness of his frame'.[52]

He hung for thirty minutes. R. R. Madden delivered a partisan but none the less poignant assessment of Emmet's death: 'and God's noblest work was used as if his image was not in it'.[53]

The punishment for treason was very specific. Emmet's body was taken down and placed on a table by the scaffold. The executioner then removed a sharp blade from his tunic and cut the head from the corpse. Grabbing the head in his hands he carried it to the front of the gallows and proclaimed in a loud voice: 'This is the head of a traitor, Robert Emmet.' Emmet's blood seeped down from the table and ran on to the pavement. Some women came forward to dip their handkerchiefs in it and take them away as souvenirs. The sonorous voice of the executioner continued to boom: 'This is the head of a traitor, Robert Emmet. This is the head of a traitor.' As the blood seeped into the gutter, some dogs gathered to lap it up.[54] Robert Emmet had risked his life in a courageous and idealistic attempt to liberate his country. He failed and paid the price for that failure on the scaffold. He was twenty-five years old.

2

ROMANCE REVISITED: THE SARAH CURRAN STORY

~

'I long to know how your wife and ten small children are. Good-bye my dear friend, but not for ever.'
(Sarah Curran in her final letter to Robert Emmet, August 1803)

'Ominously the childish voices become more and more tragic, and at the end die out in a whimper. In the last movement he described himself and his downfall; or as he later said: "It is the hero, on whom falls three blows of fate, the last of which fells him as a tree is felled."'
(Alma Mahler on Gustav Mahler's Sixth Symphony)

Shortly after Emmet's execution the artist James Petrie decided to sketch his portrait from the death-mask he had taken. One of his previous subjects had been Lord Edward Fitzgerald, the United Irishman leader who had died in 1798, and his sympathies were clearly engaged by the rebel cause. According to his son George Petrie, the future antiquary and vice-president of the Royal Irish Academy, the portrait attracted much interest. One morning a heavily veiled woman called to the house to see it and was admitted to the studio despite the artist's absence. George Petrie, only fifteen or sixteen years old at the time, hid in one corner of the room and observed the woman lift her veil to examine Emmet's countenance in the portrait. Overcome with emotion at the sight of it, she walked unsteadily to the far wall, pressed her forehead against it and began to cry hysterically. Then, 'with a sudden effort, she controlled herself, pulled down her veil and left the room as quickly and silently as she had come into it'.[1] He was later told that this woman was Sarah Curran.

The story of Sarah Curran's life has been the subject of much myth and anti-myth. She has suffered almost as much at the hands of Emmet's admirers as she has from his detractors. Both sides have distorted her final years, for their own purposes, and there has been much confusion about what happened to her after the failed insurrection of 1803. Her tragic life was immortalised in the work of Thomas Moore, the childhood friend of Robert Emmet, who romanticised her death in verse:

She is far from the land where her young hero sleeps,
And lovers around her are sighing;
But coldly she turns from their gaze, and weeps,
For her heart in his grave is lying.

She sings the wild song of her dear native plains,
Every note which he lov'd awaking;
Ah! little they think you delight in her strains,
How the heart of the minstrel is breaking.

He had liv'd for his love, for his country he died,
They were all that to life had entwin'd him;
Nor soon shall the tears of his country be dried,
Nor long will his love stay behind him.

Oh! make her a grave where the sunbeams rest,
When they promise a glorious morrow;
They'll shine o'er her sleep, like a smile from the west,
From her own lov'd island of sorrow.[2]

The tradition that Sarah Curran died of a broken heart in Sicily, far from her lover's grave, was deliberately constructed to maximise the heroic legend of Robert Emmet. It was encouraged by the American writer, Washington Irving, and reached its apotheosis in the late nineteenth century when a short biography of the rebel leader was published anonymously in Nottingham. Moore's poem was quoted with approval and it was stated that Sarah 'retired into a nunnery after the execution of Emmet where she died broken hearted'.[3] None of this was true. Like Moore's verses themselves, the account owed more to the imagination than to the reality. Sarah Curran was buried at Newmarket, Co. Cork, not in Sicily. Nor did she die in a nunnery; she in fact married a British officer, Robert Henry Sturgeon, and happily accompanied him to Sicily and then back to England, where she died at Hythe, in Kent, in 1808.

These facts proved uncomfortable for Emmet's hagiographers and were conveniently discarded for the sake of a simpler interpretation. Critics were quick to seize on them, however, and use them for their own purposes. Leslie Hale, the robust biographer of John Philpot Curran, Sarah's father, refused to reproach his subject for his conduct in 1803. For him, Sarah was a 'silly, misguided girl' who had 'compromised the reputation of her father' by her association with

Emmet.[4] Insisting that Sarah's real love was her future husband, Hale refused to accept the romantic account of her relationship with Emmet. While he did not doubt Emmet's feelings for her, he denied that she reciprocated his passion or even that she was capable of doing so: 'There is little to show that she ever loved him, or anyone but herself.'[5] Indeed he went so far as to blame her coldness for Emmet's capture and death, as 'her reluctance to give any assurance of permanent fidelity, or to agree to join him abroad, cost him his life'.

The biographer had assimilated the views of his subject. John Philpot Curran was horrified to discover his daughter's connection with a captured rebel and was quick to portray the relationship as strictly one-sided in his correspondence with Dublin Castle. Curran insisted that Emmet had invented an interest in his daughter and denounced his behaviour vehemently. Furious that Sarah had become 'the subject of the testamentary order of a miscreant', he claimed that Emmet had laboured by 'foul means and under such weak circumstances to connect her with his infamy' and had only acquired a 'posthumous interest in her person or her fate'.[6] Nevertheless Curran did not follow the logic of his own argument. Having insisted that Sarah was innocent of any involvement with Emmet, he then conceded that in his eyes she was irrevocably tainted. Although he would not cast her adrift absolutely, he admitted that she was 'blotted . . . irretrievably . . . from my society'.

Neither of the main interpretations about Sarah Curran's relationship with Robert Emmet are correct. Sarah was just twenty-one when the tumultuous events of 1803 took place, but her genuine feelings for Emmet cannot be doubted. The fact that she married someone else afterwards in search of happiness can only be criticised by doctrinaire absolutists who believe that she should have remained single for ever, or by those who feel she tarnished Emmet's memory by marrying a British soldier. Robert Emmet himself would have strongly disapproved of both these sentiments. By his own admission he had 'intended as much happiness for Sarah as the most ardent love could have given her';[7] he would not have begrudged her some happiness after his death. His own 'dying request' to his brother Thomas Addis Emmet and his sister-in-law Jane was about Sarah. Deeply concerned for her future, he begged his family to 'treat her as my wife, and love her as a sister'.[8] Even as he was about to be brought to the scaffold, he was barely able to conceal his genuine feelings:

> I did hope to have had her my companion for life. I did hope that she would not only have constituted my happiness, but that her heart and understanding would have made her one of Jane's deepest friends. I know that Jane would have loved her on my account, and I feel also that had they been acquainted she must have loved her on her own.

Imagining that she would be protected by her father and brother, Emmet none the less asked his family to intercede if she was abandoned by them and if 'no other should replace them'.

Sarah Curran's life was brief and blighted by tragedy. Born at Newmarket, Co. Cork, in 1782, she was the seventh child of the successful orator, lawyer and politician, John Philpot Curran, and his wife Sarah Curran (née Creagh). Raised at the Priory in Rathfarnham in County Dublin after 1790, her childhood was unhappy and she later wrote painfully about her 'melancholy home and confined circumstances'.[9] Curran's favourite daughter was Gertrude, a musical prodigy, who fell from a window to her death at the age of twelve in 1792. The loss was a harsh blow for Curran and he never stopped grieving it; he insisted on burying Gertrude in the grounds of the Priory and would spend hours watching her grave from his study.[10] A couple of years later his marriage collapsed. His wife found herself pregnant by a clergyman, the Rev. Michael Sandys, and an enraged Curran threw her out of the house. Unmindful of public attention or his children's feelings, he then brought a case for damages against Sandys and refused to allow contact between his family and his wife. The court case was humiliating for everyone involved. Sandys was represented by William Plunket, who was reduced to tears when his mentor, Curran, asked him, 'et tu fili?'[11] Richard Curran, the eldest son in the family, was forced to testify by his father and provided enough evidence of his mother's adultery. The defence, however, lost no time in revealing the darker side of John Philpot Curran's own character. He was accused of being a serial adulterer and his affairs with various women were brought before the court. Curran won the case, but lost some of his reputation, and was awarded only £50 in damages. He never saw his wife again and later revealed that he regarded his marriage as the worst mistake he ever made in his life.[12]

With the break-up of her parents' marriage Sarah was sent to Waterford where she stayed with the family of the Rev. Thomas Crawford at Lismore. Developing into a talented musician, she was an able pianist and harpist and also had a fine singing voice. Music was a comfort for her throughout her life and she loved in particular the works of Mozart.[13] Clothes were another passion and she had a playful obsession with new shoes. The favourite child of her mother, Sarah was deeply affected by her loss and found the Priory an even more melancholy place upon her return. Her father's parsimony was a large problem, but an even greater one was his meanness of spirit. As she later confided to her best friend, Anne Penrose, in a discussion about her childhood, 'What little kind encouragement to improve ourselves have either [myself or my sister Amelia] ever received? What was our position? To bear tyranny with injustice, to submit.'[14] This did not make for a happy household, especially when 'the additional weight' of an '*unnecessarily* parsimonious' father was added into the equation. The passing of time did little to assuage the bitterness she felt about her upbringing, and her treatment in 1803 only kindled her feelings of resentment. Sarah herself believed that the events of her youth, including the death of Robert Emmet, had cast a long shadow over her life. Attempting some measure of self-analysis in late 1807, she revealed that she had 'read somewhere that in youth a long succession of violent griefs and strong emotions are as likely to corrode as to correct the heart'.[15] And she added, 'I fear it is so.' Sarah showed a remarkable degree of self-awareness and maturity for someone still only twenty-five years old. She was perfectly aware of the destabilising effect of these 'griefs and strong emotions' and recognised that 'it creates a leaven of bitterness in our nature which breaks out now and again in spite of ourselves'.

Religion provided some measure of comfort. Sarah had a deep faith and studied the bible carefully; she was frequently able to refer to scripture in her adult years. As a child the only thing she knew by heart, apart from her prayers, was the 29th Psalm and she found it 'an unfailing soporific', putting her mind at ease when she had difficulty getting to sleep.[16] She would remember this 'hymn to the lord of the storm' in August 1803 when she had trouble sleeping once more. There was also a playful side to Sarah which has often been ignored. Even in the middle of a crisis, her capacity for laughter and her sense of humour were often able to sustain her own spirits as well as those around her. Sometimes dismissed as 'neurotic',[17] in her early years at least she had a deep reserve of strength which she could draw on in times of trouble. When Emmet was in hiding in August 1803, she concealed her dark gloom from him as best she could and attempted to maintain his morale with words of love and encouragement. As she reminded him in one of her final letters, 'you know I can laugh at the worst of times'.[18]

Developing into a 'remarkable' beauty,[19] Sarah made her social début at a ball at Castle Rath in County Wicklow in 1799. Barely seventeen, she won praise for her elegance and musical accomplishments and made a considerable impression on the assembled guests. One of these was Robert Emmet.[20] A friend of Richard Curran from their time at Trinity College Dublin, Emmet was soon spending much of his time at the Priory and increasingly was drawn there by Sarah's presence. Small and slender with dark hair and 'eyes large and black', Sarah possessed great charisma. Anne Devlin later insisted that 'her look was the mildest, and the softest, and the sweetest you ever saw'.[21] A friendship quickly developed between Robert and Sarah, but it is impossible to date precisely the beginning of their romance; it is likely that it did not develop until his return from the continent in the autumn of 1802. Shortly before his death Emmet revealed that he had 'idolised' Sarah from an early stage, but insisted that 'it was not with a wild or unfounded passion'.[22] Rather it was with 'an attachment increasing every hour, from an admiration of the purity of her mind, and respect for her talents'. The affair was kept secret, and even Richard Curran was unaware of it until after the insurrection.[23] On numerous occasions the couple discussed marriage and the number of children they would have, but their hopes were dashed in the summer of 1803. As Emmet admitted to Richard in his final hours in a letter that he wrote for Sarah's eyes, 'I did dwell in secret upon the prospect of our union.'[24] And Sarah's own thoughts on the subject are clear from her playful comment in her final letter to Emmet while he was still in hiding: 'I long to know how your wife and ten small

children are.' Events would later add an extra poignancy to her fond valediction: 'Good-bye my dear friend, but not for ever.'[25]

The collapse of the rebellion threw Robert Emmet's plans, personal and
political, into disarray. He remained in Dublin and stayed near Rathfarnham
so that he could continue to see Sarah. The letters they exchanged during this
period, both moving and passionate, revealed the depth of their mutual feelings. One letter which was discovered on Emmet after his capture contained
much evidence of her concern for his plight. Anxious for news of his safety,
Sarah confessed that she had been afraid her 'poor greyhound was lost, or still
worse might have been found'.[26] It is impossible to mistake the emotion in her
letter. After admitting that her health and spirits had been low, Sarah revealed
that she had 'feared the worst and was never more unhappy'.[27] It was only
when she received a letter from Robert confirming that he was still at liberty
that her mind was put at rest: 'I will never forget the sensation of agony I felt
while reading your letter. I assure you that my head suddenly felt as if it was
burning and for a few minutes I think I was in a fever.' Much of this fresh
anxiety was caused by the news that Robert planned to flee the country, at his
mother's request. After admitting that she longed to see him again, she made
it clear that he must do nothing to compromise his security: 'You must therefore attribute to *mental* derangement my wish of seeing you at present. Do not
think of it unless it might be done with safety.'[28]

After his capture Robert Emmet lied during his cross-examination to protect Sarah from prosecution. Although her letters provided clear proof that
she was aware of his plans, he attempted to dismiss this as unimportant with
untypical male bravado: 'a woman's sentiments are only opinions and they are
not reality . . . with a woman the utmost limit is only opinion'.[29] In truth he had
confided deeply in her and she had shared many of his fears about what might
happen after the insurrection. Sarah was aware of the possibility of a French
invasion taking place, and wrote to Emmet in hiding requesting information
about 'his hopes from abroad, and what you think they mean to do'.[30] But she
shared his suspicions about the likely behaviour of the French troops in
Ireland and wondered 'whether, if they pay us a visit, we shall not be worse off
than before'. The bond between Sarah Curran and Robert Emmet was deep
and genuine and they understood each other perfectly. There could be no
question of a breach of faith or a lack of trust. For, as she told Emmet, 'Such
is the perfect confidence that I feel subsists between us that I have no fear of
misconstruction on your part . . . I cannot bear to conceal anything from you.'[31]

The capture of Robert Emmet shattered their plans for happiness. It was
days before Sarah discovered his fate; as no one knew of their relationship, she
was not informed of his arrest and continued to believe he was safe. Despite
her appeals to Emmet to destroy her letters he had not done so and a number
were discovered on his person. Even though they were unsigned he believed
that she had been compromised and was desperate to protect her reputation;
in doing so he was finally tricked into revealing her identity. Fearing that Sarah

was under arrest, Emmet was willing to offer the government any terms. He was more concerned with Sarah's fate than the future of the rebellion or his own life, and was even prepared to remain silent at his trial if she went free. No deal was made by the Castle administration, in yet another miscalculation, because it feared little from the final speech of just one more captured rebel.

Desperate to communicate with Sarah, Emmet wrote her a letter from prison to beg forgiveness for having implicated her in the rebellion. It was intercepted by the prison officials and never reached her. His petitions for forgiveness went instead to the chief secretary, William Wickham, who was moved to read Emmet's insistent claim that he had 'no anxiety, no care about myself, but I am terribly oppressed about you'.[32] The letter was written in the dark as Emmet had been afraid that it might be discovered during the day, and ended with the tender plea: 'My dearest Sarah, forgive me.' The very next day the Priory was raided by Major Henry Sirr in an attempt to discover more incriminating evidence against Emmet. John Philpot Curran was not present and there was no one to protect Sarah, who was still asleep, from the determined visitors. The arrival of armed police into her bedroom, the capture of her lover and her own implication in the conspiracy was more than she could bear. She had exhausted her reserves of strength and was unable to withstand this new psychological blow. Wracked with grief, she fell to the floor crying hysterically. Meanwhile her sister Amelia went upstairs to try and destroy the bundle of love letters, and succeeded in burning most of them before the officers stopped her. Sarah became distraught and tearful, and her plight moved William Wickham when he read the official report; he admitted that he was 'much distressed at hearing the state of Miss Sarah Curran's mind'.[33] Her father had less sympathy on his return, fearing that his own ambitions would be stymied by his daughter's folly. This was perhaps not surprising, although Curran had shown no such squeamishness in 1798. As William Theobald Wolfe Tone, the son of the United Irishman leader, later revealed: 'he had opened his mind to my father; and, on the main point — the necessity of breaking the connection with England — they agreed'.[34] But while Curran 'avoided committing himself in the councils of the United Irishmen . . . had the project of liberating Ireland succeeded, he would have been amongst the foremost to hail and join her independence'.

The morning of his execution Robert Emmet wrote one final letter to Sarah Curran. It was addressed to her brother Richard, but almost every line was intended for a different reader. In the penultimate paragraph the pretence was dropped and he spoke to Sarah directly:

> My love, Sarah! It was not thus that I thought to have requited your affection. I did hope to be a prop round which your affections might have clung, and which would never have been shaken; but a rude blast has snapped it, and they have fallen over a grave.[35]

Battling against depression during his imprisonment, Emmet admitted that he was sustained by 'public motives' from sinking to despair. But when his thoughts returned inevitably to Sarah his peace of mind deserted him and on these occasions he viewed death as 'a refuge'.

After Emmet's execution Sarah Curran was banished from her father's home and sent to live with the Quaker family of Cooper Penrose at Woodhill, Co. Cork. There her dark sorrow gradually lifted and she developed an enduring friendship with Anne Penrose, who helped her through her grief and was soon loved as a sister. Sarah later thanked her for all she had done: 'You found me once, I may say, placed low by a cruel storm, and you raised my head and spoke comfort.'[36] But the emotional scars from this time were never completely healed. Sarah also admitted: 'I often think the effects of that period on my mind are not to be done away radically.' Anne Penrose was her 'Balm of Gilead' and her 'medium of life' and Sarah firmly believed that God provided support for the just through 'a faithful friend'.[37] From her youth she had found comfort in her strong religious faith, but she suddenly became superstitious and darkly pessimistic about her existence. Dreams began to assume a deeper significance and were regarded as portents of the future. She also had premonitions of her death and on her final visit to the Crawford family predicted that she would never see them alive again.[38] Increasingly in her correspondence she made references to her impending decline, and even though she retained her sense of humour, she was often afflicted with bouts of melancholia. According to a descendant of the Penrose family, Sarah was 'highly strung, hot-tempered and a terrific talker'. She was also prone to fiery tantrums. When a butler annoyed her during one evening of music she smashed a fiddle on his head.[39]

Feeling abandoned and alone, Sarah accepted the proposal of marriage offered by Captain R. Henry Sturgeon, a talented engineer in the royal staff corps. It seems that Sturgeon was a nephew of the late marquess of Rockingham, who had been prime minister during the granting of Irish legislative independence in 1782.[40] Two years after her marriage, Sarah reflected on how unhappy she had been at Woodhill and admitted that for long intervals she was 'to speak the truth, *engrossed* by self. It was a period passed either in a fruitless grief over past sorrow, or the anxious contemplation of new prospects and engagements, by which I hoped to be relieved from the recollection of the former.'[41] Washington Irving, in his short story 'The broken heart', claimed that the couple met at a masked ball in Dublin. For the critics of Sarah Curran this was taken as further proof of her fickleness. Irving saw it differently and described a more pathetic picture with Sarah 'wandering like a spectre, lonely and joyless'.[42] However the scene, like the story, is nothing more than fiction and it is surprising that it has since been used as a credible source. Irving ended the tale with a triumph of his story-telling imagination. The depressed and mournful Sarah began singing 'a little plaintive air' to the assembled guests who were so moved by her condition 'that she gathered a crowd, mute and silent, around her, and melted every one into tears'. Sarah Curran and

Henry Sturgeon married on 21 November 1805 at Glanmire Church in County Cork, where according to a Penrose family tradition she was brought to the chapel in tears.[43] The newly-weds moved to England where they resided briefly at Hythe in Kent. That winter Sarah caught a bad cold, which affected her singing voice, and she had still not fully recovered a year later. She was miserable at Hythe and detested the place, so was delighted when her husband was sent with his regiment to Sicily. She accompanied him and for a brief time found happiness with a husband who loved her and whom she loved in return.

The long voyage to Sicily did not pass without incident. Sarah suffered from seasickness for the first part of the journey, but soon recovered and read the first book of Euclid and then a history by Plutarch. Just after leaving the Barbary coast the ship was caught in a terrible storm and many passengers began to panic that it would capsize. Sarah later admitted, with heavy irony, that she was '*not frightened much*'.[44] They were forced to eat their dinner on the floor and had 'an unhappy goose literally *nailed* down to keep it steady'. As the ship was tossed around in the storm the men kept sliding against each other and Sarah admitted she 'never laughed more in my life'.[45] Arriving safely at Tangier Bay, in North Africa, Sarah expressed an agonising desire to look at some new faces and different clothes. With typical self-deprecation she admitted that she was only 'a poor little bog-trotter' and had never seen 'anything worse than myself'. Waiting for her in Tangiers was her brother John who had decided to join her on the journey to Sicily. This reawakened Sarah's supernatural sensitivities — she remembered that when she had first arrived at Woodhill she had dreamt of meeting John in Africa 'and that we were surrounded by blacks'; she wondered if this was not 'a very curious coincidence'.[46]

Arriving in Sicily, Sarah was immediately struck by the beauty of the island. As she stood on the deck of the ship with her husband she was enchanted by the view from the harbour at Messina and in a flight of fancy she told him that she 'could now by magic show this scenery to our friends at home'.[47] Her description of the countryside captured the colourful imagery perfectly: the 'orange groves and the vines in this season contrasted with the dark green verdure of the trees, looking like the red autumnal leaves strewn very thick on the ground'. A Sicilian sailor boarded the ship whom the English officers bombarded with questions which he struggled to understand. One intrepid sportsman asked him, 'Is there a good place for playing cricket?' But Sarah had her own concerns and was anxious to know when the last earthquake had taken place. On this occasion the sailor understood the question perfectly. Sarah was not reassured to learn that it had only been six weeks previously; nor was she encouraged by his description of the disaster as 'the murder of God'. In the beginning she found the heat 'intolerable' but was soon pleased that the island was 'very amusing' and educational.[48]

By this time Sarah had become partially reconciled to her father and greeted the news of his election to Westminster with 'high spirits' in October 1806. Her husband, who was a constant support, was adept at cheering her up on the many occasions when her melancholy returned. As Sarah confided to Anne, 'My dearest Henry behaves (as the French would say) like an angel to me.'[49] Nevertheless she felt obliged to portray all the outward signs of happiness to him and learned to mask her depression. Only to Anne Penrose did she open her heart and admit that she had 'of late, learned to suppress many wishes that I formerly thought very allowable'.[50] In private the charade sometimes proved too much for her and she confessed, 'My heart often rebels and *many many tears* have I shed which no-one witnessed.' She did not ask for sympathy from Anne, but ended the letter by quoting a verse which she thought particularly appropriate:

Me and my cares in silence leave,
Come not near me while I grieve.

Settling at Messina, Sarah carefully tended to her 'little stock of cheerfulness'.[51] In her sleep, however, unable to suppress her true feelings, she frequently suffered from nightmares. Sturgeon often had to wake her 'weeping violently when I have been under the influence of some melancholy dream'.

In an interesting coincidence General Henry Fox, the commander-of-the-forces in Ireland during Emmet's rebellion and therefore his leading military adversary, was also stationed in Sicily during some of Sarah's time there. He had been sent to Messina because of his failure in Ireland in 1803, and resided with his wife at a castle near the Sturgeons. Mrs Fox decided to look after Sarah and was 'very kind',[52] their friendship providing an ironic counterpoint to the events of 1803 when the men they loved were on opposite sides. Sarah also became very close friends with Catherine Wilmot, the Irishwoman who had known Robert Emmet on the continent.[53] In general Sarah enjoyed the company of the women she encountered, but sometimes found them a little too much to endure. The Fox family treated her with consideration, but many others were 'so rude and overbearing'. There were some moments of levity. For example, Sarah was bemused to discover that even the 'musical people' on the island had never heard of her beloved Mozart. Mrs Warrington, 'a vulgar, but rich lady who knows not a syllable respecting music', was astonished when Sarah insisted that Mozart was a greater composer than Domenico Cimarosa. Possessing a natural talent for put-downs, Sarah revealed that Mrs Warrington differed from her 'in that decided manner which ignorance *alone* could induce her with'.[54] In private Sarah spent hours venting her 'spleen against these people'. Fortunately her husband agreed with her and Sarah was relieved that 'our tastes are as much in unison as our hearts'.

Disappointed at the dearth of good music on the island, Sarah noted wistfully that she would have to settle for what she could find. To celebrate the Christmas of 1806 Mrs Fox threw a lavish party for her friends and invited some famous opera singers and orchestral performers. Sarah was highly critical of the talent on display and particularly disliked Caldarara, supposedly 'the best female singer', who had come over from Vienna. In an acerbic commentary she noted that Caldarara sang in a 'handsome, hackneyed style'. A few nights later at Mrs Warrington's party Sarah brought her harp with her, as it was the only one on the island. Towards the end of the evening her host arranged 'a formal circle' around the instrument and the women took turns singing. 'Frightened to death', Sarah performed for the group, but she was not satisfied with her song and privately blamed the weakness of her voice on her lingering cold. Mrs Warrington was next to perform and Sarah noted with malicious glee that she sang 'horribly out of tune, and badly'. While Sarah's effort might not have been up to her usual standard, it must have been reasonably good for she was later asked to sing a second piece. This time she claimed she was 'worse than before' and became so 'tired and disgusted with the whole business' that she followed it with a short Scottish song, 'Had I a cave'. Mrs Warrington took the opportunity to put Sarah in her place by telling her daughter in a loud voice, 'Arabella, my dear, you have a Scotch song too. Do sing it my love. I like those little easy things sometimes.' But Sarah had the last laugh as Arabella Warrington chose to sing 'Donald' which was 'squalled out of tune, out of time'.

It seems that Henry Sturgeon was the only person on the island who was brave enough to challenge the redoubtable Mrs Warrington. Sarah was immensely proud that he could '*manage* this lady and act towards her in her own decided style'. At the end of the party, as the guests were leaving, the Sturgeons decided to leave the harp behind and collect it the next day. Upon hearing this Mrs Warrington boldly suggested that it could remain there permanently so that Sarah could practise with Arabella. Sarah was mortified, but her husband settled the matter decisively. He told her abruptly: 'My dear Mrs Warrington, you must excuse me, I could no more part with the harp than with my life. I eat my music, I drink my music.' Then he packed up the harp then and there and brought it with him, much to the 'great astonishment' of his host.

Sarah's sojourn in Sicily had not lessened her interest in clothes and she begged Anne Penrose to keep her up to date with all the latest fashions. As she added whimsically in a postcript: 'In what corner of the world can one be squeezed where a woman forgets them?'[55]

In the summer of 1807 Sarah became pregnant. She was delighted by the news and longed to have a healthy child. In July she wrote to Anne Penrose asking her to be the child's godmother.[56] The letter was a strange mixture of hope and depression. She complained light-heartedly that 'Good servants are *impossible* to find here' and described Mount Etna as one of the finest sights in the world. But she also spoke about her fear of dying and promised that '*if I live*' she would tell her baby all about her godmother. Sarah and her husband toured around Sicily in a *lettiga*, a carriage on poles, which was driven by mules. Morning sickness affected her mood, however, and she suffered from 'violent' illness for two months. Reflecting on her life, she became depressed about 'the accumulation of misfortune I have suffered' and wondered how she had survived for so long 'after the anguish of the blow had fallen'.[57] She was echoing some of the final thoughts of Robert Emmet, who had written to her father from prison about the 'great deal of that misfortune which seems uniformly to have accompanied me'.[58] Reflecting from Sicily, Sarah now remembered that 'there do exist men of *pure* and honourable minds'. Even in her lowest moments she found the sound of people practising music uplifting and it rescued her from 'the very lowest ebb of idleness and abomination'.[59] The plight of her brother filled her with concern. It seems Richard had suffered a nervous breakdown after Emmet's death from which he never fully recovered. In 1807 he was forced to flee the country after his affair with an actress was revealed and her husband sued for damages. Sarah hoped that he would visit her in Sicily and admitted that 'his late ill-luck has pained me to the quick indeed'.[60] Whenever she was asked to sing or play the harp in public, Sarah was struck by stage-fright. She believed that people only wanted 'to find out that you had no merit'.[61] By now she was able to converse freely in Italian, although she admitted it was with a strong Sicilian accent.

On 26 December 1807 Sarah gave birth to a son. Her husband had been recalled to England and the premature delivery took place on board the ship home. At Gibraltar, Sarah had been beset by fears that she would go into labour on the voyage and she begged to be allowed to remain on shore. Sturgeon put in a request for leave but it was rejected. Sarah later revealed that she had suffered 'misery and hardship in many a shape' and had 'dreaded' the idea of continuing on the journey. All her old fears returned and she began to doubt whether she would survive the voyage. Her agony increased when the ship was caught in a storm on Christmas Day. She went into labour a few hours later, while the storm still raged, and had only one soldier's wife for assistance. For five and a half hours she 'lay on my berth on the floor of a cabin where no fire could be made', and gave birth with 'a freezing cold paralysing us all'.[62]

The difficult labour took its toll on Sarah's health and she was extremely weak afterwards.[63] She was unable to breast-feed or care for her son for thirteen days and she later admitted that 'from the first hour the child's cries disturbed me, close in the berth by him'.[64] Tormented by the belief that her son would die, on 2 January she had some kind of breakdown, or as she described it 'a brain fever', which threatened her life. Her husband discovered her in the cabin 'raging mad, I may say, repeating poetry' and prayers. In her delirium she began thinking of 'the mercies and promises of the Great Redeemer' and developed a fervent belief, based on scripture, that 'He shall gather the lambs with his arms' and let no harm come to her or her child. The ship arrived safely in Portsmouth on 7 January 1808 and Sarah immediately wrote to Anne Penrose about her 'godson', praising her husband's behaviour which had been 'beyond the power of words'.[65] Sarah was now breast-feeding her son, whom she decided to name John, like her father and beloved brother. She even began making clothes for him and completed a small cap for his head.

Tragedy struck three days later. Her very first sentence to Anne Penrose explained everything: 'My darling child is lying dead.'[66] It was the final blow for her already fragile mind and she never recovered from the loss. The pain was too much and she became assailed by doubts and nervous anxiety, admitting that 'I suffer misery you cannot conceive. I am often seized with heavy perspirations, trembling, and that indescribable horror which you must know if you ever had fever.'[67] Her poignant letters to Anne Penrose make it clear that she had given up all interest in life: 'We shall leave this immediately for London. I rely on you to come and see me before I die there. My heart is bleeding and broken, and can't pray to God for he has forgotten me.'[68] Her deep faith, which had previously provided solace in times of adversity, was now shattered. Even when the storm had raged around the ship during her difficult labour she had found strength that her child would survive:

> When all seemed adverse to hope, it is strange how an overstrained trust in certain words of our Saviour gave me such perfect faith in his help, that, although my baby was visibly pining away, I never doubted his life for a moment. 'He who gathers the lambs in his arms', I thought, would look on mine if I had faith in him. This has often troubled me since.[69]

Sarah never recovered from the death of her beloved Johnny and in her grief was able to predict her own rapid decline: 'My angel is in heaven I hope, and I will follow him and nurse him there.'[70] After all her suffering she now felt betrayed, especially after 'heaven seemed to promise happiness'. She kept remembering that she had made clothes 'for my boy, but a shroud will now do for him'.[71]

To add to her misery Anne Penrose did not write or visit. She later discovered that her friend had been prevented by her guardian, but at the time the apparent rejection only added to her feelings of isolation and abandonment. In a second letter to Anne, three days after the first, she begged for an answer: 'I cannot think you do not mean to come to me.'[72] Sarah's account of her dead child could not have been more miserable: 'My little angel was pretty perhaps to no one but us, but oh Anne, my heart will know peace no more. He was the image of your poor Sarah. Would you have loved him?' Her pleas became more desperate as the letter continued. It ended with an ultimatum: either Anne would visit or Sarah would never contact her again. The conclusion was a pathetic cry: 'I conjure you on my knees to come. On your dear breast will I repose a bleeding and broken heart. Farewell. Remember me.'

It was only in March that Sarah discovered the truth behind Anne's ostensible coldness. By now she was back at Hythe in Kent, the place she admitted she 'always detested beyond every other'.[73] Although Sarah quickly forgave her friend, her feelings of impending doom were not lessened. A shadow of her former self, she was haunted by her memories and became increasingly desperate and indistinct. The soldier Charles Napier, who had been stationed in Ireland in 1803, was at Hythe at this time. In his journal he wrote about Sarah Curran, whom he described as 'the betrothed of Robert Emmet'.[74] He revealed that 'She seemed a perfect ghost and could not speak without stopping to get breath at every word.' The uncomfortable surroundings at Hythe only added to Sarah's gloom and she felt that she 'was brought to die here'.[75] Sadly she was correct. On 3 May 1808 she died at Hythe, having succumbed to illnesses both physical and psychological. Her final request was that she would be buried at the Priory, in the garden beside her sister Gertrude. John Philpot Curran refused. And so she was buried at the place where she was born, Newmarket, Co. Cork. R. R. Madden, the biographer of the United Irishmen, was not inclined to be too hard on Curran, and set his behaviour towards Sarah against his good work for Ireland: 'If there was aught in his treatment of his poor daughter of harshness and of undue severity, let the fault be remembered and dealt with uncharitably only by those who forget his services to his countrymen.'[76]

Overcome with grief at the death of his 'favourite sister', John Curran predicted that 'some of the most precious tears of our country' would fall on her ashes.[77] Mourning deeply her loss, he found little comfort except by thinking that she was in heaven 'where her sorrows are at an end'. In a highly emotional letter to John Crawford in Lismore he broke the news that 'our *dear beloved* Sarah is torn from us' and mentioned that the dying wish of 'the refined and elegant Sarah' was to be buried at the Priory. Now he remembered her prediction that she would never see the Crawfords alive again and was unsettled by just how prescient she had been. Sarah had cared deeply about John Crawford but had 'long since foretold, that she would never see you after your party . . . True it is. She never has!' Her vivid dreams also preyed on his mind and he nervously admitted that there had certainly been 'some curious coincidences'. John Curran had loved Sarah the best of all his family and he bitterly attacked 'the envious hand of death' for having destroyed his happiness. This was the grief talking, but it is none the less an indication of just how much Sarah meant to him. All he wanted now was to 'secure a life eternal with her in a better world beyond the grave'.

Captain Henry Sturgeon did not survive the Napoleonic wars. He was distraught by the death of his wife and child and seemed anxious to seek an early death. Charles Napier worried about his health and recorded: 'He bears his sorrow too well to forget it easily' and suggested that 'The endeavour to get killed . . . would save him much anguish and perhaps cure him.'[78] It seems Napier was worried that Sturgeon would attempt to sacrifice his life and recognised that 'the world to him is void'; he also regretted that his son had died as he might have given him 'some interest in life'. Promoted to major on 1 June 1809, Sturgeon was transferred to the quartermaster general's department and served with the royal staff corps in the decisive Peninsular campaign. His abilities soon brought him to the attention of the duke of Wellington who thought him a very 'clever fellow' and praised his engineering exploits in various dispatches in 1812. At Ciudad Rodrigo, Wellington noted that without his construction of a bridge over the Agueda the advance could not have taken place, and praised his command of the second battalion's fifth regiment.[79] Promoted to lieutenant-colonel on 24 July 1812, Sturgeon won further commendations for his role in the crucial victory at Salamanca. Further successes, constructing a temporary bridge at Alcantra and a bridge of boats over the Adour enhanced his reputation, but his promotion to postmaster undid everything. He was unable to come to terms with the administrative responsibilities of the office, preferring to spend his time designing bridges. The result was an incompetent delivery system, with some letters taking six days to arrive instead of one.[80] Wellington was furious with him after the battle of Orthes, and it seems Sturgeon's spirits never recovered from this criticism.

On 19 March 1814 the British army marched on Vic Bigiarre, where the beautiful countryside was surrounded for two miles by vineyards. In the evening Sturgeon decided to carry out some reconnaissance work on his own, recklessly endangering his position. He was killed by a sniper's bullet. There was immediate speculation that he had deliberately sacrificed his own life. The obituary column of the *Gentleman's Magazine* regretted the death of 'this gallant officer' who had 'unguardedly advanced', and noted that 'his loss is greatly lamented'.[81] He was only thirty-three years old. Because of his distinguished career in the British army Henry Sturgeon was given a short entry in the *Dictionary of National Biography* published at the beginning of the twentieth century; his marriage to Sarah Curran is not mentioned.

Writing of Robert Emmet's love for Sarah Curran, R. R. Madden concluded that such was his noble character that he 'was not likely to fix his affections lightly, or on one unworthy of them'.[82] The story of Sarah Curran has been interwoven into the romantic nationalist interpretation of Robert Emmet's life. What happened to her after 1803 deserves to be an essential part of this tapestry. Her marriage to Henry Sturgeon, her fleeting happiness in Sicily and her rapid decline in England are all important elements for understanding her story. There was always something fey and ethereal about Sarah; perhaps this was what attracted Robert Emmet to her in the first place. His idealism and her fatalistic tendencies created a shared affinity and forged an enduring bond that cast a long shadow over their short lives. Sarah Curran and Robert Emmet's love affair was more complex, and less comfortable, than has sometimes been portrayed. But it is a much richer tale for all that. It was a relationship touched by tragedy and marked by the inescapable questions of love, death, pain and regret.

3

CONSPIRACIES AND CONNECTIONS

~

'I never pronounce the name of Pitt but I feel death on my shoulder.'[1]
(Alleged comment of the imprisoned Queen Marie Antoinette, *c.*1791)

Colonel William Pitt spent the autumn of 1803 preparing his corps of volunteers to repel French invasion from the shores of England. Britain had declared war on France on 18 May 1803 and there was a widespread fear that a Napoleonic invasion was imminent. As constable of Dover Castle and admiral of the Cinque Ports, Pitt raised two battalions of militia to meet the threat and purchased manuals on tactics and arms so that he could study the art of warfare.[2] Based at Walmer Castle in Kent, he went 'through the fatigue of a drill sergeant' and spent his days riding from place to place inspecting the volunteers and practising drills, 'parade after parade, at fifteen or twenty miles distant from each other'.[3] Wearing his regimental colonel's uniform at almost all times, he delighted in his responsibilities, preparing contingency plans in the event of a successful landing and ensuring that his volunteers were well trained and knowledgeable about manoeuvres and weaponry. Nevertheless not all of the military appreciated the efforts of the volunteer colonel. Major General John Moore, the commander of Pitt's district, was highly sceptical about the possible benefits of part-time soldiers. When Pitt once informed him that 'on the very first alarm' he would march to aid him with his corps, he received a sarcastic response when he enquired where his men would be stationed. Moore pointed to a nearby hill and told him that they would be positioned there where they could 'make a formidable appearance to the enemy while I, with the soldiers, shall be fighting on the beach'.[4] Pitt was bemused by the retort as it echoed some of his earlier criticism of conscript militias. But others were more impressed with Pitt's endeavours and Lord Mulgrave reported that he was 'already an excellent soldier'.[5] It was difficult to believe that less than three years previously William Pitt had been the prime minister of the country.

THE PITT CONSPIRACY

The major conspiracy theory surrounding the insurrection of 1803 is that William Pitt masterminded the whole affair for his own purposes. At least two influential biographies of Robert Emmet assert this strongly and it was stated originally by Dr Thomas Addis Emmet, the grandson of his namesake, in his history of *The Emmet family* (1898).[6] In 1880 Dr Emmet, who was born in New York, visited Ireland to conduct research into the events of 1803. At Dublin Castle he encountered Sir Bernard Burke, the keeper of the state papers, who aided him in his endeavours but was unable to grant him access to all the material. A few years later, or so it was claimed, Burke made a confession to Emmet which became the basis of the entire conspiracy theory. According to Dr Emmet's account of the meeting, Burke revealed that he had read secret documents relating to the passing of the Act of Union of 1800, as well as some relating to the rebellion of 1803, but had decided against making them public. The key letter was one from Prime Minister William Pitt in October 1802 to Alexander Marsden, the under secretary at Dublin Castle, directing him to encourage another rebellion 'at all hazards' and suggesting that 'Robert Emmet, who was in Paris, should be approached for the purpose'.[7] This discovery prompted Dr Emmet to conclude that Pitt had been 'a demon incarnate in Irish affairs'.[8] He was also disturbed to learn that there was 'an unbroken chain of evidence' which proved that an *agent provocateur* had been sent to France by the British secret service to entrap his granduncle and trick him into returning to Ireland to lead a doomed rebellion. Burke claimed he sealed these documents in a box and placed them in the tower of Dublin Castle with instructions that they were not to be opened for a certain number of years. However on a subsequent visit to Dublin, Dr Emmet discovered that the box had disappeared and the documents were lost, presumably destroyed. Continuing with his attempts to establish the truth behind the rebellion of 1803 on a subsequent trip to Ireland, Dr Emmet was visited by police officials and told to leave the country within twenty-four hours. As Helen Landreth later claimed, 'Even after more than eighty years the real story of Robert Emmet's rising was still being concealed.'[9]

J. J. Reynolds in his useful book, *Footprints of Emmet* (1903), restated the conspiracy theory with complete conviction.[10] And in 1949 when Helen Landreth published her book, *The pursuit of Robert Emmet*, the 'lost' letter of William Pitt was central to her argument. In fact, in a later defence of her book, in an article in *The Dublin Magazine* she went so far as to describe the conspiracy as 'the whole thesis of my book'.[11] The question of why the British prime minister would want to provoke a rebellion was rarely discussed in as much detail. According to Dr Thomas Addis Emmet, in a second work, Pitt

deliberately determined to punish the Irish people for their opposition to the proposed union, urged by him between England and Ireland; and to justify its establishment, resorted to the most discreditable measures of oppression, thus obtaining a pretext to check the continued turbulency and dissatisfaction of his own making, then existing among the Irish people.[12]

This had a certain resonance with the alleged comment of Thomas Russell in 1803 that 'this conspiracy originated with the enemy'.[13] Whether Sir Bernard Burke actually made these claims to Dr Emmet is impossible to prove. But what is certain is that the 'lost' letter of Prime Minister Pitt never existed. The entire theory crumbles when one major flaw is exposed: William Pitt was not prime minister in October 1802. He had resigned at the beginning of the previous year over the refusal of King George III to accompany the legislative union of Great Britain and Ireland with Catholic emancipation.[14] Nevertheless Landreth did not allow this uncomfortable fact to destroy her faith in Dr Emmet's conspiracy theory. As she argued in her preface: 'The doctor's integrity cannot be doubted.'[15] Explaining Pitt's involvement in the affair, Landreth claimed that he was expecting to be recalled to office at any moment and,

> His acute and ruthless statesmanship *may have* suggested the idea of a frustrated rebellion as an excuse for suspending the Habeas Corpus Act and thereby obtaining the means of keeping in gaol the most dangerously disaffected of the Irish people, not to mention the pacific effect that some well-publicised hangings would have on would-be patriots.[16]

There are a number of problems with this analysis, not least of which is the fact that the Habeas Corpus Act had previously been suspended in 1794 in England and the parliament could find more convenient excuses to do so again. Nor was Pitt the power behind the British government. He had been a peripheral figure since leaving office and had become increasingly distant from his successor, Henry Addington. Still regarded with suspicion in some quarters for his Catholic sympathies, he certainly did not have the authority to encourage an Irish rebellion, especially when the plot could backfire spectacularly.

For biographers of Emmet the main advantage of the conspiracy theory was that it provided a neat explanation for the failure of the insurrection. As Emmet had been the pawn of the British government from the beginning, therefore he could hardly be blamed for how it turned out. Landreth claimed that she had discovered many documents that confirmed the existence of a government conspiracy, the missing box that Sir Bernard Burke had sealed, insisting that she had 'stumbled upon a great mystery. For reasons that will become apparent, the true story of Robert Emmet's insurrection that took place in 1803 has never been told, and for generations efforts have been made to keep it a secret.'[17] The character of Robert Emmet, 'gallant, tender, and idealistic', was contrasted with the cold and enigmatic figure of William Pitt:

> His ability as a statesman and the efforts of idealising biographers have kept in the shadow one interesting aspect of Pitt's character. He was an extremely

sardonic individual, famous among his contemporaries for his bitter, freezing sarcasm and his love of a malicious joke. It *may have* amused him to think that in sending for Robert Emmet he was using the young man's blazing patriotism as a means of keeping enslaved the country he longed to free.[18]

Thus Robert Emmet had been chosen specifically because of the prestige of his family's name, with the deliberate intention of destroying him.

There were many similarities between William Pitt and Robert Emmet. Both were the youngest sons in their families and both had inherited their father's name. They also shared a youthful idealism, a love of mathematics and a rare precocity. Pitt became prime minister of Britain in December 1783 at the age of twenty-four and would remain in office for the next seventeen years. Emmet led an insurrection in Ireland at the age of twenty-five. Each man was an accomplished orator capable of speaking brilliantly for hours without notes. William Pitt did not choose Robert Emmet as his pawn in an elaborate conspiracy; there was no government plot. For one thing, Pitt had succeeded in passing the union in 1800 after much effort and had wanted to create a genuine bond between the countries through the granting of Catholic emancipation. He would not have wished to encourage a rebellion in Ireland in 1803, even if he had been in office. But, more importantly, it was not in Pitt's character to create a grand scheme that involved sacrificing a young man for the sake of 'a malicious joke' and some negligible security gains. The conspiracy theory is implausible, impractical and unsustainable. But it does give an example of some of the coincidences and connections which occurred during the turbulent events of 1803. For there is a final reason why the former prime minister would not have selected this particular victim for his conspiracy: William Pitt and Robert Emmet were distant cousins.

Both the Emmet and the Pitt families traced their lineage back to the Temple political dynasty based at Stowe in Buckinghamshire. Robert Emmet the elder and William Pitt the younger were fourth cousins. Even distant relationships were extremely important in the eighteenth century and the Emmet family profited from their useful Temple connections.[19] One cousin, George Grenville, the 3rd Earl Temple and later 1st marquess of Buckingham, was twice lord lieutenant for Ireland in the 1780s. The American branch of the Temple family was even more intimately connected to the Emmets and Sir John Temple, the 8th baronet of Stowe and first British consul-general to the United States, was a first cousin of Dr Robert Emmet. The 8th baronet's grandfather left two children. His daughter Rebecca Temple (1700-74) did not emigrate to America but instead remained in Ireland where she married Christopher Emett (as he spelt his name) and had two sons, Thomas and Robert. Her youngest son became state physician for Ireland and was the father of Robert Emmet, the subject of this book. On 4 February 1782 the British government awarded an annual pension of £50 to Dr Robert Emmet as a grant to be kept in trust for the children of the American branch of the Temple family who had lost property during the War of Independence.[20] Dr Thomas Addis Emmet, the family genealogist and historian, was proud of his family's connection with the Temple family and acknowledged the link with the marquess of Buckingham.[21] But Buckingham was the first cousin of William Pitt the younger, and this fact was either not known or conveniently ignored. It certainly adds an extra dimension to the conspiracy theory.

The Emmet family remained in close contact with their relatives in America. Robert Temple, a second son of Captain Robert Temple and Mehitable Temple (née Nelson), married Harriet Shirley and had a daughter, Anne Western Shirley Temple. She married her second cousin Christopher Temple Emmet in 1781. Sir John Temple and his wife were in regular correspondence with the Emmet family and they often did favours for each other. Dr Emmet regularly invited him to Dublin and insisted that his wife accompany him, adding mischievously, 'for without her, we, one and all, object to your coming'.[22] Grenville Temple, who succeeded his father as 9th baronet of Stowe in 1798, spent almost three years with the Emmets in Ireland. As Mrs Elizabeth Emmet wrote to her son Tom, in prison in 1801: 'You will recollect what Sir Grenville Temple said when he was last here, that he would not, by the profits of his profession, pay for the expense of his books.'[23] Mrs Emmet had been very insistent on Grenville Temple and his cousins visiting Ireland and informed his mother in 1773 that 'our boys insist upon it' as they couldn't wait to meet 'their little kinsmen'.[24] Later when Thomas Addis Emmet was campaigning against Rufus King in New York in 1807, he reminded him that he should be aware 'of my near relationship and family connection to the late Sir John Temple'.[25] On the two occasions when Buckingham was lord lieutenant for Ireland the Emmets were able to profit from his patronage. On the first occasion Dr Emmet succeeded in having his patent as state physician split in two so that his son Thomas Addis could share the sinecure. As William Drennan shrewdly noted, Dr Emmet had 'some interest' with the viceroy.[26] And in 1787 Christopher Temple Emmet wrote a lengthy poem, 'The decree', which he dedicated to his kinsman on his second period as viceroy. The story of how Dr Emmet managed to get his son included on the patent as state physician, even though he had not yet qualified as a medical doctor, is revealing. It followed the death of William Pitt the elder, as Dr Emmet made careful use of his distant connection to advance his family.

On 11 May 1778 William Pitt the elder, earl of Chatham, died suddenly after making a dramatic return to parliament. He had been assisted to the House of Lords by his youngest son and namesake, but collapsed before he could finish his speech in favour of conciliation with the American colonies. The funeral for the former prime minister was not attended by the peers of the realm as a body after some pressure had been exerted by the king. A monument to the elder Pitt in Westminster Abbey was also opposed by George III as he considered it a 'rather offensive measure to me personally'.[27] This all made an impression on the young William Pitt who was then approaching his nineteenth birthday.

With icy contempt he noted that 'the court did not honour us with their countenance, nor did they suffer the procession to be as magnificent as it ought'.[28]
In Ireland, Dr Emmet decided to raise a subscription to erect a statue to the
elder Pitt in County Cork.[29] Buckingham was the nephew of the late statesman
and was so impressed with this 'patriotic gesture of his relative' that he later
agreed to include Thomas Addis Emmet on the patent as state physician even
though he had not yet qualified as a doctor.[30] To defray the high costs of Tom's
education, Dr Emmet attempted to get a raise in his salary as state physician in
1784. On 23 October he wrote to John Temple asking him to remind the new
prime minister about the statue that had been erected in his father's honour.
His calculated and shrewd approach paid off. The following year his salary was
doubled to £400 per annum.[31]

WILLIAM PITT AND POLITICS, 1759–1801

William Pitt the elder raised his second son to be prime minister. Born on 28
May 1759 the younger Pitt had been worryingly underweight and delicate after
childbirth but was nursed carefully through infancy. His father called him
'Little Mr Secretary' and would practise speeches with him in their back garden
with the trees representing the packed benches of the House of Commons.
The young child's precocity was widely reported. On discovering that his
mother had been awarded a peerage he expressed his delight that he was not
the eldest son as he did not want to inherit the title and sit in the House of
Lords; instead he wanted to follow his father into the lower chamber and one
day become prime minister.

Brilliant but unstable, his father was forced to resign as prime minister in
1768 after succumbing to illness and insanity.[32] He never held high office
again. Rousing himself for one final speech about the American War of
Independence in 1778, he collapsed and died shortly afterwards. According to
his nephew Thomas Pitt Jr, he 'lived and died without a friend'.[33] Even the earl
of Shelburne, one of his closest allies, described him as 'a complete artificial
character', while Lord Waldegrave wrote that 'his political sins are black and
dangerous', although he conceded that Pitt had the 'finest genius' and that
'his private character is irreproachable'.[34]

The younger Pitt inherited his father's cold and aloof public persona, but
he had a more resilient temperament that was better suited to the disappointments of politics. At the age of twenty he stood for election to parliament but
came bottom of the poll. In 1781 his friend from Cambridge University, the
duke of Rutland, found him a safe seat and he entered the House of Commons
where he soon impressed with his clever oratory and cool manner. His arch-
rival was Charles James Fox, the son of Henry Fox, who had been his father's
adversary some years earlier: 'they were heirs to their fathers' conflicts, and
their own lifelong opposition satisfied a gladiatorial sense already aroused'.[35]
When Lord North's ministry teetered on the brink of collapse in 1782 Pitt made
an extraordinary declaration to the house. He informed the chamber that he

would never accept a 'subordinate situation' in any new administration.[36] It was a claim that exposed all of Pitt's pride and arrogance, but also his genuine belief in his own character and ability. Lord Shelburne became Pitt's mentor, and when he formed his ministry in July 1782 he invited Pitt to sit in cabinet as chancellor of the exchequer. The administration was fragile, however, and in 1783 needed the support of either North or Fox to survive. Pitt was given the responsibility for negotiating with the latter and met him on 11 February. When he asked Fox his terms for entering the ministry, he was told bluntly that there were 'None, while Lord Shelburne remained.' Upon hearing this Pitt walked out. As he informed Fox, 'I did not come here to betray Lord Shelburne.'[37] John Ehrman records that 'According to tradition the two men never met alone in private again.'[38] With the collapse of the Shelburne government King George III invited Pitt to form his own administration. It was an extraordinary offer for an inexperienced politician still only twenty-three years old, and perhaps what was even more surprising was that Pitt refused. He would not assume the responsibility unless he was sure that his government would be strong enough to survive; but he also wanted to mark his independence from George III. A Fox-North coalition was formed instead but it foundered that winter over the controversial East India bill. The king dismissed the ministry and once again invited Pitt to receive the seals of office. This time he accepted, and on 19 December 1783 became prime minister at the age of twenty-four.

Dominant in the House of Commons, Pitt secured his position in the general election of 1784 by winning a large majority. After the regency crisis of 1788–9 he consolidated his grasp on the premiership and Sir Gilbert Elliot commented:

> Pitt is the only object the nation can perceive, and the only thing they think valuable in the world; and I rather think they would be content and pleased to set aside the whole royal family, with the crown and both houses of parliament, if they could keep him by it.[39]

Pitt's distant manner, which was as much a mask he wore for protection as anything else, continued to cause him problems and he was popularly regarded as cold and arrogant. William Wilberforce noted with regret in his diary that 'Pitt does not make friends' and in the House of Commons he showed scant regard for the feelings of his backbenchers:

> From the instant that Pitt entered the doorway . . . he advanced up the floor with a quick and firm step, his head erect and thrown back, looking neither to the left nor the right, nor favouring with a nod or a glance any of the individuals seated on either side.[40]

The French revolution disrupted Pitt's plans for reform; his ministry in the 1790s was marked by conservatism and repression. On 1 February 1793 France declared war on Britain and Pitt was forced to adopt increasingly severe security measures. The alien office, a shadowy subsection of the home office, was established to direct secret service activity and its leading agent on the continent was the brilliant spymaster, William Wickham. New legislation to combat subversion and treason was also passed. Using the statute of King Edward III, dating from 1351, treason was rigidly defined in the eighteenth century as 'when a man doth compass or imagine the death of our lord the king'.[41] The 25 Edward III had only been intended as a 'Declaratory' Act, but instead it was now taken as a definition of the crime. The loose interpretation of what constituted treason had serious legal implications in the 1790s for it allowed the government to arrest and imprison suspects on very limited evidence. It was 'enough to make men shudder', admitted one concerned lawyer.[42] In a controversial case a prophet was arrested for dreaming about the demise of George III as this involved 'imagining the death of the king'. Richard Brothers had predicted that the British parliament would be destroyed by an earthquake, having identified it as the beast of the apocalypse because it contained almost 666 members.[43] He was arrested and tried for treason as the government attempted to make examples of people they regarded as dangerous radicals. This led to ironic comparisons between the character of Brothers and the prime minister:

Mr Brothers is a quiet lunatic.	Mr Pitt is a distracted politician.
Mr Brothers is a lunatic of good memory.	Mr Pitt is a politician that cannot remember.
Mr Brothers in his sphere is as harmless as a sporting porpoise.	Mr Pitt in his sphere is as dangerous as a shark.[44]

In 1795 the Treasonable Practices Act was passed, giving a new legal basis to the definition of treason:

if any person or persons whatever . . . shall . . . compass, imagine, invent, devise, or intend death or destruction, or any bodily harm tending to death or destruction, maim or wounding, imprisonment or restraint of the person of . . . the king . . . or to levy war against his majesty . . . shall be deemed . . . to be a traitor and traitors.[45]

With the passing of the Seditious Meetings Act the same year, the government now had a vast array of powers to combat revolutionary activity in Britain. Magistrates could send people for trial for having expressed treasonable views without them having actually committed any overt crime. The sentence for treason was also modified from the original post-hanging punishment of being drawn and quartered. Instead the traitor was to be taken down and his head cut off and held up to the crowd with the pronouncement, 'This is the head of a traitor.'[46]

In 1798 tensions were running high; the war with France was not going well and Ireland was on the brink of open rebellion. The ambiguous political views of Charles Fox infuriated many conservatives and when he toasted the sovereignty of the people, an expression of revolutionary sympathy, at a public gathering, Pitt considered imprisoning him for a time in the Tower of London; instead he had him dismissed as a privy councillor. There were genuine fears that Britain might be invaded and various volunteer corps were formed to assist in the defence of the country. One of Pitt's most acerbic put-downs dates from this period. A London body of volunteers had sent him an offer to enlist and fight but attached a lengthy set of conditions and difficulties. At the end of the letter there was a proviso that the men could never be ordered to leave the kingdom. Bemused, Pitt lifted his pen and wrote in the margin 'Except in case of actual invasion'.[47] On 27 May 1798 Pitt scandalised polite society in England by fighting a duel with George Tierney, the Irish-born whig MP who was his leading adversary in the Commons. They met on Putney Heath and exchanged shots but no one was injured and both men retired with their honour satisfied. The very next day, his thirty-ninth birthday, Pitt received news of the outbreak of the Irish rebellion. His response was immediate and decisive: he resolved to follow up the suppression of the violence with a legislative union that would merge the two parliaments and create a new imperial security. The first attempt to introduce the union failed in 1799 when a determined Irish House of Commons rejected the principle of the measure. Led by William Plunket and George Ponsonby, the opposition urged armed resistance to prevent the destruction of the Irish parliament. The British government was not to be denied however and the union was re-introduced in 1800. The Irish chief secretary, Lord Castlereagh, skilfully directed the measure through the House of Commons, having built a solid majority through the use of patronage and corruption. The support of the Catholic bishops had also been enlisted, and there was an implicit understanding that emancipation would follow the passing of the union. These factors combined to neutralise opposition to the measure outside of parliament, while creating an unbeatable majority within the House of Commons.

On 1 January 1801 the United Kingdom of Great Britain came into effect and with it a new imperial flag, the Union Jack. But the plan to make the union complete by accompanying it with Catholic emancipation was foiled. King George III was secretly influenced by a cabal of ambitious politicians and in a dramatic public confrontation with Castlereagh thundered that he would never tolerate giving Catholics the right to sit in parliament. With his cabinet splintered and his health shattered, Pitt tendered his resignation. He was insistent that a prime minister must be free to submit whatever policies he believed were the best for the empire. But he was also concerned with the way he had been undermined and was defending his conception of the role of prime minister as much as anything else. Henry Addington, the son of the doctor who had tended Pitt's father during his madness, was selected by the king as

Pitt's successor. As far as George III was concerned Pitt's withdrawal was final: 'You are closing, much to my sorrow, your political career.'[48]

COINCIDENCES AND CONNECTIONS: SHELBURNE, PITT, FOX AND EMMET

Determined to sustain his political independence, there had been no room for the earl of Shelburne in any of Pitt's administrations. The most detested politician of his day, Shelburne was distrusted and disliked by almost all sides. Born William Petty in Dublin on 2 May 1737, he succeeded his father to the title in 1761, but was seen as too 'un-English' for many people's comfort.[49] Horace Walpole, an inveterate enemy, insisted that 'His falsehood was so constant and notorious . . . that he could only deceive by speaking the truth.'[50] There is little evidence for Shelburne's duplicity but it seems his erratic and at times unstable character alienated colleagues and infuriated opponents. Samuel Johnson wrote that he was 'a man of abilities and information' but added that he 'acted like himself, that is, unlike anyone else'.[51] It had been expected that Shelburne would serve in Pitt's first cabinet, but instead his protégé ignored him politically while advancing him further in the peerage as the marquess of Lansdowne in 1784. Bitter about his treatment in later years, he derived little solace from the career of his eldest son and heir, John Henry Petty. Born on 6 December 1765 and styled Earl Wycombe between 1784 and 1805, he was groomed by his father to follow him into parliament and become prime minister. As Lady Holland later shrewdly noted, Shelburne was making his son 'a tool for his ambition, to live over again his political career'.[52] Wycombe showed great promise in his youth but became 'somewhat eccentric in his habits and amusements' when he reached adulthood.[53] MP for Chipping Wycombe in the British House of Commons (1784–1802), he began to dabble in radical politics and dangerous revolutionary causes. Visiting Ireland in 1798, he reported on Irish affairs back to Charles James Fox and the British whigs. He lived in a villa in Sandymount with his mistress, Rosy, whom he described as a 'sporting heifer'.[54] But according to some contemporaries he 'conducted himself in such a manner, associating with persons who were well known to be disaffected and plotting' that the government was forced to threaten him with arrest unless he left the country.[55] His father had always worried that he had too much interest in the sea and the 'spirit of adventure',[56] and Wycombe proved this by remaining in Ireland for much of the next five years. Increasingly embittered by events, he remarked in 1798 that there was 'scarcely an error or misfortune in my life which I cannot trace directly or indirectly to my father'.[57] Suspicious of everyone and seemingly intent on punishing his father by sabotaging his own career, in 1803 he became mixed up in Robert Emmet's plan for a rebellion. The chief secretary William Wickham learned from his informants that Wycombe had 'entered deeply into the virus' of the conspiracy, but that when it reached its climax he 'became timorous and retreated'.[58] In its terrible aftermath Wycombe was terrified that he would be arrested, but lack of evidence and an unwillingness to embarrass his father, a former prime minister, led to his escaping unpunished.[59] As Lord Holland later remembered, in Wycombe's life 'he had perversely persuaded himself . . . to guard against every kind affection of the heart', even though this was 'a quarter in which he was not by nature very vulnerable'.[60]

Related by marriage to Lord Wycombe was Henry Fox, the commander-of-the-forces in Ireland during the insurrection.[61] A highly regarded military general, he was also the brother of Pitt's arch-rival in politics, Charles James Fox. Born in 1755, 'Harry' suffered from comparisons with his spoilt but dazzling older brother, who received most of their father's attention. Writing about his sons in 1756 Henry Fox found Charles 'very well and very pert and very argumentative', but his namesake less playful: 'I called him Squeaker and he looked at me and laughed, but upon the whole seemed to like my horse better than me.'[62] William Pitt the elder detested his rival and considered him 'one of the blackest men that ever lived'.[63] He was also highly critical of the way he had raised his children. Henry Fox spoilt his sons with abandon and was profligate with the extravagances he showered upon them, especially Charles James. He allowed his favourite to break his watch, 'because if you must, I suppose you must', and refused to allow any punishment: 'Let nothing be done to break his spirit: the world will do that business fast enough.'[64] When Fox took the fourteen year old to Paris for a visit, he not only encouraged his gambling but also provided women for his enjoyment. Horrified by this example, the elder Pitt, with uncharacteristic hyperbole, blamed him for the corruption of the nation's children: 'he educated his children without the least regard to morality, and with such extravagant vulgar indulgence, that the great change which has taken place among our youth has been dated from the time of his son's going to Eton'.[65] Escaping some of these excesses, Henry Fox Jr preferred to spend his childhood on more equestrian pursuits, much to his father's disappointment: 'He lives with the horse, stinks, talks, and thinks of nothing but the stable, and it is not a very good companion.'[66] Entering the army at an early age, Henry appeared to have all the makings of a fine soldier. Although opposed to the British government's policy during the American War of Independence, he none the less fought with distinction against the colonies. His relative, Sarah Lennox, left a highly flattering description of him in 1779: 'His looks, his manners are all delightful; he has the most true, *good*, military air . . . I think I can't give you a better account of a young officer.'[67] Robert Emmet would destroy his reputation in Ireland in 1803.

PART II

~

THE LIFE

4

'AN IRISH WASHINGTON':
THE EARLY LIFE OF ROBERT EMMET

~

Robert Emmet was born on 8 September 1771 at Molesworth Street, Dublin, the eleventh child of Dr Robert Emmet, the state physician, and his wife Elizabeth Emmet (née Mason). A sickly child, he was susceptible to illness and his parents were unable to nurse him through infancy. He died before he reached the age of three.[1] In 1774 Elizabeth Emmet gave birth to her fourteenth child and he was also given the name Robert, after his father. Of Mrs Emmet's children only three had so far survived past infancy, and another son, John, who had been born on 3 September 1772, also passed away. The second Robert Emmet suffered the same fate; he died within a few days of childbirth. A fifteenth child was born in 1776. It was a son. Determined to have someone inherit the paternal name, his father called him Robert. But he was no stronger than the previous Robert Emmets and he succumbed to illness soon after delivery. In 1777 Elizabeth Emmet gave birth to another son; he was also called Robert and he too died shortly afterwards. By this time Dr Robert Emmet had moved premises from Molesworth Street to a larger house at 109 and 110 St Stephen's Green in central Dublin.[2] It was here that the fifth Robert Emmet was born on 4 March 1778. He was the seventeenth and final child of his parents.[3]

THE MAKING OF A PATRIOT

Baptised on 10 March 1778, Robert Emmet was a precocious youth.[4] Despite the difficulties his mother had endured during her numerous pregnancies, his health was good although he was never particularly big or strong. Educated at Oswald's School in Dapping Court near Golden Lane, he entered the academy earlier than was usual for young boys. The school was renowned for its success at teaching mathematics and Emmet was regarded as the brightest student in his year.[5] Moving from there, Emmet entered Samuel Whyte's 'English grammar school' at 75 Grafton Street near his home. Whyte was an exceptional educator who infused his students with a love of drama; he also tutored them in recitation. A first cousin of Frances Chamberlain, the wife of the theatre impresario Thomas Sheridan, Whyte had a distinguished list of alumni including his relative Richard Brinsley Sheridan and the playwright John O'Keefe. He also taught Thomas Moore and it is likely that his friendship with Robert Emmet dates from this time. One of the most respected and expensive teachers in the city, Whyte taught his students (both male and female) a broad curriculum which included geography and the use of the globes, history, astronomy, philosophy, writing, mathematics, book-keeping, music, dancing, languages and fencing.[6] Every year for the annual examination the students would perform a play at a nearby theatre which gave Robert Emmet his earliest introduction to public speaking. Without any doubt this was the area where Whyte truly excelled. He spent many hours training his students in the finer points of oratory and firmly believed that accent and emphasis were the 'body and soul' of eloquence.[7] At school Emmet learned the art of projecting his voice and the crucial importance of varying and modulating his tone. Whyte was cruelly dismissive of speakers who constantly mumbled 'as if they were conjuring up spirits' and was even less impressed with those who 'bawled as loudly as the vociferous vendors of provisions in London streets'.[8] Emmet was also trained on the vexatious subject of what to do with his hands while speaking; Whyte believed that 'a judicious speaker' should be master of 'a variety of decent and natural motion' and did not believe that he should throw his hands about as if he was performing magic tricks.[9] But, most importantly of all, Emmet learned at this early stage of his life the different components of what constituted a good speech and the different styles that could be used to make an argument. Whyte was particularly good at explaining what made 'a courageous speech' and taught that the speaker should be 'steady and cool', using his countenance to give his 'whole form an erect and graceful air. The accents should be strong, full-mouthed and articulate, the voice firm and even.'[10] And so in his early years Emmet received invaluable instruction from one of the finest teachers of the time which would serve him well in the future. He left the academy having learned that 'a just delivery consists in a distinct articulation of words, pronounced in proper tones, suitably varied to the sense and the emotions of the mind . . . and the whole accomplished with expressive looks and significant gestures'.[11] Before entering university Emmet's final teacher was the Rev. Mr Lewis of Camden Street.

Brimming with self-confidence, at the age of nine Robert Emmet promised his father that he would win more prizes at university than either of his older brothers.[12] Dr Emmet believed that good spelling was a sign of a good education and encouraged high standards in his children.[13] From an early age he also 'inoculated' his youngest son with strong 'moral and patriotic principles', determined to teach him the importance of virtue and values. At the different schools Robert studied a range of subjects, such as Latin, French, philosophy and fencing, but his favourite discipline was the sciences and as Madden notes, 'his predilection for mathematics and chemistry continued during his life'.[14] From a story of his father it is also clear that he enjoyed studying military history and delighted in learning tactics and imagining troop manoeuvres.[15] William Drennan, the future United Irishmen leader, met him in 1790 and was very impressed with the twelve-year old, describing him as 'a fine boy'.[16] He would bestow higher praise in the years ahead.

Inspired by a desire to investigate various scientific phenomena, Robert Emmet built a laboratory in his father's house so that he could carry out his experiments. John Patten, after 1791 the brother-in-law of Thomas Addis Emmet, would occasionally visit and assist him in his endeavours. Once, when he was about fourteen years old, Robert's refusal to give up a difficult problem almost cost him his life. He had been struggling to complete an algebra puzzle which his teacher later admitted was one of the most difficult he had ever set. Deeply engaged in thought, Robert began biting his fingernails, as he always did when he was nervous. Unfortunately he had previously been working on a dangerous science experiment and some of the poisonous chemicals had seeped under his nails. Ingesting some of the corrosive sublimate, Robert was 'seized with the most violent inward pains'.[17] Although aware of the danger he was in, he refused to call out to his father and thus concede defeat on his homework. Instead he went to the library and took down one of the medical encyclopaedias which he used to diagnose his problem. Reading carefully under the 'poisons' section he discovered that chalk could be used as a preventive medicine to counteract the effects of corrosive sublimate. Robert remembered that Patten had been using some earlier that day in the coach-house and went outside to search. Despite the intense cramps in his stomach, he managed to break open the locked coach-house door and find the chalk. Swallowing some with water, he returned inside to continue working on his algebra problem. The next morning Robert appeared as usual at the breakfast table, but his makeshift medical solution had not worked and in Patten's words, he 'looked as small and as yellow as an orange'.[18] His father rushed to tend to him and Robert admitted that he had suffered 'excruciating tortures' all night. The algebra problem, however, had been finished and the correct answer was resting on the table.

Robert Emmet the elder was a successful doctor with a considerable practice, and specialised in fever cases.[19] He was 'remarkably punctual and precise in money details'; once Thomas Addis Emmet went days without speaking to him after he was too parsimonious with a relative.[20] However it seems that Tom also inherited some of this concern about money, even though he was always punctilious about paying his debts.[21] When living in the United States, Tom reminded his daughter that as she knew he was very 'stingy about cents'.[22] In politics Dr Emmet was a patriot, despite his position as state physician, and was not afraid to make his views known in public. As one observer wrote to Benjamin Franklin in America, although Dr Emmet held an official situation, he 'yet votes and speaks on the side of the constitution at all public meetings and elections'.[23] The struggle of the American colonists against Britain had a tangible influence upon the politics of the Emmet family. It dominated discussions in the household, just as it did in many homes in Dublin, and may have contributed to Dr Emmet's growing radicalism. Soon Mrs Emmet found the entire subject extremely tiresome and she became bored listening to stories about the American colonists at the dinner table. As she complained in 1773, a full two years before the outbreak of the War of Independence, Dublin was so preoccupied with the plight of the colonies that no one had time 'to eat, drink or sleep'.[24] But she shared the cynicism of her husband towards many of the career politicians and noted acerbically that she feared the discussions were 'to very little purpose save their own private advantage, which is too often the only object that even our greatest *patriots* have in view'.[25] One of the greatest of these patriot figures was Henry Grattan, who would help win legislative independence for Ireland in 1782. Dr Emmet regularly discussed politics with him. During the general election in 1790 he asked him if he was a friend of proper representation; Grattan replied ambivalently that he supported some kind of parliamentary reform.[26] Cynical of the carnival atmosphere that accompanied Grattan to the hustings — 1,400 marching men, bands of musicians, numerous banners, and a well-dressed black boy holding the cap of liberty — Dr Emmet accused Grattan of forming a party around himself and that the 'people who were once the principals' had become a secondary consideration. This exchange prompted William Drennan to take a long look at the character of Henry Grattan, 'that little man there with the triangular phiz, so genteely ugly, so full of soul . . . with that fine enthusiasm without which it is impossible to be a great man'.[27] Few of Dr Emmet's eccentric opinions found favour with Grattan, who alternated between humouring and mocking him. Grattan had little time for the elderly physician, whom he viewed as a dangerous 'quack',[28] and was particularly bemused by some of his political recommendations. Once when he was going into the Irish House of Commons he was followed 'with much bustle' by Dr Emmet who implored him 'not to lose a moment'. Insisting that he had devised a solution to the difficult question of parliamentary reform, he told Grattan that he must 'Go in and propose my plan. It is the only thing that can save the country.'[29] Emmet then handed him his 'prescription', which Grattan later admitted was 'the most extraordinary compound' he had ever seen: 'one part of it was to increase the votes in the house, not by increasing the number of members, but by giving each member a number of voices'.[30] The House of Commons would therefore continue with 300 members, but the MPs would all be weighted differently, with the number of votes depending on their prestige. Thus Henry Grattan would have five votes, John Philpot Curran would hold four and other politicians would have three or less depending on their status.

From an early age Robert Emmet had been encouraged to share the patriotic beliefs of his father; he inherited his father's name and also his radicalism.

As he confided to Leonard MacNally on the day of his execution, from the time of his infancy he had been brought up 'with principles of refined liberty' and that these 'had increased with his years'.[31] It became his dream to win independence for Ireland just as George Washington had done for the United States.[32] Robert studied closely the dramatic events in the colonies and it was a major source of inspiration for him in the years ahead. The American War of Independence had a profound influence on the entire Emmet family. For Robert it offered a model for how Irish freedom could be secured. Not only did he study the military history of the conflict but also the important diplomatic manoeuvres which had been so crucial in the eventual victory. Of particular relevance was the treaty which Benjamin Franklin had negotiated with the French and which had been signed on 6 February 1778, a month before Robert was born. This alliance had a decisive influence on the course of the war and Robert recognised that such support would be necessary in any future Irish conflict. In his speech from the dock he referred to Franklin's mission and revealed that he had sent his own agent to Paris to negotiate a similar pact for Ireland. Critics of Robert Emmet would later censure his father for inculcating these radical sentiments. According to Henry Grattan Jr, his father, Dr Emmet, was obsessed with winning Irish freedom and would insanely encourage his sons to commit the most extreme acts. This was blamed for much of his sons' misfortunes. Apparently John Philpot Curran would regularly mimic Emmet giving his children their 'morning draught': 'Well, Temple, what would you do for your country? Addis! Would you kill your brother for your country? Would you kill your sister for your country? Would you kill me?' This led Henry Grattan Jr to decide that 'he misdirected the natural spirit of youth, and infused into their minds an extravagant sort of patriotism'.[33] The critique of the elder Emmet concluded with the view that he was a liability as a doctor and Henry Grattan was quoted as saying that he was forever talking about his 'pill and his plan', mixing 'so much politics with his prescription that he would kill the patient who took the one, and ruin the country that listened to the other'.[34] R. R. Madden denied these extreme claims, insisting with some vehemence and much sentiment:

> Dr Emmet was a man of warmth and feeling, frank, upright and steadfast in his opinions. His lady was a person of noble disposition and of a vigorous understanding, fit to be the mother of three such children as Christopher Temple, Thomas Addis and Robert. The parents of such children ought to have been exempt from the attempt to represent them as unfaithful to their parental duty, or unfortunate in their notions of its obligations.[35]

Nevertheless there does appear to be a certain element of truth in the claims; certainly Dr Emmet seemed proud to have produced two rebel sons and no loyalists.

THE EMMET FAMILY

The elder Robert Emmet was born on 29 November 1729 at Tipperary or Cork, the second son of Christopher Emett and his wife Rebecca Emett (née Temple). He married in November 1760 Elizabeth Mason, the twenty year old daughter of James Mason and Catherine Mason (née Power) of County Cork. Residing at a house at Dunscombe Marsh, he also leased a villa with five acres of land at Gilabby on the south bank of the River Lee, about fifteen minutes' walk from the city.[36] He had a 900-year lease on the house for twenty guineas a year and rented the villa for thirteen guineas. As he prospered he also bought an estate about half a mile from the town of Killarney. In 1761 his first child was born, named Christopher Temple Emmet after his paternal grandparents. The next son, Henry, died shortly after childbirth; a third, William, did not survive infancy. Their fourth child was born in Cork on 24 April 1763 and was christened Thomas Addis Emmet. Eight more pregnancies followed over the next nine years, but none of the children survived. In 1770 the family moved to Dublin where they lived at Molesworth Street. On 10 October 1773 a daughter was born in good health, Mary Anne Emmet; she survived to adulthood. There were four more failed pregnancies before the fifth Robert Emmet was born on 4 March 1778.[37]

On 25 February 1770 Robert Emmet was appointed state physician for Ireland, an office which he had purchased from the widow of the former holder for £1,000.[38] To raise this money he sold some of his land in Cork, as he was anxious to secure the office. He also became a governor of Swift's Hospital for the insane, and was later presented with a large plate from that body in recognition of his many services.[39] Normally physicians for a hospital received no salary, but Emmet earned about £300 a year for his work at Swift's and a further income of £200 for holding the office as state physician; this was increased to £400 in 1785 after the intervention of John Temple who persuaded the prime minister and the chief secretary for Ireland to increase the allowance.[40] Dr Emmet had been annoyed to learn that the physician-general to the army earned £1 a day, and admitted that his 'pride is hurt by the inferiority of my salary'.[41] While he insisted that 'my ambition is not very great, and my avarice perhaps still less', he acknowledged that 'there is a point in which both are engaged'.[42] Dr Emmet served as 'physician to his majesty's state in this kingdom' until his death in 1802, although he retired from active duty after the events of 1798. A wealthy man, Dr Emmet subscribed £2,000 to the new Bank of Ireland in 1782 to help it raise the required amount of capital.[43] Thomas Addis Emmet followed his father into medicine, and for a time shared his responsibilities as state physician. In 1783 Dr Emmet made use of his family connections with the lord lieutenant, the 3rd Earl Temple, and his brother, William Wyndham Grenville, who was chief secretary for Ireland, to advance his son's medical career.[44] It seems the viceroy was so impressed with Dr Emmet's gesture upon the death of his kinsman, William Pitt the elder, that he decided to reward him.[45] The patent was split to include two people and

Thomas Addis Emmet took up the second part of it. He resigned the office in 1788 and Dr Stephen Dickson of Bride Street, Dublin, purchased the half-share from his father for £1,000.[46]

The most talented member of the Emmet family was the eldest son, Christopher Temple. Educated at the school of Mr Kerr, he entered Trinity College in 1775 at the age of fourteen. He was 'remarkably short-sighted', of average height and with a large build,[47] and earned considerable prestige in university. Academically he was by some distance the finest student of his generation. In Trinity College Dublin there were quarterly examinations, with a premium of books to the value of £2 for the student who performed best in either the science or classics subjects. A person could only win one premium per academic year, however, and if they excelled in subsequent examinations they were instead presented with a certificate. To be awarded a degree, candidates had to pass exams in eleven terms over at least four years. As at Oxford there were four terms in Trinity College Dublin, most of which were based around religious feast-days. Hilary term began on the Monday after the feast of the Epiphany (6 January) and ran until the day before Palm Sunday (the Sunday before Easter). The Easter term began eight days after Easter Sunday and ended on Whitsun-eve (seven weeks after Easter). Whitsun term (called Trinity term when Robert Emmet was at university) began a little over a week later on Trinity Monday and ended on 8 July. The Michaelmas term started on either 1 or 2 October and ended every year on 16 December.[48] The exams were held at the beginning of each term, when the students were divided into groups of less than forty, and then questioned publicly by two examiners, one for the science subjects and the other for the classics. In his very first examinations in Hilary term 1776, Temple won a premium because of the brilliance of his answering. At the Easter term examinations he again came first and this time was awarded a certificate. He won a further certificate at the Whitsun term exams and a fourth at Michaelmas.[49] It was a clean sweep for the entire year.

As a senior freshman in Trinity College, Temple again excelled in his exams. His second year went almost as well as his first and he won a premium and two certificates. In 1778, his junior sophister year, he went for the scholarship examination and was successful. He also took exams in two terms and won a premium at Michaelmas, which was the most difficult of the lot. In his final year, now a senior sophister, he went for all four examinations and won a premium at the start of the Hilary term and a certificate for the third. In total he had won ten academic awards (premiums and certificates) at Trinity College Dublin in the space of four years, a remarkable achievement. He graduated with a B.A. in the spring of 1780.

But perhaps Temple's greatest exploits were in the debating rooms of the College Historical Society. At about the age of fifteen, Temple (as he was always known) made a 'memorable' speech that deeply impressed his contemporaries; it was considered one of the 'most remarkable speeches' that had ever been heard by the members.[50] The Historical Society traced its fairly recent origin back to Edmund Burke, the great political theorist, who had established a debating club in Trinity College during his time there. It attracted the best and the brightest students and was a training ground for many orators who would later achieve fame as lawyers, politicians and revolutionaries. Not only a great speaker, Temple also had a prodigious memory: 'he recollected everything, it stuck to him with singular tenacity'.[51] At times his extraordinary ability even amazed his own friends. There was always an examination in history prior to each debate in the society, based on thirty pages of text chosen the week before. At one meeting the books had been mislaid, but Temple was in the chair and refused to be distracted. Instead of cancelling the test he questioned all the students himself, having memorised all the relevant chapters.

Towering over his contemporaries because of his prodigious talent and intellectual ability, Temple was a leading figure in Trinity College. His oratory was brilliant; the only flaw, according to Henry Grattan Jr, was that he could not speak prose. Everything was poetry.[52] Ending one meeting from the chair with a rhetorical declamation, Temple's imagery was imprinted on the memory of his close friend, Peter Burrowes: 'America! America! The land of arts and of arms, where that goddess, liberty, was wooed and won, and twelve young eaglets springing from her nest, bore freedom upwards on their soaring wings.'[53] Temple was so concerned with his tendency to speak in images rather than facts that he subsequently gave this speech to Burrowes to amend. Burrowes returned it unaltered; he had been unable to do anything with it as it was all poetry.

A year after graduation Temple got married. His wife was Anne Western Temple, a second cousin from the American side of the family; they had one daughter Catherine (known as Kitty). Having entered the Middle Temple on 5 February 1779 and the King's Inns, he embarked upon a career in the law and was called to the Irish bar in 1781. There had never been any doubt but that he would pursue a legal career; he possessed a brilliant legal mind and had an encyclopaedic knowledge of the law. As Henry Grattan Jr later recounted with some awe and a little envy:

> Temple Emmet, before he came to the bar, knew more law than any of the judges on the bench; and if he had been placed on one side, and the whole bench opposed to him, he could have been examined against them, and would have answered them all. He would have answered better, both in law and divinity, than any judge or bishop in the land.[54]

Dr Emmet was immensely proud of his eldest son and cherished him as the most talented member of his family. On 28 October 1784 he boasted that Temple was already 'reaping a very early harvest': he had 'not any thing to ask — a seat in parliament and king's counsel gown he has already refused'.[55] Temple was still only twenty-three years old. His father predicted that 'in all probability' he 'will be an object of government's attention without any felicitations on his part'. With such ability Temple rose rapidly at the bar and he finally agreed to become a king's counsel in 1787. In that year his (and his wife's) relation, Earl Temple, returned to Ireland as lord lieutenant. His distant cousin, who had since become the marquess of Buckingham, succeeded the duke of Rutland as viceroy and Temple wrote a poem, 'The decree', in his honour. The theme of the piece was the Anglo-Irish relationship and how the two countries should co-exist peacefully. One of the verses contained a powerful warning about what would happen if Ireland was mistreated or abused:

> But if ere, in thoughtless hour,
> Freedom's rights she should invade,
> Struck with lust of lawless pow'r,
> Britain's laurels, then, shall fade.[56]

Grenville Temple, the son of John Temple, finally visited his 'little kinsmen' in late 1784. He stayed with Dr Emmet and then his cousin Temple for most of the next three years. Mrs Emmet had long insisted upon seeing the 'little boy', having heard in 1773 that he was already 'a lovely fellow'.[57] Now sixteen years old, Grenville was studying to be a lawyer. He made an immediate impression on the family and Dr Emmet soon considered him one of his own sons.[58] Through his friendship with Temple he matured rapidly and Dr Emmet informed Sir John Temple in 1787 that 'he has indeed had an opportunity of improvement in both legal and moral advancement from his residence in my son's house'.[59] Dr Emmet was confident that Grenville would prove 'an honour to his friends and an advantage to his country'. However he was worried by his relative's prodigality and was often forced to be strict, reminding Grenville of what expenses he allowed his sons 'and recommending economy'.[60] Dr Emmet warned Sir John that 'extravagance would produce waste of time and destruction of talents', but he was not sure if Grenville would follow his advice, even though he accepted 'the weight of the reason'. In a gesture of gratitude Sir John presented Dr Emmet with a bottle of Madeira 'of excellent quality' and a draft for £100 as a reward for all his assistance. Although Dr Emmet had a reputation for being careful with money, he was none the less capable of great acts of generosity. He endorsed the draft and gave the entire sum to Grenville 'for clearing any little calls which may be upon him'.[61] Delighted to have been able to help the Temple family, Dr Emmet predicted that Grenville would 'one day make as great a figure in his country as Temple will in Ireland; and he will then I think be the first lawyer in America'.[62]

Described as 'one of the brightest ornaments of the bar' by his first cousin St John Mason, Temple was considered to be the most eloquent man in his profession.[63] His fame even reached Benjamin Franklin in America who was told in 1786 that Temple was 'one of the most promising lawyers in this kingdom'.[64] There was much talk of finding him a seat in parliament and a prediction that he would prove as great a politician as Henry Flood and Henry Grattan, with the aside, 'and I am sure as honest as either of them'.[65] Revelling in his son's fame, Dr Emmet noted that he was 'on the high ground of his profession, loved and esteemed by everyone who knows him'.[66] Temple's promising career ended abruptly in February 1788. Tragically he died suddenly after a short illness. His parents continued to venerate his memory and mourned deeply the loss of their favourite son. Even in 1801, when Thomas Addis was considering moving to America, Temple was still referred to in reverential tones by his mother. She informed her middle son that although his departure would hurt her, she would not attempt to prevent it. 'No, not even a Temple Emmet would I wish to retain under such circumstances.'[67]

Temple's death altered the destiny of Thomas Addis for ever. Until then he had shared the office of state physician with his father and had graduated M.D. from Edinburgh University in 1784. In Trinity College Dublin he had also been a brilliant student although not to the same extent as Temple. He entered in the summer of 1778 and was initially overshadowed by his precocious older brother who was then completing his degree. Tom did well in his exams in his first two years, but won no premiums. However he came into his own in 1781, his junior sophister year, and came first in the exams in the final two terms winning a premium and a certificate.[68] In his senior sophister year he won another premium and completed his Michaelmas examination with the high distinction of *valde bene in omnibus*. His close friend, William Plunket, also won a premium in the same year.[69] Emmet graduated with a B.A. in the spring of 1783. At university he was a popular student and an excellent debater, although he possessed a style that was more prosaic than his older brother. But then this was possibly an advantage. Around five feet eleven inches in height, Thomas Addis had a physical stoop and was very near-sighted. His daughter Jane Erin inherited the stoop and Tom later explained to her that the 'fault' was 'a personal deformity'.[70] Possessing a great sense of humour, he delighted in entertaining his family and would attempt to sing 'with a most discordant sound — to create a laugh — which he always heartily joined in'.[71] Music was very important for all the Emmets and Thomas Addis believed that it offered a solution to the problems of the world: 'I think those very lucky who can get through its troubles by dancing and singing.'[72] In 1787 he toured Europe, spending his summer 'botanizing' in the Alps. Then he wintered in Vienna 'for further improvement'.[73] After Temple's death his father encouraged him to pursue a legal career and he returned to Trinity College where he graduated LL.B. in 1788. Entering Lincoln's Inn in London on 13 June, he was called to the Irish bar in 1790.[74]

In a character sketch of Thomas Addis written in 1800, his sister's husband, Robert Holmes, expressed his belief that Emmet 'would not have committed a dishonourable act, though secure of everlasting concealment'.[75] It was a testimony that was supported by many who knew him. Health-wise he was 'not robust' and his appearance was 'careless, almost negligent'; he barely gave any concern to what he was wearing.[76] He had also inherited many of his father's beliefs: 'those who came into contact with him felt the presence of a man of inflexible principles and fixed, well considered opinions'.[77] Henry Grattan Jr recalled that he was 'a very clever man. He possessed a powerful and logical mind, great talent and spirit.'[78] But it seems the elder Grattan had little time for Thomas Addis and viewed him as another 'quack' like his father. He was not impressed with his radical views on parliamentary reform, including a scheme which he claimed was based around holding three hundred elections each year, all over the country, with every man having the right to vote. As far as the hardened parliamentarian Henry Grattan was concerned, Thomas Addis did 'much mischief': he 'forgot that elections and representation are a work of art, he considered them as one of the operations of nature'.[79] On 11 June 1791 Thomas Addis Emmet married Jane Patten, the daughter of the late Rev. John Patten, a Presbyterian clergyman from Clonmel, Co. Tipperary; they had ten children. By his own admission Tom had 'old-fashioned' views on marriage, women and the education of children.[80] He believed that a woman should 'be habitually studious' to make her appearance agreeable and that 'the lady who is inattentive to this point neglects one of the minor virtues of her sex and station'.[81] Indeed when his own daughter turned seventeen and made her début in American society, he warned her that 'she puts at hazard the happiness through life' if she ignored the 'constant neatness and attention to her person'. It was not advice that would have found favour with the followers of Mary Wollstonecraft, but it was well-meaning, and Tom insisted that 'woman is to study and know, and to depend for her welfare, as much perhaps on the follies and weakness as on the virtues of man'.[82] Despite this view his position on the status of women in society was far more enlightened than that of many of his contemporaries. For example he was adamant that 'woman has talent and intellect to obtain the highest pursuit of science' and later wanted his daughter to marry a man who could 'meet your understanding and delight in its brilliancy' and also someone 'who in loving you can control the effervescence of your temper'. Just like he had found, he wanted his daughter to choose 'a cheerful partner to charm and beguile the tediousness and difficulties of life', who could become 'a faithful and judicious counsellor, a devoted friend and an unwearied comforter'.[83] A brilliant orator and a shrewd lawyer, Thomas Addis made £700 in his first year at the bar, a feat that was considered highly impressive.[84] He was less successful in the years ahead; it was said that he sometimes gave back legal fees if his client did not win.

On 7 December 1792 Thomas Addis joined the Dublin society of the United Irishmen. Becoming increasingly radical, he served on its committee for parliamentary reform and wrote an 'Address to the poorer classes'. Earlier that year had had first come to national prominence when he defended James Napper Tandy on a charge of treason. In a stirring oration at the trial Thomas Addis challenged the legitimacy of the entire Anglo-Irish connection. Asserting that 'there has been no legal viceroy in Ireland for the last six hundred years',[85] he caused a sensation in the courtroom. A few years later he achieved further notoriety when he defended men charged with being members of the now suppressed United Irishmen. Insisting that there was nothing illegal in the oath of the society, in a moment of high drama he made an extraordinary gesture that shocked the entire court. In the presence of everyone he took the prescribed oath, kissed the bible and sat down. No attempt was made to arrest him and the prisoners received a lenient sentence.[86]

Fearful of the threat posed by Thomas Addis Emmet's obvious talents, the government made secret attempts to win him over. Acting through an intermediary, 'F', who had been a close friend of Christopher Temple in university, it made an unofficial offer to Tom in May 1794. In return for leaving the United Irishmen and disavowing all radical activity, he would receive a lucrative sinecure and the promise of future advancement in the legal profession. The offer was declined. Thanking 'F' for his concern, Thomas Addis set out his thoughts on the subject. He agreed with his friend that this was the most important decision he would ever make in his life:

> You said this was the crisis of my life. I believe you said truly, and therefore it is the moment in which I sought to adhere most strictly to those principles of honour and morality which I have been taught to consider unerring guides. I believe this is the crisis of my life. God grant [that] I may have decided prudently; I feel I have decided honestly.[87]

In 1797 Dr Emmet retired from his public practice and decided to move to a smaller house at Casino in Milltown, near Rathfarnham. William Drennan, now one of the United Irishmen leaders, dined with the family and was disappointed to discover that he had decided to sell after carrying out so many improvements to his home. A contributory factor in the decision, or so Drennan believed, was financial insecurity. He regarded it as a

> shame on the persecuting and exclusive spirit of this protestant government when a liberal protestant and excellent man such as Thomas Addis Emmet has not gotten higher in his profession, while those whose nature it is to lick the dust, wind their way, like the serpent, to the top of the tree of life.[88]

But there were some weaknesses in Thomas Addis Emmet's advocacy, as one of his greatest admirers admitted in a biography after his death. Sometimes he would become too animated and passionate in his orations and allow his zeal to 'cloud his judgement, and obscure the perception of his mind'.[89] In January 1797 Thomas Addis became a member of the executive directory of the United Irishmen and supported the idea of a French invasion taking place instead of a popular uprising. But the Castle was monitoring carefully the movements of suspected dissidents and on 12 March 1798 it arrested leading members of the Leinster directory of the society; Thomas Addis Emmet was captured in one of the raids. He remained in prison for over four years.

According to Richard Madden his parents never recovered from this blow: 'Poor Dr Emmet and his wife, from the time of the arrest of their son, Thomas Addis, gradually sank under the calamity which laid the proud hopes of their old age into the dust.'[90] Lady Anne Fitzgerald, the widow of Maurice Fitzgerald, knight of Kerry, later claimed that Dr Emmet knew nothing about Tom's revolutionary activities: 'He in the most solemn manner declared so to me, and, in truth, condemned it.'[91] But there is no trace of censure in Dr Emmet's own correspondence with his son in prison, and so it seems highly unlikely. Furthermore when Lady Anne made these claims she was attempting to disassociate herself from the Emmet family in the wake of the 1803 rebellion.

The only daughter who reached adulthood in the Emmet family was Mary Anne who was born on 10 October 1773. When she was thirteen her father delighted in her good character and beamed that she 'promises happiness to whoever shall make her his partner'.[92] A writer and poet, she campaigned against the Act of Union in 1799 and 1800, and published at least two pamphlets against the measure. In autumn 1799 she married Robert Holmes, a barrister and radical, and helped raise some of the children of her brother while he was in prison. Of all the Emmet family, William Drennan was least impressed with Mary Anne. On the many occasions when he dined with her parents in the early 1790s he found her the least civil, but there is little to be deduced from this. Of the rest of the household he liked the 'amiable' Mrs Emmet very much and thought that Thomas Addis's wife Jane was 'very pretty'.[93] As for Tom himself, Drennan thought he was 'very studious' but suspected that some of this was for show. Nevertheless he admired all the men in the Emmet family and believed they were 'very clever in speech', possessing 'a vein of elegance, taste, and all that'.

Lord Macaulay, the distinguished nineteenth-century politician and historian, was not impressed with Robert Emmet and preferred the character of Thomas Addis. He believed that egotism and not idealism had been the younger brother's controlling impulse, and that this had driven him to attempt the doomed rebellion. As he wrote to R. R. Madden, 'I fear the vanity of a young man, with no principles, was his [Emmet's] ruling motive in the murderous affair of 1803.'[94] Macaulay was not the first person to express doubts about Emmet's character. He was barely understood even by his own father. John Patten later admitted that Dr Emmet had 'strange notions' about his shy and enigmatic son.[95] Concerned with the 'difference of appearance' between Robert and his brothers, his father was worried that 'he had not the gravity and sedateness of Temple and Thomas Addis Emmet'. Patten added that the youngest son's 'boyishness of air, and apparent unfitness for society, or unwillingness to engage in active intercourse with men of the world, made the old doctor uneasy about Robert's destiny'.[96] John Patten attributed this unease to Robert's diffidence: he was 'so modest, reserved, and retiring, that he seemed unconscious of his own powers'.[97] Dr Emmet disagreed with Patten's analysis and insisted that all of Robert's superficial nervousness disappeared whenever he made his mind up on a subject. Then he had 'no diffidence, no distrust, no fear of himself'. Dr Emmet went on to tell Patten an anecdote that summed up Robert's self-confidence; it also illustrates his own belief in his son:

> If Robert was looking out of his window, and saw a regiment passing that was about to be reviewed, and was informed the colonel had just fallen from his horse, and was incapacitated for his duty, and it was intimated to him that he might take the colonel's place, and put his taste for the reading of military tactics and evolutions to the test, Robert would quietly take his hat, place himself at the head of the regiment, and give the necessary commands without any misgivings or *mauvaise honte*.[98]

Upon hearing this story recounted to him many years later, R. R. Madden wondered if Robert Emmet's boldness could be interpreted as vanity. Questioning John Patten about what this self-confidence showed, he asked him if Emmet was 'personally vain; was he vain of his talents, of his intellectual superiority over others in any attainment, in argument of discourse?' Patten's answer has been recorded for posterity:

> From vanity! Oh, dear, no! Robert had not a particle of vanity in his composition. He was the most free from self-conceit of any man I ever knew. You might live with him for five years — aye, for ten years — in the same house — in the same room, even, and never discover that he thought about himself at all. He was neither vain of his person nor his mind.

Reflecting on his children in the spring of 1785, Dr Emmet was delighted with how they were developing. In a subjective appreciation to John Temple he acknowledged that 'few parents can look with the contented pride and satisfaction which I do on both my grown-up sons'. Casting a shrewd parental eye on his youngest son Robert, who had just turned seven, he admitted that 'the young one seems to stand as fair for honourable fame; if I may judge of a child's talents'.[99] Robert was in no way intimidated by the achievements of his older brothers, not even those of the brilliant Temple. Refusing to be in any way overshadowed, in 1787 he promised his father that 'he will bring home more premiums from college than either Temple or Tom did'.[100] This was some challenge. Temple had won ten premiums in Trinity (if certificates are included in the total) and Tom had received three. It would be a difficult tally to match, let alone better, but it was a measure of Robert's infectious enthusiasm, even at such an early age, that he thought it possible. Before entering university, or else while a student, he studied carefully the works of the philosopher John Locke and made annotations on his second treatise of government on 'The origin, extent, and end of civil government'. Of particular interest was a section discussing how people owed no obligation to a government forced upon them. Like Temple, Robert also had a prodigious memory and was sometimes called upon to demonstrate it. In April 1790, when Dr Emmet questioned Henry Grattan about whether he was a friend to parliamentary reform, he told him that the people were 'no longer the principals' as 'the nation has become a Ponsonby party'.[101] In the course of the conversation William Drennan's name was mentioned and Dr Emmet called Robert into the room to recite 'a certain' letter he had received from him. Drennan was enamoured of this story when he heard it, admitting to his friend Sam McTier that 'you will smile, but as I have little profit at present, you ought to allow me a portion of praise'.

Part of the paradoxical nature of Robert Emmet was the curious combination of poet and warrior. Like his father, brothers and sister he wrote a number of poems, mainly on political themes, and a number of them survive. It is impossible to establish the provenance of all of them; for some we must rely on family tradition, while others were collected by R. R. Madden during his extensive research. In an example of Emmet's penchant for ingenious experiments some of the poems were written in invisible ink and only became legible in purple characters after the parchment was treated with chemicals.[102] Emmet's earliest effort was said to have been a poem written around 1790 when he was twelve. However there are hints from the radical content that it may have been composed later, in 1793. Entitled 'Erin's call', the work was full of youthful enthusiasm and high idealism, encouraging Irish resistance to English oppression:

Brothers arise! Our country calls —
Let us gain her rights or die.

The political message was unsurprisingly simplistic, displaying Emmet's boyish enthusiasm and spirited defiance:

Erin's sons, for freedom fight:
England's legions we defy
We swear to conquer or to die.[103]

It was hardly subtle, but it was stirring; Emmet's political philosophy would become much more sophisticated in the years ahead.

THE TRINITY COLLEGE YEARS

On 7 October 1793 Robert Emmet entered Trinity College Dublin. He was fifteen years old and Mr Richard Graves was assigned to him as his tutor.[104] As a 'pensioner' he paid an annual fee of £15 and was thus classed with the majority of students who were 'persons of moderate income'.[105] Even as a freshman his academic gown gave him a certain status and privileges, among which was an entitlement to entry into the gallery of the House of Commons. At Trinity his close friends included Thomas Moore, the young poet who entered the following year; Dacre Hamilton, who shared his love of mathematics; and Richard Curran, the son of the famous lawyer, John Philpot Curran.[106] Thomas Moore, a year younger than Emmet, had also been taught by Samuel Whyte and would spend much time recollecting the exploits of his friend in university. He wrote that Emmet was 'altogether a noble fellow, and as full of imagination and tenderness of heart as of manly daring'.[107] But he also revealed that it was only when roused by a cause that Emmet became animated, otherwise he was 'as mild and gentle in his manner as any girl'.[108] Robert's first exam was at the start of Hilary term 1794 and he was questioned out loud on four subjects, logic, Greek, Latin and a theme. He performed very well and was awarded the grade *valde bene* for the first three and the lower *bene* for the fourth. However it was not enough to win a premium. Richard Curran, who would be his academic rival for much of the following years, did less well with two *valde bene* awards, a *bene* and only a *satis bene* for his theme. In the Easter examinations the positions were reversed with Curran scoring three *valde bene* grades and Emmet receiving only two. At the start of the Trinity term Curran again did better than his friend and was awarded *valde bene in omnibus*; Emmet had to be satisfied with two *valde bene* and two *bene* grades. Robert completed his junior freshman year by sitting the Michaelmas term exams, where he was awarded *valde bene* in logic, Greek and Latin, but only received a *bene* for his theme. His first year was over and he had won no premiums.[109]

In Emmet's senior freshman year his exceptional academic promise began to show through. Again he took all four exams at the start of each term and this time was awarded *valde bene in omnibus* for each one. He also won his first premium for his answers in Trinity term, when Dr Thomas Elrington was examining. Richard Curran also won a premium on the same day. Beginning his third year in university, Robert decided to follow his brothers in a career in the law. On 2 November 1795 he entered the King's Inns in Dublin to study to become a barrister. In doing this he also followed in the footsteps of some of the radicals of 1798 such as Theobald Wolfe Tone and the Sheares brothers.[110] Two of Robert Emmet's admission papers to the King's Inns are extant, including his memorial in which he attested:

> That he is at present a student in the university of Dublin and of the rank of junior sophister therein. That he never followed any profession or business. And he now humbly requests admission *specially* into this honourable society as a student of law therein. [signed] Robt. Emmet.[111]

His memorial also had to be signed by a barrister of at least forty terms' standing and Richard Frankland wrote underneath: 'I certify that I know the above named Robert Emmet Jnr. and the contents of the above memorial to be true and think him a fit and proper person to be admitted a student in this honourable society.' A bond of admission had to be provided by two people for the sum of £100 as security that the law student would 'conform himself to the rules, orders and regulations of the said society'. This was given by Thomas Addis Emmet and Dr Emmet. As Robert never entered an English Inn, however, either Gray's Inn, Lincoln's Inn, the Middle Temple or the Inner Temple, he was never eligible to be called to the Irish bar. This was possibly a sign that his heart was not set on becoming a barrister, or else it reflected the fact that events in Ireland soon displaced his own personal ambitions.

1796 marked the zenith of Robert Emmet's academic career. The curriculum was much broader and more difficult, with students studying logic, mathematics, astronomy, Greek, Latin as well as a theme. Emmet indicated his intentions in the very first exam at the start of the Hilary term, when he was awarded *valde bene in omnibus* and won a premium. He turned eighteen years of age in March and continued in his impressive vein of answering in the exams at the start of the Easter term when he was again awarded *valde bene in omnibus*; as he had already received a premium that year, this time he was given a certificate. The Trinity term examination was another success and he secured a second certificate and the same result, *valde bene in omnibus*. The Michaelmas exams were the toughest of the year and the odds were against him completing his clean sweep. But he had set his mind to the task and completed it in style: he was awarded *valde bene in omnibus* and received another certificate. It was his fifth premium (when certificates are included in the total) in his academic career, beating Thomas Addis by two, and while it was not as many as Temple it none the less marked Robert as one of the brightest scholars of his generation. Ethics was added to the curriculum for the fourth year, with physics replacing maths, and he answered in two of the examinations. In Easter 1797 he was awarded *valde bene* in five subjects, and *bene* in the remaining two, but did not win a premium. In the Michaelmas term he was a candidate for his B.A., having completed thirteen terms of examinations already. He was awarded *valde bene* for everything except his theme which was just *bene*. Having completed the requirements for his B.A. degree, he was all set to graduate in the spring or summer of 1798.

On 21 October 1797 a poem was published in *The Press* under the name of 'Trebor'. Emmet delighted in word-games and this was an early example of his style: when reversed the letters form the word 'Robert'. The poem was entitled 'The London pride and shamrock' and was described as 'A fable'. In reality it was a lengthy political allegory describing the history of the Anglo-Irish relationship. Emmet acknowledged that the relationship between Britain and Ireland had not always been unequal, but had become so over time. In it the Irish shamrock asks its oppressor if it is policy:

To thwart my offspring as they rise,
To break my heart, to blind their eyes?

The verses are pure political propaganda, written in inflexible rhyming couplets that are sometimes strained to breaking point. More interesting is the final section or the 'Moral'. The message here is that Britain and Ireland should be allies, but only if all injustice was removed from the relationship.

Emmet argued that the two countries could create a strong and genuine union if they only worked together: 'Two twists will make the strongest cable/ To bind a friend and keep him steady.' Thus Emmet urged the British empire to 'keep a good friend while you can', recognising that 'To strengthen him doth strengthen you.'

A clubbable young man, Emmet had many friends in Trinity. Apart from Richard Curran he also spent much time with Thomas Moore. Often when Moore was playing melodies on his piano, Emmet would come and sit beside him to listen and reflect. In 1796 Edward Bunting, the young ward of the McCracken family, which had United Irishmen connections, published sixty-six airs in *A general collection of the ancient Irish music*.[112] One of these, 'Let Erin remember the days of old', particularly inspired the young Emmet. One day while Moore was playing the piece, Emmet seems to have fallen into a reverie before waking with a start to exclaim passionately, 'Oh, that I were at the head of twenty thousand men marching to that air.'[113] The 'spirited tune' included the lines:

> Let Erin remember the days of old,
> Ere her faithless sons betray'd her;
> . . .
> When her kings, with standard of green unfurl'd,
> Led the red-branch knights to danger;
> Ere the emerald gem of the western world
> Was set in the crown of a stranger.[114]

Moore would subsequently downplay his own involvement in any radical activity while he was in college. He claimed strenuously that he had been unaware of Emmet's connection with the United Irishmen, insisting that his friend had sympathised with his difficult position at home where he had been 'constantly tied to my mother's apron strings'.[115] But there are various inconsistencies in Moore's story. On a separate occasion he boasted that he had been 'a young sucking rebel in college'.[116] And in the same passage where he denied any knowledge of university radicalism, he admitted that he had published a letter in *The Press*, the newspaper of the United Irishmen, addressed to the students of Trinity. This letter, in reality an article, appeared under the name 'Sophister' on 2 December 1797. It was an early example of Moore's work and bore little resemblance to his later conservative writings. He urged Ireland's heroes, 'their Buonapartes', to come forward and encouraged the students to:

> study to be a scourge of tyrants; study to deserve well of your country, that sunk, that injured country! And if your hearts are yet free from the infections of a court, if they are not hardened by ministerial frost, can you see poor Ireland degraded, tortured, without burning to be revenged on her damned tormentors?[117]

Moore accused the British crown of having 'murdered' the happiness of Ireland. In a savage indictment of the Dublin Castle officials, he accused them of being:

> wretches whose souls are the emblems of the government, rotted by pollution, and prolific in damnable machinations, who exult in the wages of prostitution and, like an animal that feeds on its own ordure, live by the corruptions which themselves have generated.

The final section ended with an exhortation to 'you, my fellow-students'. Rejecting the 'extremities of oppression' under which Ireland suffered, he called on the undergraduates to take action: 'Ireland is singular in suffering and in cowardice. She could crush her tormentors and yet they embowel her. She could be free and yet she is a slave.'

Strolling in the countryside one afternoon, Moore confessed his authorship of the article to his friend. Emmet's reaction was tender but contained an implicit rebuke as,

> with that almost feminine gentleness of manner which he possessed, and which is so often found in such determined spirits, he owned to me that on reading the letter, though pleased with its contents, he could not help regretting that the public attention had been thus drawn to the politics of the university, as it might have the effect of awakening the vigilance of the college authorities, and frustrate the progress of the good work (as we both considered it) which was going on there so quietly.[118]

Impressed with his friend's wisdom, Moore was even more excited by his pronouncement that the only thing that mattered in times of crisis was action. As he later remembered:

> Even then, boyish as my own mind was, I could not help being struck with the manliness of the view which I saw he took of what men ought to do in such times and circumstances, namely, not to *talk*, or *write*, about their intentions, but to *act*.[119]

Another of Emmet's friends in university was Archibald Douglas, who entered college the same day; he later became a Protestant clergyman renowned as a pulpit orator in Dublin. The two had known each other since childhood and Emmet spent much of his time at Douglas's home, 'indeed . . . he almost lived in our house'. The recollection of Douglas on 6 November 1842 was a subjective but worthy tribute: 'So gifted a creature does not appear in a thousand years.'[120] Moore's own account of what it was like to know Robert Emmet was even more awe-struck:

Were I to number indeed the men among all I have ever known, who appeared to me to combine in the greatest degree pure moral worth with intellectual power, I should, among the highest of the few, place Robert Emmet. Wholly free from the follies and frailties of youth, though how capable he was of the most devoted passion events afterwards proved. The pursuit of science, in which he eminently distinguished himself, seemed at this time the only object that at all divided his thoughts with the enthusiasm for Irish freedom, which in him was an hereditary as well as national feeling.[121]

Again Moore emphasised that it was only when Emmet was seized by an important issue that his features changed and his inner strength became apparent. Then his charisma was clear for all to witness:

Simple in his habits, and with a repose of look and manner indicating but little movement within, it was only when the spring was touched that set his feelings, and through them his intellect in motion, that he at all rose above the level of ordinary men.

There were four committees of the United Irishmen in Trinity College and Robert Emmet was the secretary of the first; the other organisers were Peter McLaughlin from County Mayo, James Thomas Flynn from Dublin and William Corbet from County Cork.[122] These four men also served on the 'higher committee' of the United Irishmen in Trinity College. The membership fee to be enrolled in the society was sixpence. To maintain secrecy the meetings took place in different students' rooms each week. The United Irishmen was a proscribed organisation nationally from 1794, so the committees were illegal and Emmet faced criminal prosecution if his membership was discovered. He also faced expulsion, as the college had passed a decree in 1795 which was approved by the visitors forbidding students from attending any political meetings outside the college. Four students were publicly admonished in 1796 for violating this order.[123] Robert accompanied his brother Thomas Addis to many United Irishmen meetings and helped design the seal for the executive directory in the south of Ireland. For this purpose he used an emerald that had been given to his father by Sir John Temple. The seal incorporated a fine drawing of a harp and a harpist and was apparently much sought after by the government, which went to great lengths to copy it.[124]

Five feet six inches tall during his time in Trinity, Robert Emmet was slightly above average height for a man of his age.[125] The mean height for the European national population between 1760 and 1960 was about 65 inches or five feet five inches.[126] Calculations for men are usually based on military sources for the period, and the mean height for someone born in 1777 (one year earlier than Robert Emmet) is estimated to be 67 inches or five feet seven inches.[127] From the various records historians have worked out that five feet five inches would have been tall for an eighteen year old male born between 1750 and

1916, but slightly below average for a male twenty-one to twenty-three years old; similarly five feet eight inches would have been tall for an adult male aged between twenty-four and twenty-nine.[128] From these calculations the adult Robert Emmet (who grew about an inch between the age of twenty and twenty-five) was about average height or just slightly below. He would have been too small to join the British heavy cavalry (had he wanted to) but would have qualified for the light cavalry and infantry.[129] In June 1803 a senior academic in Trinity College Dublin, Thomas Elrington, was asked to supply the government with a description of Robert Emmet as they had no idea what he looked like. The portrait was not flattering, nor indeed was it intended to be (and it reveals the personal prejudices of Elrington), but it is worth quoting all the same:

> In 1798, [Emmet] was near twenty years of age; of an ugly, sour countenance; small eyes, but not near-sighted; a dirty brownish complexion; at a distance looks as if somewhat marked with the small pox; about five feet six inches high; rather thin than fat, but not of an emaciated figure — on the contrary, somewhat broad made; walks briskly, but does not swing his arms.[130]

The final part of the account was probably of little help to the government in the summer of 1803, but its portrayal of Emmet's nervous energy is confirmed by a second description of his person. The Countess d'Haussonville, whose grandmother Madame de Staël had known Emmet in France, wrote:

> He was above the middle stature, rather slight and delicate, although endowed with nervous strength which enabled him to support great fatigue. He walked with a quick step, and all his movements were rapid. The portraits remaining of him have been made after his death, and the painter, it is said, preoccupied with his tragic fate, has given him a sad sombre expression which he had not in the happy days of life. His countenance was pleasing and *distingué*. His hair was brown and his complexion quite pale; the eyebrow was arched, and the eyes black and large with dark eye-lashes, which gave to his looks a remarkable expression of pride, penetration, and mildness. His nose was aquiline and his mouth was slightly disdainful.[131]

Haussonville also confirmed that his charisma only became apparent when he was animated by an important issue; then he suddenly grew in stature and seemed to be a different person:

> Energy, delicacy, and tenderness are expressed in his melancholy and ardent features. Such was, however, his total absence of affectation and his simplicity, that modesty of his character, joined to a sort of habitual reserve, hid the working of his mind in the ordinary circumstances of life, but, were any subject started which was deeply interesting to him, he appeared quite another man.

Apart from the famous Historical Society there was also a smaller debating club in Trinity College. Emmet was a leading member of this second body during his time in university and was universally accepted as its most brilliant orator. When Thomas Moore eventually joined he found Emmet at the height of his fame, 'not only for his scientific attainments, but also for the blameless-ness of his life, and the grave suavity of his manners'.[132] Moore has left many stories of Emmet's dominance at these debates, for example at the meeting which discussed 'Whether an aristocracy or democracy was most favourable to the advancement of science and literature?'[133] On this question Emmet took the side of democracy and Moore remembered that 'the power of his eloquence was wonderful, and I feel, at this moment, as if his language was still sounding in my ears'.[134] Drawing his arguments from the classical world as well as the example of France, Emmet presented the image of Julius Caesar crossing the river with only his sword, before making a striking comparison with the republic on the continent:

> Thus France at this time swims through a sea of blood; but while in the one hand she wields the sword against her aggressors, with the other she upholds the interests of literature, uncontaminated by the bloody tide through which she struggles.

In another speech Moore remembered that Emmet posed and answered the question:

> When a people advancing rapidly in civilisation and knowledge of their right look back after a long lapse of years and perceive how far their government has lagged behind them, what then, I ask, is to be done by them in such a case? What but pull the government up to the people?[135]

At one debate Emmet was answered by a former auditor and medal winner of the Historical Society, Thomas Lefroy, who had graduated in 1795 but had returned because of the young orator's burgeoning reputation. Lefroy was an admirer of *Tom Jones* and was 'a very gentlemanlike, good-looking, pleasant young man'.[136] The author of this flattering description was none other than Jane Austen. The two had met at Hampshire in England during the Christmas of 1795 and a youthful romance had quickly developed. In Austen's earliest surviving letter, written after one of their encounters, she admitted that she was 'almost afraid to tell you how my Irish friend and I behaved. Imagine to yourself everything most profligate and shocking in the way of dancing and sitting down together.'[137] The affair was ended almost immediately by Lefroy's disapproving relatives and he was ordered back to London before returning home to Dublin. It was as a guest at Trinity that he witnessed first-hand Emmet's astonishing debating powers. Rejecting the motion, Lefroy delivered an excel-lent rebuttal of the previous arguments. Given permission by the chair to reply to these comments, Emmet rose to his feet and delivered an unscripted speech that left no one in doubt that his much-hyped talents had not been exaggerated. Answering his opponent point-by-point, Emmet's oratory and impassioned gestures settled the question; as one observer recalled, 'to attempt to give an idea of the eloquence or animation of the speaker was impossible'.[138]

It was only in December 1797 that Emmet decided to join the College Historical Society, where his late brother had made his reputation.[139] Whether he was nervous at following in Temple's footsteps or just wanted to concentrate on his studies is not clear, but he did not apply for membership until 6 December 1797, when he was proposed by William Corbet. The debate that evening was on the question, 'Was the second Punic war just on the part of the Romans?' The motion was defeated by thirty-one votes to seven.[140] Emmet's candidacy came up for debate at the next meeting, on Wednesday 13 December, but a mistake was spotted on his ballot paper and his membership was delayed for another week; the Historical Society voted on Emmet on 20 December and he was successfully admitted. He almost certainly attended his first debate the following Wednesday (the attendance page is missing), when he would have heard the discussion of the question, 'Does luxury tend to the destruction of national greatness?' But he was definitely present on 3 January 1798 when the question debated was, 'Is a spirit of commerce inimical to the preservation of constitutional liberty?' (It was narrowly defeated.)[141] A measure of just how highly Emmet was regarded was the fact that on 10 January he was given responsibility for chairing a five-man committee to prepare and bring in questions to be debated over the following months.

The Historical Society, then as now, was one of the leading student bodies in Trinity College. Theobald Wolfe Tone had been auditor or president back in 1786, but the society had declined after he and other key members left. Revived and restructured in 1794, it had a detailed constitution. In Emmet's time the society met every Wednesday throughout the year and the debates took place in the Historical Room. The meetings began at 6 in the evening and continued until midnight. Members were punished if they left before 11 o'clock. There was also a serious component to the society, with all members except graduates required to study thirty pages of history each week for examination. A motion for debate was decided by a select committee and announced two weeks in advance, with two students (or 'pleaders') given opposing sides to argue. There was also a convivial element to the evenings. Tea and cakes were made available to everyone before the meetings commenced.[142]

There were about 110 members of the Historical Society in Trinity College and around sixty attended each week. Its relationship with the college authorities had always been fraught with difficulties and numerous attempts had been made to suppress the society. For the board of the university the idea of a student debating body was anathema and in the 1790s it was seen as a breeding ground for jacobinism, republicanism and other dangerous creeds. In a humorous twist, when the college expelled the Historical Society from the university in 1794 it was applauded by an unholy alliance of the capital's vintners, publicans and courtesans. At a meeting chaired by the notorious Margaret Leeson, the group thanked the board for helping their 'respective trades'. It seems that the Historical Society 'considerably injured' their profits as it kept their 'best customers' occupied during the week studying history and preparing for the debates. An uneasy compromise was reached between the society and the college authorities later in the year, with the students promising to avoid the discussion of any questions relating to modern politics or even to allude to contemporary events. In return the society was allowed back on the university grounds and was once again given access to the Historical Room.[143] One further condition was that former members were forbidden from attending, although this rule was changed in 1798 as the college authorities increasingly attempted to control the proceedings of the society.

On 10 January 1798 the meeting of the Historical Society debated the proposition, 'Is the study of the science of more advantage than the study of the belles-lettres?' Both William Corbet and Thomas Moore spoke against the question and it was defeated by twenty-two votes to ten. The meeting the following week was to discuss a motion that might have appeared to be close to Emmet's heart, but he arrived late, after 7 o'clock, and left early: 'Was the discovery of America of more advantage than injury to the human race?' This was the famous question which had been posed by the French philosopher, Abbé Guillaume Raynal, after the Declaration of Independence in 1776. Indeed he had even offered a prize of 1,200 francs to the Academy of Lyons for the best essay written on the subject; eight responses are extant which are evenly divided on the matter.[144] When the Historical Society debated Raynal's question in 1798 there was a heated exchange of views, but the 'advantage' side won by twenty-one votes to ten. At this meeting Emmet delivered his report on the sixteen motions he and his committee had prepared for the following months. The house voted on his recommendations and they passed by fourteen votes to ten, with Emmet acting as the teller for the ayes. Buoyed by this victory, Emmet and five friends (including Thomas Moore) left the meeting early and were punished for going before 11 o'clock. The next week the house, by a clear majority (twenty-three votes to three), defeated the question, 'Were the Athenians justifiable in engaging in the sacred war in defence of religion?' But for the discussion of whether the suicide of Cato was justified, on 31 January, Emmet had less interest and arrived after 8 o'clock. The motion was defeated by thirty votes to thirteen.

Two speakers were always chosen a fortnight in advance to debate each motion. On 7 February James Carter and Richard Cuthbert were meant to speak on the question, 'Is unlimited freedom of discussion the best means of stopping the progress of erroneous opinions?' However they failed to turn up and were fined 11s. 4d. With the named pleaders absent the chair asked for replacements from the assembled members. Robert Emmet immediately volunteered to propose the motion and thus made his maiden speech without any preparation. Thomas Moore spoke alongside him, with Richard Moore (no relation) speaking against.

A maiden speech is always an intimidating rite of passage but, whatever he was privately feeling, Emmet displayed no fear at the dispatch-box.[145] It was a bravura performance and left a lasting impression on those who were privileged to hear it. Even listeners who subsequently rejected his political views never refrained from applauding the ability he displayed in college. Richard Madden interviewed many people who had been contemporaries of Robert Emmet in Trinity, 'some of them of very decided Tory politics, and I never heard but one opinion expressed, of the transcendent oratorical powers he displayed there'.[146] The new rules (introduced after the compromise of 1794) forbade any reference to modern politics but Emmet managed to make clever allusions to the Anglo-Irish relationship while still remaining within the narrow confines of the question. Proposing the motion, Emmet argued that a good government encouraged freedom of discussion and he emphasised the advantages that accrued from such a policy. He then compared the historical governments of Greece and Rome, while also 'portraying the evil effects of the despotism and tyranny' that could sometimes be found in the ancient world.[147] Concluding his speech, he issued a challenge to any state which restricted the liberties of the people:

> If a government were vicious enough to put down the freedom of discussion, it would be the duty of the people to deliberate on the errors of their rulers, to consider well the wrongs they inflicted, and what the right course would be for their subjects to take, and having done so, *it would then be their duty to draw practical conclusions.*[148]

The debate was one of the most closely fought in the Historical Society. When the question was finally put to the house to decide, Emmet acted as the teller for the ayes. It was his first speech to the society, and his first victory: the motion passed by twenty-seven votes to twenty.[149] The debate was closely observed by a former member of the society, James Geraghty, who had been given permission by the board to attend. Almost twenty-nine years old, Geraghty had been a brilliant debater during his time in university and a successful career beckoned in the law (he had been called to the bar in 1794). The college had become increasingly uneasy about the Historical Society and feared that it would become a meeting place for the disaffected in the university. Therefore it enlisted Geraghty because of his conservative leanings and asked him to watch the proceedings and report on what was said. The extraordinary début of the young Robert Emmet and his clever disregard of the prohibition on modern-day politics chilled the college board. Deeply disturbed by Emmet's growing importance in the society, it plotted ways of bringing his debating (and university) career to an end.[150]

An extraordinary general meeting of the Historical Society took place on

Friday 9 February. It was called to discuss an amendment by one of the members who wanted the sixteen questions that Emmet had presented to the house to be debated in a more traditional order. This amendment was supported by the auditor and opposed by Emmet, but this time the young orator was defeated. Fifty-six members were present and thirty-four voted for the amendment with only nineteen on Emmet's side. It was the first sign of a split in the society, which was beginning to divide on narrow lines between what Thomas Moore called 'the supporters of power' and those who followed Robert Emmet on 'the popular side'. The meeting on Wednesday 14 February began with the normal examination in history: the subject was 'Conspiracies in England'. Afterwards the question under discussion was whether the peasant was a more useful member of society than the soldier. This was overwhelmingly supported by the house, by fifty-four votes to three. Emmet was one of the first people present for the meeting on Wednesday 21 February and he listened carefully to the history examination which was on 'Philip's invasion of England'. He was probably more interested in the debate, which was on a motion of his choosing. It had a classical theme: 'Ought the institutions of Lycurgus excite our admiration or abhorrence?' The opposition won at the end of the night by thirty-nine votes to ten.

In private Emmet was quiet and unassuming, but he shed these inhibitions once he stood to speak. Then he was like a different person and Moore claimed that 'No two individuals, indeed, could be more unlike to each other than was the same youth to himself, before rising to speak and after.'[151] And he went on to explain: 'The brow that had appeared inanimate, and almost drooping, at once elevated itself to all the consciousness of power, and the whole countenance and figure of the speaker assumed a change as of one suddenly inspired.' Moore admitted that he was writing from 'youthful impressions', but he insisted that he had heard little oratory since those days that had been of a better quality; indeed few had ever been able to match Emmet's eloquence. Possessing complete mastery over his fellow speakers, Emmet dominated the debates in university; quite simply there was no one else who 'enchained the attention and sympathy of his young audience'.[152]

So great was Emmet's influence over his fellow students that the college authorities increasingly regarded him as a serious threat. The year was 1798 and Ireland was on the brink of open insurrection; therefore steps were taken to neutralise his support and damage his reputation. Emmet was seen as a dangerous demagogue and the authorities were taking no chances in their attempts to curb his power. Not only was his brother a leading radical, but he himself was the head of one of the United Irishmen cells in the university, and was suspected of being involved in the purchase and smuggling of guns. In addition the effects of his inflammatory oratory were feared, 'from the susceptibility with which his audience caught up every allusion to passing events' as well as from his speeches' 'own exciting power'. Led by the reactionary bursar, Thomas Elrington, the senior fellows of the college began attending the meetings of the Historical Society to observe the proceedings. Elrington was present at the debate on 21 February and was horrified to discover that the motion in a fortnight's time was on the question: 'Is duelling of advantage to society?' It was another topic that Emmet had suggested and Elrington was determined to prevent it ever being discussed. Another controversial question was due to be debated in seven days' time on Wednesday 28 February, 'Ought a soldier to consider the motives of a war, before he engages in it?' The political and philosophical bent of the motion was an indication of where Emmet was taking the society. A number of members were anxious to speak, including Emmet himself, and the college authorities decided it was time to put the troublesome students in their place. As Thomas Moore later recounted, a former member of the Historical Society was brought in, 'a man of advanced standing and reputation for oratory . . . expressly for the purpose of answering Emmet, and endeavoured to neutralise the impressions of his fervid eloquence'.[153] This man was James Geraghty. Elrington had decided to turn the debate into a battle for supremacy between 'the supporters of power' and the radical 'popular side' that was championed by Robert Emmet.[154]

The debate at the Historical Society on the final day of February was eagerly awaited. It was another opportunity to hear Emmet speak and the room was filled with students wanting to listen to his views on the contentious question.[155] Also present was a delegation from the college board including three fellows and Elrington himself. Emmet arrived just before 7 o'clock. Speaking in favour of the motion he delivered a brilliant oration that was full of dramatic rhetoric and youthful sensibility. Posing the question of whether a soldier was bound on all occasions to obey the orders of his commanding officer, he claimed that such a proposition was dangerous to society and degrading to human nature. His speech electrified the audience. One observer later reported to R. R. Madden that Emmet spoke with 'his back to the fire place, his hand moving backwards and forwards along the chimney piece', with his graceful movements reinforcing his superior arguments. In a thrilling oration Emmet talked in a 'most impassioned manner' and 'gave utterance to language of singular force and beauty'.[156] Colourful images abounded in his oration and he invited the audience to imagine the example of a soldier who had fought blindly for an oppressor in a war. Emmet then described this man

> rushing, after death, into the presence of his creator, and exclaiming in an agony of remorse, whilst he holds forth his sword reeking still with the blood of the oppressed and innocent, 'Oh God! I know not why I have done this.'[157]

The atmosphere at the debate was tense as students jostled each other to watch Geraghty challenge the 'chief champion' of the Historical Society. The older man was joined by seven other speakers in opposing the motion, while Emmet had only one other student on his side. After Geraghty's speech, Emmet was given an opportunity to reply to his arguments. For the first time in his life he was subjected to sustained heckling and interruption as his opponent did everything he could to disturb him. Unused to such tactics, Emmet struggled valiantly to deliver his remarks but his confidence deserted him. He lost control of himself and 'broke down', returning to his seat in the middle of his address. As his friend Thomas Moore later remembered:

> Whether from a momentary confusion in the thread of his argument, or possibly from diffidence in encountering an adversary so much his senior (for Emmet was as modest as he was high-minded and brave), he began, in the full career of his eloquence, to hesitate and repeat his words, and then, after an effort or two to recover himself, sat down.'[158]

When the question was put to the house it was defeated, narrowly enough given the circumstances, by twenty-one votes to sixteen. For Emmet the whole experience was a crushing blow and his distress was keenly felt by his friends; Moore recorded that it 'left us deeply humiliated to see our hero, for the first time, inferior to himself'.[159] Emmet would be prepared for such tactics when he encountered them five years later.

Showing much spirit, Robert Emmet attended the next meeting of the Historical Society on 7 March. It was to have been the debate on duelling but there was little chance of it being allowed to take place following his defeat the previous week. For the third week in a row Elrington was present, this time accompanied by Emmet's tutor, Richard Graves. Graves, himself a distinguished former member of the society, interrupted the meeting to ask that the question on duelling 'be not agitated'. This request, in reality a demand, passed without a division. The auditor then asked the house to choose an alternative motion from Emmet's list and have an extempore debate on the question. At this the students rebelled and, displaying their independence, voted overwhelmingly against the suggestion by thirty votes to ten. There was no debate that night. Instead a number of poems were read and Tom Moore won a prize for an entry that he had submitted under the name 'Tresmagestus'. However the young poet was punished at the end of the night for leaving the chamber before 11 o'clock. Emmet did not speak. He remained silent throughout the evening and never attended the Historical Society again. Five days later his brother was arrested by the government and, realising that his own position had now been compromised, Robert decided to drop out of college. He was marked absent for the debate the following week on Wednesday 14 March. The question being debated that evening would have been of particular interest to him: 'Was that a good law of Solon's which declared neutrality in an insurrection infamous?' It was passed by the house by twenty-six votes to eleven. Emmet also missed the important meeting of the Historical Society on 28 March when medals were awarded for oratory. James Heard came first when the returns were counted with 164. Thomas Moore was second with 115.

And in third place with 88 returns was Robert Emmet. As a result Heard was awarded the society's medal for oratory and Moore and Emmet both received the 'remarkable thanks of the society'. It was an impressive showing for Emmet, given that he had only spoken twice in the period when the returns were made; in contrast Heard had spoken five times and Moore three times. Thus Emmet had an average of 44 returns per debate compared to 38.33 for Moore and only 32.8 for Heard. By no means modest in his memoirs, nevertheless Moore always acknowledged that Emmet was his better in college when it came to intellect and debating ability. As Moore insisted, he had heard 'little, since, that appeared to me of a loftier or, what is a far more rare quality in Irish eloquence, purer character' than the oratory of Robert Emmet in college.[160]

At the meeting of 'the Hist' on 21 March Emmet was again absent, but he was none the less selected to speak at the forthcoming debate in two weeks' time. As he no longer attended student events in college he asked Thomas Moore to act as his substitute. This was not good enough to avoid punishment and on the evening of the debate Emmet was still fined over five shillings for not speaking. The motion was an entertaining one and it would have been interesting to see what the young Emmet would have made of it: 'Is individual happiness more promoted by matrimony or celibacy?' He was marked absent for the following two weeks, after which his name was erased from the membership list of the society by the order of the college authorities.[161] In the years ahead Thomas Elrington would continue to view the Historical Society with distaste and suspicion. When he became provost of Trinity College in 1811 the feud intensified and he seized upon an opportunity in 1815 to eject the society from the university.

The question of whether Robert Emmet was expelled from Trinity College or withdrew voluntarily to escape punishment has vexed historians. With tensions rising throughout the country in 1798, two students were expelled at the start of the year after admitting to membership of the United Irishmen. A third, Nicholas Purcell O'Gorman, was also sent down for publishing a paper which questioned this decision. Disturbed by tales of subversive activity emanating from Trinity College, on 31 March the board decided to call in the visitors (men with a statutory duty to investigate matters of discipline) to root out the radical contagion and restore order.[162] After the arrest of his brother on 12 March, Emmet effectively withdrew from college. He stopped attending debates and probably realised that like William Lander, who was prevented from graduating in the spring, he would never receive his B.A., even though he had fulfilled all the requirements. To anticipate any moves for his expulsion, he went to his university tutor, Richard Graves, and asked to have his name taken off the books. He had decided to drop out of college rather than disobey his conscience and follow the regulations of the board. However the Irish lord chancellor, the earl of Clare, was determined that no guilty student should be allowed to escape punishment and ordered the provost not to allow anyone to take their name off the college books.[163] Emmet's request was denied.

On 19 April 1798 the University of Dublin held a formal visitation by the earl of Clare, who was also the vice-chancellor of the university. He had been called in to investigate the reports of sedition among the students, and was accompanied by Dr Patrick Duigenan, the resolutely anti-Catholic MP, who deputised for the archbishop of Dublin. In part they had been brought there by Thomas Moore's article in *The Press* from a few months earlier, the one that Robert Emmet had been critical of for drawing attention to the college. Emmet was right; the visitation would bring to an end his brilliant if troubled debating career at the Historical Society less than three months after it had started, and with it his time at university. With Duigenan acting as his assessor, Clare gathered all the students in the dining hall to examine their loyalty. The inquisitors sat on a raised platform at the upper end of the hall and watched the ceremonial entry of all the university figures. As one student, John Edward Walsh, recounted in *Ireland sixty years ago*:

> Then followed, in order, the provost, senior and junior fellows and scholars as members of the corporation; then the graduate and undergraduate students; and lastly, the inferior officers and porters of the college. The great door was closed with a portentous sound and shut in many an anxious heart.[164]

Robert Emmet was not present. Ignoring the provost's refusal to allow him to withdraw, he scorned the idea of giving satisfaction to his enemies and dropped out anyway.

Clare's inquisition at Trinity left an enduring imprint on those who witnessed it. As Walsh remembered:

> Those who have seen Lord Clare in his visitorial capacity never will forget him, the hatchet sharpness of his countenance, the oblique glance of his eye, which seemed to read what was passing in the mind of him to whom it was directed. Silence was commanded and the multitude was still.

Beginning his speech in a loud voice, Clare declared:

> We have thought it necessary to come down to hold a general visitation of this college principally in consequence of rumours, too well founded I fear, that principles of a treasonable nature have made their way within these walls. . . . It is incumbent on you all as you value your characters to come forward and acquit yourselves of this most infamous libel . . . to vindicate your characters and to vindicate the reputation of the university from the foul aspersions thus cast upon it.[165]

He added that:

he should neglect an important duty if he were to suffer it [Trinity] to continue stained with the infamous imputation of disaffection and rebellion if unfounded; or permit any guilty member thereof to poison and destroy the prospects of the uninfected.

One student then arrived wearing boots. Clare immediately ordered him to leave and return properly attired. When the student promised that he would do his best, Clare snapped, 'I will have no ifs; you shall do so or be expelled.'[166] Referring to Moore's infamous article, Clare claimed that assassination and regicide had been advocated by one student in a clarion call to the others. A roll call was taken of everyone who should be present, starting with the provost and working down, and few excuses for absentees were accepted. When Robert Emmet's name was called there was complete silence and, although his tutor half-heartedly argued his case, he was still marked down as wilfully disobedient or 'contumacious'. The fact that his brother had been arrested the previous month as part of the government's counter-revolutionary measures did little for his cause.

Everyone present was then questioned by the lord chancellor, starting with the provost and ending with the porters. The examination of Dr Whitely Stokes, a junior fellow, caused much excitement in the hall. Theobald Wolfe Tone, who knew him during his time in Trinity, once said of Stokes that he was 'the very best man I have ever met'.[167] Stokes admitted that he was aware of illegal groups in the college, but when asked what they were, he replied that they were Orange societies. Clare was not amused: 'If the chancellor had been struck a violent blow he could not have shown more surprise and indignation. He actually started on his seat at the audacious sincerity of the simple-minded man, and another murmur ran through the hall.'[168] After much favourable testimony from colleagues and students, Stokes was eventually allowed to return to his seat, but Clare did not let him go unpunished. He announced that Stokes should have 'no pupils, nor be raised to the board of senior fellows for the space of three years' as a trial period to see if he would wipe himself clean 'as a person countenancing a system of treason for the subversion of the established government of this country'.[169]

Before examining the undergraduates Clare lectured them on the value of evening classes as a way of keeping them out of mischief. Insisting that they take an oath on the bible to confirm their loyalty, he then interrogated them about what they knew. About fifty refused to comply and they were marked as contumacious and threatened with expulsion. Among this number was Thomas Moore. As Duigenan attempted to hand him the bible, Moore's reactions made the scene, as Walsh later described it, unintentionally hilarious:

The book was presented to him. He shook his head and declined to take it. It was thrust into his right hand. He hastily withdrew the hand, as if he was afraid of its being infected by the touch, and placed it out of the way behind his back. It was then presented to his left hand, which he also withdrew, and held behind his back with his right. Still the persevering book was thrust upon him, and still he refused, bowing and retreating, with his hands behind him, till he was stopped by the wall.[170]

Moore's own account of the incident continues the story. On the second day of the visitation the fifty students were given a second opportunity to take the oath. Clare explained that the college was like one large family; therefore the authority that was being exercised was merely parental. He also promised that anyone who came forward and confessed their guilt, but gave their word that they would abandon their radical opinions, would be forgiven their error.[171] Moore remembered that he dreaded coming before 'the terrific tribunal' a second time and was intimidated by the sight of

> the formidable FitzGibbon [Clare], whose name I had never heard con-
> nected but with domineering insolence and cruelty; and by his side the
> memorable 'Paddy' Duigenan, memorable, at least, to all who lived in those
> dark times for his eternal pamphlets sounding the tocsin of persecution
> against the catholics.[172]

Moore again refused to take the oath, insisting that he had an objection. When asked to explain his reluctance he replied, 'I have no fear, my lord, that any-thing I say would incriminate myself, but it might tend to affect others; and I must say that I despise that person's character who could be led under any circumstance to criminate his associates.'[173] When told that he would not be allowed to remain in university unless he confirmed his allegiance, Moore backed down and took the oath. But he insisted that he reserved the right not to answer questions about others; the lord chancellor dismissed this statement impatiently, 'We do not sit here to argue with you, sir.'

The political ideology of Robert Emmet was the real concern for Thomas Moore. Worried about 'the plot uncovered', he was unsure about how 'the fearful drama' would conclude for his friend.[174] Emmet's absence from the tri-bunal made Moore uneasy, and every roll-call that he missed only served to confirm his guilt in his mind. Claiming to be surprised at how far the United Irishmen had infiltrated Trinity, Moore insisted that he was astonished to hear the damning testimony of so many students, which underlined that the lord chancellor had not been mistaken in his concerns: 'It was really most startling and awful to hear the disclosures which every new succeeding witness brought forth.'[175] And with Emmet, the two Corbet brothers, John Browne and others all refusing to attend the investigation, 'their total absence from the whole scene, as well as the dead silence that daily followed the calling out of their names, proclaimed how deep had been their share in the transactions now about to be inquired into'. Dacre Hamilton, Emmet's close friend who shared his passion for mathematics but not his politics, fell victim to the witch-hunt. A scholar in 1797, Hamilton had an excellent brain but a simple mind, and his naivety and innocence often provided much amusement for his friends. Nevertheless he was still regarded with much affection and Emmet and he 'had long been intimate and attached friends'.[176] But, because of his association with Emmet, the brother of a captured rebel, he was examined thoroughly to prove a link between him and the United Irishmen's college organisation. Moore later insisted that Hamilton was innocent of any real involvement, blaming an informer for selling him out, and claimed that he was persecuted for his refusal to answer questions that would have incriminated Emmet. In the event Hamilton was expelled from Trinity and because of his contumacy was prohibited from entering any of the professions. The fear of following his example encouraged other students to come forward and testify, and many won their safety at the expense of associates and friends.[177]

Having taken the oath on the second day, Moore was interrogated by Clare about his knowledge of subversive activity. The existence of United Irishmen cells had already been established and Moore was asked if he had been a member of any of them. He replied with a firm assurance, 'No my lord.'[178] He was then asked if he had any knowledge of the groups' proceedings; he also denied this, 'No, my lord.' The third question revealed the depth of the lord chancellor's anxiety. Moore was asked if he was aware of any schemes of the students to buy guns and ammunition. Again he insisted, 'No, my lord.' The final question was about the proposals for assassination which ironically Moore himself had advocated in his newspaper article. Lying under oath, he denied any knowledge of this conspiracy, 'Oh no, my lord.' After hearing all of this Clare conferred with Duigenan for a few minutes. Then, returning to face Moore, he asked him why he had objected to taking the oath when he had not been aware of any seditious activity. The young poet answered with a mocking smile, 'I have already told you, my lord, my chief reasons; in addition to which, it was the first oath I ever took, and it was, I think, a very natural hesitation.' Upon hearing this, Dr Whitely Stokes turned to a friend and said, 'That's the best answer that has been given yet.' Moore was given permission to stand down and returned to his seat happy with the answers he had given. Nevertheless he still looked nervously to the rest of the students, anxious for their approbation and straining to see 'what sort of verdict their looks and manner would pass on my conduct'.[179]

It was Robert Emmet's turn to be examined on the second day, 20 April. Again he was not present and his tutor, Graves, 'made some observations relative to Emmet who long since wished to have his name taken off the college books'.[180] Upon hearing this Lord Clare roared into life and launched into a vehement denunciation of Emmet:

I have been for some time in possession of everything that has been going forward in the college — and I know that Emmet is one of the most active and wicked members of the society of United Irishmen — and I did desire the provost not to suffer any person to take his name off the college books, that I might bring him and others of his association to punishment.

He then ordered Emmet to appear before the visitation and warned that he would be expelled if he did not. The next student to be examined, Mawe, admitted that he had attended a meeting of the United Irishmen in Trinity about a fortnight earlier. It had taken place in Thomas Corbet's room and had been called to discuss appointing sergeants and corporals. The avowed object of the committee was Catholic emancipation and parliamentary reform, and Mawe denied any knowledge of gun-running. He revealed that the members of the society were to be organised into units or splits of twelve men each, with ten splits (of 120 men) forming a company.[181]

There was some unexpected light relief when Martin Farrell, a Roman Catholic from Cork, was questioned by the lord chancellor. Farrell denied attending any meetings of the United Irishmen, although he did concede that he 'did once become a member'. With some spirit he told Clare that he would always follow his conscience. Immediately Clare asked him if he would follow his conscience if it justified murder, but Farrell replied that this was 'an impossible case'. Rejecting his position, Clare said that it was not impossible. The only reply Farrell could make was, 'Why then I should be mad.' With a sardonic smile, Clare cut him down: 'In truth you seem a little foolish as it is.' Michael Farrell, the son of a Catholic farmer from Longford, was also summoned to appear, but his tutor, Graves again, explained that 'the disturbed part of the county in which he is, prevents his attendance'. Clare was having none of it and Farrell was one of the students marked down for expulsion. As the lord chancellor explained: 'If I had not reason to suspect that a considerable part of the disturbance of that county might be traced to him, I might perhaps be induced to excuse him.' Tensions were high on the campus and the finger of suspicion was not slow to be pointed. A few students who were expelled challenged suspected informers to duels; at one, the men exchanged four shots but neither was hurt.[182] The talk in Dublin was of nothing but the visitation. William Drennan reported that everyone was commenting on it and he himself was disgusted that the earl of Clare could give 'lectures on morality and religion' when his own 'conversation is a tissue of obscenity and lies'.[183] He hoped that Robert Emmet would be around to provide further details, and he was clearly impressed with the young man. He thought that Emmet was 'a wonderful orator, though so modest and diffident in company'. The visitation ended on 21 April with a speech from Clare at 2.45 in the afternoon. He revealed that there was substantial evidence that within the last two weeks 'there was an order given for arms within your walls' and that the United Irishmen in the college had held 'a deliberate assembly' for the purpose of 'appointing assassins to take off all those who might be supposed inimical to their measures'. Accusing the suspected students of contaminating the university, Clare announced that 'overt acts of rebellion were committed within your walls, under the influence of these pestilent associations . . . It remains only for us to discharge a painful part of our duty in purging this society of some of its pestilent members.' His speech ended with 'great clapping and applause from all parts of the hall'.

The lord chancellor's intervention ended Emmet's university career. Nineteen students were expelled from Trinity College as a result of the visitation. These included George Keogh, the son of the Roman Catholic leader John Keogh, the Corbet brothers, Peter McLoughlin and James Flynn. Because Robert Emmet had refused to testify, his name was included on the list, even though he had anticipated the punishment and had written a letter to the board of the university attempting to withdraw from the college. It marked the end of his academic studies and the beginning of his career as a revolutionary. Michael Dwyer, the Wicklow rebel who conspired with Emmet in 1803, claimed in his examination by Dublin Castle that Emmet would have been a fine man if he had but 'brains to his education'.[184] Time would show that there was a certain amount of truth to this observation. But a less critical commentary was provided by Charles Philips, the friend of John Philpot Curran, who included it in his recollections of the barrister. Having interviewed Emmet's friends and contemporaries in Trinity College he concluded that Emmet's education had a lasting influence on his subsequent adventures:

> His mind was naturally melancholy and romantic — he had fed it from the pure fountain of classic literature, and might be said to have lived not so much in the scene around him as in the society of the illustrious and sainted dead. The poets of antiquity were his companions, its patriots were his models, and its republics his admiration. He had but just entered upon the world, full of the ardour which such studies might be supposed to have excited, and unhappily at a period in the history of his country when such noble feelings were not only detrimental but dangerous.[185]

Philips applauded the education Emmet had received in Trinity College. But he also paid tribute to the influence the young man had wielded on the university. He had entered at the age of fifteen a young patriot and left under a cloud five years later a committed revolutionary. It was clear to Philips that Emmet 'was gifted with abilities and virtues which rendered him an object of universal esteem and admiration. Everyone loved, everyone respected him; his fate made an impression on the university which has not yet been obliterated.' Philips concluded that only 'an ungenerous loyalty' could 'not weep over the extinction of such a spirit'.[186]

5

WARFARE AND TECHNOLOGY: THE IMAGINATION OF AN INSURRECTION

~

'Only vulgar minds harbour the thought that a physical possibility is impracticable because it has not already been done.'
(Robert Fulton discussing submarine warfare with the British prime minister, Lord Grenville, 2 September 1806)[1]

In September 1800 the British fleet off Le Havre was attacked by the *Nautilus*, a submersible boat designed and commanded by the brilliant American inventor Robert Fulton. Warned in advance by spies, the British navy was prepared for the raid and prevented the *Nautilus* from attaching a 'torpedo', in modern terms an underwater mine, to any of its hulls.[2] The attack marked the culmination of three years of intensive research and development, financed by the French government, and it ended in failure. Fulton retreated to the French coast and continued to refine his invention, but the *Nautilus* began to fall to pieces and he was forced to sell the parts for money a year later. While carrying out his experiments in France he encountered the young secretary of a delegation of United Irishmen which had been sent to the continent. They shared a passion for mathematics and chemistry and quickly became friends. Robert Fulton's association with Robert Emmet, who had been chosen for this crucial mission because of his growing reputation, was to have an important bearing on subsequent events in Ireland.

THE CAREER OF ROBERT FULTON, 1797–1806

Born in Pennsylvania in 1765, Fulton had studied to be an artist and even exhibited six paintings at the Royal Academy in London (1791–3). Changing professions in England he benefited from the patronage of Charles Mahon, 3rd Earl Stanhope, who encouraged him to become an engineer. Stanhope was himself a scientist and inventor and had supported the French revolution in its early stages. Fulton studied methods for improving canal navigation, and shared lodgings in Manchester with Robert Owen, who later became famous for his utopian radicalism. Travelling to Paris in 1797, Fulton joined the *émigré* American community there and decided to offer his services to the French revolutionary government. His submission to the Directory on 12 December 1797 made an immediate impact. It proposed the construction of a 'mechanical nautulus' (sic) which could be used 'to annihilate' the British navy.[3] Fulton was the first person to call a submarine after the nautilus, an ocean mollusc which has a shell of air-filled chambers. At this time he was also experimenting with underwater mines so that the submarine could become a deadly weapon of war; these could be attached to the hulls of enemy ships to explode after the submarine had slipped away. This was not an original idea. David Bushnell had created a similar weapon during the American War of Independence but had failed in his ambitious attempt to sink the British HMS *Eagle* with his submersible craft, the *American Turtle*, on 6 September 1776.[4] Fulton was determined to improve on this quixotic experiment and make underwater warfare an indispensable part of modern naval conflict. A French report in 1798 concluded that the weapon devised by Fulton was 'a terrible means of destruction, because it acts in silence and in a manner almost inevitable'.[5] Fulton himself claimed that his submarine would transform international relations by extending 'the principles of liberty' throughout the world and establishing 'a lasting peace among the nations'.[6] The British government initially feared little from Fulton. Although as the leading naval country it had a lot to lose, it was confident that his ideas were too fantastical and would never succeed. As Joshua Gilpin, an American correspondent, reported to Stanhope on 28 August 1798 there was little danger of Fulton's designs becoming a threat to British security. Gilpin was convinced that the French government and Fulton were only 'amusing each other (I think however to little purpose) on his new invention of the submarine boat'.[7] But at exactly the same time Fulton was proudly writing to Stanhope informing him his ideas, including proposals for canal navigation, had 'created a revolution in the mind of all the French engineers'.[8] With the rise to power of Napoleon Bonaparte in 1799, Fulton's proposals were given conditional government support and the *Nautilus* was completed in the summer of the following year. When briefed about the scheme, the French first consul wrote a perceptive comment: 'I have just read the project of Citizen Fulton, engineer, which you have sent me much too late, since it is one that may change the face of the world.'[9] The *Nautilus* was launched on 24 July 1800 and made its 'shake-down' voyage five days later on the Seine; Fulton succeeded in submerging the shell-like vessel, which was twenty feet long and five feet in diameter, for eight minutes on one occasion and for seventeen minutes on another. Preparations complete, in September he set out on a journey of almost seventy miles to intercept the British navy, having calculated that the *Nautilus* had enough air for three men and a candle to survive underwater for three hours.[10] Failure off Le Havre in September tainted Fulton's reputation. The British navy had been warned by the admiralty about his attack and successfully evaded his attempts to mine its ships. Unwilling to give the French government access to his plans and drawings, Fulton's claims were undermined and Napoleon quickly lost patience: the first consul declared in 1801, 'Don't mention him again'.[11]

Not willing to give up on his invention, Fulton continued refining the design of his submarine. By 1803 he was convinced he had a practical weapon of war and he persuaded the French military to give him another opportunity to test it in action. Reluctantly the government gave him permission and he began preparations for an audacious attack on London. The plan was to strike at the heart of the British navy by mining the River Thames and thus sink every ship near the capital. This mission was set to take place in July 1803, the exact time that Robert Emmet was preparing to revolt in Ireland. Once again the British secret service came to the rescue of the empire when the plan was discovered in June. There was uproar at the admiralty. The prospect of a submarine moving stealthily up the Thames, releasing mines underneath the British fleet, was a terrifying possibility especially as there was little hope of preventing it. Evan Nepean, a key agent at the alien office, received secret information of the scheme and sent it to key members in the admiralty on 19 June. His message was blunt: 'A plan has been conceived by Mr Fulton, under the influence of the first consul of the French republic, for destroying the maritime force of this country.'[12] Nepean had uncovered the full extent of the destructive mission, including intelligence that 'the sole submarine vessel is uncommonly manageable'. Appalled, he acknowledged that the entire plan 'may be easily executed and without much risk; that the whole ships and vessels in the port of London are liable to be destroyed with ease, and that the channel of the River Thames may be ruined'.[13] In the event, the mission did not go ahead; it seems that Napoleon again lost faith in Fulton and following the failure of Emmet's rebellion the attack was forgotten about. By now the British government had come to realise just how much a threat Fulton's weapons posed and it resolved to prevent him assisting the French in the future. A plan was formed to persuade him to defect.

Disillusioned with his treatment by the French, Fulton agreed to open negotiations with the British. He was offered a lucrative contract to develop his submarine and his plans for 'torpedo war' with a bounty of approximately £40,000 for every French ship he hunted and sank.[14] Stanhope helped sell the deal and Fulton arrived in London on 23 April 1804, shortly before William Pitt returned to power. For the next three years he worked on various projects for the new administration, using the alias Robert Francis. The British government, wisely, had little interest in developing submarine warfare; it recognised that the existing system maintained its mastery of the seas. But Fulton's experiments with underwater mines and torpedoes had a real appeal and the special commission set up to investigate his proposals spent most of its time examining these areas. Five people studied Fulton's drawings, one of whom was Major William Congreve, who had been appointed to the panel by the admiralty. Congreve would soon achieve fame for inventing an advanced type of 'fire rocket', which would even bear his name, but there is evidence that Fulton (and possibly Emmet) deserves some of the credit. Pitt was intrigued by Fulton's designs for 'instantaneous submarine bombs', and because of his newly acquired interest in military tactics decided to oversee some practical tests.[15] On 15 October 1805 Fulton successfully blew up the *Dorothea* near the walls of Walmer Castle. The explosion took place fifteen minutes after he fired the submarine bomb into the water and split the brig in two. As Fulton recorded with satisfaction: 'The ends sank immediately, and nothing was seen but floating fragments . . . her annihilation was complete, and the effect was most extraordinary.' The ship was destroyed like 'a shattered eggshell'.[16]

Delighted by the results of his test, Fulton sent detailed reports to Pitt and Lord Castlereagh. Full of pride in his achievement, he was convinced that he had transformed the future of naval warfare. His report betrayed signs of a dangerous hubris:

> Now, in this business, I will not disguise that I have full confidence in the power which I possess, which is no less than to be the means, should I think proper, of giving to the world a system which must of necessity sweep all military marines from the ocean, by giving to the weaker maritime powers advantages over the stronger, which the stronger cannot prevent.

Needless to say, key figures in the British admiralty were disturbed by these claims. Shortly afterwards Fulton had an interview with the earl of St Vincent, one of the most distinguished admirals of the day. St Vincent recognised the true significance of Fulton's plans for submarine warfare and later raged:

> Pitt was the greatest fool that ever existed, to encourage a mode of war which they who commanded the seas did not want, and which if successful would deprive them of it.[17]

Fearful of a French invasion of England, the government devised contingency plans for mining the English channel to prevent enemy ships from getting through.[18] Fulton's designs also assisted the British engineers in the development of a war-rocket, but the real credit for this new technology can be traced to events on a different continent.

THE TIGER OF MYSORE

On the night of 5 April 1799 Colonel Arthur Wellesley and his men were attacked by the rocketeers of Tipu Sultan, the infamous 'Tiger of Mysore'. Wellesley had been ordered to seize the village of Sultanpet, a strategic position in the British plans for conquering Mysore, the leading state in southern India.

The prince of the region, Tipu Sultan, had been since 1783 a major irritant to successive British governor-generals, including Cornwallis, by challenging the power of the East India Company and encouraging the French to join him in an alliance. Attacked in the darkness by rockets and musket-fire, the future duke of Wellington was neither able to command nor inspire his men. The rockets flared like crimson lightning through the sky. Unused to dealing with such weapons, the British troops panicked and fled into the countryside. It was one of Wellesley's worst ever defeats and he failed to report on time the following day as he struggled to rally his men.[19]

Tipu Sultan had recognised the enormous potential of the missile and had enlarged his father's rocket companies to 5,000 men, almost one-tenth of his total army. As with all his weapons, the rockets were inscribed with the motif of a tiger-stripe.[20] It was Tipu Sultan's proud and distinctive symbol. His personal motto was that it was better to live two days as a tiger than 200 years as a sheep. The terror displayed by the British soldiers was not an aberration and in the years ahead the first reaction of even battle-hardened troops was to be put to rout when attacked by rockets. At the battle of Seringapatam on 4 May 1799 the Tiger of Mysore's luck finally ran out. His 48,000 men were comprehensively defeated by the 8,700 European and 27,000 native troops of the British army.[21] Surrounded by the enemy, Tipu Sultan received two bayonet wounds and one gunshot injury, but he refused to reveal his identity and surrender, shouting defiantly at an aide, 'Are you mad? Be silent.' A grenadier shot him through the temple and his corpse was trampled on in the subsequent confusion.[22] Wellesley was appointed governor of the fort and some captured rockets were sent back to England for investigation.[23]

Rocket technology in Europe in the late eighteenth century was very limited. In India and the Far East however it was more advanced and had been used with varying success for centuries. As the East India Company evolved from being a mercantile to an imperial operation, it sometimes encountered the weapon which was loud and colourful though not particularly accurate; nevertheless its sheer novelty surprised and terrified soldiers. Various people were working on prototypes for a practical European rocket in the early 1800s, but it was William Congreve who eventually emerged to claim the credit. In 1807 his rockets were used to attack Copenhagen, to prevent the Danish fleet falling into the hands of the French, and over three days around 25,000 missiles rained down on the city bringing much terror and destruction. Over 1,500 civilians were killed and Denmark was forced to surrender its ships to the British; present at the carnage were General Cathcart and Sir Arthur Wellesley. The weapon was also used against the Americans during the War of 1812 and the 'rockets' red glare' made such an impact during an attack on Fort McHenry that it inspired Francis Scott Key to write the national anthem. During one battle in 1814 a British officer mocked the way American troops fled when greeted with rocket-fire: 'Never did men with arms in their hands make better use of their legs.'[24] Even when he was out of office, William Pitt received much information about the combat capabilities of this new weapon. On 22 October 1803 Captain Meares, an officer in the East India Company, sent the former prime minister a detailed report as well as 'the original rocket of Scindia'.[25] Scindia was the maharajah of Gwalior, who had led the Mahratta confederation against British rule in India. This particular rocket was probably captured at Assaye on 23 September 1803 when General Arthur Wellesley defeated the Mahratta and its French allies with breathtaking audacity; it was the battle which he was always most proud of winning, despite later victories like Waterloo. Pitt was informed that 'The war rockets of India [are] in universal use there, particularly to annoy cavalry' and that the model which he had been sent 'inflicts in its progress dreadful carnage'.[26] For maximum effect, Meares advised, the rocket should be fired in a horizontal direction when it was 'formidable indeed'. By attacking an enemy on the flanks, 'in their rear and on their line of march', the impact of the weapon was 'fatal'.[27] But by October 1803 the British government was already well aware of the danger posed by rockets to European combat. Robert Emmet had brought an improved version of the technology to Ireland.

ROBERT EMMET IN IRELAND, 1798–1800

Expelled from Trinity College Dublin in April 1798, Robert Emmet was faced with a difficult set of choices. His brother was in prison, the United Irishmen's plans were in disarray and all the time the country lurched towards open rebellion. No warrant was issued for his arrest (at least until 3 April 1799), but Emmet feared that he would be taken up by the authorities and took precautions against being captured. All this time he lived with his father and mother at Milltown.[28] The poet Robert Southey visited Dublin in late 1801 and met Emmet's 'most intimate friend', probably Richard Curran as Thomas Moore was then in England.[29] Southey had many conversations about the 'admirable man' and from all he heard concluded that 'God almighty seldom mixes up so much virtue and so much genius in one, or talents as ennobled.'[30] Apparently Southey also learned that during the 1798 rebellion, or immediately afterwards, Emmet avoided arrest by 'excavating a hiding place under the study in his father's house' where he stayed for six weeks. He had a supply of food, books and a light, and ventured out at night into the park for exercise.[31] A similar story was told by R. R. Madden who visited Casino in 1836 and talked to Michael Leonard, a servant of the late Dr Emmet and a former family gardener. Madden learned that 'Master Robert's bedroom' had a secret trap-door which led through a passage to the lawn outside.[32] To enable him to avoid capture, a tunnel ran from two basement windows on the left of the porch entrance to a summer house fifty yards away. According to a family tradition this summer house was a favourite sanctuary of Robert Emmet.[33] Deeply involved in the United Irishmen conspiracy, Emmet acted as 'a messenger and confidential agent' when 'the affairs at hand were deemed of great importance'.[34] But because the 1798 rebellion, which began on the night of 23 May, was confined to a small number of counties outside of Dublin, he did not see any fighting. Instead he waited for reports to arrive in the capital and watched as Marquess Cornwallis, the new commander-in-chief and lord lieutenant, arrived in Ireland to quell the rising. On 8 September the French general, Jean Louis Humbert, was defeated by Cornwallis at Ballinamuck, ending any lingering hopes of victory. By the close of autumn the rebellion had been crushed completely and Theobald Wolfe Tone's attempt to land with a French fleet ended in abject failure. Captured off Lough Swilly, Co. Donegal, Tone was brought to Dublin in chains and charged with treason. Wearing his ceremonial French uniform at his trial, he had 'a large and fiercely cocked hat, with broad gold lace, and the tricoloured cockade, a blue uniform coat, with gold and embroidered collar, and two large gold epaulets, blue pantaloons with gold laced garters at the knees, and short boots bound at the tops with gold lace'.[35] Tone defiantly admitted that he had enlisted foreign aid in his efforts to liberate Ireland, but he refused to accept that he was a traitor and read a defence of his actions from a paper he had written. At the start of his speech he looked flushed and agitated, but after asking for a glass of water he recovered his composure and 'behaved with great firmness'.[36] Accepting his guilt, he revealed that, 'It is not my intention to give the court any trouble; I admit the charge against me in the fullest extent.' And he also declared with some vehemence that he was fully prepared to accept the consequences of his actions:

> I have sacrificed all my views in life; I have courted poverty; I have left a beloved wife, unprotected, and children whom I adored, fatherless. After such sacrifices, in a cause which I have always conscientiously considered as the cause of justice and freedom — it is no great effort, at this day, to add, 'the sacrifice of my life'.[37]

Disillusioned by the reports of atrocities on both sides in the 1798 rebellion, Tone took the opportunity to clarify what he had intended: 'For a fair and open war I was prepared; if that has degenerated into a system of assassination, massacre, and plunder I do again most sincerely regret it.'[38] In his peroration Tone acknowledged that 'in this world success is everything', and he admitted that he had attempted to 'follow the same line in which Washington succeeded and Kosciusko failed'. But as he had been unsuccessful in the attempt to 'establish the independence of my country', he accepted that his life was 'in consequence forfeited'. Ending his speech with great equanimity he stated: 'The court will do their duty and I shall endeavour to do mine.'

Sentenced to death, Wolfe Tone cheated the executioner; he committed suicide in prison. Among his closest friends had been Thomas Addis Emmet and Thomas Russell, with whom he had enjoyed 'a fellowship in our labours; a society on our dangers; our hopes, our fears, our wishes'.[39] His widow Matilda (born Martha Witherington) remained in Paris and dedicated herself to raising their three children. She later revealed that she 'lived for the sole and single purpose of taking care of Tone's children; and [that] I promised him I would do this, when, in setting off for that last unfortunate expedition, he bid me that his life was gone . . . and urged the care of his darling babies to me'.[40]

After the rebellion Thomas Addis Emmet was one of the state prisoners who signed the 'Kilmainham treaty' with the government; he was subsequently moved to Newgate Prison. There were many heated exchanges between Dublin Castle and Whitehall about what to do with the men. Some of the prisoners including Emmet wanted to emigrate to the United States, but this unnerved many senior political figures. When the home secretary, the duke of Portland, expressed his preference for executing the state prisoners rather than allow them to move to America, there was an angry response from Cornwallis, the new viceroy. William Wickham shared Portland's concerns and was uneasy about letting dangerous radicals take refuge in the new republic. He helped persuade the United States ambassador to the court of St James, Rufus King, to reject any such proposal by emphasising that the British government was 'anxious that these people should not be suffered on any account to set foot on American soil'.[41] This attitude was in sharp contrast to the opinion of Lord Castlereagh, the chief secretary, who noted sardonically that 'the majority of our prisoners are not more dangerous than the general class of American settlers'.[42] The part played by Rufus King in preventing his emigration to the United States was never forgotten by Thomas Addis Emmet. In 1807 he torpedoed King's prospects of becoming governor of New York by publishing an open letter which was brimming with barely contained rage and resentment. Thomas Addis revealed that it had been his intention to bring his father and his family, including Robert, with him to America, but had been prevented by the duplicitous manoeuvring of King who had cravenly followed the instructions of the British cabinet. Because of this he had been forced to spend four of the best years of his life in prison.[43] The bitterness was never far from the surface, especially when Thomas Addis began reflecting on the fate of his beloved Robert. He icily informed King that his brother would have been a partner in his emigration and noted sharply that he was someone 'whose name perhaps even you will not read without emotion or sympathy and respect'. Now his entire family had been torn from him and he had been prevented from 'saving a brother, from receiving the dying blessings of a father, mother and sister, and from soothing their last agonies by my cares — and this, sir, by your unwarrantable and unfeeling interference'. If the entire Emmet family had emigrated to the United States in 1798 the history of Ireland would have been very different. But as Thomas Addis noted with dripping sarcasm, it seemed that Alexander Marsden had been correct in his analysis and that Rufus King 'did not want to have republicans in America'.

Robert Emmet visited his brother regularly at Newgate Prison and his movements were watched and reported back to Dublin Castle.[44] Meanwhile the executive directory of the United Irishmen was reformed and the government became convinced that 'Emmet junior' was 'certainly' a member.[45] This was both a nod to his distinguished family name but also a recognition of his abilities and growing importance in the movement. However the government decided to allow him to remain free, because 'they [the directory] cannot at present accomplish anything'.[46] Thomas Wright, a surgeon who had smuggled guns for the rebels in 1798, was asked to write a military handbook for the United Irishmen, which was amended by Emmet and Malachy Delany. When arrested by the British government on 28 April 1799, Wright agreed to become a double agent and he reported that Emmet was 'a young man with military talent'.[47] The United Irishmen decided upon a serious reorganisation of its structures, and a report was prepared on the reasons for the failure in 1798. Its main conclusion was that there had been too much 'publicity' surrounding the conspiracy, enabling the government to arrest the leaders in advance, maximise the use of informers and expose the plans.[48] The report contained a passage rich in apocalyptic fervour and excitement: 'In a period so pregnant with the future fate of Ireland . . . torpor or negligence on the one side, and publicity on the other, will draw down on us immediate destruction.' The government discovered in 1803 from its informers that the United Irishmen 'goes entirely on the old system of 1799, formed by young Emmet, etc.'[49] Lord Hardwicke wrote on the margin that this system was 'by communicating to very few, and not by visiting'.

In January 1799 visiting restrictions were imposed at Newgate and the Emmet family were prevented from seeing Thomas Addis. Beginning to despair, Dr Emmet wrote a poignant letter to the Dublin Castle officials in February pleading to be allowed to visit: 'May we hope to be re-admitted to the painful pleasure of seeing him even in that prison. Had you, sir, a son, like any son you would feel in reading what I feel in writing this letter.'[50] Thomas Addis did not remain at Newgate for much longer. On 18 March 1799 he learned that he was being moved and eight days later nineteen state prisoners were transported to Fort George in Scotland. He would remain there for the next three years.

One consequence of the 1798 rebellion was the introduction of a legislative union by the British prime minister, William Pitt. His aim was to abolish the Irish parliament and replace it with a united parliament at Westminster in an attempt to create a new imperial security.[51] Pitt was determined to prevent Ireland from being used as a base to attack Britain on a flank where it was most vulnerable. Therefore Catholic emancipation was to be a part of the scheme, and Pitt envisaged uniting the islands in a new political system for the pursuit of empire. The Irish parliament however proved resistant to the proposal and it was rejected by the House of Commons in January 1799. Pitt however was determined to see it pass, and it was re-introduced twelve months later. This time every resource of the government was strained to ensure a majority in parliament and the union passed due to the ruthless use of patronage, corruption, borough compensation and the Catholic question. John Philpot Curran was one of the barristers who opposed the measure, but perhaps the loudest anti-unionist in parliament was another lawyer, William Plunket. In one famous declaration he announced that he, for his part,

> will resist it [the union] to the last gasp of my existence and with the last drop of my blood. And when I feel the hour of my dissolution approaching, I will, like the father of Hannibal, take my children to the altar and swear them to eternal hostility against the invaders of their country's freedom.[52]

The poetry of 'Trebor' resurfaced in radical newspapers during this controversy. One interesting effort was published in *The Anti-Union* in 1799 as Emmet struggled to reconcile his imagination with what was happening in Ireland. 'The two ships: a fable' contained a subtle political subtext, but the rhyming was still as clumsy as ever. Relying on off rhymes, a device which was occasionally used by Swift, he linked the words 'creaking' and 'wrecking' and 'deny' and 'mutiny' for maximum effect. The arguments for and against the union were presented before Emmet, speaking as the Irish captain, explained the true cause of his ship's discontent:

> I know I have on board some men,
> That seem rebellious now and then,
> But what's the cause? You know full well —
> Allowance short — makes men rebel.

Reviewing the history of the Anglo-Irish connection, Emmet accused Britain of having secured the connection through deceit and treachery:

> a scoundrel few
> About the helm, betrayed the crew;
> And for a bounty, basely gotten,
> Lash'd the sound vessel to the rotten.[53]

At a time when a legislative union between Britain and Ireland was being debated, Emmet was clear than an unequal arrangement would only damage both countries. Allegorising his times, he argued that rather than risk exploitation or possible destruction, it was better for Ireland to seek her independence and break away from 'the crazy ship'.

A third poem by 'Trebor' was published in early 1799.[54] It was entitled 'Help from heaven' and began with a quotation from the 118th Psalm: 'The right hand of the Lord bringeth mighty things to pass — the Lord has chastened and corrected me; but he hath not given me over to death.' Emmet's style is slightly different in this effort and there is a new rhyming scheme. The poem ends with the lonely and plaintive figure of Ireland receiving divine consolation:

'My fervent thanks, high heav'n,' she cries,
'Be ever, ever given to thee;
Thou'st chas'd my sorrow, tears and sigh —
Thou'st sent me Hope and Liberty.'

Only one of Emmet's poems bears his initials, 'Genius of Erin', which is signed 'RE' at the end. The stanzas lack the splendour of his oratory and are at times rather crude and simplistic. Nevertheless it seems harsh to criticise Emmet for the poems he wrote before the age of twenty-one. The majority of these were either teenage expressions of national pride or hack propaganda pieces that were rushed for publication. As his oratory and letters prove, Emmet certainly had a gift for words, but he did not have a natural flair for poetry. However the poem did end with a moving and heroic rallying cry for rebellion:

Erin's sons, awake! — awake!
Oh! too long, too long, you sleep;
Awake! arise! your fetters break,
Nor let your country bleed and weep.[55]

'Arbour Hill' drew its inspiration from the burial ground for people exe-cuted for treason, and was probably written in the wake of the 1798 rebellion. The tone is initially embittered but it gradually changes to one of reconciliation and finally acceptance. The 'callous judges' whose 'hands in blood are dyed' were condemned and Emmet lamented the absence of any justice in Ireland. The poem ended with an elegiac tribute to the dead heroes of 1798:

And those who here are laid at rest,
Oh! hallowed be each name;
Their memories are for ever blest —
Consigned to endless fame.[56]

Emmet's conception of virtue and heroism, even at this early stage of his life, was clear.

On 7 June 1800 the union bill had its third and final reading in the Irish House of Commons. Two-thirds of the opposition members walked out of the house in disgust and the measure passed without a division. John Foster, the anti-union Speaker of the House of Commons, threw the legislation on the table before sinking into his chair in despair. According to a family tradition, Robert Emmet watched the concluding discussion of this question from the public gallery. Lord Cloncurry, the United Irishman conspirator who knew the Emmets on the continent, confirmed that Robert attended many of the union debates. He wrote how 'a young man in the gallery listened, in solemn silence, to what was going on, and made a secret vow that he would one day effect the delivery of his country'.[57] With the destruction of the Irish parliament complete, Robert decided it was time to search for the key to Ireland's freedom on the continent.

In the summer of 1800 Robert Emmet was appointed secretary of a secret United Irishmen delegation to France, under Malachy Delany who was made ambassador.[58] First he decided to visit and confer with his brother at Fort George. Robert arrived just as Thomas Addis was writing to John Patten, his brother-in-law, requesting him to travel over with duelling pistols.[59] At Fort George fissures had been developing between the state prisoners and there were numerous confrontations, in particular between Thomas Addis Emmet and Arthur O'Connor. The two men, leading figures in the United Irishmen executive in the 1790s (the former had succeeded the latter after his arrest in 1797), disagreed strongly about how the movement should proceed and differences of temperament only exacerbated their antagonism. Robert arrived just as these tensions were coming to a head. Fortunately he succeeded in preventing violence and he used his extraordinary powers of persuasion to bring about a temporary reconciliation. This was one of his greatest abilities, for as Madden records:

> Robert Emmet had a singular talent for composing differences, and making people who spoke harshly and thought unkindly of one another acquainted with each other's good qualities, and thereby causing them to come to terms of accommodation.[60]

THOMAS ADDIS EMMET, 1800–1802

While in prison in Fort George, Thomas Addis Emmet was joined by his wife. The governor of the prison, Lieutenant Colonel James Stuart, was a benevolent and humane man who did everything he could to make the living conditions as hospitable as possible. From June 1800 the prisoners were allowed to visit each other in their rooms and Jane Emmet was given permission to live in the same cell as her husband. Escape was never considered, and Tom later explained that the prisoners could not renege on their word, 'as soon would we have committed suicide'.[61] Gradually he returned to the idea of emigrating to America after his release, but it seems he was determined to become a farmer once there. At Fort George he forgot about the law as a profession and amused himself by solving complex algebra problems. After Robert left Ireland in the summer of 1800 his parents looked to Thomas Addis to keep their spirits raised. His mother wrote to him on 14 July 1800 expressing a hope that he would remain patient in prison. She added:

> We feel, my dearest Tom, very sensibly your kind solicitude about us. You have indeed filled your brother's place to us in every action of a most affectionate and kind son, but who can truly fill the present vacancies in our family?[62]

On 1 January 1801 the Act of Union creating the United Kingdom of Great Britain and Ireland came into effect. Robert Emmet Sr wrote to his son at Fort George wishing him a happy new year and regretting that they could not embrace each other. But he was optimistic that an Anglo-French peace might allow his son to return home to his family. The beginning of a new century filled the old doctor with excitement:

> What a period, my dear Tom, for abstract thought and philosophic contemplation — the eighteenth century closed, but the temple of Janus not shut; on the contrary every portal thrown open, and Bellona issuing forth with redoubled rage and augmented fury. When will it end?[63]

Dr Emmet missed his son deeply, but had come to accept that he would probably never be allowed to return to Ireland. Therefore he considered selling Casino, his house in Milltown, and moving to England or Wales where he could live with him. But his health would not allow him to travel further, and as his wife made clear, beyond Britain 'your father thinks he cannot venture to go'.[64] Upon discovering that Thomas Addis wanted to emigrate to America after his release, Elizabeth Emmet displayed a very natural, maternal concern. In an unsubtle attempt to persuade her son to remain in Europe she told him that the climate was not 'congenial to European constitutions'. And, she added,

> Captain Palmer mentioned to us that, independent of the yellow fever, he had perceived — and it was, he said, a general observation in America — that after the first two years Europeans generally declined in health. Do not call this a prejudice of mine.[65]

But she insisted she wanted Thomas Addis to make up his own mind. Both she and her husband asked him 'to act as if we were out of the question, consulting only what you think will be most likely to make you and them [his family] happy'. Nevertheless Mrs Emmet did not hide her own preference, even if she did acknowledge that she could not be happy in her son's society, 'if I caused in any respect sacrifices of your interests, your peace of mind, or your security'. These were her own concern she insisted, and she spoke of herself as 'the weaker vessel' before adding, 'of your father's firmness you can have no doubt'.

The letter did little to change Thomas Addis Emmet's resolve. In late October 1801 he sent his mother the news that he was determined to go to America and she acquiesced in his decision. As Mrs Emmet admitted, she had known in her heart that he would leave Europe but she claimed she was not depressed,

> though we are to be separated from the first prop of our age, the polar star by which I, at least (who often want direction and support), wished to steer for the remainder of my life; yet, though your light will be denied to us, I

trust in the just God, whom you so truly served, that he will cause you to shine in another hemisphere.[66]

Desperate to see her son again, she made one final attempt to persuade him to come to Ireland before he left for ever. But even though she was confident that he could get permission to visit his family in Dublin and sort out his affairs, she was not optimistic that he would take the opportunity. She knew that he would not want to compromise his principles and she reassured him that his father understood completely: 'you are not a more careful guardian of your unsullied honour and fame than he is'.[67] Aware that she would never see her son again, she noted with sadness: 'between you and us there will be a gulf over which we cannot pass'. Worse still, her husband's health was in decline and this was an additional concern, even though there were some signs that he might be getting better.

In the summer of 1801 Jane became pregnant and Governor Stuart gallantly maintained a protective eye over her. One night a fire broke out at a gunpowder magazine near the Emmets' quarters and as soldiers attempted to extinguish it Stuart's first priority was for the family's safety. Afterwards, concerned for Jane's health and well-being, the governor gave an order for her husband's cell to be left permanently open in case of future emergencies. He trusted in Emmet's honour and was not disappointed. On 18 April 1802 a healthy daughter was born named Jane Erin after her mother and the homeland she was exiled from.

Raising his daughter in Fort George, Tom wanted to make her as Irish as possible. When she was older he teased her about her predilection for Scottish accents, which he could not explain except that she was 'a highlander by birth'. 'Who knows', he speculated, 'but early impressions on our organs are indelible and that your musical ear was prepared for the *friendly and affectionate* sound of the dialect.'[68] When residing in the United States, Jane Erin (who later called herself Jeannette) was told by her father that it was always his wish 'to have you entirely Irish (except so far as you ought to be American)'. Elaborating on this theme he explained that he

> meant to make you Irish, in spite of your birth-place, when I gave you the name of Erin, and meant to give you the feelings which little John Bradstreet once expressed with infantile naiveté to a gentleman who asked him where he was born — 'I was born in America, sir, but I am to be brought up an Irishman.'[69]

Apologising for teasing her about her preference for Scottish accents, he assured her that 'Be you Scotch or Irish I shall always love you.' When raising his daughters Tom taught them that it was 'a daughter's duty to bear and forbear . . . for she will be uncommonly fortunate if she does not meet a husband who will be often wrong and perhaps unjust in his conduct to her'. Urging forbearance, he taught them the proverb, 'A mild answer turneth away wrath.'[70]

It seems that Thomas Addis Emmet and Samuel Neilson did not forget about the revolutionary cause. The government discovered a plot in the autumn of 1801 to spread republican principles in Scotland and destabilise the Scottish militia in the event of a French invasion. A Belfast prisoner, Robert Hunter, turned informer and approached the home secretary in a bid to buy his freedom. However his treachery was discovered by Jane Emmet who had struck up a friendship with 'an Irish patriot' who was married to one of the officers; this woman revealed everything. Hunter was immediately isolated from the other prisoners and he began to worry that he would be killed: 'Not that I fear any man in point of courage, or my character; but it was always their system, terror and dark assassination.'[71] He also revealed that only about ten men had maintained their spirits in prison: 'the rest are broken down by confinement and ill-fortunes'. Two of the most determined were Emmet and Neilson, 'men of abilities and talent' who, he said, were at the head of a faction promoting renewed conflict.

In the spring of 1802 the state prisoners were released provided they gave an assurance they would not return to Ireland, and Thomas Addis Emmet emigrated to the continent in July. Arriving at Cuxhaven, in Lower Saxony, the tensions between him and Arthur O'Connor finally reached their climax. Emmet had reacted angrily in Fort George when he heard from John Patten that O'Connor was accusing him of duplicity while at Kilmainham Prison in 1798. Now that they were at liberty, O'Connor decided to settle the quarrel by challenging his antagonist to a duel.[72] John Chambers and John Sweetman, fellow prisoners, intervened and persuaded the men to part amicably. O'Connor decided to back down and Emmet informed him, 'You are right in withdrawing your challenge. I never did you any injury; I never intended you any.'[73] They shook hands and O'Connor expressed a hope that now that their disagreement was at an end they might become friends and avoid giving satisfaction to their enemies. But Emmet was not inclined to be so forgiving and while he accepted that 'everything of a hostile nature has been done away' he wanted it to be understood that he was not interested in 'any renewal of intimacy in consequence of what has taken place'.[74] The men bowed coldly to each other and parted.

Resolving to go to Hamburg which was only seventy miles away from Cuxhaven, rather than visit Paris, Thomas Addis spent much of the next few months travelling. He proceeded from Hamburg to Holland, taking in Amsterdam and Rotterdam, before moving to Brussels where he stayed for three months. It was on the journey to Belgium that he finally met up with Robert in the summer of 1802.

EMISSARY TO FRANCE: ROBERT EMMET, 1800–1802

Travelling from Yarmouth, in England, the United Irishmen delegates, Robert Emmet and Malachy Delany, went first to Hamburg, where they waited for passports to enter France.[75] Delany was formerly an officer in the Austrian army who had risen in the ranks of the United Irishmen after the capture of its main leaders in 1798. William Wickham, a good judge of people, regarded him as 'a man of very considerable talents'.[76] Because a warrant had been issued by the British government for Delany's arrest, he travelled to the continent under the alias Bowens, but as the warrant for Emmet's arrest had never been pursued he was free to use his own name. At Hamburg the men were received by Robert Grey, their United Irishman contact, and they waited in the German city until they secured passports from General Pierre François Augereau.[77] They entered France in 1801.[78]

In Paris Robert Emmet had meetings with Napoleon Bonaparte, the first consul, and also encountered the wily diplomat, Talleyrand, with his 'scarlet velvet embroidered coat, bag and ruffles'.[79] Many plans were discussed for invading Ireland, including one for an expedition that would be led by General Humbert, the veteran of 1798. The scheme involved Humbert feigning dissatisfaction with the French government and organising a convoy to Louisiana in America. The expedition would carry French and Irish soldiers who would pretend to be 'settlers' to throw British spies off the scent, but the ships would land in Connaught rather than cross the Atlantic.[80] This plan, when it was eventually executed, caught the Irish rather than the British by surprise. The expedition sailed for the West Indies instead of Ireland, and it seems that the United Irishmen were used as a decoy by the French government. Humbert later claimed that Talleyrand had sabotaged the plans for an invasion of Ireland, first by refusing finance and then by selling the information to the British.[81] In March 1801 spies reported to Dublin Castle that Emmet would soon land in Belfast carrying 'papers of consequence and some commissions' but this journey never materialised.[82] Instead he remained in Paris where he became increasingly disillusioned with French society in general and French politicians in particular. In October 1801 Emmet received news that his father had put the family home Casino at Milltown up for sale for £2,000. He was delighted to hear this and he hoped it meant his family would soon be reunited on the continent, 'enjoying the only happiness which now remains to us — that of looking back on the past in the society of friends who esteem us with full conviction of the purity of our motives'.[83]

The brilliant general, Napoleon, made a poor impression on Emmet. The idealistic young Irishman was disgusted by the way the first consul had risen to power and disapproved of his treatment of smaller countries.[84] For his part, Napoleon was cautious when it came to Ireland and feared that the legislative union would lessen demands in the country for independence; Emmet argued persuasively against him. In private Robert spoke disparagingly about the French leader and this negative opinion was later shared by his brother Thomas Addis, who claimed that Napoleon was 'the worst enemy Ireland ever had'.[85] Meanwhile the devious Talleyrand was finding it difficult to manipulate Emmet. Unwilling to make any promises to the young United Irishman, he and the other politicians instead gave 'evasive answers' to all his enquiries about the possibility of French aid. As Robert Emmet later explained, 'I left the place without making any demands, telling them at the same time that we merited their intervention at least as much as the patriots of Naples.'[86] He resolved not to ask anything further of the government, but instead try and discover 'whether they had made any stipulation for us or not'.[87] All this time Napoleon was negotiating a peace treaty with the British, and the United Irishmen on the continent became a pawn of the French neo-imperialists. There was even an offer on the table to expel the disaffected Irish from France if Britain did the same for its French *émigré* community. Arthur O'Connor seemed to have little trouble with Napoleon's designs and supported an 'intimate political connection' between the two countries, possibly even extending to a union.[88] The schism between the Emmet and O'Connor factions in Paris crystallised around the question of French aid. For O'Connor, only support from France would make another rebellion viable, while Russell and Emmet were convinced that the French should be treated with caution rather than enthusiasm. Russell's antipathy towards Napoleon was blamed for leading Emmet to his death. O'Connor later insisted that Russell 'pushed the faction to excite Robert Emmet to the mad and utterly desperate attempt he made and which gave the finishing blow to the United Irish confederacy'.[89]

In his spare time Emmet sometimes visited the Palais Royal and the Louvre, which was 'the general lounge of all the Irish and English' in Paris.[90] Preferring to associate with English-speaking people, he felt increasingly alienated from his surroundings and became moody and withdrawn. In March 1802 he met Catherine Wilmot, the twenty-nine year old Irishwoman who was travelling on the continent and who kept a detailed diary of her adventures. It seems his reputation had gone before him as she knew that he was among 'the politically distinguished in Dublin College'.[91] In a charming description of Emmet she wrote how 'His face is uncommonly expressive of everything youthful and everything enthusiastic.' But Wilmot's portrait, which began well, ended badly as she went on to explain that 'his colour comes and goes so rapidly, accompanied by such a nervousness of agitated sensibility, that in his society I feel in a perpetual apprehension lest a passing idle word should wound the delicacy of his feelings'. In her company Emmet was shy and reserved, but occasionally he would flicker into life, 'For though his reserve prevents one's hearing many of his opinions, yet one would swear to their style of exaltation, from their flitting shadows blushing across his countenance in everlasting succession.' Wilmot had met Emmet at a particularly bad time. He had hurt his eye in February and was in much pain for a couple of months, but her description tallies with other accounts of Emmet's behaviour in France.[92] Living at Paris St Germain, Emmet often visited Matilda Tone, the widow of the late United Irishman leader, whom Wilmot found 'interesting to the greatest degree'. By her own admission Matilda had 'remained many years in entire seclusion, occupied solely in cultivating the minds of my children'.[93] Her two sons William and Frank were educated at the national schools in Paris, but her favourite was her eldest child and only daughter Maria, who stayed at home.

Immediately impressed with Matilda Tone, Catherine Wilmot noted with genuine approval that she was

> delightfully affectionate and caressing in her manner, delicately pretty and understanding *so much* of every accomplishment that she has a never-ending source of amusement and cheerfulness in herself. She is exactly what comes under the name of a *fascinating* creature.[94]

Catherine Wilmot recognised that 'Maria her daughter (a girl about sixteen) is her idol', and Matilda Tone confirmed this in her own account when she called Maria her 'younger sister and friend'.[95] Living 'almost in entire seclusion',[96] Matilda and Maria entertained few guests, but Robert Emmet was an exception. As the younger brother of Wolfe Tone's great friend he was always welcome and Maria would play the piano and sing. In a subjective maternal appreciation, Matilda wrote that Maria was 'beautiful, accomplished, enlightened and eminently endowed',[97] but this was also the opinion of the more objective Catherine Wilmot. She found Maria as delightful as her mother did and wrote that she was not only beautiful but that she 'gives one exactly the idea of a poet's nymph — long sateen auburn tresses, sylph-like figure, inexpressibly speaking eyes and elegance and deportment'.[98] But tragedy soon revisited Matilda Tone. Maria was taken ill with consumption and died before she reached the age of seventeen. Her mother's grief was absolute:

> if I transferred the drooping head of one beloved child from my bosom to the pillow for a moment, it was but to run to the grave of another, and vent my broken heart in tears of truly unutterable anguish.[99]

Spending much of her time at parties, 'quaffing liqueurs and coffee', Wilmot also became acquainted with Talleyrand and Napoleon. She was initially unimpressed by the former, but soon succumbed to his redoubtable charm. Nevertheless Talleyrand was still described as having, from a distance, a face that was 'large, pale and flat like a cream cheese' but which on closer examination displayed 'cunning and rank hypocrisy' above all else.[100] Napoleon received better treatment and Wilmot was seduced by 'his eyes [which] are reflection itself, but so charming a smile as his I never scarce beheld'.[101] At a formal dinner with the first consul the conversation turned to the failed Bantry Bay invasion of 1796. General Emmanuel Grouchy, the second-in-command of the fleet, was also present and he revealed his disappointment that he had not snapped 'the grappling irons which attach Ireland to England'.[102] With mischievous independence Catherine pointed out that

> had their philanthropic undertaking prospered as happily in Ireland as it did across the Alps I should expect by this time to see our little Ireland hung up as a curiosity in the Louvre amongst the Italian trophies.

Fortunately for Wilmot, her comments were taken in 'the highest good spirits' and everyone laughed. But she was clever enough to realise that what she had said might not in different circumstances have been taken as 'too civil'.[103]

Robert Emmet made a great effort to avoid these dinners. He had few friends in Paris, but was close to William Lawless, a former surgeon and now a general in the French army, and also Gabrielle, the marquise de Fontenay.[104] He was also friends with an unnamed 'English gentleman' who was visiting Paris. But he refused to dine in public and stubbornly insisted on meeting guests in the residence of this man. Catherine Wilmot was intrigued by the enigmatic character of Emmet. She was impressed by his reputation and obvious intelligence, but disturbed by his cold and impenetrable manner. In her profile of him she noted:

> His understanding they tell me is very bright. But I am not likely to know much about it. For his extreme prejudice against French society will prevent our meeting him anywhere except at the house of an English gentleman, who is soon returning to London. At this house we have seen the widow of the unfortunate Tone.[105]

The reports which the British government received about Emmet's movements in France confirm Wilmot's account. It was noted that he 'lived very privately at Paris' and spent most of his time preparing various papers which he delivered to the French government.[106] Some of these proposals fell into the hands of British spies, and after the rebellion in Ireland were examined by William Wickham. In a notable tribute the former head of British intelligence on the continent agreed with his contact that 'the military operations recommended to the French army . . . show talent and judgement'.[107]

After the peace of Amiens, signed formally in March 1802, Britain and France were no longer at war and, even though it was clear to most people that this was a ceasefire rather than a genuine settlement, it further dampened the expectations of the Irish in Paris. As Emmet grew even more suspicious of the French, he became convinced that the government was prepared to 'deliver up the United Irishmen, tied neck and heels' in a reconciliatory gesture to Britain.[108] It was a perceptive and accurate comment. The United Irishmen mission to the continent had proved a failure.

Refusing to be distracted from his ambition of freeing Ireland, Robert Emmet began buying books on military tactics and history. His most important purchase was a two-volume work that had been translated by Colin Lindsay entitled *Extracts from Colonel Templehoff's history of the seven years' war* (1793). Emmet spent much time studying this textbook and made numerous annotations on the margin. His copy, now at the Royal Irish Academy in Dublin, provides a remarkable insight into Emmet's military thinking, revealing the aspects that he believed were most important. Interestingly, Templehoff, a colonel in the Prussian army, seems to have been descended from the Temple political dynasty at Stowe and was therefore a distant relative of Emmet. A number of works were contained in the two volumes, and Lindsay included his own history of 1688 and the Williamite conquest of Ireland. His message in the introduction may have found some resonances in Emmet's character: 'while we certainly have no desire to be the wolves, we have as little inclination to become the lambs'.[109] The first volume contained the history of the seven years' war and a number of useful aphorisms; the second comprised of a set of instructions and various pieces of military advice. Templehoff's history was filled with much analysis about the merits of outflanking manoeuvres and this information had a great influence on Emmet's thinking.[110] There was also a sharp criticism of people who judged a general's ability on the result of one battle alone. Instead,

> The preparatory steps must be well considered, before we conclude that he deserved censure or praise. When the battle once begins, much must depend on the subordinate generals, on the commanders of battalions, on the officers, and even on the private soldier. If these do not perform their various parts, how often will the whole be lost?[111]

Templehoff insisted that military strength came only from having attention and obedience in every rank. A general could not be responsible for everything, but he was required to choose the correct strategy based on his resources: he must frame 'his designs according to the measure of his talents and the men's within his reach. Inferior minds frequently see difficulties where great men see none.'[112]

Twenty-four years old on 4 March 1802, Robert Emmet still had no first-hand experience of combat. But he was determined to avoid entering into the service of France, having decided that he would only fight for Ireland directly. By studying military history, which had always been a favourite pursuit, he hoped to be able to compensate for his deficiencies and learn what was necessary for leading men in battle. Templehoff had important advice on the respective roles of theory and experience: 'theory has been said to be the right foot, and experience the left. To move, we must have both.'[113] 'An officer of eminence' must be willing to rely on theory and experience, because only then could he determine 'when it may be prudent to abandon our designs.'[114] Another prerequisite for success was having a passion for the occupation, 'For the officer who is not attached to his profession, as he would be to his mistress, can never rise to eminence.'[115]

Of all the military tactics discussed in the book, Templehoff devoted most time to explaining echelon attacks and his beloved outflanking manoeuvres. Robert Emmet would adopt these ideas for use in Ireland. The former required the troops to move in a diagonal rather than a straight line, and thus attack in waves rather than all at once.[116] But it was the decisive area of flanking manoeuvres which Templehoff regarded as the key to victory; this opinion was shared by Napoleon, who used the tactic to spectacular success in his encounters. By attacking from the side or the rear as well as from the front, it was possible to destabilise the enemy and cause him to panic. In this way a small army could win over superior numbers, a crucial point for Emmet. As Templehoff explained, in history 'the most decisive battles have been won by armies considerably, and often astonishingly, inferior in numbers to their opponents'.[117] He cited the example of the battle of Torgau in 1759 when General Wunsch with 4,000 troops attacked and routed the Austrian and Imperial troops who numbered 14,000. As he explained:

> The nature of the order of battle makes it evident that the attack must be directed upon a flank. The main object is to make impression on a point; from hence to proceed to out-flank the enemy, and move upon their flank and rear . . . The enemy must not have time to recollect himself, but by a vigorous and unexpected attack must be overthrown before he is able to fire a shot.[118]

Surprise therefore was always essential.

The strain of years of reading took its toll on Emmet's eyesight. Like his brothers, he did not have perfect vision and was sometimes forced to wear spectacles. He later revealed that 'No. 5' was the prescription that suited him best.[119] As he spent his time in Paris studying military history he marked with an 'X' the most important sections of the first volume of Templehoff. It was a series of questions that every good commander should ask before a battle. These were: 'what am I to do further if I gain the battle?' and 'what am I to do if I lose it?'[120] They were questions that Emmet would reflect upon on the night of 23 July 1803.

The second volume of Templehoff's work contained more useful teaching. Emmet took many detailed notes in blue ink, especially on the crucial matter of maintaining outposts in a battle. He wrote on the margin 'That the alarm posts and places of arms for the outguards . . . shall be fixed and determined.'[121] There was much underlining in the text about the importance of posts, which may explain Emmet's later reliance on depots in Dublin.[122]

Included in the collection was 'A treatise on winter posts' by a Prussian captain, C. F. Lindenau. Emmet discovered much that was relevant in this short essay, even though it was directed primarily at mountain combat. Adapting it for his own interest in street-fighting, he learned that the most effective method of assaulting an enemy was by having the troops move in parallel lines to the place of battle and then attacking at the same time. Lindenau also advised that the commanding officer should always carry out the reconnaissance before an attack is ordered. Then

> the different divisions will proceed in the utmost silence to the point of attack, led by proper guides; and as soon as it is possible that they have

gained their posts, the commanding officer will cause the signal to be made, which has been previously fixed, whether by a cannon or a rocket.[123]

The final piece of advice had already made an impression on Robert. Through his meetings with Robert Fulton he had already begun considering how to apply the new advances in rocket technology for use in Ireland.

'AN OFFICER OF EMINENCE'

When the British government carried out a searing investigation into the insurrection of 1803 it was most disturbed by the discovery of a supply of rockets and other explosive devices. William Wickham was shocked to learn that Emmet's depot in Patrick Street had not been for the manufacture of gunpowder, but rather for 'making rockets, and other combustibles for the purpose of filling hollow beams that were to be laid across the streets and caused to explode in the line of march of the troops'.[124] It was in Paris that Robert Emmet developed his interest in unorthodox military weapons, in part due to the influence of Robert Fulton, but also because the use of gadgetry appealed to his scientific nature.[125] It is not clear how much Fulton contributed to Emmet's rocket design, but there were similarities between the underwater mines tested at Walmer in 1805 and the explosive devices discovered in Dublin. Impressed with the ingenuity of the American inventor, Robert told his brother all about him when he went to Brussels. Fascinated by his anecdotes, Thomas Addis made sure to meet Fulton when he travelled to Paris in 1803. He was intrigued to discover that Fulton was planning to go to Ireland to use his new torpedo against the British fleet.[126] When Thomas Addis finally emigrated to the United States he remained in contact with Fulton and even represented him in a number of important legal cases in New York in the 1810s.[127] A passionate defender of the inventor's reputation, he protected him from 'malignant calumny' spread by jealous competitors and was adamant that 'no disinterested person' could have 'the least suspicion of Mr Fulton'.[128]

William Congreve would later claim the credit for inventing the modern war-rocket but, by his own admission, Emmet's prototype pre-dated his improvements. In his memoir, *A concise account of the origin and progress of the rocket system*, published in London in 1810, he wrote that it was only in the spring of 1806 that he 'conceived the plan, and obtained permission to proceed in making still larger rockets, and forming them with iron cases instead of paper'.[129] But as Emmet's associate, Miles Byrne, made clear, Robert Emmet designed the motor case for his own rockets and his specifications were that they 'be twenty inches long, two and a half inches in diameter, [and] cut out of sheet iron'.[130] Mitchell R. Sharpe, in his account of Robert Emmet's role in the development of the war-rocket, places too much emphasis on the fact that both men decided to use iron rather than paper for their motor cases. The rockets of the Tiger of Mysore also used an iron cylinder and this would have been the model for both their designs. Bernard Duggan, another conspirator, later made a statement that Emmet had told him he was improving upon the rocket used by the East India Company and that someone had helped him perfect his design; Duggan then suggested that Congreve had improved on both of these.[131] This is unlikely. What does seem plausible is that Emmet discovered the Mysorean rocket while in France, perhaps through Fulton who had been shown it by the military, and decided to adapt it for use in Ireland. When some of his rockets were captured in July 1803, they assisted the British military in their search for an effective combat rocket. It was perhaps too much of a coincidence that Pat Finerty, one of the captured rebels, avoided prosecution by agreeing to work for the British government. Eventually sent to the Royal Arsenal in Woolwich, he helped assist on various projects under William Congreve.[132]

In the plan for the insurrection in Dublin one function of the rockets was to signal the different groups of rebels.[133] This was in keeping with the advice of Captain Lindenau in the textbooks Emmet had studied. For example, for the attack on Island Bridge 'three rockets were to be the signal that an attack on any part was made, and afterwards a rocket of stars in case of victory, a silent one of repulse'.[134] The men were to be armed with hand grenades which they could use to disrupt British troop movements. Rocket-batteries were also to be set up in certain areas like Market Place, where they could fire horizontally at advancing soldiers while pikemen prepared an outflanking manoeuvre. In another ingenious innovation, Emmet even proposed using land-mines against cavalry: these would be wooden beams filled with glass and nails to create maximum carnage when detonated.[135] Given the reaction of every other group of European and American soldiers when they first encountered rockets (not to mention other exploding weapons) it is almost certain that the British soldiers in Dublin would have fled if successfully fired upon. The rocket may still have had limited destructive capabilities in the summer of 1803, but as a weapon of psychological warfare it was lethal. The significance of Robert Emmet's rocket supplies cannot therefore be over-emphasised. It gave his band of rebels its best hope of defeating a much greater army and offered a genuine opportunity of removing entire regiments from the conflict at a single strike.

Robert Emmet suffered an eye-injury in February 1802. It took him almost two months to recover, despite consulting a physician, and during that time he debated what to do with his life. Weighing heavily on his mind was an offer from Thomas Addis to emigrate to the United States with him and abandon his plans for liberating Ireland. Around this time also he was approached by some leading men in the United Irishmen and informed of a new scheme to have simultaneous rebellions in Ireland and Britain. Emmet may have met, but was certainly given the name of William Dowdall, the associate of Colonel Despard and friend of Philip Long. His mission was to meet with him in Dublin and discover the state of affairs in the country. Dowdall was the key figure linking Despard with Ireland and he would become one of the most important conspirators in Dublin. In Emmet's own phrase, 'some of the first men of the land' invited him to return to Ireland and investigate whether a successful rebellion was possible.[136] He was persuaded to consider the proposal and return home to assess the chances of it working. Well aware of the risks in travelling to Ireland and conscious that he would probably forfeit his life if a rebellion failed, Robert admitted privately: 'If I only thought of myself, if I only took into consideration the sorrows that are before me in Ireland, and the advantages I would find in the society of my brother, I would joyfully share his fate.'[137] His parents however had given him their blessing to choose whatever course he felt was best, just as they had with his brother, and this left a deep impression. They had 'made the sacrifice of their own wishes' and that sacrifice had convinced him that he could not allow himself 'to be carried away by personal motives'. Swayed by this and by his own eager idealism he made his decision. Writing from Paris on 24 April 1802 to his friend Gabrielle, the marquise de Fontenay, he announced:

> I have therefore determined on returning to Ireland, provided I can do so without contracting any engagement that might compromise my honour. No one better than you, dear madame, knows how much it has cost me, the resolution of returning to a country where, in the presence of all that must awaken the souvenirs of the past, I must forget everything — that I had hopes, friends, tender ties, perhaps.[138]

From the newspapers he learned that the state prisoners at Fort George were being released, but this only added to his pessimism. He admitted in a post-script: 'I doubt more and more that I can return to my native country.'

THE DESPARD CONSPIRACY

There has been much confusion among historians about the degree to which the revolutionary conspiracies of Colonel Despard and Robert Emmet were connected.[139] Marianne Elliott, whose ground-breaking scholarship in this period has been so important, contends that 'the plots of Despard and Emmet were premature manifestations of a larger conspiracy which included risings in England and Ireland' and were both part of a larger and more important revolutionary strategy.[140] Edward Marcus Despard, later dismissed as 'another three-named madman', was a disaffected radical who became embroiled in a revolutionary scheme in 1802 which had some superficial similarities to efforts in Ireland the following year. Born on 6 March 1751 in Queen's County, Despard left Ireland to serve in the army and was stationed in the West Indies with the 50th regiment. In 1779 he was promoted to captain and served with the young Horatio Nelson on a secret British mission in Nicaragua. Later based at Jamaica, Despard was promoted to colonel in 1782 and received the thanks of King George III for his bravery. His increasingly autocratic manner, however, made him many enemies and he was recalled to England in 1790 to answer charges. Angered by his treatment at the hands of the government, he drifted into radical politics and was a member of the London Corresponding Society and, after 1796, the United Englishmen. Now heavily involved in supporting France and fomenting revolution, he was a founding member of the United Britons in 1797, another organisation which attempted to imitate and assist the United Irishmen in the struggle for independence. Co-ordinating the efforts of the English radicals with France, on 22 April 1798 he was arrested on suspicion of treason and imprisoned for three years without trial. Released in March 1801, he returned to his home at Queen's County, apparently deter-mined to quit all radical activities. A meeting with William Dowdall in January 1802 altered his destiny and he decided to revive the United Britons in London. His friend Lord Cloncurry later remarked that he 'looked like a man risen from the grave' and he took to his work with added bitterness and renewed vigour. However the government discovered his plans, informers having infiltrated his circle, and he was arrested on 16 November 1802 with about thirty men at the Oakley Arms in Lambeth. Accused of plotting to assassinate the king on his way to the opening of parliament a week later, Despard was tried by a special com-mission in February 1803. Despite supporting references from Evan Nepean and Admiral Nelson, he was found guilty under a weight of manufactured and circumstantial evidence and sentenced to death. On 21 February a crowd of 20,000 people came to watch him die at Borough Jail in London. With the help of his black wife, Catherine, Despard prepared in advance a speech to deliver from the scaffold. His short oration drew much applause and cheering as he insisted that he was about to die 'for a crime of which I protest I am not guilty'. And, he added,

> though his majesty's ministers know as well as I do that I am not guilty, yet they avail themselves of a legal pretext to destroy a man, because he has been a friend to truth, to liberty and to justice. [Interrupted by applause] Because he has been a friend to the poor and the oppressed. But citizens I hope and trust, notwithstanding my fate, and the fate of many who no doubt will soon follow me, that the principles of freedom, of humanity, and of justice, will finally triumph over falsehood, tyranny and delusion, and every principle hostile to the interests of the human race. I have little more to add, except to wish you all health, happiness and freedom, which I have endeavoured, as far as was in my power, to procure for you, and for mankind in general.

As the crime of high treason demanded, Despard was hanged and beheaded, although the surgeon botched the decapitation with his dissecting knife. He 'missed the particular joint aimed at, and was haggling at it, till one of the exe-cutioners took the head between his hands, and twisted it round several times, and even then it was with difficulty separated from the body'.[141] Finally Despard's head was raised to the crowd as the executioner intoned: 'This is the head of a traitor.' His supporters led his coffin in an elaborate procession to St Paul's churchyard and he was buried in a grave 'fourteen and a half feet deep to deter body-snatchers'. The crowd attending was so large it was reported to be 'beyond belief'.[142] It seems clear that Despard had no intention of assassinating the king; this was the idle talk of drunken conspirators which had been dismissed by the leaders out of hand. On the contrary, Despard urged caution and would have preferred to wait for French aid before leading a rising. To the working classes he became a martyr who died proclaiming liberty from the gallows. One firebrand in a pub in Leeds provoked uproar with a tirade damning 'the jury that found Colonel Despard guilty — I wish they were all in hell — and Colonel Despard's head crammed down the king's throat.'[143] The man was immediately arrested and charged with sedition, but escaped punishment.

The home office was quick to assert that the Despard plot had no 'connection with treason in Ireland'.[144] But the role of Dowdall in the events in England and later in Ireland belies the confidence of this claim. Dublin Castle received a report from their confidential agent 'JW' — Leonard MacNally — who would himself play an important role in the Emmet story, revealing that he had 'good reason to believe that several persons in Dublin expected to hear of an attempt at partial insurrection in London so long ago as September last'.[145] The shadowy role of Dowdall in the insurrectionary activities of 1802–03 remains unclear. Born around 1768, in County Westmeath, he was the illegitimate son of the politician Hussey Burgh, and benefited from the patronage of Henry Grattan in his early life. A member of the Dublin whig club, he worked for a time under the chancellor of the exchequer (and later Speaker), John Foster. However it appears he provided Grattan with confidential information to assist him in a debate and as a result was dismissed from office. Becoming involved in the United Irishmen conspiracy in the 1790s he was arrested in the summer of 1798 and imprisoned at Newgate. According to a government spy he was a tall man (about 5' 9") with pale skin and brown hair who walked 'very erect seemingly to show his figure which all together is the most perfect model of a well-made man than can possibly be seen'.[146] He refused to deal with the government and was sent to Fort George in March 1799. Because he had not done a deal with the government, however, he was released in December 1801 after the restoration of habeas corpus. Spending some time in London, he visited Paris to consult with United Irishmen figures there before returning to Dublin. Back home he got drunk one evening in a public house and began boasting of his radical connections. His embarrassing indiscretion came to the attention of the United Irishmen leadership and James Hope was called in to give him a stern warning.[147]

A DIVIDED CONSPIRACY

The United Irishmen in Paris were split into two factions: the first was a Francophile group of *émigrés* led by Arthur O'Connor; the second formed around those who were cynical about French intentions. Robert Emmet, deeply uneasy about the ambitions of Napoleon, also shared his brother's distrust of O'Connor. During many of the discussions about liberating Ireland,

Emmet and O'Connor found themselves arguing vehemently on opposing sides. For the latter, there was no point in planning an Irish insurrection unless French support was guaranteed. Robert Emmet disputed this, believing that the United Irishmen should 'try the thing alone'.[148] Frequently the debates grew heated as tempers flared, but Emmet was an experienced debater and consistently refused to give way. Before leaving Paris he and Michael Quigley had 'a very serious quarrel' with O'Connor. Thomas Russell, a key United Irishmen leader, sided with Emmet and voiced serious objections about accepting French support. He detested Napoleon's government and, in particular, blamed Talleyrand for having betrayed previous expeditions to Ireland.[149] The rift between the supporters and the opponents of French aid was never healed and played a significant role in undermining the rebellion in Dublin in 1803.

There followed an uneasy compromise between the supporters and opponents of French aid for Ireland. This helps explain much of the confusion about whether Emmet's rebellion was part of a larger conspiracy or an isolated event. There were men like Dowdall who were convinced Ireland should form part of some wider scheme, but this was opposed by Emmet who just wanted to win Irish independence and not fight a proxy war with Britain on behalf of France. As Michael Frayne, a Kildare conspirator in the summer of 1803, later testified, there was a real division between those who supported a French invasion and those who did not. He was convinced that Emmet only used France 'to encourage the lower orders of people', as he often heard him say: 'that bad as the English government was, it was preferable to a French one, and that his object was a separation of Ireland from England, to have it an independent state brought about by Irishmen only'.[150] The real originality of Emmet's rebellion was that it deliberately cut the French-Irish nexus and attempted to introduce a new model for self-determination. The old United Irishmen alliance with France was abandoned, at least as far as Emmet was concerned, and he courageously decided to lead a rebellion without French troops. He wanted to first win independence with Irishmen and then use French aid to defend what had been achieved. Certainly many of the other conspirators disagreed with this analysis and believed a rebellion was certain suicide without a French landing. This tension contributed significantly to the weakness of the attempt on 23 July 1803. But Emmet stubbornly pursued his own agenda, fully convinced that his scheme alone could save Ireland from French imperialism as much as from British domination.

While in France Emmet practised disguising his handwriting. He learned to write in different styles and with different hands to prevent documents being traced back to him. This created enormous problems for the government when it attempted to build a case against him, as it became almost impossible to link him with key incriminating documents. Sometimes Emmet wrote in large letters and sometimes small ones, taking care all the time to alter how he formed his words. William Wickham later feared that Emmet would go free because of 'his act in changing frequently his manner of writing'. He was worried about having to produce as samples of Emmet's handwriting 'different papers written *apparently* by different persons'.[151]

Missing Ireland, Emmet attempted to express his feelings in poetry. His effort, 'The exile', is his shortest poem and also perhaps his best. A more mature style is evident in the two stanzas and from the content it seems certain that it was written during this period when he was on the continent. Its final lines could be read as Emmet's own manifesto for Ireland as he contemplated making a final decision about his future:

Ah! where is now my peaceful cot —
Ah! where is my happy home?
No peaceful cot, alas! is mine —
An exile now I roam.

Far from the country I am driven,
A wanderer sent from thee,
But still my constant prayer to heaven
Shall be to make thee free.[152]

Before embarking on his mission to Ireland Emmet decided to visit his brother who had been released after the peace of Amiens. The night before he left for Holland and Belgium he met with Lord Cloncurry, a conspirator in the 1798 rebellion who had been imprisoned for a number of years on a justified suspicion of treason. They had dinner in Paris and Cloncurry later provided two different and at times contradictory accounts of this meeting.[153] Although Madden insisted that 'Nobody who had the pleasure of knowing the late Lord Cloncurry could for a moment doubt the truthfulness of the man', he was forced to concede that on this occasion he had to question 'the accuracy of his lordship's memory'.[154] The version that is most suspect is Cloncurry's recollection in his memoirs that he dined with both Emmet brothers in the French capital. As Thomas Addis was in Amsterdam, this could not have happened. In a subsequent interview with Madden, Cloncurry changed his story and said that he had dinner with Robert alone. According to this second account,

Robert Emmet confided to him the object of his return to Ireland; that a plan had been formed for a renewed effort to free the country; and that his return was connected to this effort; and that he spoke in the most sanguine terms of the probability of its success.

Again Cloncurry's version is problematic. However as Emmet was committed to liberating Ireland, even if he was not fully committed to any conspiracy, he would have been likely to converse with Cloncurry on this theme. The description Cloncurry provided of the impassioned Emmet was an accurate portrait of the young orator in full flow:

while he was speaking on this subject became so excited that his features glowed with animation — and his lordship noticed drops of perspiration glistening on his forehead during the conversation. His lordship in vain attempted to dissuade him from that attempt.

Going to Amsterdam to meet his brother in the summer of 1802 and then on to Brussels, Robert Emmet was not certain what path his future would take. This was the recollection of William J. Macneven, a United Irishman on the continent, and it corresponds with Emmet's own statements at his trial.[155] In September Robert decided to return home, again rejecting his brother's advice to accompany him to America. According to an Emmet family tradition his sister-in-law Jane also pleaded with him not to return to Ireland, but to no avail.[156] He had made up his mind and was determined to follow his destiny.

Emmet made friends easily and no matter where he went he was always able to find people who were willing to help him. The official government investigation later discovered that he passed through Hamburg for a stopover, and there is some evidence that he took a long route home.[157] In his search to find a ship he entered France and travelled through Normandy. According to an Englishman called Lawrence, whom Madden accepted as a reliable source, Emmet passed through Andemar on his journey to Ireland. Lawrence was a tanner in the town and claimed that on a cold, dark night he was visited by a young man who 'asked for shelter, saying that he had been travelling on foot, and had lost his way'.[158] Giving the stranger a bed for a few days, Lawrence soon struck up a friendship with his guest and learned that his name was Robert Emmet. Deciding to remain in the town for a few weeks, disguised as a labourer, Emmet took a great interest in Lawrence's tanning business. During this time he also revealed that his ambition, 'his desperate enterprise', was to liberate Ireland; this treasonous talk made Lawrence uneasy and he 'did all in his power to dissuade him from it'. Emmet stayed for some weeks in the town, keeping a low profile so as not to attract the attention of any British spies, before going to Honfleur, a nearby seaport. Madden concluded the anecdote by saying: 'It would appear that poor Emmet's usual power of fascinating those who came into contact with him was felt by Lawrence, who never spoke of him but in terms of enthusiastic admiration and affection.'[159] At Honfleur Emmet struggled to find a safe passage home. But once again his luck held and he encountered a young Scottish radical called Campbell. Not only did Campbell secure him a place on a ship that was bound for England, he also provided him with an introduction to all the disaffected Scottish people who were living in Ireland.[160] This would prove extremely useful over the following months.

By the spring of 1803, five months after Robert Emmet's return to Ireland, the Dublin Castle administration became aware that some conspiracy was being plotted in Ireland, but it had little idea of the extent. There were unsubstantiated reports that Thomas Addis Emmet and Arthur O'Connor had landed in the country, but these were 'vague' and unconfirmed.[161] Unsure of what exactly was being planned, the government tried to remain vigilant. As one official noted at the end of the month, it was not clear what was going to happen, but he was certain that the administration 'must expect that a game will be played here'.[162] William Wickham later reported that no one was aware at this time of the 'treasonable mission' that Robert Emmet had undertaken.[163] But this was misleading, for Emmet had not yet decided what to do once in Ireland. On his way home after two years in self-imposed exile on the continent, he was not even sure if he would be arrested as soon as he set foot in the country. Willing to do what was necessary to free Ireland, he was cognisant of the risks involved and the scale of the challenge before him. Usually criticised for lacking pragmatism, on this occasion he fully comprehended the danger he faced and the very real possibility that he might lose his life. As he had privately admitted a few months earlier, 'I believe I am, myself, on the point of making a sacrifice by returning to Ireland', and he was well aware that it could turn out to be 'a very painful one to me' indeed.[164]

6

RETURN TO IRELAND

~

'If genius is sometimes "fey" does it not also draw from its own mysterious
lights a compelling power to affect and awe the minds of men?'
(T. M. Healy on Charles Stewart Parnell)

'He [Robert Emmet] possessed that enthusiasm which forms its projects
without deliberation, pursues them under a heated imagination, and
consequently fails in the execution of them. The plan he conceived was
wild, imaginary, and impracticable'.
(*The Times*, 27 September 1803)

Arriving in Ireland in late October or early November 1802, Robert
Emmet went back to living with his parents at Casino House in
Milltown. Concerned by his father's declining health, he remained
nearby, occasionally visiting friends but not venturing too far away.
'Slight, and under the middle size', Emmet had benefited from his experiences
abroad and had returned a confident and assured young man.[1] Someone who
knew him around this period, John Fisher, remembered him as being 'of gentle-
manly appearance, possessing handsome features, and . . . a dark complexion'.[2]
But he had no career and no visible means of support except the generous
allowance his ailing father continued to give him. While on the continent he
had received at least five payments totalling £337-14s. without which he would
not have been able to carry out his work.[3] Most of the professions were closed
to him after his expulsion from Trinity College in 1798, and he had been forced
to abandon his studies at the King's Inns. Instead he considered learning a trade.
Together with John Patten, who supplied the finance, he entered into a partnership with a tanner called William Norris, 'a notoriously disaffected but very ingenious man', at Dolphin's Barn.[4] It seems Emmet and Patten decided to give the
business a chance and if it failed emigrate to America and work as tanners there.

Renewing his old friendships and acquaintances, Robert dined out regularly. He carried a little cane for walking which he would tap rhythmically on the ground when he was deep in thought.[5] Going 'into society', Emmet spent much time 'visiting people of consequence'.[6] Men that he dined with in this period included James Ryan, at Marlborough Street, and George Evans. He also had many conversations with Philip Long, a successful merchant who lived at Crow Street and a close friend of William Dowdall. Long had been in Spain between 1789 and 1795 and visited France in 1802 to meet various United Irishmen leaders; he missed seeing Robert Emmet, however, who was in Belgium.[7] Long soon became embroiled in the conspiracy and would provide funding at a critical stage. But at this time Emmet kept protesting that he had no such plans and that he had returned to Ireland 'about his private affairs' and not on some secret business.[8]

Dr Robert Emmet died on 9 December 1802. He was buried three days later at a strictly private ceremony at St Peter's churchyard, Aungier Street.[9] Robert took responsibility for the funeral arrangements and provided much emotional support for his mother during this difficult period. For this she was deeply grateful, admitting that 'I have had many mitigations afforded to me' but that 'the presence and support of our dear Robert was one of the greatest that could have helped in such a situation.'[10] Praising Robert's attentiveness in a letter to Tom in prison, she added that she was 'consoled by all my children, for surely never parent has been more supremely blessed than I am in the affection, the virtues, and the disposition of my children'.[11] The death of her husband had been something she had long dreaded, but now that it had happened she found the strength to endure it: 'I have for a length of time lived under an uplifted axe; it has fallen, and I am not destroyed.'[12] William Drennan was upset at the death of his 'old, revered' friend. After the funeral he was sent one of Dr Emmet's scarves and hatbands by the family.[13] Drennan knew that Robert was back in Ireland but did not think he would long 'reside in this country'. In his will Dr Emmet left his property in County Kerry as well as Casino House in Milltown to his eldest son, Thomas Addis, but with a provision of a £2,500 investment for his widow. Seventy-three years old when he died, Dr Emmet had made sure that his wife would be financially secure. Through careful investments he had guaranteed that she would have an income of £350 a year, in addition to the £30 per annum that she received from her wedding settlement. Under the terms of the will, after Mrs Emmet's death, half of the money invested for her would go to their daughter Mary Anne Holmes, and then to her children. If she had no family, then the money would revert to Thomas Addis and Robert. The other half of Mrs Emmet's investment would be inherited by Robert. The daughter of the late Christopher Temple Emmet, Kitty, received a bequest of £1,500. After all these amounts and debts were paid, the residue and remainder was divided equally between Thomas Addis and Robert. This provided Robert Emmet with a legacy of around £2,000, which he received in March and which gave him the financial security to begin plotting the independence of Ireland.

The secret preparations for a new rebellion were partly compromised by the drunken indiscretions of a coachman in December. From the beginning of the long journey from Dublin to Limerick it was clear that the driver was intoxicated and he had no sooner left the outskirts of the city than he drove into a wall. Fortunately no one was injured and after a brief delay the coachman was able to continue, with one of the passengers, a Mr Mansell, joining him in his box to keep him alert. Striking up a conversation, the driver asked him if he was a friend. Mansell did not reply. At this the carriage shuddered to a halt with the coachman angrily insisting that he would not drive any further unless he was assured he was with a friend. Understandably cautious, Mansell admitted that he was a friend to Catholic emancipation and parliamentary reform. But the coachman was not satisfied and wondered if that was all he supported: was he not also a friend to the plans to overthrow the government and assist the French when they landed? Deciding to play along, Mansell pretended that he was, and the coachman shook his hand 'in a particular way'.[14] Then he entered the carriage and asked if the other two passengers were also friends and if they had been 'seven miles round the mountain'. Bewildered and not a little bemused, Mansell sat back as the journey resumed and listened attentively as the driver explained that he expected 60,000 Irishmen to aid the 25,000 French soldiers who would land. However as the carriage came closer to Limerick the driver sobered up and refused to make any further revelations.

This alerted the government when the episode was reported in January 1803 and helped bring the full glare of official scrutiny to activities in Limerick. William Wickham, the chief secretary, decided to investigate personally and discovered that the county was 'in a state of great disorders' with 'the lower orders ripe for rebellion'.[15] However he was persuaded that the numbers involved were too small to be significant and that, while they were dangerous as bandits, 'as rebels they are nothing'. Dismissing the 'vague rumour' of a new insurrection, he increased the watch over the countryside, but was confident that he would not be caught by surprise.

By the spring of 1803 Robert Emmet had completed his investigation into the rebellion that was being planned for later that year. After having met with the key conspirators in the provisional government he concluded that a new rebellion was viable and had every chance of success. Invited to become involved, he soon accepted and quickly established himself as the leading figure in the movement. As he himself explained at his trial: 'When I came to Ireland I found the business ripe for execution. I was asked to join in it. I took time to consider, and after mature deliberation I became one of the provisional government.' Resolving to gamble everything on the venture, Emmet decided to invest all his inheritance to help finance the scheme. It is a measure of the high regard in which the other conspirators held him that he was given the rank of general, with responsibility for leading the insurrection in Dublin. It would not be the last time that older and more experienced men would defer to the abilities of the precocious young revolutionary.

Around this time Emmet visited Mount Jerome to see John Keogh, one of the leading Roman Catholics in the city, whose son George had been expelled with him in 1798.[16] Also at the dinner was John Philpot Curran. Inevitably the conversation turned to politics and the possibility of another general insurrection. According to a transcript of the conversation which Madden received, Emmet spoke 'with great vehemence and energy in favour of the probability of success, in the event of another effort being made'.[17] Keogh then asked him to estimate how many counties would rise. Emmet replied that nineteen could be counted upon, before turning to Curran to ask him, 'Would you say an attempt should not be made with less?' There was a pause before Curran answered, 'No: if there were two counties that could be thoroughly depended on, I would think about it.'

Visiting the Currans at Rathfarnham with increasing frequency, Robert Emmet fell deeply in love. The object of his affection, Sarah Curran, was just approaching her twenty-first birthday but had already experienced much pain in her life. By Emmet's own admission he soon began to idolise her, although he insisted 'it was not with a wild or unfounded passion'.[18] Rather it was with 'an attachment increasing every hour, from an admiration of the purity of her mind, and respect for her talents'. It was a delicate romance which developed slowly and unexpectedly out of a strong friendship; by the time they realised what was happening, 'it was too late to retreat'. Later, Emmet revealed that 'the young woman's affections were engaged without the knowledge of her friends, and in fact without her own'.[19] That he kept the relationship a secret from everyone, including his close friend Richard Curran, would suggest it only developed seriously after he had joined the rebel conspiracy.[20] Otherwise there would have been no risk attached in letting her family know. If this was the case then the romance between Sarah Curran and Robert Emmet can probably be dated to the spring of 1803, after the death of his father. Indeed that tragedy may have helped to draw them closer together, as Emmet discovered someone who could empathise with the loss of a parent. It was perhaps inevitable that the idealistic and somewhat prelapsarian character of Robert Emmet should fall in love with someone fragile and ethereal like Sarah Curran.

Robert Emmet turned twenty-five on 4 March 1803. Charismatic and authoritative, he was growing into his leadership role every day. Even experienced campaigners fell under his spell and could not hide their astonishment at how young he was. One person who was especially moved by Emmet's 'powerful and eloquent language' was a former soldier, Sergeant Matthew Doyle, who was later recruited to the cause. He 'felt highly honoured and flattered' in Emmet's presence and was in awe of his inspirational way of explaining everything. Despite all his experience and travelling he 'could not conceive how so young a man could possess such uncommon intellect'.[21] On 5 March William Henry Hamilton and Michael Quigley arrived in Dublin from France, via England, to assist in the preparations for the rebellion. Emmet had been friends with Quigley in Paris and immediately entrusted him with recruiting the disaffected in Kildare, where he had contacts.[22] Quigley left with Thomas Wylde, his brother-in-law, on a short mission to his native county, where he had fought bravely in 1798. Meanwhile Hamilton set off for the north 'where he was to command a rebel force in the intended insurrection but where he found that his influence was not so great as he had expected'.[23] Hamilton was married to a niece of Thomas Russell and had been arrested in 1798 on board a French ship. But he avoided execution by pretending to be a French officer and instead had been exchanged. Arriving in Antrim, he was to have commanded that district in the event of popular uprising in the summer of 1803, with Russell in overall control of the northern theatre, directing the rebellion in Down, and Emmet in charge in Dublin.[24]

On St Patrick's Day a meeting for the disaffected was held at John Rourke's public house, the Yellow Bottle, on Thomas Street. Between forty and fifty men gathered, but the presence of some suspected informers caused some alarm and alerted Emmet's agents. Rather than risk having their plans revealed, as a precaution they cancelled the meeting and persuaded Emmet not to attend. The crowd was told that the entire story had just been 'a delusion'.[25] Active preparations for the insurrection began a week later on 24 March 1803.

Now fully committed to leading the insurrection, Emmet was well aware of the danger posed by spies and informers. Therefore he maintained strict secrecy and kept many details of the plans hidden from the other conspirators. He also began renting depots at strategic points in the capital, starting with one at Marshal Lane (off Dirty Lane and beside Marshalsea Lane). It was connected to a passageway at the back of the White Bull Inn on Thomas Street, but its main entrance was on Marshal (or Mass) Lane. To add to the confusion, this depot was variously known and referred to as the Thomas Street depot, the Marshalsea Lane depot and the Dirty Lane depot. But at the state trials after the rebellion, the crown established that its main entrance was on Marshal Lane.[26] The White Bull Inn was run by a widow, Mrs Dillon, and was connected to the depot by a small private entrance through a yard.[27] The Marshal Lane depot would be the primary outpost for when the insurrection broke out. During this period Emmet met Miles Byrne for the first time, a young man just twenty-three, who had been heavily involved in the previous rebellion and who now worked as a clerk in the office of his half-brother's timber yard at New Street. Emmet trusted few people completely unless they had served in the rebel cause during 1798. According to Byrne's later recollection, Emmet made a stirring speech about why a new insurrection was necessary:

If the brave and unfortunate Lord Edward Fitzgerald and his associates felt themselves justified in seeking to redress Ireland's grievances by taking the field, what must not be our justification, now that not a vestige of self-government exists, in consequence of the accursed union. Until this barbarous act or transaction took place, from time to time, in spite of corruption, useful local laws were enacted for Ireland. Now seven-eighths of the population have no right to send a member of their body to represent them, even in a foreign parliament, and the other eighth-part of the population are the tools and task-masters, acting for the cruel English government and its Irish ascendancy — a monster still worse, if possible, than foreign tyranny.[28]

The British government would later discover that Byrne was 'one of the most active men connected with Emmet in the affair of 1803'.[29]

As far as French aid was concerned, Emmet was adamant that it could only be accepted with conditions. If a French army landed it could only be on the understanding that it was there as an auxiliary force, like that provided to fight the British during the American War of Independence. Emmet did not bother concealing his dislike of Napoleon. But he informed Byrne:

That though no one could abhor more than he did the means by which the first consul came to be the head of the French nation, still he was convinced that this great military chief would find it in his interest to deal fairly by the Irish nation, as the best and surest way to obtain his ends with England.

Crucially, he would not tolerate any French attempts to make Ireland a satellite state as had happened elsewhere in Europe. With that warning sounded, Emmet declared that he was willing to gamble everything, fully confident of victory: 'He was resolved to risk his life, and to take the little fortune he possessed, for the accomplishment of those preparations so necessary for the redemption of our unfortunate country from the hands of a cruel enemy.'

An inspirational speaker, Emmet was at his most effective when he was persuading people to believe in something. He was brilliant at expressing his ideals and very quickly came to epitomise those ideals for his listeners. Byrne immediately fell under his influence. Resolving to help in whatever way he could, he was sure that 'success was certain'. In part he was swayed by Emmet's oratory, but a more crucial factor was the aura of confidence and genius which surrounded the young rebel general. As Byrne later recounted:

Mr Emmet's powerful, persuasive language, and sound reason, all coming from the heart, left it impossible for any Irishman, impressed with a desire for his country's independence, to make any objection to his plans (particularly as Ireland's great opportunity seemed now to have arrived for her freedom), save to bide the proper time and wait for French aid. For my own part, I had no objections to make.

Emmet's inspiring oratory and Byrne's own willingness to believe success was possible made for a powerful combination, dispelling any rational doubts about the idealistic venture. Both men were determined to prove that a new rebellion could win Irish independence and were not inclined to over-analyse the odds. They often met in the home of Ann 'Biddy' Palmer, at Harold's Cross, a young woman whose father and brother had fought in 1798. If the matter was urgent Emmet would call to the timber yard where Byrne worked, but instead of going inside he would wait at a nearby garden until he was spotted. Because all the people involved in the preparations for the insurrection had 'suffered in the cause of Ireland', Emmet never doubted their loyalty: 'For this reason, no test, no oath was taken by any one during those preparations and organisation, which was to extend throughout the country.'[30]

At their second meeting, Emmet briefed Byrne about his plans for the primary depots. He had already secured one at Marshal Lane off Thomas Street; one of its functions was to store ammunition, various types of firearms and pikes, which would be used to arm the men from Kildare when they came to help take the capital. Henry Howley, a master carpenter, leased the house at Marshal Lane in his own name on 24 March.[31] A place in Patrick Street was also needed to store weapons for the Wicklow and Wexford men for 'when the time of action arrived'. These depots had a second function: they were to be used to manufacture gunpowder, pikes, rockets and other weapons. Curious to learn more about what kind of pikes had been used in 1798, Emmet quizzed Byrne about the type of wood they would need. Byrne advised using red deal, as he knew that ash would be difficult to find in the required quantities. Since Byrne worked in a timber yard it facilitated the purchase of wood, and Emmet was confident enough of his numbers to buy sufficient red and some white deal to make seven or eight thousand pikes.[32] Byrne recounted that 'a trustworthy man of the name of Ned Condon, to whom he introduced me, came regularly to the timber-yard, dressed as a car-man, and took away the boards to the depot in the lane in Thomas Street'.[33]

There remained the problem of what to do once the pikes were made. It would be difficult to move them safely from the main depot to the safe-houses through the crowded streets without attracting attention, so Emmet devised an ingenious solution. He ordered the construction of 'what were called the hollow beams'. Each one was:

A piece of timber eighteen inches square, ten feet long, [which] had its outside slabs sawed off about an inch and a half thick; then one foot long of each end of this beam was cut off, and on those two blocks three of the slabs were nailed or spiked firmly, whilst the fourth slab, serving as the lid, was screwed on. When mud was carelessly spattered on the joints, no one could think that the beam was hollow, though eight feet long of it was a complete case in which the mounted pikes were packed.[34]

In this way it was possible to carry the pikes, hidden securely within the hollow beams, without arousing any suspicion. With this problem out of the way, Emmet turned his attention to firearms. He had definite ideas about what he wanted, small weapons that could be concealed easily but which would still be highly effective in close combat. Therefore he ordered the making of 'a number of pocket pistols, the barrels of which must only be four inches long, and the calibre to admit a soldier's musket cartridge'. He also wanted 'a vast number of short blunderbusses'. Unsure of where he could get these made, he asked Byrne if he could recommend a good gunsmith, one 'whose curiosity would never lead him to inquire whether the firearms were destined for smugglers or privateers'. Byrne knew just the right man, Daniel Muley,[35] a fifty-seven-year-old gunsmith who lived at 28 Parliament Street. And so they asked him to make as samples a pair of pistols and a blunderbuss to the specified design. Muley did so quickly, and although Emmet was only moderately satisfied with the quality, he was very pleased with the low price:

> he was delighted to know that the articles could be made so cheap with locks and barrels perfect, and though the workmanship might have been better, and the polish higher, still they were all that could be required for the use to which they were destined.[36]

Emmet then ordered 100 pairs of pocket pistols and 300 blunderbusses, all made out of a certain metal which was cheaper than brass. Giving instructions for the weapons to be made as soon as possible, Emmet discovered that the gunsmith would not accept any money until all the merchandise was made. For Byrne, the efficiency with which this arrangement was entered into convinced him that 'the plan was extensive and carefully carried on, so as to offer every chance of success'. But he was mistaken, and as the date of the insurrection approached the weapons had still not been finished. Another gunsmith, Michael Devereux, also made pistols for the rebel leaders.[37]

All this time Emmet was busy recruiting men to his cause, while carrying out reconnaissance around Dublin, and his ability to establish an immediate rapport with different classes of people proved invaluable. Meeting with Miles Byrne almost every day, Emmet was proud of how rapidly everything was progressing, thanks to 'the exertions of those true patriots who did not fear to identify themselves with him, if they could redeem their country, and throw off the foreign yoke'.[38] His fortuitous meeting with Campbell in Normandy was also bearing dividends as he was able to use his contacts to engage a number of disaffected Scottish radicals in his conspiracy. One difficulty remained. Emmet was having problems finding a suitable place to rent in Patrick Street for use as a primary outpost. At last he discovered a suitable venue, a house at Number 26, which was 'sufficiently extensive for the depot of military stores which we wanted'. It also had a yard with an out-house which stretched down by Hanover Alley. But for obvious reasons Emmet could not rent it himself, so he went into town to try and find someone who could, giving Byrne instructions to keep a look out for a suitable person; 'a married man would be preferable'. A few minutes after he left, a Scottish carpenter called John Macintosh (also spelt as McIntosh) arrived at the yard to buy some timber. Married to an Irishwoman, a sister of the Keenan brothers, Macintosh was one of the Scottish patriots who had been recommended to Emmet by Campbell. Therefore Byrne felt confident in mentioning the house at Patrick Street and he informed him that Emmet wanted 'some one of our friends to take a lease'. Macintosh 'immediately volunteered to go about it'.[39] Meeting with Emmet, he was given enough money to pay the rent six months in advance before taking out the lease in his own name. Robert Holmes, Emmet's brother-in-law, took care of all the legal paperwork.[40]

Immediately Emmet set to work turning the house at Patrick Street into a suitable base of operations. Macintosh volunteered to do whatever carpentry was necessary, and he was assisted in this work by Michael Quigley, who was 'a skilful bricklayer' as well as a 1798 veteran.[41] Together they began making changes to the building, following Emmet's detailed instructions, and they constructed a number of

> secret closets from the ground floor to the garret, which could never be suspected or discovered, except by those that were in the secret. These secret closets were large enough to hold pikes, firearms and ammunition for ten thousand men.

When the building was searched by the police in September, *The London Chronicle* reported that Major Henry Sirr discovered

> a concealed door, artfully formed behind bricks built in a frame, plastered over to resemble the adjoining wall, which was covered by shelves and turned out upon hinges and castors. Upon opening this door a tier of closet rooms appeared, communicating by trap-doors and scaling ladders through the different stories of the house. They were spacious enough to conceal forty men, and were provided with air holes communicating with the outer wall. In these rooms were found from 300 to 400 pikes of a peculiar construction, having an iron hinge at about half their length, by which they doubled up; and though when extended they were six feet long, yet by this contrivance it was possible to carry one of them undiscovered under a man's coat. A quantity of sulphur was likewise found, and every appearance of much more serious preparations having gone forward in the house.[42]

Sirr was so impressed that he decided to keep the concealed door as a souvenir. The town major, Sirr was the man who had captured Lord Edward Fitzgerald in 1798. Henry Howley also carried out improvements to the Marshal Lane depot as a security precaution. He built a partition of brick and mortar all the way from the ground floor through to the lofts at the top of the building. As Wickham later discovered:

On each loft a door was made in it of a very peculiar kind. It was small, and consisted of a frame of timber, in which bricks were laid in mortar. When shut it seemed to be part of the wall, so that no door appeared, and any person coming in might suppose the partition to be one of the walls of the building.[43]

The fake wall was used to create a secret storage area for the arsenal that was being manufactured. One day the curious landlord asked to see the premises, which caused much concern. However Emmet removed the danger by ordering his men to build a trap door to the lofts and then pretending that a lodger lived there.

This did not mark the extent of Emmet's ingenious designs. He also ordered Byrne to have 600 jointed pike handles made to his specifications. These would allow the six foot pikes to be folded in two, so that they could be concealed on the rebel's person and then extended to their correct length for combat. Emmet wanted one half of the pike handles to be three feet long, with the other part two and a half feet long. The second half was deliberately shorter to allow 'a small carbine bayonet, or a small pike head, not exceeding six inches in length' to be attached to it.[44] A small spring and clasp ensured that the weapon was solid when extended and Byrne was impressed with the design. As he later recorded:

[The] handle extended and stretched out was six feet long; when doubled up, it was only three feet long, which made it easier to be carried and concealed under a great coat. These handles were on the principle of a parasol handle that doubled up, joined together by a small hinge. A tube six inches long covered the joint, pressed forward three inches and then was stopped by a pin. A small spring started up behind to keep it on the joint equal on both sides. Thus it became quite solid, and easier managed than a soldier's musket and bayonet. With this weapon and a blunderbuss slung with a belt from a man's shoulder, he had great advantage in close quarters with the enemy, as it was much easier to charge [with] the blunderbuss than the musket.

As head of the Dublin district Emmet had the title of 'General' and was often called this by the men under him.[45]

Different contraptions were constructed at the Marshal Lane depot. Emmet supervised work on a set of hollow beams twelve feet long which he planned to turn into explosive weapons. There were echoes of Fulton's underwater mines in his design. First, Emmet had the hollow beams bored with a small pump auger on one side. Then they were filled with gunpowder and resealed with a plug 'a foot long, of the same diameter, well spiked to prevent it from coming out'. Wheels were then put on the beams to make them easier to move. Finally, 'two cases, five-feet long each, filled with small stones and combustibles', were put together and these 'were to be placed on the top of the beam'. The result was an easily moved weapon of destruction, a controlled bomb that could be used to disrupt infantry and cavalry on the streets. As Byrne correctly predicted: 'The explosion of this machine placed as an obstacle before the enemy must have a terrible effect.'[46] After the rebellion the army discovered just how productive the conspirators had been. At the Marshal Lane depot alone the soldiers found '36,400 cartridges, 246 hand grenades, 8 rockets, 500 pikes and large quantities of other munitions' that had been constructed.[47]

Most of the scientific experiments took place at the Patrick Street depot. Because of this, the operational staff there was kept to a minimum to avoid bringing attention to the house. Derby Byrne, a Wexford man who had fought on the rebel side in the 1798 rebellion, was employed because he had experience in making ball cartridges for the British army, in which he had served after his capture. The two Keenan brothers, in-laws of Macintosh, were also contracted to assist in the work. But perhaps the most important person at the Patrick Street house was Johnstone, a former soldier in the East India Company. He had worked with rockets in India and had valuable expertise on how to prepare them. This information, combined with detailed scientific notes that Emmet had brought with him from France, allowed the team to prepare an improved type of rocket. Emmet gave Byrne a list of what he wanted and had him visit the gunsmith to order the outer parts of the weapon. Meeting the craftsman, Byrne

> showed him a strong piece of paper shaped in a certain way, which was to serve as a model to have tubes twenty inches long, two and a half inches diameter, cut out of strong sheet iron; as soldering would be liable to melt with the fire, they were to be clasped and well hammered on the joints, which would render them quite solid. The sloped shape at one end formed a point like an arrow.[48]

Again the gunsmith made a prototype for Emmet's inspection. It was of high quality and both he and Johnstone were satisfied with the work; Emmet ordered 'several hundreds of the same description made as soon as possible'. As with the blunderbusses, Emmet was to be disappointed and less than a dozen were made by the end of July.

Working intensively on preparing the insides of the rockets, Johnstone started filling the tubes with an explosive mixture made from gunpowder, potassium nitrate and sulphur; this looked like wet mortar when it was prepared. Emmet supervised the entire process, consulting his notes to make sure it was done correctly.[49] He dictated everything: 'the way the materials should be prepared, and even the way the tubes were to be filled, the size of each portion to be put in at a time, the weight of the hammer, the plug to drive it down, [and] the number of strokes to be given before another portion was put in'. The rockets were completed by placing an iron needle in the centre of the tubes, around which the mortar was tempered, and when the needle was drawn out, the hole was then filled with powder. Thus prepared, they were to be fastened with strong wire to a slight pole about eight feet long, at one end; and from the other end a card prepared as a fuse would convey the fire to the mouth of the tube.

Supporting structures or 'trestles' four feet high, were also made as stands for the rockets. This was the delivery system which would be used to 'set off [the rocket] in the direction of the enemy'.[50] Hand grenades and other gadgets were also made at the Patrick Street out-house for use in hand-to-hand combat. As well as the two main depots, at least three other houses were rented in the city to act as secondary depots. These could store the ammunition and various weapons, as well as acting as bases of operation for the rebellion, and were located at Winetavern Street (opposite Christ Church), Irishtown and Smithfield.[51] The objective was to have enough supplies to arm the large numbers of people who were expected to join in the rebellion. With all the activity that was taking place in March, Emmet decided for security reasons to move in with Ann 'Biddy' Palmer at Harold's Cross, using the alias, Hewitt.[52]

Efforts were made to recruit as many disaffected people as possible to the cause. James Hope, a linen weaver with a loom in the city, who had been a key recruiter before 1798, was given responsibility for raising the workers and labourers. As far as Byrne was concerned, Hope was, 'without exception, the best person that could be entrusted with the organisation of his own class in the Liberty of Dublin, from which class, the fighting men were expected to come'.[53] Hope had fought at the battle of Antrim on 7 June 1798 and had sung the *Marseillaise* into combat. He had refused an offer of pardon after the rebellion and went into hiding, travelling around the country before finally setting up a small haberdashery shop at Number 8, The Coombe, in the Liberties of Dublin. Now thirty-eight years old, he was 'sober, prudent and unassuming; he spoke and reasoned justly' and had no problem rallying men to Emmet's standard:

> He soon made acquaintance with the persons of his own trade who had acquired reputation as good, honest patriots, and to them he communicated the general plan. He promised them nothing which he could not prove to them would be realised when the time for action arrived.

In less than two months Hope was able to report with bold confidence that he had 5,000 men 'organised and ready' for the rebellion. In a subsequent statement to Madden, Hope was able to confirm that 'Mr Emmet was not, as has been supposed, the originator of the preparations of 1803'.[54] He had discovered the plan in Paris and had returned to Ireland to investigate its feasibility. Once home he had joined the conspiracy and soon was given a leading role because of his conspicuous talents. At his first meeting with Hope, Emmet informed him that 'Some of the first men of the land have invited me over' and asked him if he was in favour of 'an appeal to arms'. Hope declared that he was, and after a brief conversation Emmet decided that their 'plan was formed'.[55] At their second meeting Emmet revealed that he had secured two depots in the city and had already chosen the men to work in each one. Almost forty trusted workers were employed to make weapons and ammunition at these buildings.[56]

The conspirators were anxious to maintain the goodwill of the key Irish patriot politicians. One of the most influential of these was Henry Grattan, the man who had helped win legislative independence in 1782 and who had fought valiantly in the House of Commons against the union in 1800. William Dowdall had a meeting with his old friend in the spring of 1803 and discovered that he still had a high regard for some of the leading figures in the United Irishmen. In the letters sent at this time a cypher was used to maintain secrecy: New York was the code for Ireland, Caldwell was Grattan, Mr Adams meant Napoleon, and the anti-federalists was code for the United Irishmen.[57] Samuel Neilson sent a letter to Dowdall on 3 March admitting that, 'what you say of *Caldwell* is highly gratifying to me, both in a private and public point of view. I am happy to stand well in the eyes of a man I esteem so much.' To ease Dowdall's financial problems after his release from Fort George, Grattan had sent him money, through his business agent Ross McCann, and these sums came to around eighty guineas in total.[58] Dowdall however had a serious quarrel with McCann in the spring of 1803 over a personal matter. It seems Dowdall had separated from his wife, or 'discarded her' as McCann put it, and now wanted to marry McCann's step-daughter who had a dowry of £5,000.[59] This prompted McCann to intrigue against Dowdall and he persuaded Grattan to 'give him up completely'.

Former soldiers provided much-needed experience and the arrival of Sergeant Matthew Doyle in Dublin was fortuitous. Doyle was another rebel who had been captured in 1798 but had gone on to serve in the British army. His regiment had fought against Napoleon in Egypt and he had set his mind to study military tactics so that he could use them on his return to Ireland. After the peace of Amiens he was released from the army and slowly made his way home. Meeting with his old friend, Miles Byrne, in Dublin, he asked him if he knew of any available work. Byrne recognised the possibilities and quickly went to meet Emmet and give him a résumé of Doyle's career. Emmet was delighted by his good fortune, exclaiming 'Oh! He is just the man we want. Let me be introduced to him immediately.'[60] Doyle was soon given responsibility for training the men in Dublin and the vicinity, preparing them 'to hold themselves in readiness to take arms when called on'. He was 'an indefatigable organiser' and proved invaluable in the months ahead. Emmet considered him 'a great acquisition' and 'received him most kindly and frankly, taking pains to initiate him into the preparations then going on, and telling him all his hopes and plans'. Malachy Delany also arrived in Ireland from Paris and set about raising support for a new rebellion in Counties Kildare and Wicklow.[61]

Arrested for his role in treasonable activities in 1798, he was acquitted by a sympathetic jury and returned to Dublin to assist in the preparations there.

Hugh Boyd McGuckian, the former law agent of O'Connor, was also sent to Ireland to take part in the rebellion. He was a veteran of the 1798 conflict and had been seriously wounded in one encounter with the British. Afterwards he went to Jamaica where he entered into French service and devised a plan for raising an army to seize the island; he was foiled however by the vigilant actions of General Cathcart.[62] His arrival in Ireland was at the request of O'Connor and he reported on the preparations for the rebellion. There is no evidence however that he was taken into Emmet's confidence and his influence on deliberations before the night of 23 July was negligible.

Word of Emmet's talent and activities quickly spread. Thomas Cloney, one of the leading men in 1798, heard of his reputation and the rumours that he was planning another rebellion. At a dinner held in Cloney's honour at George Nowlan's hotel in Maynooth, he asked Miles Byrne if he knew anyone who was acquainted with the younger Emmet. Byrne admitted that he could arrange contact, but he did not reveal his own role in what was going on. The next evening he brought Cloney to Harold's Cross so that he could meet Emmet. In the distance they saw Emmet approaching, 'walking along and musing, and tapping the ground with his little cane, in his accustomed way'.[63] Byrne made the introductions and then discreetly left the men together for three-quarters of an hour. The evening made a strong impression upon him and he never forgot the sight of

> two heroic patriots, equally devoted to poor Ireland, discussing the best means of obtaining her freedom. The contrast in appearance of the two was very great — Emmet slight and under the middle size; Cloney almost gigantic, being six feet three or four inches high, and well proportioned.

At the end of their conversation the men rejoined Byrne. Emmet then took his leave and 'said in a familiar tone to me "Miles, I shall call on you in the morning"' before returning to his lodgings. Walking with Byrne, Cloney informed him that although he had heard a great deal about Emmet's talents,

> certainly he far surpasses anything one can imagine. His powers of reasoning and persuasion are such, that an objection can scarcely be made to any of his plans; which indeed, if judiciously carried on, and put into execution by determined, honest and devoted patriots, must succeed.[64]

Cloney had learned from Emmet that nineteen counties were being prepared for the rising, and he resolved to keep in touch with Byrne about the business. It was becoming clear that Emmet was preparing for a national rebellion, with extensive lines of communication and a large revolutionary movement to call upon when the fighting began.

To maintain secrecy, Emmet only used trusted agents in his dealings with the counties. He had a list of names of men who had been 'good patriots' in Carlow, Wicklow and Wexford in 1798 and he met with these when they visited Dublin. Anyone who could not afford to spend the night in the capital had their expenses paid by Emmet. He briefed them individually and warned them to make sure that no weapons were stolen from the British soldiers in their districts; it was vitally important that martial law was not declared in the country.[65] Every leader from the provinces was given three ivory counters which Emmet had designed to be used as special signals. All of them had been branded with a red-hot iron, the first type with three marks, the second type with two, and the third type with one. The men in the provinces were to only trust messengers who could produce similar counters. It was possible to tell how important an agent was by whether he carried a one or two-mark counter. The least important was the one with a single mark. If a messenger from the provisional government arrived with this one, he was merely to receive a basic report about men and supplies in the area. An agent with the two-mark counter could be trusted with additional information and 'he, in conjunction with the patriots of the districts, was to devise the safest and best means of procuring arms, and he was to be instructed with the money necessary to defray all the expenses'.[66] The three-mark counter was the most important and indicated something different. If a messenger arrived from the provisional government with this one, it was to signal that the rebellion was about to begin. The bearer would also carry any final instructions about how to organise the fighting.

When Thomas Russell arrived in Ireland in the spring of 1803 he was impressed to discover just how much Emmet had organised. Russell was to be the general in command of the rebellion in the north and he would play a major role in subsequent events. Over six feet in height, he towered over Emmet and one of his female admirers wrote that while 'his appearance was not altogether that of a soldier, his dark and steady eye, compressed lip, and somewhat haughty bearing, were occasionally strongly indicative of the camp'. Born in County Cork on 21 November 1767, Russell was the son of a lieutenant stationed at Mallow.[67] At the age of fifteen he enlisted in the army and was sent to India where he was commissioned an ensign in the 100th regiment. Under the command of Colonel Norman McLeod, Russell first saw action at Mangalore against the forces of the 'Tiger of Mysore', Tipu Sultan.[68] Returning to Ireland around 1786, he lived on his meagre salary and began attending debates at the House of Commons. There he met and had an argument with a young barrister by the name of Theobald Wolfe Tone. They were soon inseparable and as Marianne Elliott has commented, it was as if they were always 'destined to be friends'.[69] Tone later revealed that he loved Russell 'as a brother' because he had 'the purest of principles and best of hearts'.[70] In September 1790 Russell went to Belfast where he was stationed with his new regiment. There he met Mary Ann McCracken who quickly became enamoured of the 'model of manly beauty'. She discovered that 'his voice was deep-toned and melodious' and then made a comment about his speaking ability, which had some similarities with future descriptions of Robert Emmet:

> though his conversational powers were not of the first order, yet when roused to enthusiasm he was sometimes more than eloquent. His manners were those of the polished gentleman, combined with the native grace which nothing but superiority of intellect can give.

Revelling in his life as a young soldier, Russell spent most of his evenings drinking and carousing: his diary entries invariably included the comment 'half drunk', 'drunk' and sometimes even 'very drunk'. On one occasion Russell fell into the gutter after a late night out with two other officers, destroyed his coat and bent his sword.[71] A complex but brilliant man, he distrusted lawyers, visited prostitutes and supported Catholic emancipation and social reform. He became a leading member of the United Irishmen, and the close confidante of Wolfe Tone, until his arrest in the autumn of 1796 on a charge of high treason. He spent the next six years in various prisons. Incarceration took a major toll on his physical and mental well-being. Sent to Fort George with the other state prisoners, Russell became increasingly caught up in millennial thinking. He fervently believed that the world was coming to an end, as foretold in the bible, and that there was overwhelming evidence that God would punish 'those individuals and those nations who obstinately persist in supporting injustice and tyranny, by fraud, cruelty and superstition'. Russell's most recent biographer, James Quinn, has shrewdly noted that his 'millennialism became the driving force behind his determination to renew the revolutionary struggle after the failure of 1798, and explains his steadfast adherence to the cause at times when many former colleagues became disillusioned and demoralised'.[72] After his release from Fort George, Russell made his way to Paris where he joined up with Robert Emmet. Highly critical of the French oligarchy, he thought that it was run by 'professed atheists and deists' who governed with 'detestable hypocrisy' and had made the dangerous error of linking 'the cause of irreligion with that of liberty'.[73] He blamed Talleyrand for frustrating expeditions to Ireland and detested Napoleon for betraying the hopes of smaller nations. From his miserable experiences in Paris, Russell had deduced that neither Talleyrand nor Napoleon wanted to see an independent Irish republic: Ireland was merely to be used as a bargaining chip in peace negotiations or as a means of facilitating an invasion of England. He became convinced that the dictatorial first consul 'hated Ireland, and would rather see it sunk into the sea than yield the disaffected in it any assistance'.[74] Thus Russell shared many of Emmet's concerns about French aid, and brought disturbing news with him from Paris. Much to some of the rebels' disappointment, he revealed that they could not rely on a French invasion but nevertheless he 'expressed his own decided opinion that the Irish people should begin at once and free themselves. He added that he was sure the north would rise to a man.'[75] To investigate whether this claim was true, Emmet decided to send James Hope and a man from Wexford to visit Ulster. Miles Byrne was given responsibility for choosing the Wexford man and he selected Michael Berney, the first cousin of Denis Lambert Redmond, who would later play a small but significant role in the rebellion. After a fifteen-day tour Berney and Hope reported that,

> at every meeting the greatest veneration and admiration was expressed for the honourable part that Thomas Russell had acted in the years '97 and '98 and those present seemed proud to have him once more at their head to lead them to victory: and when they were told by Berney and Hope that Dublin should be taken, which would be the signal for all Ireland to rise, 'Oh then,' they cried, 'we pledge ourselves not to be the last.'[76]

This was also the confident opinion stated by the men in the other provinces which were visited around the same time.

Towards the end of April Robert Emmet decided to disappear.[77] He realised that the conspiracy could not run the risk of having its leaders arrested by the government in a pre-emptive strike, as had happened in 1798. Emmet was deliberately following the United Irishmen revolutionary strategy he had been so instrumental in devising in 1799. Finding an isolated house in Butterfield Lane in Rathfarnham, he rented it using the alias, Robert Ellis.[78] This was another example of Emmet's fondness for word games — like Trebor in his youth — and Ellis was chosen precisely because it was so similar to his own surname: five letters, an 'E', a double consonant, a vowel and a final consonant. Nor was it a coincidence that he decided to live in Rathfarnham, where he could visit Sarah Curran as often as possible; Wickham later discovered that the house was 'within a short distance' of the Priory.[79] Emmet had workmen build fences to maintain privacy before he moved into the house around 5 May.[80] William Dowdall, William Henry Hamilton and Thomas Russell all stayed with Emmet at Butterfield Lane, which became the new base of operations, but it soon became a drain on the conspiracy's resources. Given the rank of lieutenant colonel, Dowdall was second-in-command to Emmet (who had the rank of general) in Dublin, while Russell was the general with responsibility for the northern theatre. In personality Emmet and Dowdall had some similarities: they were both shy and diffident except when excited by something that was said in conversation. As an informer revealed, Dowdall was 'modest to a degree of sheepishness' on 'ordinary subjects' but 'when roused speaks with much warmth'.[81] However he possessed an icy ruthlessness and a predilection for intrigue that was alien to the idealistic Emmet. Despite this, he proved much less suited to deception than Emmet. Upon his return to Dublin in September 1802 he became drunk at a dinner and began talking indiscreetly about his relationship with Despard. Friends of the government were present and later some United Irishmen had to censure Dowdall for his conduct. It would not be the last time that drink would affect Dowdall's participation in events.

Michael Dwyer, a 1798 veteran who had been in hiding in the Wicklow mountains for the past five years, provided a few 'trusty attendants' for the rebel executive at Butterfield Lane. These included the young Anne Devlin, and even though they were 'honest and frugal, and their service was considered a safe-guard and an acquisition', they added to the mounting costs.[82] The men slept on mattresses on the floor and 'lived very plainly', but the expenses were still high and were soon resented by some of the men. John Palmer, Ann's father, who was in charge of supplies and purchased the provisions in Dublin, grew quite bitter about all the 'waste and extravagance' at the house, which he nicknamed 'The Palace'. The conspirators would regularly meet at Butterfield Lane and Byrne was sometimes worried about what would happen if they were raided; on one occasion thirty men were present for dinner.

Soon after taking the lease Robert Emmet was visited by Michael Dwyer, the young Wicklow 'mountain general'.[83] This was probably around 7 May. Paranoid about being captured, Dwyer refused to allow anyone to leave the house while he was there. He remained awake for the entire three days so that he could keep watch on the group. They all 'drank brandy freely' and discussed the plans for the rebellion.[84] Emmet claimed that he had 60,000 men committed to the attempt, an extraordinarily optimistic prediction, and insisted that he would 'astonish the government' and make Ireland 'independent of all the world'. Dwyer later revealed that if he had known Emmet 'depended on the lower orders' he would have corrected him about his misplaced confidence in this regard. Agreeing to help Emmet, he offered him 800 men, and 5,000 more once the rebels captured Dublin and held it for forty-eight hours. Privately Dwyer was sceptical about the possibility of success and even critical of Emmet's character. He later informed Dublin Castle that 'if Emmet had brains to his education he'd be a fine man'.[85] To maintain secrecy Dwyer was not told the names of the other leaders of the conspiracy. Dwyer had his own conditions. There was only one signal he would accept as proof that the capital was in the hands of the rebels: the sound of cannon firing. When the conversation turned to France Dwyer was surprised to learn that neither Emmet nor Russell would welcome an invasion. They held General Humbert in high esteem but not Napoleon and were sorry he had come to power. Dwyer heard much that was ambitious but little that was convincing, and lost respect for Emmet's grandiose schemes. He soon became convinced that 'many people promised to support Emmet who had no intention of doing so'. A discussion of the land question drew a swift rebuke from William Hamilton. Expressing Emmet's own opinion, Hamilton insisted that Dwyer must not use the opportunity presented by a new rebellion to attempt to recover 'the forfeited estates' as 'it would only create a civil war amongst us'.[86] On the third day of his visit Dwyer looked out of the window and noticed a young woman nearby cutting paper and watching him intently. No one knew her identity and Dwyer panicked. Fearing that his security was compromised he decided to leave the area and return to the Wicklow mountains. But despite his cynicism, even he was caught up in

Emmet's enthusiasm and he began to grow confident of victory. On 28 May he got very drunk at John Doody's pub at Eadestown in Wicklow after a successful piece of highway robbery. His victims, the Thorp family, were present as Dwyer decided to entertain them after liberating their pistols and money. Growing in confidence with his consumption of alcohol, Dwyer informed the Thorps that he had been 'fighting five years for liberty and that the sixth would gain it'.[87]

A niece of Michael Dwyer, Anne Devlin proved a valuable addition to the house. She became Robert's trusted helper and would serve him loyally in the months ahead. There is some confusion about how old she was in 1803. According to an inscription on her tomb she would have been twenty-two years old, but R. R. Madden believed that she was a 'young woman of about twenty-five or twenty-six-years of age'; the government's files however confirm she was twenty-two.[88] An inaccurate account provided by Luke Cullen stated she was born in 1789 in County Wicklow, but this meant she would only have been fourteen years old when she served Emmet.[89] Many years later she visited the house at Butterfield Lane and was moved to tears when she saw the bedroom that Emmet had slept in. She remembered that there had been very little furniture around and that the men usually only travelled out at night-time. As she informed Madden, spirits had been high and

> Mr Emmet sometimes hummed a tune, but he was no great singer. But he was the best and most kind-hearted of all the persons she had ever known; he was too good for many of those who were about him.[90]

Another important addition to the conspiracy was Thomas Branagan, a timber merchant from Irishtown in Dublin, 'whose daring, resolute designs for this purpose could not be surpassed'.[91] Meeting with Emmet, he suggested that an attempt should be made 'to surprise and take the Pigeon House when the signal from the city should be given'. Delighted with this 'bold offer' Emmet gave his agreement and promised to have small depots of arms made available nearby as soon as possible. Married and with several children, Branagan was a determined and ambitious man. Upon being given the Irishtown command by Emmet he immediately rushed out to buy a general's epaulettes, 'fully determined to prove that he was worthy of wearing them'.[92] Recognising something of his own character in Branagan, Miles Byrne fully approved of his spirit. Emmet often visited Branagan at his home in Irishtown to discuss the plans for the insurrection and carry out reconnaissance. When the tide was out Emmet and Branagan would walk across the strand making notes for seizing the Pigeon House and studying the terrain.[93]

One day while travelling from Thomas Street to Butterfield Lane, Hope and Emmet had a lengthy conversation about the land question. They had been discussing the state of the country and Hope expressed his conviction that there would never be peace in Ireland, especially in Ulster, until 'the rights of the people in relation to the soil . . . were recognised'.[94] This made Emmet uneasy and he replied that it would be dangerous to address that question until after independence had been won; otherwise there would be civil war in the country. He was convinced there could only be equality in Ireland once justice had been secured. He would have no hand in tearing the country apart over the land question and he insisted:

> I would rather die than live to witness the calamities which that course would bring on helpless families; let that be the work of others — it shall never be mine. Corruption must exhaust its means before equity can establish even its most reasonable claims.

Russell and Hamilton were in agreement with Emmet on this point. As the millenarian Russell made clear with almost religious fervour,

> we are now in the vortex. If we can swim ashore let it not be through innocent blood; if the people are true to themselves, we have an overwhelming force; if otherwise, we fall, and our lives will be a sufficient sacrifice.

Upon hearing this, Emmet smiled and made a half-serious assessment of their cause. If they failed, then 'One grand point at least will be gained. No leading Catholic is committed — we are all Protestants — and their cause will not be compromised.'

Finance for the rebellion was precarious. Emmet had invested all his inheritance in the conspiracy but it was not enough. His reluctance to involve France in his plans prevented that resource from being tapped, but he was determined not to compromise his principles. For Emmet this was to be Ireland's war of independence and not a game played by France against Britain. Foreign support would be accepted once Dublin was captured and the counties had risen. But it would not be as part of a plan to attack England; the French soldiers would come as allies to assist the Irish or else they would not be allowed to land at all. Instead he looked for money elsewhere and found a willing patron in his merchant associate, Philip Long. In May, Long agreed to help finance the conspiracy and he gave Emmet the first instalment of cash; his contributions eventually totalled £1,400.[95]

In an attempt to liaise with the United Irishmen in Paris, Emmet sent Patrick Gallagher over to maintain the strained links. Once there, Gallagher reported that lines of communication had been established between north and south and that 'very proper and respectable men' had offered to assist in any rebellion.[96] Thomas Addis was also enlisted by his brother to try and rally support for the Irish cause among the French politicians. He arrived in Paris with his family and found a house at the Vallée de Montmornecy.[97] Of crucial importance was the need to secure a promise of 'money, arms, ammunition and officers', and it is significant that soldiers were not also a requirement.

Both Emmets were of the opinion that the insurrection must be won by Irishmen, and while they were prepared to accept French officers to lead the men, they were determined to preserve its character as an army of national liberation. In a deliberate attempt to follow the model of the American War of Independence, Robert wanted a treaty signed between the United Irishmen and France in advance, 'as a guarantee similar to that which [Benjamin] Franklin obtained for America'.[98] It was not forthcoming and Tom Emmet's mission in Paris proved to be a prolonged failure. The ministers vacillated and dissembled, all the time refusing to give any definite commitments. Worse, Napoleon refused to see him and he had to be content with meeting uninterested subordinates and indifferent courtiers. It became increasingly clear that the impetus for their involvement would have to come from elsewhere.[99]

Thomas Addis Emmet remained in touch with his brother during these months. He sent the letters to his mother who then passed them on to her son. One was discovered at the Marshal Lane depot which began 'My dearest Robert'. It seems he also kept Robert up to date with the latest in French publishing. A copy of Constantin François de Volney's *The ruins, or, Meditation on the revolutions of empires* was discovered at the Patrick Street depot after the rebellion.[100] This translation of the classic was only published on 1 November 1802 in Paris, so Robert possessed one of the few copies in Ireland. Volney was a leading French intellectual and his book was an introductory text for anyone interested in the ideologues. Drawing on his eastern travels, Volney's work was essentially an eccentric collection of thoughts and ideas and included chapters on the principles of society, religious beliefs and the law of nature. There was also a curious final section on the signs of the zodiac. Emmet's own star sign was Pisces, the two fish, and Volney described the background to this twelfth symbol of the zodiac. He wrote how 'The fisherman succeeded the shepherd. The precession of the equinoxes produced a new avatar; a new sign arose in the heavens; and a new saviour was born to save mankind.' However there is little evidence in any of Emmet's writings or statements that he was influenced by Volney, although the proclamation of the provisional government does echo some of his views on the promotion of morality. Overall it seems that Tom's attempts to educate him in French philosophy were wasted. As it happened, hurling proved to be of far more use to Robert Emmet than horoscopes.

Hurling was a popular sport in Ireland at the beginning of the nineteenth century. When reporting on the tranquillity of County Galway in early 1803, Lord Ashtown explained that it was usually only 'at fairs and hurling matches' that the peasants 'got drunk and broke heads'.[101] But he recognised the irony that this was 'an extraordinary proof of a peaceable disposition', while explaining that it was 'none but an Irishman could give'. As the preparations for the rebellion gathered momentum in the summer of 1803, it was decided to use hurling matches as a pretext for meeting with conspirators. In May, William Dowdall established a hurling society in Dublin, which met regularly at a tavern in Donnybrook.[102] This was also a brilliant ruse to facilitate covert training, with the hurling stick an adequate substitute for guns and pikes. As the government learned too late, these exercises 'were said to be hurling matches . . . [and were] attended by all the disaffected who had been in Fort George and Kilmainham'.[103] Judge Robert Day was impressed with the dealings of 'the famous Hurling Society' and believed that it was 'instituted no doubt to bring together without alarm or hazard, and to recruit for traitors'.[104]

On 18 May Britain declared war on France. Conflict had been inevitable for some time and the resumption of hostilities brought the return of William Pitt to the House of Commons. He did not look well upon entering the chamber and the Foxite MP, Thomas Creevy, noted that he looked 'much changed and fallen' and concluded with smug satisfaction that the former prime minister 'was done'.[105] It was a bad misjudgment for five days later Pitt rose to his feet to deliver one of his finest ever war speeches. Even Creevy was abashed and conceded that 'the great fiend outdid [as it was thought] all former performances' by his 'miraculous perspicuity and fluency'.[106] But on 3 June Pitt made a serious miscalculation. A motion of censure had been tabled against the government and he vacillated between supporting and opposing it. Seeking to avoid making a decision he attempted a clever tactical manoeuvre, proposing a motion of his own to pass to the orders of the day and thus avoid a vote on the question. It backfired. Both the government and the opposition wanted to discuss the motion of censure and Pitt's manoeuvre was embarrassingly rejected by 58 votes to 335. Upon hearing the result Pitt walked out of the house. He later admitted that his strategy had not been 'good *generalship*'.[107]

Two days after the resumption of hostilities with France, General Henry Fox arrived in Ireland to succeed Sir William Medows as commander-of-the-forces. He formally took over on 1 June and gradually set about familiarising himself with the military state of the country. Lord Hardwicke, the lord lieutenant, briefed him about the possibility of a French invasion on 10 June and they also discussed various measures to improve the coastal defences. Both men agreed that it was important to be able to arrest suspected persons, but neither seemed inclined to bring in a new Martial Law Act.[108] Alexander Marsden, the under secretary at Dublin Castle, also met with Fox and discussed the troop deployments in the country. Anxious to get first-hand experience for himself, Fox decided to leave Dublin on 13 July and travel west, spending time at Athlone and Galway. He was out of the capital for the next eight days. His military secretary, Colonel Beckwith, left a detailed itinerary for the lord lieutenant, but nevertheless when a crucial report was sent to him on 18 July about the discovery of a rebel depot, he did not receive it until after his return to Dublin. Nervous and indecisive, Fox would have been an adequate commander-of-the-forces in peacetime, but was a disastrous person to have in charge of the army when the country was on the brink of open rebellion. The most fortunate development in the history of the conspiracy was the arrival of Henry Fox. A competent commander would have been able to mobilise the full force of the army to crush the insurrection at the first sign of trouble. But Fox's bungling and ineptitude combined spectacularly to give Emmet's ambitious schemes every chance of success.

If Robert Emmet was lucky to have Henry Fox based in Ireland for the summer of 1803 then this good fortune was more than counter-balanced by the presence of William Wickham, the brilliant chief secretary. He had been formally appointed to the office on 13 February 1802 and had arrived in Dublin with Charles William Flint in attendance as his private secretary. Few in Ireland were aware of the extent of Wickham's activities in the 1790s or just how dangerous a figure he was. For years he had been the effective head of British intelligence on the continent and was one of the most feared spymasters in Europe. He was ruthless and determined, with years of experience detecting and preventing conspiracies, provoking counter-revolution, and other covert activities.

Born in England in November 1761, Wickham was educated at Winchester and Harrow before entering Christ Church Oxford. There he became friends with William Wyndham Grenville who was to be an invaluable contact in the years ahead. Wickham decided upon a career in the law and entered the University of Geneva in 1782 where he fell in love and married Eléonore Madeleine Bertrand, the daughter of Professor Louis Bertrand, who was connected to a powerful Swiss banking family. Returning to London, Wickham was called to the bar in 1786 but he was not a success at the law. His old friend, now Lord Grenville, intervened and, recognising his potential as a spy, decided to employ him in the government's service.[109] One of his first assignments in August 1793 was to infiltrate the London Corresponding Society, a radical working-class movement which was campaigning for the vote and parliamentary reform. His mission was a success, leading to the arrest of its leaders in May 1794 and the suspension of habeas corpus. Pitt announced in the House of Commons that the corresponding societies had attempted the 'total subversion of the constitution, the annihilation of parliament and the destruction of the king himself'.[110] As a reward for his services Wickham was appointed superintendent of aliens and began his work for the alien office, a shadowy subsection of the home office. Ostensibly set up to monitor the activities of foreigners in the country, in reality the alien office acted as a fully efficient intelligence organisation that was soon referred to, in official reports, as 'His majesty's secret service'. In October 1794 Wickham was sent to Switzerland on a clandestine mission to investigate an overture for peace that had been received from two French deputies. His instructions were written by Grenville but deliberately left unsigned so that his activities could be disavowed if he was captured.[111] This mission marked a deliberate shift in the government's policy and signalled the beginning of a new counter-revolutionary strategy against France. Wickham was accompanied by Charles Flint, who acted as his private secretary and who was one of his most important agents on the continent. Exposed as a spy in 1797, Wickham was forced to leave Switzerland and return to London. He resumed his work as superintendent of aliens and was also appointed an under secretary at the home office. Part of his work involved gathering intelligence on the state of Ireland, including the planting of agents to discover details of the United Irishmen conspiracy, and it bore dividends with the arrest of sixteen members of the directory, including Thomas Addis Emmet, on 12 March 1798. On 5 July the alien office was divided into three sections. Charles Flint was given responsibility for monitoring the home office police in Britain and John King and Wickham jointly directed foreign activities. After his rise to power in 1799 Napoleon was soon acknowledged to be one of the greatest threats to British security and the alien office helped finance various schemes to overthrow him. Assassination was unofficially countenanced and on Christmas Eve 1800 a bomb exploded on the Rue Niçaise, but Napoleon escaped unhurt. At the beginning of the new year Wickham, who was based in Austria, grew anxious that the prime minister, William Pitt, should be made aware of the full workings of the alien office. He wrote to Lord Portland, the home secretary, advising him to show Pitt all the secret records and registers that had been carefully compiled. Wickham was certain that if Pitt spent but half an hour studying the material 'a mind like his could not fail to see at once' its importance and how the government possessed 'the most powerful means of observation and information, *as far as their objects go*', that ever existed.[112] Roger Wells has revealed 'there can be no doubt that Wickham played a major role in the genesis of an efficient secret service while working in the alien office between 1794 and 1801',[113] and that the alien office provided Pitt with a potent form of 'social control' to 'construct some of the machinery of an authoritarian state'.[114] In Wickham's own words the office could provide 'the best system of *preventative* police that ever yet was made use of by any government'.[115]

The collapse of Pitt's government over the Catholic question in 1801 caught Wickham by surprise. His first reaction was to applaud the ministers' 'honourable retreat' and he decided to resign with them in sympathy.[116] But as he admitted to Grenville before he left office, he was not indifferent to any honour that might be bestowed on him '*as a reward for my past services*', and neither was he afraid to return home and 'live in confined circumstances'. In a delicate reference to his espionage work he revealed that

> too much of the public money has gone through my hands for me ever to wish to be rich, and I had rather leave a good name and a good example to my son than the first fortune in the United Kingdom.[117]

Back in London as superintendent of aliens, Wickham did not resign after much persuasion from Grenville who believed that he was too important to retire. Instead he sought the prestigious appointment of ambassador at Berlin, but unfortunately his reputation as a spymaster preceded him and no European government was prepared to tolerate his presence. Wickham's diplomatic ambitions came to an end in July 1801 when the French ministry published papers detailing his espionage activities on the continent. Now no longer able to function as a secret agent abroad, he was forced to remain in Britain where he was made a privy councillor. On 13 February 1802 he was appointed chief secretary for Ireland and was delighted to take up this new appointment.

Leaving for Dublin on 20 May, Wickham and Flint regretted that they would no longer have access to the vast resources of the alien office. Therefore they decided to continue gathering intelligence on their own by turning the Irish office into their 'principal office'.[118] Ostensibly the Irish office was the place where the chief secretary could work while in London and keep his papers and records, but Flint used it to continue his secret service correspondence with agents on the continent. The cabinet did not fully approve of this development and in March 1803 downgraded the office by amalgamating the jobs of under secretary and assistant secretary and giving the new position the status of chief clerk.

Reports reached the alien office in April 1803 of disaffection in Ireland. The Rev. Ralph Fletcher informed John King that on the third of the month a man had passed through Manchester who 'spoke confidently of the French invading Ireland in case of war'.[119] As more suspicious activity was uncovered in the following months reports were sent to Wickham of the possible danger. On 19 July Fletcher discovered further evidence of several Irishmen passing through the English countryside 'in the character of delegates who represent the state of Ireland', making noise that they were 'highly favourable to what they call the state of liberty'.[120] King sent the information to the home secretary, who in turn instructed him to pass it on to Wickham. The report was dispatched from Whitehall on the morning of 23 July. Other information came, ironically, from sources close to Emmet and Russell. The barrister Peter Burrowes received information that a rebellion was being planned and passed it on to his friend, George Knox, the MP for Dublin University (Trinity College) in the imperial parliament. He had discovered 'an invisible revolutionary government in great forwardness and activity' with 'numerous partisans in the city of Dublin, and all through Leinster, in the city of Limerick, and other parts'.[121] After the rebellion Knox always insisted that he sent the detailed report to Wickham and that it was not acted upon.[122] The inactivity was inexcusable. Knox met Wickham in London on 3 June and arranged for Burrowes to write to Marsden, back in Dublin Castle, using the signature, Junius. Further information was discovered on 10 June when Knox learned:

> The design of the rebels is to prepare the common people for a rising, but not to organise them; not to arm them individually, but to have depots of arms for them when the insurrection was to begin. The great object was then to be to seize the capital.

No word of this new intelligence was sent from Wickham to Ireland until after 23 July. With reports coming in about the role of 'young Emmet' in the plans for rebellion, efforts were made to locate him. This proved impossible, not only because he had covered his tracks carefully but also because the authorities had no idea of what he looked like. Emmet's old enemy from Trinity College Dublin, Thomas Elrington, came to the government's rescue. On 7 June he provided his famous sketch of Emmet in 1798, describing him as having an 'ugly sour countenance, small eyes . . . [and] a dirty-brownish complexion'.[123]

The plan for taking Dublin was breathtaking in its precision and audacity. It was nothing less than an ambitious blueprint for a dramatic *coup d'état*. Emmet had spent months preparing the details, reconnoitring Dublin to assess locations and plot strategies and counter-strategies. He divided his plan into three parts: what he called lines of attack, points of check, and lines of defence. Four targets in Dublin were to be attacked. The opening assault would be on troops and arms at the Pigeon House, with 200 men to meet beforehand at the strand between Irishtown and Sandymount. They would divide into two groups and attack at low tide, with one party climbing the wall and the other crossing at Devonshire Wharf. They would regroup at the Pigeon House where six men from each group would storm the gates, half armed with blunderbusses and the other half with jointed pikes. After the sentries had been taken the rest would rush inside. Once the location was secured a rocket would be fired into the Dublin sky to signal that the other three attacks should begin.[124]

Island Bridge was the second target. Four hundred men were assigned to this mission, who were to meet opposite the arms depot at the quarry-hole and burying ground. Nine men, armed with pistols and one blunderbuss, would seize the sentry and then rush the gates. Once inside, the main party would attack the installation from all sides by climbing over the walls using the scaling-ladders. After gaining control, the men had instructions to drag two cannon over the bridge and face them towards the barrack road to use against any soldiers who approached. More cannon were to be sent to James's Street and also to Rathfarnham, to give the rebels the benefit of heavy artillery. An attack was also planned for the Cork Street barracks, but the intention here was to set fire to it, rather than capture the position.

Each attacking group was given a supply of rockets. At the start of every attack the leader was to fire three into the sky, to signal the start of the attempt. Afterwards, if the mission was successful a noisy rocket of stars would be fired into the air; if unsuccessful, a silent one would be used to signal defeat. The main attack, which Emmet planned to lead himself, was to take place simultaneously: a daring raid on Dublin Castle. Two hundred men were assigned to this mission, and the place of assembly was the Patrick Street depot. Emmet also hoped to secure a house at Ship Street, beside the Castle, and launch a second assault from there. Half the men were to be armed with jointed pikes and blunderbusses, the rest would act in support armed only with ordinary pikes. Two rebel coaches were to drive into the courtyard of the Castle and from there attack the guard-house. At the same time the rest of the men would attack the building from all sides, using the scaling-ladders. There was also a quixotic hope that the rebels could mine under the walls of the Castle, and attack from underneath. Emmet was convinced that he could capture the lord lieutenant and the principal officers of government in this bold assault.[125] His plan was to send them, under an armed escort, to a rebel commander in Wicklow, probably Dwyer, to use as hostages in any subsequent negotiations.

The points of check were offensive-defensive positions which were to act as links between attack and defence. Three hundred men were to gather at the old Custom House, with instructions to seize the gates and prevent reinforcements getting through to relieve the other areas. Similarly, sixty men were to take up positions at a house-painter's house opposite the Mary Street barracks. Twenty-four of the men would be armed with blunderbusses and draw the fire of the soldiers. The remainder of the group would be armed with pikes and wait in the alleys to repulse any sorties. The corner house at Capel Street, overlooking Ormond Quay, and the house of Dixon the shoemaker were also to be seized. These could be used to attack the flank of the British army when it attempted to move through the city.

Holding the positions for any length of time posed the greatest challenge. Therefore Emmet made extensive plans for his lines of defence. Bedford Street was of great strategic significance as it was the focal point for seven areas: Church Street, Coleraine Street, King Street, Stirrup Lane, Mary's Lane, Pill Lane and the quays. A blockade there would seriously disrupt any advances through the city, so Emmet planned to use large double chains to seal off the street. In addition, some coaches would be overturned, and tied to butcher's blocks, to further obstruct the road. Men would be waiting in the houses, armed with hand grenades, pistols and stones, to pick off any advancing troops. Two hundred pikemen would also be on hand to attack anyone who managed to make their way through the obstacles and cross-fire. The intention here was to force the army to head to Dublin Castle by a different route, and so herd it into an ambush.

The second line of defence was on Merchant's Quay. Chains and barriers would block the army at Bridge Street, John Street and New Row, with rocket batteries waiting in reserve to open fire if soldiers attempted to get through. This was intended to force the army from Bedford Street back on to the line of defence, where the rebels would be better placed to deal with them. On the quay, rebels armed with muskets, grenades and stones would occupy strategically placed houses and warehouses and fire down upon the soldiers. Emmet designed a three-pronged ambush so that a body of pikemen in Winetavern Street could instantly rush on them in front; another body in Cook Street to do the same by five lanes opening on their flank; and by Bride Street in their rear.[126] Exploding beams would be placed in adjacent streets to disrupt the army's movements. One beam would prevent access to Bridge Street; another one would close off Cook Street. In addition, two rocket batteries would be placed near the Market House, with an exploding beam in front of it, and pikemen waiting alongside to offer support. This would scatter cavalry charges and create havoc with the columns of infantry. Prepared for the worst possible scenario, Emmet devised points of retreat in case things went badly, and he marked certain places where the rebels could regroup and continue the fighting. A final retreat was at Cork Street, as from there the men could escape to Templeogue. Finally, the bridges of the Liffey were also to be blocked, with boards full of long nails bound by two iron bars, with spikes eighteen inches long driven through them into the pavement, to stop a column of cavalry or even infantry.[127] Once these attacks began, the rebellion would spread to the rest of the city and county, with different groups poised and ready to join the fighting.

All in all, it was an extraordinary revolutionary programme, fully justifying Emmet's reputation for military planning. It successfully combined elements of guerrilla warfare and street-fighting, and displayed a masterful grasp of the requirements of battle. But, crucially, it depended on two factors: arms and men. The ambitious plan was contingent on both and Emmet convinced himself, despite some evidence to the contrary, that the rebellion would not be found wanting. In so many ways, Emmet's optimism and enthusiasm provided the rebellion with its driving force and dynamic. But they were also its undoing. For arms and men would be the very, indeed the only things lacking when the time came for fighting in the summer of 1803.

Apart from co-ordinating the details of the conspiracy, Robert Emmet also spent some time co-ordinating his love life. He endeavoured to see his beloved Sarah Curran as often as possible, and when this was not possible he sent her letters by messenger reaffirming the depth of his feelings. Most of this correspondence was destroyed, but what survived provides genuine evidence of their strong attachment. When the Marshal Lane depot was raided after the insurrection a number of important documents were discovered, one of which was the draft of a letter from Robert to Sarah. Probably written only days before the rebellion, it began by putting her mind at rest that 'whatever account you may have heard of my not being well, be assured that I never was in better health and spirits, nor looked forward with stronger hope to the accomplishment of all my wishes'.[128] Robert regretted not having made his last rendezvous but explained that he feared 'it would not be right for me to call on you at the time I promised, not on my own account but on your father's'. Nevertheless he had been desperate to catch a glimpse of her and had thus 'called two or three times to the same place in hopes of seeing you, and would have continued it but for the circumstances of which the bearer can inform you'. He did not wish to compromise John Philpot Curran and was careful not to do so, but he admitted to Sarah that he could not stay away from the Priory if she requested him to come: 'on this head I will do whatever you wish'. The letter ends with a solemn declaration that he would see her soon, no matter what. For if he had life he would see her 'the day after and prove to you that however other objects may for a time occupy my mind, my ultimate object to which it looks forward above every other for its own happiness is that which it now seems to neglect'.

To relieve the tension Emmet resumed writing poetry. Again his efforts showed his penchant for ideological imagery, patriotic fervour and strained rhyming couplets. One poem was discovered at the Marshal Lane depot when it was raided, and although only fragments survive it is none the less an interesting work. Rich in militaristic images of 'battlement walls' and 'dungeons', it contains a pervasive feeling of death. The hero is faced with much pain:

> While with innocent conscience his eye is intent
> On the fetters that link him to death,
> When from the dark synod of a blood-sucking fiend,
> To his chamber the *monarch* is led.[129]

Standing in opposition to the monarch is 'the suffering *patriot*' who is facing 'oblivion'. As Emmet develops this theme he explains the demise of his hero:

> A thousand sharp punctures of cold sweating pain
> And honour shall leap at his heart.
> But now he half raises his deep-sunken eye,
> And the motion counsels a tear.

Emmet's plan was for Dublin to rise first and the other counties to join in once the capital was taken. On 3 July Byrne recorded in his diary that the preparations were going well everywhere in the city 'with the greatest caution however and circumspection; no one meddling with the concerns of others, solely occupied with his own part'.[130] Everything was set for the end of the month, but gradually the conspiracy spiralled out of control. Emmet's luck began to desert him and the rebellion slowly unravelled from the centre. At the beginning of July Matthew Doyle was badly burnt while working in one of the arms depots and he lost the use of limbs. This was only the first of a litany of problems that were to bedevil Emmet that month.[131]

Men from Kildare had arrived in Dublin to assist in the production of pikes in the Marshal Lane depot and they worked 'day and night' preparing them and the 'other war implements'. Once each batch of weapons was produced they were moved to safe-houses which were used as secondary depots. Around the same time Thomas Russell decided to set off for the north with James Hope as his aide. The Wexford men and the workers from the Liberties were disappointed to be losing Hope and wanted him to remain by their side for the fighting in the city. Russell relented and informed everyone: 'You may keep him. You certainly take off my right arm, but I shall march myself with an imposing force from the north on Dublin.' Upon hearing this Emmet smiled and the conversation turned to other matters. In the event, Russell remained in Dublin for a few days longer, but when he finally left he brought Hope with him anyway.

Anxious to make sure that the rockets were fully operational, Emmet decided to test one out. He gathered a few men at night, including Johnstone, Russell,

Dowdall and Hamilton, and brought them to a quiet and secluded place in the countryside near Irishtown. A rocket was tied with wire to a long stick to stabilise it during launch and then placed on one of the trestles or support stands that had been constructed to hold it. A match was used to light the fuse and everyone stood back to watch the consequences. The result was spectacular as the crimson flare from the rocket lit up the sky:

> it went off like a thunderbolt, carrying the pole along with it, and throwing flames and fire behind as it advanced, and when it fell, it went on tearing the ground till the last of the matter with which it was filled was completely consumed.[132]

Johnstone and Emmet were delighted with the result and stepped up production of the rockets. One problem that had been noticed was that 'the card which was placed along the pole to serve as a train or match did not communicate the fire quick enough', but this was remedied by preparing a more flammable liquid back at the depot. Some veterans of the 1798 rebellion were suspicious of Emmet's reliance on this high technology. Thomas Cloney, for one, voiced his unease and was concerned about the amount of money that was being spent on the experiments. Instead, he believed that the leaders should be buying more guns and ammunition, but despite his qualms he was unable to persuade the headstrong Emmet to change his strategy.

One minor member of the conspiracy had had enough and decided to defect. Upon hearing the news Emmet remained stoical and reflected:

> There were many who professed to serve a cause with life and fortune, but if called on to redeem their pledge, would contrive to do it with the lives and fortunes of others. For my part, my fortune is now committed; the promises of many whose fortunes are considerable are committed likewise, but their means have not been as yet forthcoming.[133]

Remembering the advice of Templehoff, Emmet insisted that he would not be to blame if the rebellion failed because of the treachery of his allies. If they chose to break faith then so be it. He explained to Hope:

> If I am defeated by their conduct, the fault is not mine. Even my defeat will not save the system which I oppose; but the time will come when its greatest advocates cannot live under the weight of its iniquity. Until that time my reasons for the present attempt will not be fully understood, except by the few who serve and may suffer with me.

He ended his remarks with a dark prophecy: 'The elements of dissolution are gathering round the system by which these two islands are governed, and the Pitt system will accelerate its fall.' Shortly after the rocket test Russell departed for

Ulster, taking Hamilton and Hope with him. The loss of Hope was a major blow for the rebellion in Dublin and Miles Byrne recognised that had he remained,

> He would have been useful beyond measure, carrying the despatches and giving the verbal orders of the chiefs; besides, there was no-one appointed to replace him with the Liberty people, whom he had organised for action.[134]

It was a bad mistake by Emmet and it would not be his last.

At about 6.30 in the evening on Saturday 16 July an explosion ripped apart the Patrick Street depot.[135] Some of the men had been working on making fuses for the rockets and gunpowder in the out-house and a moment of carelessness had led to an accident. One of the Keenan brothers and Derby Byrne were injured in the blast and to escape suffocation from the smoke Keenan had smashed one of the windows with his arm to breathe; he ruptured an artery and began to bleed to death. Afraid to shout for help and draw attention to the work of the depot, the men remained silent until some locals decided to investigate what had caused the noise. John Macintosh who had been supervising the work immediately went to the door and put a padlock on it. Then he went to the window and told the crowd which had gathered that some dyers had been doing an experiment.[136] One man shouted that the house was falling, while another 'saw a splinter of fire drop from a window'. A fire engine was called, but when it arrived Macintosh refused to allow anyone inside the house.[137] This aroused further suspicion and a police officer was soon on the scene; the men were discovered and rushed to Dr Steevens's Hospital. There is some confusion about who was responsible for the explosion. According to Miles Byrne it was the fault of Johnstone who had been perfecting the fuses in an inner room and somehow had allowed a spark to escape into an adjoining chamber. In his account the room burst into flames, the windows were shattered and the men were thrown out on to the street. But both Bernard Duggan and James Hope blamed George McDaniel, a dyer, who had been working on the rockets while drunk.[138] However it seems more plausible that one of the men discovered at the scene was responsible. The *Dublin Evening Post* noted three days later that two men were 'dreadfully wounded' in the accident; Keenan died in hospital from his cuts. A second fatality was Emmet's comprehensive plan for rebellion a week later.[139] Philip Long brought news of the explosion to Robert Emmet, who was dining at Joe Alleyburne's house in Kilmacud.[140] Also present were some of the other conspirators including William Dowdall, John Allen, John Hickson, John Hevey and John Madden. Emmet immediately returned to the depot at Marshal Lane to supervise the movement of the hidden weapons. Never one of strong character, Philip Long was so terrified at the prospect of the conspiracy being exposed that he spent the next week hiding in the house of William Cole, a shoemaker, on Ormond Quay.[141]

There remained the problem of how to move the weapons from Patrick Street to safety. Miles Byrne volunteered to take responsibility. Gathering together a few men at dusk, a few hours after the explosion, he got them to carry the blunderbusses, jointed pikes, ammunition and everything else concealed under their greatcoats. They walked 'two by two, and at a certain distance from one another, so as to attract no notice', making as many journeys as necessary to transfer everything. Anything that was not ready for movement was left behind hidden in the secret closets. One cask of ball cartridges, flints and pike-heads however was brought to John Palmer's house in the early hours of the morning to be sent to Dwyer in Wicklow. The party's nocturnal activities were observed by two night watchmen, who believed the men were smugglers. They asked the men where they were going but were jeered in response, 'Come along with us, and you shall see.'[142] Arriving at Palmer's house, on the corner of the Coombe and New Street, the men rested the cask by the door and gave a signal. When Palmer went outside he was immediately alerted by the sight of the police, closed the door and pretended he was going for an early morning walk. Unfortunately the cask had fallen open, alerting the officers that something was afoot. The comical sight of a fully dressed Palmer pretending to be going for a walk at 4 o'clock in the morning only made them more suspicious.[143] Miles Byrne discovered what had happened and set out with a group of men to recapture the cask, which he did successfully, mocking the police for thinking they could keep possession of it. In the meantime, Emmet had also heard the news and set out from Marshal Lane with some armed men to intercept the watchmen, but was relieved to discover his mission was unnecessary when he came across Byrne's triumphant party. The next day Palmer was interrogated by the police, but they had no power to detain him and he

> persisted in professing his ignorance of the contents of the cask or the person to whom it belonged, refusing in a rather flippant manner to account for his being dressed and going out of his house at so early an hour as four o'clock in the morning.[144]

Palmer met with Emmet shortly afterwards and assisted him in transporting gunpowder from the 'grand rebel depot' at Marshal Lane to the others.[145] Many of the key meetings between the conspirators were held at Palmer's house, 'in an inside room', with 'Palmer himself directing the persons that came to the room where Emmet sat'.

Edward Wilson, the chief peace-officer of the workhouse division of the Dublin police, investigated the house for anything that looked suspicious. He did not discover all the weapons, thanks in part to the secret compartments but also the quick thinking of Macintosh who had removed compromising materials. But on Sunday 17 July he did find, in an adjacent house, 'a machine for making powder with an apparatus . . . and up a chimney some bayonets that had been fixed on poles, and a number of handles prepared for others'.[146] He also discovered Emmet's copy of Volney's *Ruin of empires* and about fifty musket-balls.[147] This should have been enough to alert the authorities that an insurrection was being planned. Byrne was interrogated several times, but he claimed to be just a simple labourer and nothing of consequence was learned. Nor did the authorities have any luck in tracking down Macintosh, who went underground. Lord Hardwicke, however, was alarmed and sent a detailed report to the new commander-of-the-forces, General Fox, on 18 July. But Fox was touring the country investigating the strength of the military forces, and because of some fatal confusion the report was lost in transit; he did not receive the news until the afternoon of 23 July.[148] Caught by surprise, many observers were complacent and refused to recognise the danger. With magisterial authority the *Dublin Evening Post* pronounced that there was no reason for people to be afraid. On 19 July it confidently declared:

> Various reports have been founded on the circumstance, according to the different views and prejudices of the reporters, and alarmists have not been idle; but from the inquiry made by us, we have reason to believe that nothing of a political nature is connected with the transaction.[149]

Meanwhile the authorities carried on in blissful negligence and later defended their inaction by insisting that the explosion was 'not sufficiently loud to occasion a very general observation of it'.[150]

A new depot was needed to store the weapons and ammunition taken from the depot on Patrick Street. Fortunately Michael Berney was able to recommend a house owned by his cousin, Denis Lambert Redmond, who was renovating it to live in when he got married. Flattered by the interest from Emmet, Redmond agreed to let him have the keys to the property, which was at 14 Coal Quay, not too far from Dublin Castle. He was also briefed about the plans for the rebellion, which he only learned about for the first time. Berney had not told him anything sooner, 'lest he should neglect his business, and particularly his marriage'.[151]

Major Sirr was asked to carry out another search of the house at Patrick Street and he discovered more ball cartridges. Details of all of this were included in the report that was sent to Fox on 18 July but which never reached him on his travels. According to Miles Byrne's *Memoirs*, Emmet was terrified that the entire conspiracy would be exposed and decided to bring forward the date for the attack on the city. This belief was shared by the government after the rebellion and it has been accepted without question by historians. The overwhelming consensus is that Emmet was forced to act hastily because of the explosion on Patrick Street and that this was the reason why the rebellion was so disorganised. It is a view which Emmet himself challenged. As he admitted after his capture, the date of 23 July had been decided in advance and the leaders in the rest of the country were already briefed. Therefore 'to change the day was impossible, for I expected the counties to act, and feared to lose the advantage of surprise'.[152] The confusion about the date for the rebellion was a by-product of the extreme secrecy of the preparations: few knew that the date of 23 July had been fixed in advance, so they assumed it had been brought forward after the explosion. On the night before his execution Emmet informed his defence lawyer, Leonard MacNally, 'in a most solemn manner and as a dying man, that not more than ten persons knew that the rising was fixed for the 23rd before the 21st or 22nd'.[153] After the explosion he convened a war-council of all the leaders then in Dublin to consult them about their opinions; at this meeting he gave the order that the rebellion would still go ahead. Confirmation of this decision was quickly sent to all the other counties.

For Emmet it was important that the rebellion had the symbolic trappings of a campaign of national liberation. Therefore he was determined that his officers should be properly dressed in full military uniform as befitting the army of the republic. On Sunday 17 July he enlisted the help of Terence Colgan, a tailor from Lucan, as well as other tailors to make what he required. At his trial Colgan spun a highly elaborate tale of how he had come to work for Emmet. He claimed that he had been brought to John Fleming's inn on Thomas Street by a friend, where he kept drinking until he fell unconscious. He awoke in a large out-house, filled with arms and poles, unaware of how he had come to be there. At this depot he was put to work making 'white pantaloons and green jackets' for the rebels who were being directed by Robert Emmet.[154] What is more likely is that Colgan voluntarily agreed to do the work, and was well paid for it, for when he was released he showed no desire to report the matter to the authorities. Indeed he only testified against Emmet because someone informed on him and he was arrested.[155] The rebel uniform consisted of white pantaloons, a green jacket, a white waistcoat and a cocked hat with a feather. Colgan's workmanship was good and he made a number of outfits for the leaders and with gold lace and epaulettes (as befitted a general) for Emmet's green jacket. Nicholas Stafford, a barber, was enlisted in the conspiracy in the final fortnight of preparations. He was a childhood friend of Quigley and went to the White Bull Inn in July to escape his creditors.[156] On 21 July he met Emmet for the first time and became embroiled in the work at the Marshal Lane depot.

All the leaders in Dublin were visited in the run-up to the rebellion. Miles Byrne met with many of them and later felt betrayed by their inactivity on the night of 23 July. In his *Memoirs* he revealed that not all of them had gone to the posts that were assigned to them, and if they had

> been exact and done their duty, or even had they come to the depot to assist Mr Emmet in the first bustle, their presence then might have caused more discipline, and in spite of mistakes and accidents, we should have taken the Castle.[157]

According to Bernard Duggan, one of the conspirators, Emmet had a scheme to kidnap the commander-of-the-forces in Ireland, Henry Fox. A few days before 23 July he met with Duggan and informed him that Fox 'had the habit of walking very early every morning on the Circular Road, in the neighbourhood of Kilmainham'.[158] Emmet planned to force him into a carriage and take him prisoner. According to Duggan the plan was frustrated by the timidity of Emmet's staff. But as Fox only returned to Dublin on the evening of 21 July it would have been very difficult to execute the plan successfully in time. Thus, after making all the necessary preparations, Duggan was informed that the plan had been aborted. According to James Tandy, the son of Napper Tandy, Emmet also had a plan to have armed horsemen kidnap the leading members of the administration and take them to the hills, 'to throw the government into confusion'.[159] Tandy had served under Cornwallis in India and dismissed this scheme as nonsensical: 'I must have been but a poor scholar of my Lord Cornwallis to have acted on such *sage*, political or military plans!!!' But these were thoughts in 1807, when he was making an appeal to be freed from prison, and wished to dissociate himself from the events of 1803. However it does seem that he was innocent of any involvement in the conspiracy and was arrested because of his name rather than because of any evidence against him. In his published pamphlet he wrote sympathetically of 'the unfortunate Mr Emmet', but attacked the rebellion as 'so truly genuine, ridiculous and puerile' and later referred to Emmet himself as 'that highly-gifted but infatuated boy'.[160] In a frank assessment of the various people involved in the rebellion, Duggan had much respect for Emmet but very little for the other leaders. He later wrote:

> Mr Emmet had three plans that would effect a revolution without blood-shed, if put into execution at any period; and the reason why none of them was resorted to was the timidity of some of his own staff and advisers, the general officers of districts and counties.[161]

Pat McCabe, a calico dresser from Francis Street who was one of the conspirators, also confirmed that there was a plan to capture the 'most active and intelligent members of the government' in their houses.[162] Duggan insisted that, to his knowledge, Emmet had 'secret friends connected with the government, who gave him intelligence of all the movements of the Castle'.[163]

The only two figures of distinction that James Hope recognised at the Marshal Lane depot were Lord Wycombe and Gerard Fitzgerald, the brother of the knight of Glin. As the son of a former British prime minister, Wycombe was a notable participant and Hope had no doubt that 'he was cognisant of Robert Emmet's plans in 1803, and privy to the plans for insurrection while they were carrying on at the depot in Thomas Street'.[164] It seems Philip Long recruited Wycombe to the conspiracy and encouraged him to enter 'deeply into the virus of the party'.[165] When the time came to take arms, however, Wycombe vanished and he drifted out of the conspiracy before he could be compromised irrevocably. The knight of Glin, Colonel John Bateman Fitzgerald, died on 18 June 1803, but this did not deflect Gerard Fitzgerald from his support for the insurrection; he was the leader of the Limerick insurgents in the months ahead.[166] One man whom the government believed was implicated in Emmet's schemes was John Keogh, the successful merchant and Catholic committee leader. His house was raided on 29 July 1803 and his papers were seized, but it seems he was innocent of any real involvement. After all, Emmet had been happy to reflect that, as no leading Catholic was committed to the conspiracy, 'their cause will not be compromised' if it failed.

At daybreak on Tuesday 19 July two cheese shops on Patrick Street were broken into and the tills were robbed.[167] Whether this was connected to the activity of the rebels is unclear. During this week the hollow beams were used to transport the pikes from house to house, while ammunition and firearms were moved by trusted people at night-time underneath their greatcoats. One observer noted during this period that all the rebels looked to Emmet for leadership and advice. Indeed 'from the instant he came in they would not do anything without applying to him'.[168] Friday 22 July was a market-day and Thomas Street was filled with grain and meal merchants and their produce. Working from the Marshal Lane depot, Emmet spent the night before the rebellion preparing his manifesto and finalising the details for the insurrection. 'Running from reflection', he convinced himself that his conspiracy had every chance of success. Very quickly things went badly wrong. A lot of people had promised Emmet money, but as the date of the insurrection approached they grew hesitant and backed off. As a result there were insufficient funds to buy blunderbusses for the men, and the conspiracy began to unravel. As one conspirator remembered, 'When money failed, however, treachery in the upper ranks began to appear, as in all former struggles.'[169] Meanwhile gross incompetence sabotaged the plans for the exploding beams. The fuses and rammers had not been prepared and the man whose responsibility it was, probably George McDaniel, chose to go to Kildare instead to raise men and did not return until the morning of 23 July.[170] Robert Emmet later explained that as a result 'all the beams were not loaded, nor mounted with wheels, nor the train bags of course fastened on to explode them'. Struggling to find solutions to these problems, Emmet's control over events began to drift steadily away.

Sometime after 9 o'clock on the evening of 22 July a grocer's steward, Patrick Farrell, passed through Marshal Lane. He had been working all day at the market and was returning home after completing his business. Hearing noise coming from the arms depot, which he thought was a waste house, he stopped to investigate. Within a couple of minutes he was discovered at the door and dragged roughly inside. There he was confronted by about fourteen or fifteen men and asked if he knew Graham (this was the code-name for Quigley). When Farrell admitted that he did not, they asked him what he was doing there, and when he couldn't answer satisfactorily they decided he was a spy. One man gave the order to 'Drop him immediately!' Terrified that he was about to be shot, Farrell was brought upstairs 'and after some consultation, which I could not hear, they agreed to wait for some person to come in'.[171] This person was Robert Emmet. The rebels had wisely decided to maintain discipline and wait for their general to return before acting. Shortly before 10 o'clock Emmet arrived back at the depot. He questioned Farrell himself and discovered that while he did not know a Graham, he did recognise Michael Quigley from years earlier when he had been a bricklayer in Maynooth. Some of the rebels wanted to kill Farrell, but Emmet ordered that he should be looked after but kept at the depot so that he could not inform the authorities about the weapons he had seen. As one government agent reluctantly conceded, Farrell's 'life had been spared by Emmet, contrary to the desire of the sanguinary miscreants around him'.[172] He remained a prisoner until the following evening, when he used the confusion of the rebellion to effect his escape.

The detailed plan for the insurrection, brilliant in theory, failed on every level. But even years later Miles Byrne was not inclined to be too critical of it and insisted that, 'The memory of the ever-to-be-lamented Robert Emmet will never cease to be revered, down to the latest posterity, and his plans will ever be consulted by all those wishing for the independence of poor Ireland.'[173] The lesson for future generations, he argued, was clear: 'whenever Irishmen think of obtaining freedom, Robert Emmet's plans will be their best guide. First, to take the capital, and then the provinces will burst out and raise the same standard immediately.'[174] Byrne was convinced that Emmet's 'views and plans for the independence of my country [were] so much superior to anything ever imagined before on the subject'. And he was proud that he had done all he could to try and make them succeed, 'otherwise I should have been sad indeed'.[175]

Waiting patiently for the fateful night of 23 July, Robert Emmet displayed few nerves in front of his men. He was fully confident of success, and if he failed he was prepared to accept the consequences. The government later learned that one day, in a 'playful and sporting mood', he got dressed in his military uniform and told 'his admiring audience what mighty feats he expected to perform' in it.[176] In one of the final things he wrote before the rebellion, he admitted that he had long dreamt of freeing Ireland and was now prepared to accept his destiny:

I have little time to look at the thousand difficulties which still lie between me and the completion of my wishes. That those difficulties will likewise disappear I have ardent and I trust rational hopes, but if it is not the case, I thank God for having gifted me with a sanguine disposition.

In later years Thomas Addis Emmet rarely referred to his brother's fate. It was an intensely personal and painful subject which affected him deeply. In his diary entry for 14 September 1803 he recorded: 'I have my own disasters to regret, but I do so in private.'[177] Not surprisingly he studied carefully the transcripts of the trial and his brother's poignant words became imprinted on his memory. These thoughts of Robert, written just before the insurrection, were quoted in court and made a particularly strong impression. Years later Thomas Addis would use almost identical phrases in his own correspondence, for example when referring to 'the vision of the happiness' that he wished his daughter Jane Erin to enjoy.[178] It was the exact phrase which his brother had used while contemplating the liberation of his country. As the date of the insurrection approached, Robert Emmet shied away from introspection and self-examination, and drew instead on his natural reserves of enthusiasm and optimism. Aware of the great danger he faced, he hoped for the best, but believed he was prepared for the worst. Choosing to 'run from reflection', he freely admitted:

if my hopes are without foundation, if a precipice is opening under my feet, from which duty will not allow me to run back, I am grateful for that sanguine disposition which leads me to the brink, and throws me down, while my eyes are still raised to the vision of happiness, that my fancy formed in the air.[179]

7

COUP D'ÉTAT AND BLOODY PROTEST: 23 JULY 1803

~

'It is not true that the government was surprised. Never had government better information of the persons concerned in a conspiracy.'
(William Wickham to Henry Addington, 9 August 1803)[1]

'I find a universal dissatisfaction at the conduct of government. They were certainly taken by surprise and were in no way prepared.'
(John Foster to Lord Sheffield, late July 1803)[2]

Robert Emmet's plan for the rebellion was ingeniously flawed. Having learned from the lessons of 1798, he devised a conspiracy whose greatest strength (and weakness) was its secrecy. In the wake of the insurrection waves of abuse fell upon the government, which was sharply criticised for its inactivity and ineptitude. Some of this was unfair, for despite warnings and a nocturnal explosion in Dublin there were not sufficient reasons for a general alarm before 23 July. The lord lieutenant, Hardwicke, found it 'remarkable that the plan for the rising in Dublin, and the mode by which it was to be effected, as well as the moment, was a perfect secret among the leaders themselves'.[3] But he recognised that the key problem with maintaining such security precautions was that while 'it diminishes our chance of procuring good information, it must [also] greatly diminish their chances of success at any point'. William Wickham, the chief secretary, was in England when the crisis broke and was completely outflanked by events in Dublin. He had been complacent about the dangers of rebellion and had disregarded some tell-tale warning signs. Writing to his under secretary, Alexander Marsden, on 13 July, he even concluded with a joke about possible trouble: 'If all people thought as lightly of invasion as I do, we should, I have no doubt, be in real danger.'[4]

Afterwards Wickham justified his neglect by insisting that the extreme secrecy of the conspiracy made intelligence-gathering impossible. As a former
spymaster he admitted that 'I am much used to this sort of trade, both at home
or abroad', but in Ireland the problems were 'infinite'.[5] He had been unable
to discover reliable information because the rebels were 'ready to march at any
moment, without knowing what they were about, and scarcely where they were
going'. This was precisely what Emmet had intended, although the extreme
security precautions brought their own difficulties.

While Wickham was relaxing in London, Emmet was busy at the Marshal
Lane depot refining the final details for the fighting. His plan for the rebellion
in the capital was complex and precise. Miles Byrne was to go to the house of
Denis Redmond on 14 Coal Quay and distribute pikes at dusk to the men from
Wicklow and Wexford. Other rebels were to be waiting at a house on Ship
Street ready to break into Dublin Castle when the signal was given. Emmet
himself was to leave from Thomas Street with six hackney coaches, each one
carrying six armed men. They would pass by Coal Quay, which would be the
signal for Byrne's men to join the fray.[6] Events soon overtook Emmet however
and reduced substantially the chances of success. First he discovered that
Michael Dwyer's men from Wicklow refused to take part. Emmet later blamed
this on the mistake of a messenger, but it was more likely an indication of
Dwyer's scepticism about the plan and its leaders. As the government later
learned, Dwyer had informed Emmet that

> he would not commit his brave men upon the faith or good conduct of the
> rabble of Dublin: however if the latter could accomplish any point of
> moment, or he could perceive the green flag (the colour of the rebels)
> flying above the king's, on the tower of the Castle, he would be at hand to
> cover or second the enterprise.[7]

Worse news followed. A report circulated around Dublin that the rising had
been postponed until Wednesday. Whether this was deliberate sabotage or not,
it had a serious effect on reducing the number of men who came forward in
the evening.

THE IDEOLOGY OF THE INSURRECTION

> '[This] solemn declaration we now make. We war not against property. We
> war against no religious belief . . . We war against English dominion . . . If
> we are to fall, we will fall where we fight for our country.'
> (Draft proclamation of the provisional government)[8]

The proclamation of the provisional government, addressed 'to the people
of Ireland', set out in detail the ideological concerns of the leaders. It gave
form to Emmet's convictions and outlined the code of conduct by which the

rebellion should be fought. Some members of the government would later become convinced that William Dowdall had written the proclamation, as incriminating papers were found in his house, but although it is probable that a number of people contributed to the final document, it is clear that the driving force was Robert Emmet.[9] In addition a draft of the proclamation in Emmet's normal handwriting was discovered in his desk after the rebellion.[10] It was an eloquent and finely crafted declaration and when the men gathered at the Marshal Lane depot, Emmet read it out loud to inspire them for the battle ahead.[11] He took the original manuscript out of his writing desk and read it 'to the rebel guards which surrounded him'.[12] Some men were impressed with the content and thought 'it was very good', but others were critical and complained that it 'was too merciful'. As Emmet insisted on revealing at his trial, at least one man 'objected to the paper when it was read' and thought it highly 'improper'.[13] Thousands of copies of the document were printed, to be distributed throughout the country as a constitution for the new republic. The opening paragraph foreshadowed the peroration of Emmet's speech from the dock and contained a suggestion about Ireland taking her place among the nations of the earth. This proclamation was Emmet's declaration of independence and it closely echoed, sometimes explicitly, the American revolutionary example. The United States, not France, was the ideological progenitor of the rebellion and the American War of Independence provided the inspiration for how Irish freedom should be won. This was precisely what Emmet had stated repeatedly in the Marshal Lane depot, that 'his object was a separation of Ireland from England, to have it as an independent state brought about by Irishmen only'.[14] Central to this belief was Emmet's determination to begin the rebellion without any aid from France. He wanted to send a clear message that Irish independence would be won by Irishmen fighting for Ireland. French support would be accepted afterwards to help maintain that independence, just as it had been accepted by the American colonists. But France would never be allowed to exert any control or influence in Ireland, where it could threaten to usurp and betray the freedom of the country. As he informed Leonard MacNally before his execution, 'if Ireland was once separated from England by treaty she ought to establish her independence against both France and England by beating the French out of the island, if they remained as conquerors'.[15] He had no problems with accepting French aid: 'he only objected to France conquering Ireland for herself'.

Addressing 'the nation', Emmet began the proclamation with a dramatic exhortation to the people of Ireland:

> You are now called in to show the world that you are competent to take your place among nations, that you have a right to claim their cognisance of you as an independent country, by the only satisfactory proof you can furnish of your capability of maintaining your independence by your wresting it from England with your hands.[16]

Outlining the work that had been done by the conspirators 'within the last eight months', Emmet explained that they acted 'without the hope of foreign assistance'. And in a reference to the Despard conspiracy and the resumption of war between Britain and France, he revealed that neither event had 'retarded . . . nor accelerated' their plans. Rather 'a spirit of perseverance' guided their conduct, and Emmet called on Britain to make 'a prompt, manly and sagacious acquiescence, of our just and unalterable determination' for independence. Moving on to discuss the great secrecy which had accompanied the conspiracy, Emmet urged his enemies not to underestimate the preparations which had been made. He called on the expected nineteen counties to rise and promised that 'our object is to obtain a free and independent republic in Ireland', adding that 'the pursuit of this object we will relinquish only with our lives'. There would be no negotiations with the British government except over the exchange of prisoners 'until the acknowledgement of its independence from England'.

Then Emmet addressed each part of Ireland individually. He began with the place 'where the flame of liberty glowed' and he called upon 'the north to rise up and shake off their slumber and their oppression'. Next he addressed the men of Leinster and urged them to 'stand to your arms'. He reminded them that they had risen 'without arms, without plan, without co-operation' in 1798 and had valiantly held out 'in open defiance of the government'. Praising them for the 'courage which you have already displayed', he predicted that their enemies would be overwhelmed with anxiety 'when they shall find this effort to be universal'. But he then issued them a challenge. Their honour had been questioned by the authorities in 1798 and he explained: 'You are accused by your enemies of having violated that honour' by committing 'excesses which they themselves had in their fullest extent provoked, but which they have grossly exaggerated.' It was a clever ploy, for he was anxious to maintain discipline in the countryside and was determined to prevent the rebellion degenerating into a sectarian conflict or an excuse for pillage. He explained that 'the opportunity of vindicating yourselves . . . is now for the first time before you'. And he called upon them to 'give the lie to such assertions by carefully avoiding every appearance of plunder, intoxication or revenge', reminding them that they 'lost Ireland before, not from want of courage, but from not having that courage rightly directed by discipline'.

To protect captured prisoners Emmet issued a clear statement that 'the nation alone' possessed the right of executing the death sentence. This was something that was emphasised at regular intervals throughout the document and was clearly something he believed passionately. He issued a general order that 'whosoever shall put another person to death, except in battle, without a fair trial by his country, is guilty of murder'. He was determined to be in a strong negotiating position with Britain after taking the capital, and recognised that he might be able to cut a deal for the return of the state prisoners from 1798. This would allow his brother to come home to Ireland, but he was also thinking about the other men who had been banished or transported. Any British soldiers that were captured would be retained as hostages for the safe return of the Irish exiles. To safeguard this, the provisional government called 'upon the people to respect those hostages, and to recollect that in spilling their blood, they would leave their own countrymen in the hands of their enemies'.

Following victory in war, the provisional government would cease to exist. It would quickly 'resign its functions' as soon as 'the nation shall have chosen its delegates'. However until this change of power it would continue to maintain order in the country and prevent private grievances taking precedence over national concerns. The critical issue was the contentious land question. Emmet realised that disaffected tenants might seize the opportunity provided by a national rebellion and attempt to reverse the land settlement of Ireland. But, as he had convinced his associates, the property issue could not be agitated at that time. Therefore the provisional government explained that 'it, in consequence, takes the property of the country under its protection, and will punish with the utmost vigour any person who shall violate that property, and thereby injure the present resources and the future prosperity of Ireland'.

Next to the land question, Emmet was afraid that the rebellion might be allowed to degenerate into a war of religion. Therefore he issued another order that 'whoever presumes by acts or otherwise to give countenance to the calumny propagated by our enemies that this is a religious contest, is guilty of the crime of belying the motives of his country'. He went on to explain:

> Religious disqualification is but one of the many grievances of which Ireland has to complain. Our intention is to remove not only that, but every other oppression under which we labour. We fight that all of us may have our country and, that done, each of us shall have his religion.[17]

Emmet also included instructions for how the war should be fought. Soldiers would be obliged to follow the instructions of their superiors and go wherever they were sent. There would be no exceptions and whoever 'refuses to march to whatever part of the country he is ordered, is guilty of disobedience to the government which alone is competent to decide in what place his services are necessary'. The key point was that every rebel had to constantly remember 'that in whatever part of Ireland he is fighting, he is still fighting for freedom'. He was aware that the men would be apprehensive about 'quitting your own counties' and leaving their wives and children 'in the hands of your enemies'. But he urged them to 'have no uneasiness', assuring them:

> If there are still men base enough to persecute those who are unable to resist, show them by your victories that we have the power to punish, and by your obedience that we have the power to protect, and we pledge ourselves to you, that these men shall be made to feel that the safety of everything they hold dear depends on the conduct they observe to you.

Having given this encouragement, Emmet ended the section with a brilliant piece of impassioned rhetoric. It was a bold exhortation to arms:

> Go forth then with confidence, conquer the foreign enemies of your country, and leave to us the care of preserving its internal tranquillity; recollect that not only the victory, but also the honour of your country, is placed in your hands. Give up your private resentments and show to the world that the Irish are not only a brave, but also a generous and forgiving people.

The third section was addressed to the men of Munster and Connaught. It began: 'You have your instructions, we trust that you will execute them.' This was followed by an intriguing reference to the provinces wanting to rebel five months earlier, in March 1803, and Emmet now called upon the rebels 'to show, what you then declared you only wanted the opportunity of proving, that you possess the same love of liberty and the same courage with which the rest of your countrymen are animated'. Moving quickly on to a discussion of 'The Orangemen of Ireland', although this phrase was deleted from the published version, Emmet attempted to bridge the divide that existed in the country.[18] He referred to the 'prejudices' of one community and insisted that he wanted the provisional government to 'overcome [them] by a frank declaration of our intentions' rather 'than [by a] conquest [of] their persons in the field'. By 'making this declaration' he suggested that the provisional government did not 'wish to dwell on events which, however they may bring tenfold odium on their authors' would only keep alive 'both of the instruments and victims of them, a spirit of animosity which it is our wish to destroy'.

Embarking on a brief justification of his desire for independence, Emmet declared that he had no wish to enter into details 'of the atrocities and oppression which Ireland has laboured under during its connection with England'. Instead he justified the decision of the provisional government to revolt 'on the broad historical statement': 'that during six hundred years she [Britain] has been unable to conciliate the affections of the people of Ireland; that during that time five rebellions were entered into, to shake off the yoke'. Continuing with a sketch of recent Irish history, he made a direct reference to the Act of Union, a measure which he regarded as inherently corrupt. Britain had

> broken every tie of voluntary connection by taking even the name of independence from Ireland, through the intervention of a parliament notoriously bribed, and not representing the will of the people; that in her vindication of this measure she has herself given the justification of the views of the United Irishmen, by declaring in the words of her ministers, 'That Ireland never had, and never could enjoy, under the then circumstances, the benefit of British connection . . . [and] that the interests of the lesser will be borne down by those of the greater'.

The minister quoted by Emmet was none other than Lord Castlereagh, the chief secretary who had worked tirelessly to pass the union. Lord Auckland was also quoted because of his observation that 'Ireland had been left in a state of ignorance . . . and barbarism'. To address these claims Emmet posed a number of powerful rhetorical questions:

> Did the curse of the almighty keep alive a spirit of obstinacy in the minds of the Irish people for six hundred years? Did the doctrines of the French revolution produce five rebellions? Could the misrepresentations of ambitious and designing men drive from the mind of a whole people the recollection of defeat and raise the infant from the cradle with the same feelings with which his father sank into the grave?

Angered by these reflections, Emmet went on to make the most exciting part of the proclamation, his 'solemn declaration' to the entire people of Ireland. This was issued 'in the face of God and our country' and was a sophisticated statement of the aims and objectives of the rebellion:

> We war not against property — We war against no religious sect — We war not against past opinions or prejudices — We war against English dominion.

But this was immediately followed with a chilling message for those who 'violated the common laws of morality' and were guilty of 'torture, free quarters and rape'. The provisional government conceded that it would not 'hazard the influence we may have with the people and the power it may give us of preventing the excesses of revolution'. In other words some people would fall outside its protection and would be liable to be punished, not for supporting 'the government of our oppressors', but because they betrayed the universal moral code. Emmet explained that he had hoped to catch the Irish loyalists by surprise and to have taken control of the country before they had time to act. This was no longer possible, but he was still confident that they would not take the side 'of those who have deceived them', a government which, by its own admission, had 'forfeited its claim to their allegiance'.

At all costs Emmet wanted to avoid a return to the 'system of terror' which the Irish people had endured in 1798. This was addressed in the final section of the proclamation and it was dedicated to an unlikely audience, the British government. He challenged it directly to accept the independence of Ireland and questioned if it would 'force us to employ the law of retaliation in our defence'. Warning that the system of terror had failed in the past, he explained that it had not prevented 'the people of Ireland from coming forward to effect their freedom'. He urged the British not to resort to such tactics again, and he explained that while it might lead to victory in the short term, it would be at an unacceptable cost. It would only 'increase the acrimony' of the people's minds and 'leave us under the melancholy delusion that we have been forced to yield, not to the sound and temperate exertions of superior strength, but to the frantic struggles of weakness, concealing itself under desperation'. He cleverly played with the fact that the distinction between 'rebel and enemy' was 'of a very fluctuating nature', reminding the government that their own recent experiences showed how quickly it could change. Here he was making a reference to the American colonists, and how the rebels soon became the friends of the British government after winning their freedom. He warned that this would be more difficult in Ireland's case if the government acted unjustly in its attempts to suppress the rebellion. He explained:

> you cannot hope to do so [become allies of Ireland] as tranquilly as you have done towards America, for in the exasperated state to which you have raised the minds of the Irish people, a people whom you profess to have left in a state of barbarism and ignorance, with what confidence can you say to that people, 'while the advantage of cruelty lay upon our side, we slaughtered you without mercy . . .' [or say] 'let us mutually forget, that we never gave quarter to you'.

Emmet was making it explicitly clear that the British could not fight ruthlessly against the moves for Irish freedom and then seek to do a deal when their casualties mounted.

In a profoundly moving and eloquent passage, Robert Emmet then pleaded with the British government to fight the Irish war of independence with justice and honour. He wanted its army to treat the Irish soldiers as if they were equal protagonists in a conflict and not to suppress the rebellion brutally with unlawful force. It was a remarkable request which showed that Emmet was all the time looking to the future. If the rebellion was defeated, he wanted to be reassured that the Irish people would not be persecuted for his failure. But if it succeeded he was already thinking about re-forming the Anglo-Irish relationship, except this time on an equal footing, so that Ireland could work peacfully with its nearest neighbour. His argument was potent: a system of terror would be disastrous if the rebellion failed, and even more damaging if it succeeded. This gave him the confidence to make his audacious demand:

> Cease then we entreat you uselessly to violate humanity by resorting to a system inefficious as an instrument of terror, inefficious as a mode of defence, inefficious as a mode of conviction, ruinous to the future relations of the two countries in case of our success, and destructive of those instruments of defence which you will then find it doubly necessary to have preserved unimpaired.

But even if the British government would not act justly, Emmet still insisted that the Irish provisional government would not dishonour itself. Prisoners would be respected and there would be no system of cruelty. However if Irish soldiers were summarily executed after their capture, then he was prepared to be ruthless in response and would reciprocate with violence. The passage makes grim reading, and was used by the government to incriminate the state prisoners, but Emmet undoubtedly felt it was necessary. As he explained to the British government in rather severe terms:

> if your determination be otherwise, hear ours. We will not imitate you in cruelty; we will put no man to death in cold blood. The prisoners which first fall into our hands shall be treated with the respect due to the unfortunate; but if the life of a single Irish soldier is taken after the battle is over, the orders thence forth to be issued to the Irish army are neither to give [n]or take quarter.

The proclamation closed with a sweeping call to arms: 'Countrymen, if a cruel necessity forces us to retaliate, we will bury our resentments in the field of battle, if we are to fall, we will fall where we fight for our country.' It ended with a final appeal to 'the sword and to heaven' as the rebels prepared to take to the field of battle:

> Fully impressed with this determination, of the necessity of adhering to which past experience has but too fatally convinced us; fully impressed with the justice of our cause which we now put to issue, we make our last and solemn appeal to the sword and to heaven, and as the cause of Ireland deserves to prosper, may God give us victory.

Attached to the proclamation was a list of thirty regulations which would be stringently enforced while the provisional government was in power. These were aimed at maintaining law and order and preserving the stability of society. The first regulation abolished all tithes and confiscated the church lands which would become 'the property of the nation'. The second and third prevented the transfer of property, bonds or public securities until courts of justice were established; this was aimed at preventing violence against landlords and unscrupulous profiteering. The Irish generals in charge of the various districts were given permission in the fourth regulation to 'seize each of the partisans of England as may serve for hostages' and were authorised to tell their opposite numbers in the British army that 'a strict retaliation shall take place if any outrages contrary to the laws of war shall be committed by the troops under his command'. However there followed a stern injunction that the Irish generals were to treat all captured English soldiers as 'prisoners of war' and behave accordingly, except where retaliation demanded an example. Any Irishmen captured on the enemy side would not be treated as well, and there was a sombre admission that they 'would be considered as rebels, committed for trial, and their properties confiscated'. No one was to be put to death, except in the case of rebel soldiers who mutinied. In all cases justice was to be administered by court martials, and military offenders would be tried under them. However even if a sentence of death was passed it could not be executed until the provisional government 'declares its will'. Emmet was determined to keep the number of deaths of innocents as low as possible, although he did not shy from supporting violence when it was necessary. Flogging was declared illegal, and no form of torture was to be administered. In addition, he laid down strict rules of conduct for how soldiers should behave on duty. Regulation eight punished anyone that should 'disgrace themselves by being drunk in the presence of the enemy'.

The generals in charge of the districts were given the power to promote from the ranks. Soldiers could rise all the way to colonel but the generals could only create one colonel for every fifteen hundred men and one lieutenant-colonel for every thousand men. The provisional government was the supreme body in charge, and the army had to defer to it at all times. Once each county was 'cleared of the enemy', a county committee would be elected, following the constitution of the United Irishmen, to administer the 'civil direction' of the region. Co. Cork was a special exception because of its size and it would be divided into two areas, north and south. The county committees would have full power to govern effectively, but they had to keep a record of everything that was done for inspection by the provisional government. They were also warned to take great care of the state prisoners and see that they were treated 'with humanity' and support, 'however great their offence'. Emmet was determined to ensure that 'the world may know, that the Irish nation is not actuated by the spirit of revenge but of justice'.

Once the country had been secured by the provisional government, and the British army had been defeated, it would immediately commit 'the sovereign authority to the people'. A meeting would take place in Dublin of representatives from all the counties. Once they assembled the provisional government would resign its functions. In total there would be 300 representatives from the counties, the same number that sat in the old Irish House of Commons; the delegates for each area were chosen 'according to the best return of the population of the cities and counties'. In alphabetical order the 300 representatives would consist of: 13 from Antrim, 9 from Armagh, 1 from Belfast town, 3 from Carlow, 7 from Cavan, 8 from Clare, 14 from North Cork, 14 from South Cork, 6 from Cork City, 10 from Donegal, 16 from Down, 1 from Drogheda, 4 from Dublin County, 14 from Dublin City, 5 from Fermanagh, 10 from Galway, 9 from Kerry, 4 from Kildare, 7 from Kilkenny, 6 from King's County, 5 from Leitrim, 10 from Limerick County, 3 from Limerick City, 9 from Londonderry, 4 from Longford, 4 from Louth, 12 from Mayo, 9 from Meath, 9 from Monaghan, 6 from Queen's County, 8 from Roscommon, 6 from Sligo, 13 from Tipperary, 14 from Tyrone, 6 from Waterford County, 2 from Waterford City, 5 from Westmeath, 9 from Wexford and, finally, 5 from Wicklow.

Ending the list of regulations was a final reminder about the code of conduct that must be followed. There was a strong moral and religious tone to the message, as well as a philosophical understanding that only through justice and mercy could liberty be established:

> The provisional government strictly exhort and enjoin all magistrates, officers (civil and military), and the whole of the nation, to cause the laws of morality to be enforced and respected, and to execute as far as in them lies justice with mercy, by which alone liberty can be established, and the blessings of divine providence secured.

The proclamation of the provisional government, and the thirty regulations that were attached, was printed and published in time for the night of 23 July. Many copies were still wet with ink when the soldiers raided the depot. It was a powerful and incendiary document and deserves far more recognition than it has received. Certainly the British government understood its significance, taking great pains to destroy all the copies it discovered. Indeed it seems that apart from a draft version in the rebellion papers, only a handful of others are extant.[19] The proclamation was nothing less than a complete programme for administering the country during and immediately after the rebellion, and it also set down comprehensive rules of conduct for the Irish soldiers to follow. It was a sophisticated document, making references to the 'will of the people' and other enlightenment notions, but it was also grounded in harsh realities about how the war should be fought. It was an important statement of the ideology of the rebellion and the moral beliefs which underpinned it, and it had Robert Emmet's imprint all over it.

A shorter proclamation was also printed for distribution. This was an abridged and edited version of the full text, and it is believed that Philip Long prepared it.[20] A much less sophisticated document, it contained far more aggressive language and abandoned the attempts at conciliation. Addressed simply to the 'Citizens of Dublin' it announced that 'A band of patriots, mindful of their oath and faithful to their engagement as United Irishmen, have determined to give freedom to their country, and a period to the long career of English oppression.' It revealed:

> In this endeavour, they are now successfully engaged, and their efforts are seconded by complete and universal co-operation from the country; every part of which, from the extremity of the north to that of the south, puts forth its warriors in support of our hallowed cause.[21]

The proclamation then called on the people of Dublin to rally around 'the long degraded green' and assist the rebellion in whatever way possible. It urged them to 'impede the march of your oppressors, [and] charge them with the arms of the brave, the pike'. Even those staying indoors could help the crusade by throwing 'stones, bricks, bottles, and all other convenient implements on the heads of the satellites of your tyrant, the mercenary, the sanguinary soldiery of England'.

The Orangemen were addressed by name in this proclamation and the language used was deliberately menacing: 'attempt not an opposition, which will carry with it your inevitable destruction; return from the paths of delusion; return to the arms of your countrymen, who will receive and hail your repentance'. It then called on 'countrymen of all descriptions' to 'act with union and concert' but to prevent 'excesses, pillage and intoxication'. Neutrals were also warned 'that during public agitation, inaction becomes a crime'. The final section was a propagandistic call to arms and asked the people to remember

> your oppressors for six hundred years, remember their massacres, their tortures, remember your murdered friends, your burned houses, your violated females; keep in mind your country, to whom we are now giving her highest rank among nations. And in the honest terror of feeling, let us all exclaim, that as in the hour of her trial we serve this country, so may God serve us, in that which will be last of all.

GENERAL EMMET V. GENERAL FOX

The exact details of what happened in Dublin on the night of 23 July remain unclear. It is a complex jigsaw with crucial pieces missing and some others which don't fit neatly. The various accounts provided by the rebels, including Emmet himself, and the different reports commissioned by the government are conflicting, incomplete and often self-contradictory interpretations of what happened. Some of the testimony at the state trials was deliberately exaggerated to secure a conviction, while at the same time captured rebels deliberately downplayed their involvement to avoid execution. Adding to the confusion is the fact that many of the key protagonists on both sides distorted the truth by overstating their own importance. The fog of war only added to the inexactitude. Piecing together a coherent narrative of what happened on the fateful night becomes an exercise in historical methodology, drawing together connecting strands of testimony.

At 10 a.m. Robert Emmet met with the leading Dublin figures to co-ordinate the plans for the rising in the evening. It was the first of a number of conferences during the day and probably took place in John Allen's warehouse at College Green.[22] Anxious to rally the men behind the cause, he was flanked by his lieutenants Nicholas Stafford and Michael Quigley, who were wearing the 'splendid green uniforms' of the republic.[23] After a frank exchange of views it seems few believed that the rebellion should go ahead. With a characteristic sense of misplaced optimism, Emmet argued against them, fully confident that victory was still possible, despite the disorganised state of the preparations. Notwithstanding his skilful presentation of the case, no one was convinced. Nor it seems were the men impressed with the quality of Emmet's lieutenants, having recognised Stafford as a simple baker from Thomas Street. The 'grand consultation' ended with all but Emmet objecting strongly 'to having anything to do with the business'. The first stage in the unravelling of the conspiracy had taken less than an hour. At around 11 o'clock a delegation of about ten men arrived from County Kildare to investigate the status of the preparations; they met with Emmet at the White Bull Inn on Thomas Street. When they discovered that the men from Dublin were sceptical about rising they insisted upon meeting with the other leaders and examining the main arms depot. Determined to maintain security, Emmet 'refused peremptorily to introduce them to the other leaders but consented to show the depot to two of them immediately'.[24] Agreeing reluctantly to this, the Kildare delegation sent two of their number to accompany Emmet to Marshal Lane where they conducted a careful inspection of the collection of weapons. They discovered a quantity of pikes, a supply of ball cartridges and some 'combustibles' (the grenades and rockets), but were horrified at the shortage of firearms. Going back to the White Bull Inn, the men were scathing of the preparations. Adding to their unease was the figure of Emmet himself: they were unwilling to risk their lives for so inexperienced a leader. They privately mocked 'the youngster' and concluded that 'the boy' wanted 'to put the rope round the necks of decent men'.[25] After a few hours the Kildare delegation made its decision: they would return to their homes and have nothing to do with the rebellion. On the long journey they turned back any Kildaremen they encountered going to the capital. Undaunted, Emmet still went ahead and gave the order to assemble the 'lower orders of the people' in their respective neighbourhoods in the afternoon, and await further instructions. He also instructed Bernard Duggan to raise the workers in Palmerstown as well as the men recruited in the Liberties by James Hope. It was now midday.

With all the activity taking place in the city, unsettling reports soon reached Dublin Castle. At 2 p.m. the under secretary, Alexander Marsden, asked the commander of the Dublin district, Major General Sir Charles Asgill, to call to the Castle. He also wrote to the lord lieutenant, Hardwicke, informing him that upon his arrival in town he had discovered 'a considerable degree of alarm on the apprehension of a rising this night or tomorrow in Dublin'.[26] As far as Marsden was concerned the administration was now facing a dangerous threat. All the half-reports and warnings suddenly assumed a terrifying significance and he revealed, 'I have reason to think that something serious is intended.' Advising Hardwicke to leave immediately for the Castle in his carriage with General Fox, he emphasised that 'I would not request [it] upon any light grounds.'

As it happens Fox was already at the viceregal lodge in the Phoenix Park when this message arrived. Hardwicke had requested his presence the night before and the commander-of-the-forces arrived a half an hour late at 2.30 p.m.[27] Once there he was briefed about the explosion on 16 July in Patrick Street and the suspicions of Edward Clarke, a justice of the peace from Palmerstown. Clarke owned a large cotton factory near Dublin and employed about 300 men, including a number of workers from the Liberties. On Thursday 21 July he noticed that his men were acting suspiciously, 'that some mischief was going on', and immediately reported this fact to Marsden. The next day he assembled the workers and questioned them about their loyalty. They assured him 'with one voice that they had no complaint whatever, but on the contrary were perfectly satisfied and contented'.[28] Well-meaning but gullible, Clarke took them at their word and visited Marsden later in the evening to inform him that he had been mistaken in his opinion. Fox had no sooner listened to this narrative, when the confidential report from Marsden arrived. The news made disturbing reading. Clarke had arrived in the Castle earlier that day, distraught that he had been deceived: 'it was with pain he felt himself obliged to unsay what he had [previously] stated' with confidence. That morning he had noticed that the men were distracted, had requested permission to leave early and 'above all, [made] a pressing request, urged in an unusual manner, that they might receive their week's wages at an early hour in the afternoon'. All these symptoms 'revived former suspicions' and Clarke left to pay Marsden his third visit in three days.

Hardwicke was now convinced that something serious was afoot. He immediately left in his carriage for Dublin Castle, accompanied by Fox, and arrived at 3.15 p.m. There the two men heard more disturbing news from Marsden, who had been receiving a steady stream of intelligence reports. One of them had come from Alderman Manners, who claimed that a Roman Catholic priest had learned that morning that a rising was planned. Marsden revealed that the garrison at Naas, Co. Kildare, was under arms because of all the activity there, a fact which Fox admitted he already knew. There were also rumours that

considerable numbers of persons from the country had come into town in the course of the morning, and that large bodies were then on different roads from the county of Kildare, particularly on those from Naas and by the Grand Canal.

In part this news came from Lieutenant Colonel Aylmer, of the Kildare militia, who had left Naas at 8 a.m. because the town appeared 'deserted by its inhabitants'. Heading for Dublin, he was alarmed to notice many women coming from the city, as if they were escaping some imminent disaster.[29] Marsden also learned that 'an extraordinary number of people had come into town' and he recognised that this made a rising inevitable: the people would act even if the leaders did not. There was even more information coming through. A 'confidential correspondent in the North' had revealed that 'a rising was intended both in Belfast and Dublin'. This convinced Marsden that an attempt would shortly be 'directed at the metropolis'. Fox was bewildered by all this intelligence and it was left to Marsden to take control of the crisis. He suggested various methods of defending the capital from attack and recommended sending a guard to Clondalkin to protect the powder mills there. Urging vigilance, he also advised Fox to double the twenty-man guard at Chapelizod 'to counteract the manufacturers at Palmerstown'. Another area which needed reinforcing was the Pigeon House and the arms magazine at the Phoenix Park, and Fox was briefed about just how important these stra-tegic points were. Hardwicke, for his part, worried that attempts would be made to seize the Bank of Ireland, 'particularly pressed' that it should be protected. Other potential weak spots were the jails at Kilmainham and Newgate and fears were expressed that they might be taken. The activities of Bernard Duggan were then discussed. Marsden explained that he had been under sus-picion for some time, but could not be arrested because habeas corpus was not suspended, and this prevented any form of internment without trial. However the authorities were aware of Duggan's location, and Marsden told Fox that he 'lived near one of the avenues of the town which was particularly named and described by a reference to a bridge'. Fox's reply was remarkably casual: he 'observed that he was too little acquainted with Dublin and its environs to know in what quarter that bridge was situated'. Unable to believe what he was hearing, Marsden began to despair about Fox's military leadership.[30] Worse, none of them had noticed that there were no supplies of ammunition in Dublin Castle, except for 'one cask of pistol castings' which a captain had left there by mistake 'and contrary to his orders'.[31] A month later Hardwicke would make a vehement attack on this 'insanity of arms'. Fox's inept management of the city's defences was now taking an ominous turn.

Paralysis gripped the administration. One critical problem was that as martial law had not been declared, the military could only act under civil authority. But the lack of magistrates — police and ordinary — on hand to issue orders as the day progressed, contributed to the breakdown in dealing with the rebellion. The Police Act of 1786 had created a new but not fully efficient constabulary which still aroused some controversy as it was seen as a tool for the dispersal of patronage. Having listened to the detailed reports of an impending crisis, Fox decided to return to his barracks at the Royal Hospital, Kilmainham. His carriage had followed him to the Castle from the viceregal lodge and he imme-diately took his leave. On his way to the yard he remarked to Marsden and Hardwicke that 'it was a fortunate circumstance that so sensible a man and so good an officer as Colonel Vassal was field officer of the day, adding that he would immediately send for him'. This prompted a jittery Hardwicke to exclaim, 'For God's sake, let everything be done with as little alarm as possible!'[32] It was now 4.30 in the afternoon.[33] Arriving back at the Royal Hospital, Fox sent a note to Colonel Vassal to call on him at 9.15 p.m. He issued no further orders but waited patiently for other news, oblivious to the growing danger. His com-placency was almost fatal for British rule in Ireland. Fully confident that 'all that was required at the moment was military vigilance and precaution', he did not inform the lord chancellor or the lord mayor of what was happening; Wickham later wrote that this behaviour was unjustifiable.[34] Nor did Fox even attempt to mobilise the army to deal with any sudden eruption of violence. Instead he did nothing, telling anyone who listened that 'an idea prevailed at the Castle of a rising in Dublin but he could not believe it'.[35]

Remaining in Dublin Castle, Hardwicke had conversations with Sir Edward Littlehales, the military secretary, about his meeting with Fox. Sometime between 5 and 6 o'clock he decided to return to the Phoenix Park, fully convinced that the commander-of-the-forces had given 'immediate notice' to the 'officers and troops of the garrison to hold themselves in readiness' so that 'any rising which might be attempted in the city, or any attack upon it from without, would be immediately suppressed'.[36] It was clear to anyone with military experience, except Fox of course, that a real and serious threat existed. If the rebels succeeded in taking control of the capital then the rebellion would spread like wildfire throughout the rest of the country, and cripple the army's attempts to restore order. To lose the Castle was unthinkable, for psychological as well as practical reasons, and the rumours that an organized rebellion was about to commence in Dublin, which had been spared fighting in 1798, were deeply distressing. Further on in the evening new intelligence of rebel activity was passed on to the languid General Fox. Again he chose to ignore the information.

Unfortunately for Emmet he was unable to capitalise on these errors of judgment. His preparations throughout the afternoon of 23 July were constantly disrupted by unforeseen circumstances. The men at the Marshal Lane depot had not finished making their weapons, so Emmet was forced to issue hourly instructions for them to continue getting the pikes and other arms ready. However this became almost impossible as there was a constant stream of people entering and leaving throughout the day and in the confusion little was done. Patrick Farrell, who had been captured the previous evening, was ordered to assist the men. He helped to fill the small bottles with gunpowder, so that they could be used as grenades, and was also involved in preparing the beams and the pikes.[37] Money shortages were debilitating, with 'scarcely any blunderbusses bought up': Emmet sent a message to Philip Long that £500 was necessary. Again there were problems and it was late in the evening before the money was secured; even then it is not clear if it ever reached Emmet.[38] The only money that Emmet had left out of his own fund was sixty guineas, not enough to buy sufficient weapons. He instructed George McDaniel to purchase some blunderbusses and he in turn paid a gunstocker from Nicholas Street called James Toler to secure two. McDaniel was satisfied with the weapons he brought back and asked him to get more, informing him that 'there was to be an insurrection on that night and that if Toler would not buy the blunderbusses he should be shot'.[39] Terrified, Toler insisted that he would 'act no further in it'. Not only a bully, McDaniel was also a rogue. When Emmet could find no one else to collect and pay for weapons he had ordered from a gunsmith on Dame Street, he dispatched McDaniel with the remainder of his sixty guineas. The unscrupulous McDaniel took the money and never returned.

Just as things were beginning to get desperate, at 5 o'clock Emmet finally received the necessary finance to proceed with his plans. This was probably the money from Long, or it may have come from another source. He immediately dispatched 'the trusty men of the depot, who alone knew the town' to 'buy up blunderbusses, for the people refused to act without some'.[40] They only managed to secure six.[41] The rebels also had two muskets which they had secured from two soldiers who deserted.[42] Meanwhile one of the conspirators had been given responsibility for preparing the special 'slow matches' or fuses for the rockets and other explosive weapons. Once again luck was not with Emmet and the man bungled the operation: he mixed the fuses that had been prepared with the ones that had not, and it was impossible to distinguish them. The combat rockets, perhaps the most innovative part of the rebellion, were now inoperable. Exasperated, Emmet admitted that 'all our labour went for nothing'. Worse news followed. The fuses for the grenades were lost by the same man, and when he went to search for them he could not find them in the crowd. Adding to the problems, the blacksmiths were unable to provide the cramp irons in time, and only a single scaling-ladder was completed. Though wearied by the mounting difficulties, Emmet refused to postpone the rising: as he later admitted, 'I expected the counties to act, and feared to lose the advantage of surprise.' In a frank assessment of what went wrong, he afterwards revealed:

> Had I another week — had I one thousand pounds — had I one thousand men, I would have feared nothing. There was redundancy enough in any one part to have made up, if complete, for deficiency in the rest, but there was failure in all — plan, preparation and men.

In a shrewd and thoughtful observation, Sarah Curran later blamed the failure of the rebellion on 'barbarous desertion and want of unanimity'.[43]

One characteristic of great generals is an ability to remain calm in the face of apparent disaster. For E. L. Muson leadership is essentially 'the creative and directive force of morale'.[44] On the night of 23 July, with his plans in tatters, Robert Emmet displayed ice-cool nerve. He never lost control of his emotions and at all times maintained an outward air of confidence and determination. Bernard Duggan studied him carefully during the day (until 7 p.m.), anxious to spot any tell-tale signs of weakness:

> At all times Mr Emmet seemed cool, tranquil, and determined . . . He appeared to be confident of success; he was never light or thoughtless in his manner, nor absent nor agitated in his mind. He talked familiarly with the men, but still with something of seriousness — nothing of jocularity.[45]

Only twenty-five years old, Emmet acted with a maturity beyond his years. With a firm control of his emotions, he displayed remarkable composure and never let any difficulty shake his resolve. He chatted to the men, encouraging them, but never joked or compromised his leadership position. Because of this, 'the people had great confidence in him; they would venture their lives for him'.[46]

A little after 6 p.m. he had a second meeting with his officers. Again they were of the same opinion, that the rebellion should be aborted.[47] As the general in command of the district it fell to Emmet to make the fateful command decision. He gave the order to strike at 11 p.m.

At 6 o'clock Major General Sir Charles Asgill, the commander of the district in Dublin, arrived at the Castle. It was four hours since he had been sent for by Marsden, but his presence helped the civil authorities formulate a coherent response to the crisis. Assisted by Major Swan and Colonel Finlay, Marsden and Asgill discussed the disturbing reports which were still coming in from all parts of the city. Then Asgill set out for the Royal Hospital in Kilmainham at 7 o'clock to discuss these events with the commander-of-the-forces. Several magistrates and captains of yeomanry kept arriving at the Castle to await instructions, but it was 'thought prudent to restrain the yeomen from assembling their men and, by their so doing, increasing the alarm'.[48] There was a faulty logic to this reasoning. Marsden was still convinced that Fox had spent the afternoon issuing orders for the soldiers in the barracks and at the various posts. Because of Fox's dislike of the yeomanry they had no weapons: he had confiscated them a few weeks earlier.[49] The garrison of Dublin consisted of 3,000 men, and Marsden believed that this was sufficient to quell any rising, especially if they were ready to act 'on the first intelligence of the assembling of the mob'.[50] Thanks to Fox however the army was still unaware that anything was amiss in the city.

Between 6 and 9 o'clock the rebels gathered at the Marshalsea Lane depot to receive their orders. The plan was for the men to be armed after everyone had assembled. Emmet would then lead an assault on Dublin Castle one hour before midnight. The wait was for Henry Howley, who had gone off to bring six double carriages to the depot. These carriages were central to the plan. The drivers would be dressed in fine liveries and the coaches would be filled with some of the leading rebels, including Emmet himself, all armed with blunderbusses. Using subterfuge, they would attempt to gain entrance to Dublin Castle by pretending they were all going to a party and, once inside, they would seize the courtyard. Simultaneously men would storm the main gate of the Castle and in the confusion other rebels would break through a wall on Ship Street and sneak inside to aid the attack; houses had been secured on the street for this purpose. Emmet intended to capture the privy council which, he had learned through 'private information', would be sitting that evening.[51] At about 7 o'clock Emmet received word that Edward Clarke from Palmerstown had set out for the Castle with further intelligence about his workers' movements. This could not be allowed, so Emmet instructed his trusted aide, Bernard Duggan, to intercept him. Duggan set out with some men and established check-points on all the likely routes to the Castle and the Royal Hospital.[52] Miles Byrne was still at Denis Redmond's house on Coal Quay waiting for the Wexford and Wicklow men to arrive. Afterwards Byrne would reassure Emmet that the 300 Wexford rebels turned up and by 8 o'clock formed a considerable group. He insisted that he began distributing the pikes to the men and waited patiently for the signal from the coaches before he marched on the Castle.[53] But the government reports directly contradict Byrne's account. When its agents searched Redmond's house they discovered that 'not one of the pikes . . . had been used' and were still in their hiding place.[54] When Emmet was told this he refused to believe that Byrne had lied to him. But when he was reminded that 'he had been grossly imposed on in many other instances', he admitted that 'he had in many other instances been most cruelly deceived'.

As daylight faded on the evening of 23 July, Emmet waited for the rebels to arrive at the main depot. To ensure they were properly fed before setting out to fight he had arranged for 240 loaves of bread to be freshly made in the ovens at his disposal.[55] He expected 2,000 men to appear. Eighty turned up. Worse, before assembling, most of them had been to the Yellow Bottle public house on Thomas Street, run by John Rourke, where they had been 'drinking and smoking, in the highest spirits, cracking jokes, and bantering one another, as if the business they were about to enter on was a party of pleasure'. Despair set in and Emmet was 'quite mortified' that the support he had been promised had not materialised.[56] The other leaders, including William Dowdall, assembled at John Hevey's house at 41 Thomas Court where, Madden discreetly mentions, 'refreshments were not wanting'.[57] Emmet gave the order to begin distributing the weapons, which were tied in bundles, to the men. The eighteen blunderbusses, four muskets and large numbers of pikes were passed around as he got ready to lead his ragged group on to Thomas Street. There was only one sword which was retained by Emmet. Messengers kept running back and forth between Hevey's house and the depot, carrying news and orders, but few it seems were taking the evening seriously. Shortly before 9 o'clock their complacency was shattered.

THE FOG OF WAR

With so many people gathering around the lanes off Thomas Street, the police became suspicious. The chief peace officer of the workhouse division, Edward Wilson, who had investigated the explosion at the Patrick Street depot the previous week, learned at 6 o'clock that riots were expected in the evening. Perturbed, he sent an order for the other officers to meet him at the watch house on Vicar Street, which ran on to Thomas Street near the Market House.[58] Also reconnoitring the area were three other police officers, including Oliver Carleton, the high constable of the watch. On the night of 23 July he was the acting head of the police, as the superintendent magistrate, Alderman William Alexander, had 'irresponsibly decided to absent himself from Dublin'.[59] It seems that once Alexander had briefed Carleton about the danger facing the city that night, he then made sure to get as far away as possible.[60] Carleton at least was no lightweight. He was an experienced campaigner; indeed five years earlier he had been the officer who arrested Thomas Addis Emmet. Upon

A pencil sketch of Robert Emmet made in 1802.

The west front of Trinity College in the late eighteenth century.

ROBERT EMMET

MICHAEL DWYER.

LORD EDWARD FITZGERALD.

THEOBALD WOLFE TONE.

JAMES NAPPER TANDY.

HENRY JOY McCRACKEN.

THE PATRIOTS OF '98.

[COPYRIGHT.] Published by BERNARD DOYLE, Franklin Printing Works, 9 Upper Ormond Quay, DUBLIN.

A nineteenth-century remembrance of the patriots of 1798, showing Wolfe Tone in the centre and Emmet at top left. The others shown (in clockwise order) are Michael Dwyer, Lord Edward Fitzgerald, Henry Joy McCracken and James Napper Tandy.

COLLEGE LIBRARY, DUBLIN.

The long room of Trinity College Library as it was in Emmet's day. The ceiling shown here was replaced in the mid nineteenth century by the more dramatic barrel vault that one can see today.

Thomas Addis Emmet.

A nineteenth-century view of the Upper Castle Yard in Dublin Castle.

John Philpot Curran.

College Green showing Daly's Club, left foreground, and the Parliament House, left background, the statue of King William III in the centre and the front of Trinity College in the background.

A view of the Wicklow Hills, where Emmet and his small band of followers fled after the failed rebellion in a desperate attempt to elude capture.

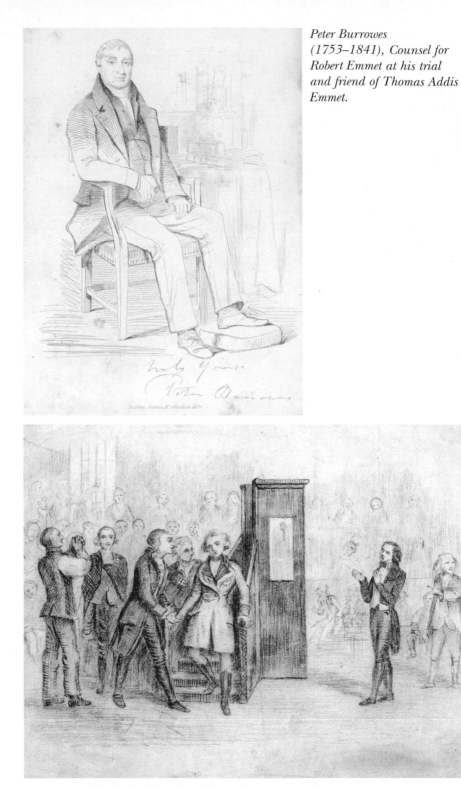

*Peter Burrowes
(1753–1841), Counsel for
Robert Emmet at his trial
and friend of Thomas Addis
Emmet.*

Robert Emmet in the dock.

A highly stylised nineteenth-century view of Emmet's speech.

Illustration from a broadside showing Emmet speaking at his trial.

Robert Emmet's execution.

arriving at the Market House he saw 'women with bundles of pikes laying them down in the near corner'.[61] When he went closer to investigate he 'saw several men pass by me with pikes on their shoulders'. The peace officers, Shee and Wilkinson, urged him to retreat, but he held his nerve and kept going. Unfortunately one of the rebels recognised his colleague and shouted 'There is bloody Shee.' In the pandemonium Carleton narrowly escaped.

A short time later at the watch house, Wilson had formed a party of a dozen men, half of whom were carrying pistols; he himself wore a pair of pistols and a sword. After checking that everyone's weapons were loaded, he set out with them to patrol the city. They did not have to go far. When Wilson looked down Dirty Lane (the popular name for Bridgefoot Street), he noticed a group of men wearing grey frieze-coats acting suspiciously by the fountain and decided to investigate. Calling on them to disperse or be taken into custody, he began to pursue the men down the street. As he passed a public house he noticed an armed man rushing out and shoved him aggressively back inside. Wilson knew the landlady well, having fined her for serving after-hours in more peaceful times, and ordered her to shut the door. Once this was done he resumed the chase, closely followed by his colleagues, and turned the corner on to Marshal Lane at full pace. He ran right into a column of pikemen. To his 'utter astonishment' he was now confronted by a large number of dangerous men marching aggressively towards him. Too close to the rebels to turn and run, Wilson was forced to stay and fight. Drawing a pistol, he challenged the men to lay down their arms or he would shoot. Caught by surprise, some of the rebels placed their weapons against the nearest wall. But one tall well-dressed man, 'muffled up with a great coat to his chin', refused to be intimidated and lunged at Wilson with his pike.[62] Struck in the belly, Wilson aimed his pistol at his opponent's chest and fired. The rebel was dead before he hit the ground. Seriously injured, Wilson also collapsed. By his own admission he 'bled immensely' and was convinced that he was fatally wounded. The peace officers rushed to his side and prepared to fight. The noise had alerted Emmet, however, and he went outside and began shouting instructions to the pikemen.[63] In a skilful manoeuvre the rebels suddenly parted to the right and to the left to allow 'some men in the rear to fire'. One of the watchmen was shot dead. The others returned fire with their pistols and, as the smoke cleared, dragged Wilson to safety. They escaped to Thomas Street where they were not pursued. The first shots had been fired in the 1803 rebellion.

With his hand pressed against his bleeding stomach, Wilson made his way to the guard-house at the Coombe, where he raised the alarm and took the opportunity to reload. There his wound was treated, but he refused to remain inside to recuperate. He was terrified that he would 'be taken in bed' and 'continued on duty the whole night'.

Realising he could not fight the rebels without reinforcements, Oliver Carleton rushed to Dublin Castle. He demanded entrance but was refused until Major Swan agreed to let him through. Major Sirr, who was also on duty, was not pleased to see Carleton and told him abruptly, 'Sir, you can't get a party [of troops] here.'[64] Because Swan and Sirr were appointees of the Castle and Carleton was a corporation official, the lines of command were compli-cated by party factions and a large degree of tension existed between them. Therefore, despite what was happening, Sirr refused to allow Carleton to take some soldiers to fight the rebels and told him to go instead to the barracks. This was impossible, as the route was blocked, and Carleton became increas-ingly agitated. He told Sirr that he 'had always trusted him as a gentleman' but now scorned him for remaining inside where 'he was safe with his army and palisades to protect him'. Leaving the Castle, still seething from his treatment, Carleton made his way to Alderman Exshaw at the Exchange and told him what he had witnessed on Thomas Street. Exshaw replied that he had no ammunition. Beginning to despair, Carleton informed him that if he did not get some 'he would be annihilated in five minutes'.

The activities of the police created panic in the depot. Michael Quigley, Emmet's trusted lieutenant, lost his nerve and concluded that the conspiracy had been exposed. Raising the alarm, he shouted: 'We are lost, the army is coming on us!' Only Robert Emmet remained calm. Walking to one of the desks, which had a secret compartment, he took out his green military uni-form and began getting dressed.[65] First he put on 'a white waistcoat and white pantaloons', his sash and a pair of new black boots. Over this came the green military jacket, which had gold lace on the sleeves and several 'gold epaulettes like a general's dress'. Then he added his sword, a pair of pistols and a large cocked hat with a feather in it. Once he was dressed he asked for a greatcoat, which he said was to 'disguise his uniform till he went to the party that was to attack the Castle'. For whatever reason he was not given one, however, and he wore nothing over his uniform that night.[66] Quigley and Stafford were also in uniform; these were identical except they had only one epaulette each, the for-mer with a white feather on his hat, the latter with a green one. While getting ready it seems that Emmet gave the order to fire one signal rocket, although there is some confusion about this.[67] Expecting an attack at any moment Emmet decided to fight on the streets rather than be trapped in the depot. There was no time to wait for the carriages. That part of the plan had to be abandoned like so much else. Even the twelve baskets of bread with twenty loaves in each went uneaten. As Emmet later admitted, 'there was no mistake in the night settled for the rising in Dublin, the mistake was in the hour; it was not intended for two hours after it happened'.[68] Reflecting on the decision Emmet made to continue with the rebellion, Madden later recorded: 'Then it was that Robert Emmet determined to meet his death in the street, rather than wait to be cooped up with his followers in his den, and [be] massacred there or captured.' When he reached the door of the depot Emmet drew his sword and shouted a rallying cry to his men, 'Come on boys!'[69] With a characteristic blend of bravery and foolhardiness, he marched out on to Thomas Street, impatient to meet his destiny.

At almost the exact same moment Edward Clarke was completing his second report of the day to Alexander Marsden. Accompanied by Richard Wilcock, another magistrate from Palmerstown, he had avoided the ambushes prepared by Bernard Duggan and had arrived safely at the Castle. He revealed that 'a party is coming from Lucan' to take part in a rising and was disgusted to report that his workmen 'had appeared dressed in their best clothes, and [were] preparing to go out'.[70] Finishing his report at 9 p.m., Clarke then set out for home on horseback with Wilcock. This time they went the wrong way and at the corner of Lincoln Lane, as they turned on to Arran Quay, they encountered Duggan and his men.[71] 'You bloody villains,' shouted Duggan, 'where have you been? What brought you here?'[72] Armed with a blunderbuss, he opened fire on Clarke, seriously injuring him. Duggan's weapon however was unreliable: it burst in his hands after firing and he screamed that he was wounded. His blood was still on the street the next day. Three other men fired on Clarke, missing, as his horse took off with him to safety. The rebels ran away. Some people who were passing came to Clarke's aid and helped him off his horse. He returned to the Castle where his wounds were tended; 'thirteen slugs' had to be taken out of his side and shoulder, and his nose was broken.[73] He had the satisfaction of learning that a reward of £300 would be given to the man who captured his would-be assassin.[74] Lord Norbury later praised his vigilance and told him that he had 'proved himself as great a lover of your country as ever I met with in the world'.[75]

By now Robert Emmet had led his band of rebels on to Thomas Street but they were making slow progress. Hardly an impressive sight, the eighty men were drunk, disorganised and completely lacking in discipline. As Madden later discovered, 'The motley assemblage of armed men, a great number of whom were, if not intoxicated, under the evident excitement of drink, marched along Thomas Street . . . with their ill-fated leader at their head, who was endeavouring to maintain order.'[76] Immediately the rebels began firing their weapons at lamps and any other target which presented itself, and whatever measure of control Emmet might have had quickly disintegrated. Stafford and Emmet led from the front, with Quigley attempting to maintain order from the rear, and there soon developed 'a considerable distance' between the front ranks and the mob behind. Giving up on the men, Quigley rushed forward to rejoin Emmet and his advance guard. William Dowdall was nowhere to be seen. He had remained drinking at Hevey's house and played no part in the events which followed. Miles Byrne was later disgusted to learn this, although it was a measure of Emmet's magnanimous nature that he never once blamed Dowdall or the other men. But for Byrne, their inaction was unforgivable: he was convinced that their presence 'might have preserved discipline and prevented the disasters and false alarm which produced such bad effects on the men in Thomas Street'.[77] He was particularly scathing of Dowdall, insisting that he should have come at once to Robert Emmet's assistance at this critical moment, he being his confidant and intimate all the time they were at Butterfield Lane. He could have no excuse to offer for his conduct on this occasion.[78]

John Hevey, at least, joined Emmet and became part of his advance guard. Also in this group were six Kildaremen who had not lost faith in Emmet or the plan for the rebellion: these were Thomas Wylde, John Peppard, John Mahon, Charles Keane and the brothers William and John Perrot.

Waiting at his house on 64 Plunket Street for the signal to attack was Owen Kirwan, a tailor, and about ten rebels. Apparently he saw the rocket that had been fired and shouted 'There is the signal my boys, give me my green coat.' The men who had been drinking in the house for some time immediately went to fetch their pikes. After getting ready they marched to Thomas Street, with Kirwan rallying his small command with increasing levels of enthusiasm: 'Turn out my lads, every man take a pike; this town is our own this night. God's blood! Turn out, the town is our own this night'.[79] One eye-witness, Benjamin Adams, a neighbour on Plunket Street, claimed at Kirwan's trial that he threatened people with death on Thomas Street unless they took part in the rebellion. He was quoted as shouting: 'Every man that does not turn out this night, shall surely be put to death tomorrow.' But John Philpot Curran ruthlessly destroyed Adams's credibility as a witness. Under cross-examination Adams was forced to admit that his wife had left him a year and a half previously, after spending the night with Kirwan. Adams pretended he was not angry about this, insisting that he was still on good terms with his wife, even though they were no longer living together. Few were convinced. As Kirwan and his men went back and forth from Plunket Street to Thomas Street they were joined by other rebels; Mrs Kirwan provided glasses of porter to slake their thirst.

The route to Dublin Castle which Emmet had chosen was one which avoided any army barracks and involved heading on to Francis Street and then through Plunket Street on to Patrick Street. A dragoon had the misfortune to pass through Thomas Street on his way to deliver a report and was fired upon and then piked to death.[80] Emmet heard the fateful shots but he 'did not think it right or prudent to turn back'. Elsewhere the carriages never reached the depot. Henry Howley did his best to bring them through, but he ran into trouble when he crossed the Queen's Bridge. A rebel from one of the counties was brawling with a soldier and Howley became so excited that he jumped out of the carriage and foolishly shouted, 'Fair play to the countryman.' This brought him to the attention of Lieutenant Colonel Browne of the 21st regiment who was on his way to his barracks at James's Street. He drew his sword and challenged Howley to explain himself. Losing his nerve, Howley panicked and grabbed his pistol. He fired at Browne, killing him instantly, but then abandoned the coach and ran away.[81] It marked the end of his involvement in the affair.

Still General Fox refused to believe that anything was wrong. Sir Charles Asgill arrived at the Royal Hospital after 7 o'clock and did his best to persuade him to order the soldiers out on to the streets. Again Fox vacillated and refused to accept that the capital was in danger. He informed Asgill that while Marsden was convinced something was afoot, he for his part 'cannot give much credit to it. . . . It is almost impossible such an event could take place in Dublin.'[82] Sir Charles was less sanguine: 'I have been in Ireland during the whole of the late rebellion and I have seen very extraordinary things happen, so that it is best to be on the alert and prepared for everything.' A little before 9 o'clock Fox decided to send Asgill back to Dublin Castle to learn if Marsden had any further information. He set out on horseback and decided to take the most direct route, via Thomas Street.

Colonel Thomas Spencer Vassal also had an appointment to keep. Earlier in the day Fox had asked him to report at 9.15 p.m. to the Royal Hospital and he made his way on horseback from the barracks. He rode right into the mob. Fortunately for him some of the 21st regiment came out of their barracks and a mêlée ensued. It was at this point that Asgill came upon the mob from behind. Horrified to discover a large group of pikemen marching through the city, he attempted to escape detection but it was too late. The rebels began firing at him and he was forced to flee back to the Royal Hospital with Colonel Vassal at his side. They rode abreast, drawing their swords to fight if necessary, and galloped to safety.[83] Narrowly escaping with his life, Asgill brought this damning proof of a rebellion back to the commander-of-the-forces. When Fox heard the report he rose very quickly, plainly agitated. He went to get his sword and gave orders for Asgill to make his way by a different route to the Royal Barracks, promising that he would follow immediately. Lieutenant Colonel Beckwith, the military secretary in Ireland, was also given orders to raise his horse guards and join him there. However, although Asgill arrived safely at the barracks, he discovered to his horror that he could not mobilise the army. The order had to come from Fox, and as the hours passed he still did not arrive. Worse, Beckwith decided to remain at the Royal Hospital in case it was attacked and countermanded the order that had been given to his horse guards.[84] In a critical breaking of the chain of command, he neglected to send a dispatch to Asgill informing him of this decision; thus the general waited in vain for their arrival wondering what had happened.

It was now twilight. Emmet marched his small advance group of only about a dozen men from Francis Street, through Plunket Street and on to Patrick Street. There he stopped to address the people: 'Turn out my boys, now is your time for liberty! Liberty, my boys — now turn out!'[85] Firing his pistol in the air, Emmet attempted to rally supporters to his cause. It had little effect, although his flamboyant outfit — the cocked hat, large feather, and green general's uniform — left an enduring impression on the shopkeepers. One sharp victualler noted that 'his dress was most suspect'. It was probably at this point that Emmet admitted to himself that his plan had failed. The truth had been evident since leaving Thomas Street, but he had clung to the idea of winning an unlikely victory. Now he recognised that there were only two options: stay, fight and die, or abort the entire project and escape to safety. There was nothing in Emmet's character which found the idea of a heroic sacrifice attractive. He was still only twenty-five years old and had gained valuable experience in planning a campaign and leading men in battle. True, it had ended disastrously, but there was plenty of time to analyse what had gone wrong, study Templehoff further and learn for the future. And it was with the future in mind that he gave the order to cancel the attack on the Castle. He later admitted, 'I would have given it [the night] the respectability of insurrection, but I did not wish uselessly to shed blood. I gave no signal for the rest, and they all escaped.'[86] Gathering his men, he headed south to seek refuge at Rathfarnham and then head for the Wicklow mountains. A section of the rowdy mob followed soon after. They had stopped to break every lamp on the way, and when they arrived on Patrick Street they gave 'a most savage yell and demanded to know which way the former party went'.[87] They waved their long pikes menacingly in the street, then headed back for Thomas Street. What had begun as an attempted *coup d'état* now degenerated into a vicious riot on the streets of Dublin.

With the loss of 'the generals in green', the mob was left without a leader.[88] Up stepped the surly James Bannon, a former soldier in the British army, who was wearing a distinctive scarlet coat. Attempting to rally the men, he urged them to continue in their plan to attack the Castle. It was now 9.45 p.m. The government later conceded that 'all the atrocities that were committed were the acts of the mob that remained behind with the blunderbusses and pikes in their hands with no-one to lead them but the soldier [in the red coat] I have mentioned'.[89] One of the first victims of its frenzy was a Mr Cole who was travelling from the Custom House in a hackney coach. The mob dragged him from the carriage and threw him to his knees. Ignoring his pleas for mercy, one of the rebels 'gave him a frightful pike wound in the groin'.[90] The worst atrocity was still to happen. Coming along Thomas Street, at the corner of Vicar Street, was a second carriage with a more distinguished occupant, Lord Kilwarden, one of the privy councillors. Kilwarden was travelling to the Castle, having heard the reports of trouble, and was accompanied by his daughter and his nephew, the Rev. Richard Straubenzie Wolfe. In the 1790s Kilwarden (then simply Arthur Wolfe) had been attorney general and had helped Wolfe Tone avoid prosecution in 1794. But any past services to dead heroes cut little favour with the mob. Ignoring the warnings of some onlookers to turn back, Kilwarden's driver, Thomas Moorehead, continued foolishly on his journey. Meanwhile the injured Mr Cole took advantage of the confusion and escaped to the Vicar Street watch house. The mob descended on the carriage, rattling their pikes against the door. The sixty-four year old Kilwarden refused to open the door, but he was dragged from his seat and a rebel plunged his pike into his stomach. Mortally wounded, he fell to the ground as other men joined in the attack, 'fighting to see who would get most blows at him'.[91] His nephew attempted to run to safety, but he was cut down and killed before he could get far. Only Kilwarden's daughter survived unscathed; a man 'rushed forward, took her from the carriage, and led her through the rabble to an adjoining house'.[92] David Fitzgerald, one of the young rebels, later insisted that the man was Robert Emmet, but by this time Emmet was already some distance away. It was over an hour before Kilwarden's body was discovered. According to Major Swan, he was still breathing although only just. Deeply moved, Swan later provided a transcript of Kilwarden's final conversation.

> *Swan*: My dear sir, I am heartily grieved to see you in this situation. Do you know me?
> *Kilwarden*: Swan.
> *Swan*: It will give you consolation to know that your daughter is perfectly safe.
> *Kilwarden*: Where is she?
> *Swan*: In the Castle.
> *Kilwarden*: I thank God.

At this point somebody arrived with information: 'We have taken four of the villains. What is to be done with them?' Swan's response was uncompromising: 'Executed immediately.' Upon hearing this Kilwarden endeavoured to stretch out his hand and said faintly, 'Oh no, Swan, let the poor wretches at least have a fair trial.'[93] Then he died.

Robert Emmet was horrified to discover some days later that Kilwarden had been murdered. He was disgusted by the atrocities and the fact that the rebels had blatantly ignored the military instructions of the provisional government. At his trial he had his lawyers quote the section: 'We will not imitate you in cruelty; we will put no man to death in cold blood.' But on the night of 23 July no one remembered the proclamation and Emmet's injunction that 'whosoever shall put another person to death, except in battle, without a fair trial by his country, is guilty of murder' went unheeded. The murder of Kilwarden and his nephew also shocked the political elite in Dublin. But some seized the opportunity for advancement. Kilwarden's nephew, the Rev. Richard Wolfe, rector of Kilbeggan, Co. Westmeath, had been promoted to the prebend of Ticolme and the rectory of Temple Peter after the passing of the union as a reward for his uncle's loyal support. These now fell vacant, and with unseemly haste the provost of Trinity College Dublin, Dr John Kearney, applied to the Castle on 24 July for his son to succeed in his place.[94]

Joining James Bannon at the head of the mob was Felix Rourke, the brother of the proprietor of the Yellow Bottle. Assuming a leadership role, he was called at various times in the night Captain Rourke, Colonel Rourke and even General Rourke. By now the rebels were well spread out across Thomas Street, with some on James's Street, others down Dirty Lane and a few as far as Plunket Street. There was no organisation or coherence to their movements and many began to panic. One man informed Bannon that because the groups were so far apart 'They will be cut off by the damned army.'[95] Emboldened by his newly acquired power, Bannon cut him short: 'Damn that army. We are not afraid of them. We will fight them.' But others were still concerned and wanted the men in the rear to rejoin the main group. However with a confident swagger Bannon insisted that 'They would march up to the Castle. The town would be their own in half an hour.' The rebel group had now grown in size, with some recruits press-ganged into joining and others enlisting for the adventure. John Killen and John McCann were two of the men caught up in the action. Both were publicans. Killen kept a tavern on Thomas Street near James's Street and was known popularly as 'the husband of the dirty cook'; McCann had an alehouse on Dirty Lane. Killen was given a pike and McCann a blunderbuss and they were issued instructions by Rourke. As they headed down Dirty Lane they came upon two wounded men. Rourke ordered their deaths: 'Do your duty and free your country. Pike these wounded men that make a noise.'[96] Killen impaled one of the men and McCann fired at the other at point-blank range. Having proven themselves to Rourke, Killen told him that the 'business is done'.[97] Drums began beating in a call to arms across the city. Michael Mahaffy, a pedlar and con artist, walked into the middle of the mob. He was spotted by Rourke, given a pike and told, 'Do your duty and free your country.'[98] He later claimed at Rourke's trial that he was told repeatedly to go down Dirty Lane: 'Go . . . or if you do not, I will blow your brains out.' But Mahaffy was a scoundrel and a trickster, famous for his cups-and-ball scam, and his testimony was unreliable. However his partner-in-crime, John Ryan, also became involved in the rebellion and testified that when Mahaffy went down Dirty Lane he was so overcome with fear that he began vomiting against a wall.[99] Meanwhile Rourke began shouting, 'It is the Castle of Dublin we attack first!'[100]

As it happened the first real attack was made on the barracks in James's Street. A marauding group of rebels led by Edward Kearney attacked the 21st regiment there, but they never stood a chance. One daring soldier, noticing that Kearney was a distance ahead of his men, darted forward and took him prisoner.[101] Deprived of their leader, the rebels lost their nerve. The soldiers loaded their weapons and in rapid succession fired two volleys of musket-fire. Routing immediately, the rebels dropped their pikes, turned and ran.[102] Some of them fell and were captured. Felix Brady brought Kearney and twelve other prisoners he captured under armed guard to General Fox. Losing his nerve, Kearney threw himself on the ground and attempted to escape; he would have been shot by the soldiers only for Brady's intervention.[103] Afterwards Kearney protested his innocence and before his execution made a speech 'in a firm, manly voice, and with some degree of eloquence, [urging the people] to avoid drinking in public-houses, which he said had brought him to his untimely end'. Another attack was made on the Coombe Barracks but that too was easily repulsed. Lieutenant Felix Brady of the 21st regiment deserved much of the credit for suppressing the rebellion in the Liberties. Edward Wilson's watchmen had reported their concerns to him and he set out to inform his superior, Colonel Browne, of what was happening at about 9.30 p.m. He little suspected that Browne had become one of the first casualties of the rebellion. He raised about fifty men from the Cork Street barracks and took command of the crisis, sending men to different areas to deal with the rebels.[104] Elsewhere in the city other gangs had formed to join the fight. At Ballsbridge a unit of rebels assembled and issued pikes to anyone who passed, urging them to fight for their 'country and liberty'.[105] Again, captured prisoners subsequently claimed that they only took arms because they were told that anyone 'who refused to go shall be put to death'.

At 11 o'clock Marsden finally wrote to Lord Pelham to inform him that a rebellion had broken out. He admitted that he was 'much afflicted' to have to explain the circumstances, especially as the government had received warnings in advance. Nevertheless he insisted that 'such precautions were taken as the circumstances appeared to warrant' but that 'the mischievous disposition which prevails at present is beyond what was calculated upon'.[106] He also revealed that Kilwarden had been killed. A few hours later the government was relieved to discover that the attempts to seize the mail-coaches, the signal for a general insurrection, had been foiled.

It was only at midnight that the army was mobilised.[107] The rebellion was already three hours old, and fading fast. Wickham was later astonished to learn that 'two companies of infantry were all that were engaged with the rebels' and were 'found sufficient to defeat, and did actually put down the whole insurrection'.[108] But while Wickham tried his best to spin this as a good thing, the implication was far more disturbing. For it meant that while the capital was facing potential disaster, thanks to the breakdown in the civil and military command and the ineptitude of Fox, 'the rest of the garrison remain[ed] quietly in their quarters, not even put under orders'. It was fortunate for the government that the incompetence had not been limited to one side.

In the aftermath of the rebellion there was an immediate rush to find a scapegoat. The administration did not have to look far. Wickham arrived back in Dublin at the end of the month and was disgusted by the accounts of Fox's behaviour. In a confidential report to the prime minister he conceded that Fox was 'a soldier, a gentleman and a man of honour'.[109] But that was the extent of his praise. For he continued by saying, 'his health is bad, he is fitful and undecided in his opinions, and does not appear to me to have either body or mind equal to the present emergency'. Three days earlier he had been even more critical. He admitted that if he had been in Dublin on 24 July he would

unquestionably have advised the lord lieutenant on the Sunday morning to have suspended the commander-of-the-forces and requested his majesty's government to have ordered a court of enquiry into his conduct. It is terrible to reflect on what might probably have been the consequence of his neglect had the rebels been in greater force or shown more skill and resolution.[110] It was a far cry from Wickham's response in January when he discovered that Fox was going to be the new commander-of-the-forces: 'I know no man who I should wish to select in preference to General Fox.'[111] As Wickham explained to the prime minister, someone had to take the blame: 'There is no alternative: either the government or the commander-of-the-forces were deeply culpable.'

At around 11 o'clock on 23 July Robert Emmet and his small band arrived at Butterfield Lane. Anne Devlin was outside in the yard, having just sent off a horseman with a sack of ammunition and some bottles filled with gunpowder. Hearing the men moving in the dark she shouted, 'Who's there?'[112] Emmet replied, 'It's me, Anne.' Then she realised that the plan had failed. Angry and disappointed, she rebuked the men in uncompromising terms, 'Oh, bad welcome to you. Is the world lost by you, you cowards that you are, to lead the people to destruction, and then to leave them?' Patrick Pearse would later reflect on 'poor Emmet's reply': there was 'no word of blame for the traitors that had sold him, for the cravens that had abandoned him, for the fools that had bungled'.[113] There was just a 'halting, heartbroken exculpation, the only one he was able to make for himself'. 'Don't blame me,' Emmet said dejectedly, 'the fault is not mine.' The next evening he and his men made their escape to the Wicklow mountains.

8

THE PURSUIT OF ROBERT EMMET

~

'There is something vulgar in all success. The greatest men fail,
or seem to have failed.'
(Oscar Wilde on Charles Stewart Parnell)

Only a few miles from the urban centre of Dubin lay the rugged, savage wilderness of the Wicklow mountains. With its rich forests and steep glacial valleys its landscape offered a natural refuge for bandits and rebels. Fleeing there with his ragged and exhausted band, Emmet kept moving from place to place in a desperate attempt to avoid capture. One of the group, James Commons (also spelt Cummins) from Baltyboys, knew the area well, so the men decided to take shelter at John Doyle's home at Ballynameece near Ballinascorney, some eight miles from Dublin. They arrived at about 2 o'clock on the morning of Tuesday 26 July. Knocking loudly on the door to get the attention of the farmer, Commons begged to be allowed inside. Doyle roused himself from his drunken slumber and opened the door, but he grew apprehensive when thirteen men followed his neighbour inside. He became even more frightened when he saw that the group was heavily armed, and he kept repeating that he was very drunk; he thought it was some terrible dream and would 'scarce open his eyes'.[1] Doyle later testified that he had been drinking 'pretty heavily' and had gone to bed between 10 and 11 o'clock in the evening.[2] One man poured him a glass of spirits from the party's own supply to calm his nerves, but he refused to touch it.

Emmet and Quigley were introduced to Doyle as French officers and for the duration of their stay the former spoke in French and the latter in broken English. Doyle's son and namesake was also in bed and he got up to see what all the commotion was about. He watched as Emmet entered the house and heard the other men introduce him as 'a general'. Emmet spoke in a strange language and the younger Doyle could not understand what he said, as he had never heard anyone speak in the same manner but a French priest he once heard celebrate mass in Francis Street chapel, which made him suppose the general to be a Frenchman also.[3]

The rebels commandeered the house for the night. Lighting a candle, the young Doyle took Emmet to the main bedroom. There his father was pushed to the middle of the bed so he could not escape, and Emmet and Quigley went to sleep on either side of him. Quigley joked with the farmer about the novelty value of having 'a French general and French colonel' beside him, and bet that it was a new experience; Doyle later conceded that this 'was true enough'. One man remained outside during the night standing by the ditch to guard against the rebels being surprised. Emmet's companions were Michael Quigley, Nicholas Stafford, 'Big' Arthur Devlin, John Hevey, John O'Neill, a Wexford soldier called Byrne, James Commons, the Kildaremen Thomas Wylde, John Peppard, John Mahon and Charles Keane, and the brothers William and John Perrot.[4]

Terrified that he would be murdered in his bed, Doyle struggled to remain awake. At about 5 a.m. he decided that the men were fast asleep and slipped quietly out of his room. He was horrified to discover that the group had thirteen blunderbusses, a musket and some pistols. Unable to leave the house because of the sentry outside, Doyle was forced to stay put. At about 10 o'clock everyone gathered at the breakfast table to eat. Emmet was not fully dressed. It was warm inside and he did not put on his elegant military uniform. He looked unwell and spoke only in French. Two men kept a regular watch outside for any sign of trouble and the rest of the group spent the day sleeping in different rooms. Doyle was very curious about the young man whom the other rebels called 'General'. He seemed 'to be about twenty-seven years old, slender made, about five feet seven inches high, very swarthy and rather ill-looking, dark-brown hair, thin visage and small eyes'.[5] The other man, the colonel, was about six foot and 'strong and well-made'. The rebels waited in the house until twilight, when they could take advantage of the darkness to proceed with their journey.

At about 8 p.m. Emmet finally decided to get into uniform. He gave the order for the party to assemble and prepare to move out. For the first time Farmer Doyle got to examine his attire when sober and he noted that it was a dark green outfit with a quantity of gold lace and a remarkably large cocked hat with a very long feather. With a great sense of relief he watched as the men left in formation, turned at the hill and disappeared from sight. A few hours later, two men on a black horse called to the house and asked if the party had already gone to the Widow Bagnall's farm; John Doyle Jr reluctantly agreed to accompany them and give directions. The following morning his father discovered one of the small proclamations at the breakfast table and that evening he made a full report to John Robinson, the barony constable.[6] The next day,

Thursday 28 July, he brought Robinson the proclamation to examine. This intensified the search in the area as the net closed on Emmet and his party.

The Widow Bagnall's farm, about a mile away, was indeed the next destination of the rebels. Earlier that day Patrick Loughlin, a 'jobbing carpenter' who was helping the group, told her that she could probably expect a visit from certain men that evening. She asked if they were gentlemen and Loughlin replied that 'some of them appeared to be so'. He then described the leaders in green uniform and said they appeared to be Frenchmen. Rose Bagnall lived at the Breaks of Ballinascorney and owned a large amount of land which she sublet to tenant farmers. Heading for her house, Emmet asked directions from a man who was repairing a fence nearby.[7] He accompanied the party to the farm and then prepared to leave, but Emmet told him 'You must go with us.' The rebels first visited Michael McDonagh who lived next door to Mrs Bagnall. Some of the men quenched their thirst with alcohol that was provided, and this was followed by a supper of bread, bacon and milk. Emmet instructed two of the men, who were armed with pistols and blunderbusses, to stand guard in case the houses were raided during the night.

Still continuing in his guise as a French officer, Quigley only talked to the farmers in broken English. He comically told one of them that 'me can speak English as well as you'. The rebels were joined by the two men on the black horse during the evening, bringing their number up to sixteen.[8] Some of the group were still hungry and Emmet suggested a bit of cattle-rustling. However it was thought that it was too late to kill, cook and eat a bullock, so instead they went out to steal some sheep. A few of the rebels drove a herd into Bagnall's yard and a 'low sized man' killed two of them. One of the sheep was then boiled in the kitchen and the second was cooked in a pot on a camp fire the following morning.

During the day the local farmers listened intently to the conversations of the rebels. John Devine and Michael McDonagh both counted their number and calculated that there were either sixteen or seventeen men. They were alarmed by one man's bold assertion that the French had landed and found no comfort in his comment that it would be 'a folly for the people to be killing themselves any longer at their labour' and that if they joined the rebellion 'they would all soon be gentlemen'. Someone else told the farmers that they were veterans of 'the battle on the Saturday night before'. This prompted a bout of recriminations about the insurrection, with many of the rebels cursing 'the Dublin fellows for not assisting them'. They boasted that they would some day soon take the Castle, once the 'set of cowardly rascals' from the capital found some courage. Tempers were high and one man was so angry with the Dublin rebels that he suggested that the city should be set on fire as a punishment. Emmet spent the first night at Rose Bagnall's house and the second at Michael McDonagh's.[9] He learned that the Wicklowmen were still planning to rise, but he issued a countermanding order to prevent unnecessary violence. Anne Devlin and a sister of Thomas Wylde had a rendezvous with the rebels at a glen near the

Widow Bagnall's. They discovered Emmet and the other men sitting on the side of a hill, dirty and dejected.[10] Devlin had brought some letters from the other leaders and waited to bring back further instructions. But by this time Emmet had come to a decision. He resolved to quit the party and return to Dublin with Anne Devlin. According to one of his biographers, Emmet addressed his men for the last time with the words:

> Our plan was an excellent one; it failed owing to circumstances beyond our control, and impossible to foresee. Let us now part, gentlemen, and let each look to his own safety. I shall do the best I can to quit the country, in the hope of again meeting you under happier auspices.[11]

To make himself appear less conspicuous, he discarded his cocked hat and green general's jacket and borrowed a brown greatcoat from one of the men to wear over his white waistcoat and other clothes. Then he began the perilous journey back to Mrs Palmer's house at Harold's Cross, fully aware of the danger he faced.

The rest of the country soon returned to normality, although one observer claimed that 'a smothered war' persisted.[12] Despite the frantic efforts of Thomas Russell, the rebellion in the north had fizzled out without anything happening. As James Quinn has noted: 'It produced no pitched battles and no casualties . . . it may be that not a single shot was fired in anger.'[13] Russell's attempts to rally support in Antrim and Down had proved depressing failures, and his public addresses had been greeted with indifference. Baffled by the unwillingness of people to rise up in arms, he watched as the chosen date of 23 July passed without incident. The next day he posted a number of his own proclamations around Belfast which were very similar to Emmet's. They urged the people to be 'as just and humane as you are brave' and to 'rely with confidence that God, with whom is victory, will crown you with success'.[14] The government later noted with glee that 'every instance' where he 'endeavoured to collect a numerous meeting of the people . . . has totally failed'.[15] After learning of the collapse in Dublin, Russell retreated into his own world and convinced himself that his mission would still succeed and the millennial utopia would sweep aside British domination. His biographer has shown how his 'rigid millennialist convictions drove him steadily towards an inevitable martyrdom'.[16]

On 24 July the government issued a proclamation offering a reward of £1,000 sterling to anyone who gave information leading to the capture and conviction of the first three people involved in Kilwarden's murder.[17] A pardon was also offered to anyone who was involved in the rebellion, but not Kilwarden's death, if they helped the government find the men responsible. Robert Holmes was arrested by the government almost immediately. As Emmet's brother-in-law he was an obvious suspect, although it is not clear how complicit he was in the events of 23 July. He had been in London on business and only arrived back in Dublin the day after the rebellion. Apart from the fact that he had assisted Emmet with the legal paperwork to secure the depots, it seems he had little real involvement in what was being planned, although he was certainly sympathetic and supportive. He was imprisoned for a year but was eventually released because of the lack of evidence against him. Tragedy greeted him upon his return home. The health of his wife, Emmet's sister, had rapidly deteriorated during his imprisonment and she died after his release; a romantic tradition developed that she expired on the doorstep upon seeing him. It is likely that Robert Holmes would have defended Robert Emmet in September 1803 had he not been imprisoned. Certainly he would have been an effective counsel, but even his brilliant oratory would have been unable to secure a different result. In May 1848, when Holmes defended John Mitchel on a charge of treason, he delivered an emphatic closing address which created a sensation in the country. The trial itself had some associations with Emmet; the presiding judge was Thomas, now Baron Lefroy, who had once debated against him in Trinity, while John Mitchel was later described by W. B. Yeats as 'the greatest disciple of Emmet' in the nineteenth century.[18] Beginning his closing statement, Holmes declared that 'Ireland is an enslaved country' and revealed that it would be impossible to do justice to his client without first doing justice to Ireland.[19] To murmurs of applause from the courtroom he attacked the Act of Union and then made an impassioned defence of the right of the Irish people to rebel:

> I assert an enslaved people have the right, if driven to search a course by necessity, to seek a recourse to arms by necessity, to seek a recourse to arms to obtain their liberties, even at the hazard of life. I say life. What is life? What is life worth to any man without liberty?[20]

Holmes was a staunch protector of Emmet's reputation, and as the speech progressed he made implicit and explicit references to the events of 1803. His powerful rhetoric reverberated throughout the courtroom as he hammered home the point:

> Deep, deep, deep is the guilt of those who have made Irishmen slaves, and slaves' assassins, instead of leaving brave men free. Deep, deep, deep is the guilt of England, which, by an unprovoked and unjust invasion, obtained dominion in Ireland.[21]

In his peroration Holmes referred directly to the events of 1803 as he reminded his audience that, 'A Russell once bled on the scaffold; he bled in the cause of liberty. May his name be forever embalmed in the memory of the virtuous and the brave.'[22] Robert Emmet was not mentioned by name in the oration, but Robert Holmes sampled the famous speech from the dock in his conclusion and was clearly thinking about his relative's fate. The reference to his 'lamp of

life' was taken directly from Emmet's last oration and Holmes was either con-
sciously or unconsciously mirroring that speech in his own conclusion:

> Gentlemen of the jury, I speak not here for my client merely; I speak for you
> and your children, and your children's children. I speak not here for myself.
> My lamp of life is flickering, and must soon be extinguished; but were I now
> standing on the brink of the grave, and uttering the last words of expiring
> nature, I would say, 'My Ireland be happy; my Ireland be free.'

Despite these stirring words, Mitchel was none the less found guilty and sentenced to transportation. Years later he published his history of Ireland which
included a powerful tribute to Emmet. He wrote how 'The purity and elevation
of his motives have never been questioned, even by his enemies. His ardent
spirit . . . [attempted] to do at least what one man might, to rouse the people
for one more manly effort.'[23]

A number of the rebels were taken soon after the rebellion. Pat McCabe was
arrested on 24 July at the door of his house with a blunderbuss in his hands.[24]
He had little stomach for prison and soon cut a deal with the government. His
information helped implicate and convict many other rebels in the months
ahead. An Insurrection Act was passed on 29 July which gave the government
increased powers to make arrests and capture the leaders of the conspiracy.
Denis Lambert Redmond fled Dublin and went all the way to Newry before he
was captured. St John Mason was arrested in Nenagh as he travelled to either
Limerick or Kerry. On his person were discovered many letters, including one
ostensibly from a woman in London. It 'mentioned a longing till her nails
should grow so long as to tear flesh and draw blood, and in more than one
place expressed a wish to draw blood'. Rather than believe that the erotic,
sado-masochistic sentiments in the letter were genuine, the magistrates
concluded it was encrypted and the author was Robert Emmet.[25] Anonymous
tip-offs poured into the Castle, advising the authorities to search suspicious
areas; one barely literate note revealed the existence of the house at Coal Quay
and was signed, 'A frend who cant avow it.'[26]

Hugh Boyd McGuckian, Arthur O'Connor's agent, was also captured in the
wake of the rebellion.[27] Imprisoned for a time, it seems there were some legal
problems with the attempts to transport him and he was released. Travelling to
England he spent much time 'cultivating friends and assisting other measures'
to aid 'the French in case of invasion'.[28] Orders for his arrest were issued in
London and he was forced to flee the country on board a ship bound for
Norway. It stopped at Brest and from there McGuckian made his way to
Antwerp where he lost his possessions and was arrested. O'Connor was forced
to intervene on his behalf to secure his release.

Perhaps unsurprisingly the finger of suspicion was soon pointed at the
Catholic leaders in Ireland. Archbishop John Thomas Troy of Dublin was quick
to publish a pastoral letter condemning the rebellion, but the lord lieutenant

was not convinced by his protestations of Catholic loyalty; he dismissed the letter as 'the greatest piece of craft, dissimulation and hypocrisy' he had ever read. Hardwicke was adamant that Napoleon was scheming to conquer Ireland and install a Roman Catholic government, and was certain that the pope had 'given his sanction to the measure'.[29] There was little evidence for his paranoia except the strength of his own prejudices. John Keogh, the successful Catholic merchant, had his house raided by the police. His papers were seized and brought to Dublin Castle but were later returned unopened. Keogh declared his 'positive belief that the Roman Catholics as a body had no knowledge or concern in the conspiracy'.[30]

With almost universal criticism of his handling of the rebellion, General Fox began to buckle under the pressure. Steadily retreating into his own world, he insisted on taking command of the garrison of Dublin, 'to the astonishment of everyone', and refused to answer the requests to call to the Castle.[31] Those close to him refused to question his actions and he deluded himself that everything was fine.[32] In an almost deliberate attempt to cause offence, he forbade any soldier from wearing a side-arm when off duty, which increased the hostility towards him.[33] On the night of 17 August he had a heated altercation with Lieutenant Colonel Frederick Beckwith, the military secretary in Ireland. Beckwith was so upset that he immediately wrote to Wickham, his childhood friend, at 10 p.m. seeking advice on what to do next. He revealed that he had been spoken to that night 'in a way which during twenty-four years of service I have never experienced'.[34] He decided to resign unless Wickham could assure him that Fox would soon be relieved from his position. It became inevitable that Fox would be replaced. One alternative (and Wickham's own choice) was Lord Cornwallis, who had been sent to Ireland in 1798 to quell that rebellion, but he was unpopular in some quarters because of his leniency towards the Catholics. In October it was decided to send Lord Cathcart and Wickham was delighted because of his reputation as a 'good officer'. He underlined the point by adding, 'Believe me, that is all we want here.'[35]

Rather than close ranks, some leading establishment figures only reopened old wounds after the rebellion. John Foster, the final Speaker of the Irish House of Commons, was furious at the mismanagement of events in Ireland and added his considerable weight to the chorus of criticisms. He privately censured the administration for discrediting 'every information which poured in upon them', but praised the much maligned yeomanry for saving 'the city and perhaps the kingdom'.[36] He was astonished that Fox could have stayed in his apartment for so long, oblivious to the noise of men firing weapons only a short distance away. Spencer Perceval was also outraged by 'the negligence of the Irish government in letting itself be surprised' and added that 'if it were *not* surprised' then it was even more culpable for 'not having taken greater precautions'.[37] The chief secretary did not escape criticism. The Irish chancellor of the exchequer, Isaac Corry, began briefing against him; it seems he resented his status and considered him a rival for power. The Speaker of the British

House of Commons was also angry with Wickham and jealous of the fact that the Irish regarded him so highly. Others that were hostile included Lord Hobart and his father-in-law, Lord Auckland; both were former chief secretaries for Ireland and had their own narrow ideas about how the country should be governed.[38] Even Lord Castlereagh was alarmed by the incompetence that had taken place in Ireland and was irritated because he could not 'see the change which his own great measure, the union, has effected in Ireland'. Commenting on all of these squabbles, Lord Redesdale, the Irish lord chancellor, concluded that Castlereagh was 'only mistaken', but that the others had 'selfish or mischievous views'. Nevertheless he noted acidly that Castlereagh's father 'had all the meanness of a pettifogging attorney' and that the son had 'not quite rid himself of early impressions'. With all the in-fighting that was taking place, Redesdale threw his hands up in the air and despaired about how 'little miserable piques and resentments, interested views of individuals, and often of the most contemptible individuals' could 'decide the fate of nations'.

Making his way back to Harold's Cross, Emmet left Anne Devlin at Rathfarnham and arrived safely at Mrs Palmer's house on Saturday 30 July. It was just seven days after the abortive rebellion. Returning to his old alias of Hewitt, he lived in the parlour and began contacting the other rebel leaders. On his second day back in Dublin he talked to Miles Byrne for the last time. As Byrne later recorded: 'He seemed much affected and cast down' and it was a 'melancholy interview'. 'Overwhelmed by sorrow', Emmet explained the reasons why he had not made it to Coal Quay on the night of 23 July, and Byrne assured him that he was waiting there with the armed Wexford men ready to strike. Magnanimously, Emmet did not blame any of the other leaders for what had happened.[39] He was anxious to send a messenger to his brother in Paris and entrusted Byrne with this responsibility. Finding a ship to Bordeaux, Byrne left the country taking Emmet's seal-ring with him as a proof of his credentials.

At the beginning of August Anne Devlin called to visit Emmet and was given a letter to bring to Sarah Curran. He also sent word that he was safe to his anxious mother, who urged him to leave Ireland for ever. All this time Emmet wrote using different styles of handwriting to confuse the authorities if his letters were intercepted. As the Priory was only a short distance away, Sarah Curran was able to visit him at a pre-arranged meeting place, and she often walked to Harold's Cross to see him. To cheer him up she wrote him love poems which she initialled 'SC' at the bottom. These letters comforted Emmet immensely and his spirits revived whenever he received 'her handy work'.[40] Sarah also gave him a few strands of her hair which he sewed on to the black stock around his neck. But privately she was filled with anxiety and had nightmares whenever she went to bed. Although Anne Devlin remained at Butterfield Lane, she called to Harold's Cross often, acting as confidential messenger for the correspondence between the two lovers.[41] His letters were destroyed in the raid on the Priory, but two copies of Sarah's are extant. They were almost certainly written between 17 and 24 August.

Despite the great danger which was attached to any communication, Sarah could not stop herself writing. As she confessed to him, she 'knew so well by experience the pleasure of hearing in any way from a friend, that I have not resolution to deny it to you, while I have it in my power'.[42] For her part, she was greatly relieved to receive regular letters from her love, as it meant that he was still safe. Emmet took great pains to set her mind at rest. His letters were written as if he had not a care in the world and his humorous anecdotes were highly effective in easing her worries. As she told him,

> I feel myself cheered even by the sight of your handwriting, and find more consolation from your letters than from any effort of reason on my mind. Your last, particularly, made me quite happy when I received it. You know I can laugh at the worst of times.

'New causes for anxiety' had restored her nervousness, however. A friend was returning from England and she was uncertain about whether or not to tell him about her involvement with Emmet. She feared that she 'shall not have the magnanimity of mind enough to abide by the consequences of the conduct I have chosen'.

As daily reports of the arrest of the rebels reached the Priory, Sarah became increasingly concerned for Robert's safety. She told him that she longed 'to hear from you again' and hoped that Anne Devlin 'will have a letter if she comes this day'. Gently, Sarah asked him to destroy her previous letter, adding mischievously, 'at all events, you ought to be tired of it by this time'. She hated making this demand and admitted, 'I know I should find some difficulty in complying with such a request from you.' In fact she so enjoyed his last letter that she said she would not give it up for all the others. But she warned him, 'Do not let this be any encouragement to you.' She was well aware that he would be reluctant to do as she asked and she joked about his disobedience: 'Indeed, I see plainly you are turning out a rebel on my hands.' Then she teased him that if she caught him with copies of her letters or 'handy work, as you call it, it should be anything but a moment of delight to you'.

Emmet had attempted to shield Sarah Curran from what had happened and had not told her all the details of the rebellion. This drew a playful rebuke. She revealed that she 'had heard a great many things lately which in your great wisdom you would not tell me of, which adds to my resentment'. Therefore she longed to see him again 'for the purpose of mortifying you'. Enclosing a 'bit of ribbon', she merrily noted that it was 'not originally intended for a willow' but nevertheless it might 'break with dumb eloquence the tidings of my inconstancy'. She teased him that she was about to get married, but there was a touching subtext to the tale: 'I intend shortly to make a worthy man happy with my heart and my hand, which unhappily for you do not always go together.'

Ending the letter, Sarah admitted that her 'thoughts are running almost equally on the past and future'. She begged him to forgive her jesting and instead 'believe me always the same as you would wish'. To raise his spirits she insisted that she was 'quite well, except that I sleep badly'. This prompted her to recollect that when she was a child she found 'an unfailing soporific in the 29th psalm, which, except my prayers, was the only thing I had by heart'. She claimed that it was better than anything to be found in an apothecary's shop as 'its effect increased every time, instead of growing weaker'. The letter was unsigned and ended with only a simple 'Adieu, my dearest friend.' After finishing it, she remembered something else and wrote on the cover: 'I am very uneasy about the poems I wrote for you. There were initial letters under them all. Tell me if there is any danger to the writer.'[43] These poems were reluctantly destroyed by Emmet to protect her identity, but he disobeyed her other request and kept the letter to read and re-read.

The wealthy merchant and financier of the rebellion, Philip Long, was taken up by the government in the middle of the month. He was examined on 18 August.[44] Sent to Kilmainham Jail, it seems imprisonment took its toll on his state of mind and he became increasingly embittered and aggressive. A few months later a transcript of two conversations with some of the other prisoners was recorded by the government. Long had become 'very tipsy' one evening and launched into a drunken discussion of the rebellion. He expected to be tried at any time, but drew some consolation from the fact that his friend Dowdall had escaped, 'Yes by Jesus he is completely out of their reach.'[45] John Palmer was in a cell next to him and Long was angry that he wouldn't join in the conversation, noting sarcastically, 'I suppose he is taken up with contemplation and prayer.' The young James Napper Tandy was also a prisoner and protested that he knew 'no more about this business than my little child'. This drew a chuckle from Long, and he told him, 'There was no small laughing at your expense among us all. It shows they are all in the dark.' Long had very little sympathy for Tandy's predicament and told him harshly, 'You always had a bit of the aristocrat about you, so that I don't pity you, and what are you the better of it now?' Tandy had heard a rumour that Dowdall had been captured, but Long put him right: 'By Jesus Christ he is not in their reach.' When the conversation turned to Robert Emmet, Tandy insisted that he had never met him in all his life. This prompted a bitter recollection from Long. 'He was a man whose word could not be depended on. He owes me a great deal of money, that is the fact, a shilling of which I am sure I shall never get.' Tandy agreed that the money was probably gone for ever and wondered what had induced Long to become engaged in such a conspiracy. Long swore that he had 'been made the dupe of a pack of rascals' and expressed his desire to be executed because he was 'quite tired of life'.

It was only a matter of time before the authorities connected Robert Ellis with Robert Emmet. Orders were given to search the house at Butterfield Lane. From the conversation at the Curran dinner table, Sarah learned that it would probably be raided the next day, so she decided to send a coded message to Emmet to warn him 'of the honour intended your country residence by his majesty's troops'.[46] She was especially anxious because she knew that he regularly went there to see Anne Devlin; indeed he had been at Butterfield Lane that very day. However she could not send the message until she found 'an ambassador', and as she explained, 'unfortunately for Homer he presented himself and was unlucky to be trusted'. It is likely that 'Homer' was a reference to her brother Richard. The classical allusion was appropriate for the scholarly friend of Emmet and the fact that he was carrying a volume of Horace suggests that it was not a servant. Unfortunately the message was not delivered. As 'Homer' reached the bridge he came across a military check-point, with the soldiers searching everyone who passed. There were about nineteen people ahead of 'Homer' and, as Sarah later brilliantly described, 'he committed his precious deposit to his boot, and marched up to the gate like another Achilles, vulnerable only in the heel'. Great at telling a story, Sarah recounted that his 'pockets were turned inside out, where, to use an elegant phrase, the devil might have danced a hornpipe without kicking his shins against a halfpenny'. He was rigorously searched and they confiscated his book of Horace 'for the inspection of the government', but they did not discover the letter. 'Homer' could not risk continuing to Harold's Cross and he returned home 'in disgrace'.

The next day Butterfield Lane was raided by a magistrate and some yeomanry. Three or four of the men surrounded Anne Devlin, with their fixed bayonets aimed 'so close to her body that she could feel their points'. She bravely insisted that she was ignorant about the men who had lived in the house, claiming she was only a servant maid and that 'so long as her wages were paid she cared to know nothing else about them'.[47] The magistrate threatened to kill her unless she told the truth, but she stuck to her story and insisted she knew nothing of Mr Ellis's actions and movements. The order was given to hang her on the spot.

Anne Devlin was brought into the courtyard and put up against a wall as a makeshift gallows was erected for her execution. Watching in horror as this was being done, she was interrogated by the yeomen who kept 'prodding her with their bayonets in the arms and shoulders till she was all covered with blood'.[48] They continually asked her, 'Will you confess now? Will you now tell where is Mr Ellis?' But she kept repeating, 'I have nothing to tell. I will tell nothing.' When the gallows was ready she was dragged to it and a noose was put around her neck. For the final time she was asked, 'Will you confess where Mr Ellis is?' She replied defiantly, 'You may murder me, you villains, but not one word about him will you ever get from me.' Praying to heaven she pleaded, 'The Lord Jesus have mercy on my soul', seconds before the yeomen drew back the cart and pulled the rope tightly so that she hung in mid-air. After what seemed like an eternity she was dropped to the ground, gasping for breath, 'and a savage yell of laughter recalled her to her senses'. It had been a mock-execution to break her resolve. She was arrested and brought to Dublin Castle where she was interviewed by Major Sirr.

The authorities were closing in on Emmet and Sarah Curran became terrified that her 'poor greyhound was lost, or still worse, might have been found'.[49] She had arranged to meet him at their secret meeting place, but when he did not arrive she began to despair. Emmet however managed to get word to her that he was safe and she admitted, 'Although I may laugh now, I assure you I then feared the worst, and was never more unhappy.' She explained that when she had read his letter she experienced a 'sensation of agony' which she would never forget: 'I assure you that my head suddenly felt as if it was burning, and for a few minutes I think I was in a fever.' Emmet had revealed that he must leave the country for ever, as his mother wished. Distressed by this news, Sarah was desperate to see him again, despite the danger attached, although she accepted that this was foolish. 'You must there-fore attribute to *mental* derangement my wish of seeing you at present.' Concerned for his security she immediately warned him, 'Do not think of it, unless it might be done with safety, which I think impossible.' And to lighten the tension she asked, 'At any rate, in the present circumstances, is it not wiser to limit myself to the gratification of knowing you are well and safe?'

At Dublin Castle Major Sirr questioned Anne Devlin about her knowledge of Emmet's whereabouts. Her family had also been arrested and she was told that they had given information and had been set free; both statements were untrue. Sirr promised her a reward of £500 and told her that it 'was a fine for-tune for a young woman'. There was just one question she had to answer and she was asked it over and over again, 'Well, Anne, all we want to know is, where did he go to from Butterfield Lane?' Each time she refused to respond. Years later R. R. Madden tracked down Anne Devlin and listened in fascination to her account of this interrogation. When he heard about Sirr's offer he said 'with becoming gravity, "You took the money, of course?"' Devlin's reaction impressed him. It was a look of 'wonder, indignation and misgiving of the seriousness of the person who addressed her'. She said 'Me, take the money? The price of Mr Robert's blood! No, I spurned the rascal's offer.'[50] Sirr con-tinued trying to persuade her to confess and even quoted the lines she had said to Emmet on the night of 23 July; this made her suspect that one of the rebels present that night had become an informer.

While hiding out in Mrs Palmer's house, Emmet decided to write a letter to the government. It was one of his most extraordinary actions, as well as one of the strangest, but given his character it had a certain singular logic. Although the letter was never finished, it reveals a remarkable insight into Emmet's thinking in the aftermath of the failed rebellion. He had spent some time preparing the text and it seems he intended to sign his name to it and then send it to Dublin Castle.[51] One of the matters discussed was the fact that the government had been taken by surprise on the night of 23 July. But rather than gloat, Emmet actually attempted to exonerate it from any criticism. The letter is brimming with all his characteristic traits of youthful idealism, precocity and irrepressible self-confidence. Treating the government as an equal, he discussed the state of affairs in the country and defiantly confirmed that the struggle for independence would continue. The tone throughout was respectful rather than arrogant, and the measured approach suggested a diplomatic ambassador rather than a defeated adversary. At his trial the prosecution wanted this letter to be read as evidence, but because the handwriting couldn't be linked to Emmet, the judge had doubts about whether it was admissible. Emmet intervened and informed his counsel that he had no problems with it being used against him.

Beginning the letter in an almost apologetic tone, Emmet admitted that:

It may appear strange that a person avowing himself an enemy of the present government, and engaged in a conspiracy for its overthrow, should presume to suggest an opinion to that government on any part of its conduct, or could hope that advice coming from such authority might be received with attention.[52]

But he then explained: 'The writer of this, however, does not mean to offer an opinion on any point on which he must of necessity feel differently from any of those whom he addresses, and on which therefore his conduct might be doubted.' Rather he wished to discuss freely some issues on which he felt a certain sympathy with the government. He was careful to draw a distinction between the 'English part of the present administration' which he respected, and the Irish section supporting it which he despised. He explained that,

His intention is to confine himself entirely to those points on which, however widely he may differ from them in others, he has not intention of declaring that as a man he feels the same interest with the merciful part as an *Irishman* with at least the *English* part of the present administration.

He was anxious to warn the government that the military campaign was likely to be resumed if it pursued a system of terror. He urged conciliation as the best policy to smother the conspiracy, recognising that anything else would only provoke an immediate renewal of the conflict. As he explained, he wanted

to communicate to them in the most precise terms that line of conduct which he may hereafter be compelled to adopt, and which, however painful, it must under any circumstances be, would become doubly so if he was not conscious of having tried to avoid it by the most distinct notification.

Moving on to a discussion of 'the present conspiracy', Emmet explained that he would do little more than 'state, what government itself must acknowledge' that of recent events 'it knows, comparatively speaking, nothing'. He wanted to show that 'instead of creating terror in its enemies, or confidence in its friends' the government would only 'by the scantiness of its information . . .

furnish additional grounds of invective to those who are but too ready to censure it for the want of intelligence'. But he generously admitted that this was
not the administration's fault and 'no sagacity could have enabled it to obtain'
detailed information prior to the rebellion.

This segued into a bold warning for the government not to resort to terror
tactics. If, Emmet explained, 'it had not been able to terrify by a display of its
discoveries', then what hope did it have of crushing dissent 'by the weight of
its punishments'. In a passage rich in irony he asked, 'Is it only now we are to
learn that entering into conspiracy exposes us to be hanged?' Of real concern
to him was the fact that minor participants in the rebellion were now being
arrested and would probably be executed under the terms of the treason
legislation. In part the letter was a direct attempt to save their lives and he
questioned the rationality of such a policy. He asked the government if 'the
scattered instances, which will now be brought forward, [are] necessary to
exemplify the statute?' and also if 'the numerous and striking examples which
have already preceded were insufficient?' His appeal to reason was further
evidence of the amount of regard he had for the British administration in
Ireland; he may have rejected its legitimacy but he none the less respected it.
For Emmet it was a desire for national independence and not blind hatred
which motivated his actions. His advice for the government was to follow a
moderate course in dealing with the aftermath of the rebellion, rather than
pursue a vindictive policy which would ultimately be counter-productive:

> If government can neither by the novelty of punishment, nor the multitude
> of its victims impress us with terror, can it hope to injure the body of the
> conspiracy so impenetrably woven as the present, by cutting off a few
> threads from the end of it?

The second theme which he wanted to address was his future line of conduct.
Thus he 'notified' the government that the struggle for independence would
continue, no matter what the government did to extinguish the flame of liberty. Its policies may 'change the nature' but could make no difference to 'the
period of the contest that is to take place'. And he confidently asserted that
'the exertions of United Irishmen will be guided only by their own opinion of
the eligibility of the moment for effecting the emancipation of their country'.

Under the terms of the Insurrection Act, the owner of every house had to
post a complete list of all residents on the door. Joseph Palmer, the son of Mrs
Palmer, drew up one for the house at Harold's Cross, but Emmet persuaded
him not to include Mr Hewitt on it, freely admitting that 'he was afraid the
government would take him up'.[53] The two men had a number of conversations
about the events of 23 July and Emmet mentioned that he 'had passed part of
it in Thomas Street'. It seems Joseph Palmer was curious about the rebel uniform and Emmet told him that it was made up of the same white waistcoat,
white pantaloons and black Hessian boots that he currently wore, but with an

elaborate regimental coat. Palmer later testified that Emmet 'said it was a very handsome uniform'. They also discussed the rebel proclamation. In the event of the house being raided, Emmet had prepared a contingency plan: he would climb from the parlour window into the back-house, and from there escape through the fields.[54] Many men called to see him at Harold's Cross and whenever they arrived they asked to see Mr Hewitt and were admitted to his room.[55] Sometimes he met small groups, other times just key individuals, and it is clear that he was attempting to continue directing the conspiracy in the aftermath of the rebellion. It was foolish to meet at his hiding place, however, as it increased the numbers of those who were aware of his location. It only needed one person to be tempted by the reward for his security to be compromised. The government later discovered that around 20 August Emmet wrote to Michael Quigley, who was hiding in Kildare, urging him to keep things 'perfectly quiet' and wait until the French landed shortly before 15 October.[56] But it seems unlikely that Emmet had any real expectations of a French landing, and if he did he was gravely mistaken, so it is difficult to give too much credence to this report.

In her final letter to Robert Emmet, Sarah Curran did not bother to conceal her unhappiness. She knew that it was daily becoming more dangerous for him and nothing would ameliorate her fears. For a few days she had been intending to write a letter but she admitted that she kept postponing it because she 'was really incapable of conveying anything like consolation'.[57] Sensitive to his state of mind, she was afraid that if she revealed her true feelings it 'would only serve to irritate and embitter' his own. There was another reason for her 'degree of reluctance to writing'. She was beginning to realise 'the extent of the risk I run' as well as the 'breach of propriety it occasions' by communicating with a fugitive rebel. But she recognised that this 'may be rather inconsistent' after 'what has passed'. Despite her doubts and agitation, this letter was one of her longest to Emmet and was written very shortly after she had sent 'Homer' to warn him of the raid at Butterfield Lane. It was begun early in the morning, worked on throughout the day, and she only finished it after 2 a.m., by which time her mood had lightened considerably. Twice during the day she stopped writing to go for a walk to Harold's Cross, so that she could stroll casually by Palmer's house. Each time she was frustrated that she wasn't able to catch a glimpse of him.

Going behind her father's back was taking its toll, and Sarah admitted that every 'departure from duty has been attended with that self-reproach which is generally attached to the first breach of it'. But she lovingly insisted that these sentiments were the only thing which interrupted 'the satisfaction I feel in sharing every anxiety with you, and of preserving to you, in spite of other mischances and disappointments, the consolation of a friend'. Sarah knew that Robert would understand her concerns; indeed she suspected that he shared them. Therefore she felt no embarrassment in being completely honest and revealed that such is the perfect confidence that I feel subsists between us that I have no fear of misconstruction on your part of any uneasiness I feel. On the contrary I know you share it, and cannot think me blameable. At all events, I wish you to know me exactly as I am.

The next passage was highly revealing of her character and indirectly showed her strong feelings for Emmet. 'I cannot bear to conceal anything from you', she confessed, before making a point about their future together by discussing how much it had pained her to be disobedient:

I should wish you to recollect [when we are married] that the violation of promise or duty brought most abundantly with it its punishment; and that at a time when I was sunk by disappointment, without hope of future prospect of comfort, I almost shrunk from availing myself of the only consolation that still remained, although the one I prized above every other — that of sympathising with you, and endeavouring to atone for what you had lost.

Sarah was already dreaming about her life together with Robert. And in 'looking forward to the circumstance that might ultimately unite us' she wondered if they should not, 'like the rest of the world', judge the strength of their love by the obstacles they had overcome. She was proud of that fact that her love for him had survived the failure of all his plans; it was not therefore 'fed by any rational hope' but rather had been 'strengthened by disappointment'. Thus in the future she could look back on her 'perverse inclination' to love him and remember the 'triumph of resolution and constancy over temporary disaster and opposition'.

At Robert Emmet's trial for treason extracts from this letter would be read by the crown to prove his guilt. Sarah Curran was not mentioned by name and the prosecution pretended that it had been sent by a man. It might have amused her to hear the attorney general refer to her as a 'brother conspirator' and an 'intelligent rebel'.[58] The passages where she discussed the possibility of a French landing were of most interest to the government, and certainly they show that she was fully cognisant of his plans for the country. Not only that, she shared many of his own suspicions about the character of the French. She told him that she

should wish particularly to know from you how matters stand at present (if you would not be afraid); particularly what are your hopes from abroad and what you think they mean to do, and whether if they pay us a visit we shall not be worse off than before.

Then she discussed the views of someone close to her; Emmet marked out this name with a pen-knife so that he could not be identified. The person, possibly Richard Curran, was 'very desponding' and believed the people 'are incapable of redress and unworthy of it' especially after their failure to act on 23 July. He was also sceptical about the possibility of a French invasion and believed that Napoleon was just playing a game, hoping to bankrupt the British by forcing them to spend vast amounts of money on defence.

To cheer Robert up, Sarah told him a story about 'Homer's' romantic entanglements. He had gone to a house in the countryside to see 'a young lady' but had been discovered by her family and treated very badly. Sarah hoped that Robert was not angry with her for writing so much about this and joked that he 'ought to be obliged to me for making you laugh — *malagré vous*'. It was now close to 2 a.m. and she had been working on the letter on and off throughout the day. She admitted that she 'began and ended' it 'in very different moods'. Weighing heavily on her mind was the danger to Emmet's life and she confessed that she 'passed the house you are in twice this day, but did not see you'. She reassured him that 'If I thought you were in safety I would be comparatively happy, at least.' There were so many daily reports of what was happening that she could not help listening to them, 'and although I cannot suppose that the minute events which occur now can materially influence the grand and general effect in view, yet my mind is risen or depressed as I suppose them favourable or otherwise'.

As the letter drew to a close she admitted her great unease in sending it and that she would not be comfortable until she knew it had reached him safely. Therefore she begged him to reply immediately and she also emphasised that he should read it quickly and then destroy it: '*I request you to burn it instantly.*' She was also desperate to know 'if you are well and in spirits', well aware that the failure of the rebellion was disturbing his peace. Therefore to raise his morale she advised him to 'Try and forget the past, and fancy that everything is to be attempted for the first time.' Closing with a joke, she told him that she longed 'to know how your wife and *ten small* children are'. Her final sentences contained a fond valediction and a warning: 'Goodbye my dear friend, but not for ever. Again I must bid you burn this.'

On the afternoon of 25 August Emmet had a meeting with one of the rebel leaders who called to see him at Harold's Cross. They discussed their future plans, and after the man left, Emmet returned to writing his letter to the government. He began a new section with the words 'That administration . . .' but got no further. It was now dinner time and he sat down to eat with Mrs Palmer and her daughter; Joseph was in bed, unwell. There was a knock on the door and the young girl went to answer it. Immediately Major Sirr and one of his officers burst inside and went straight for the back parlour where they knew a stranger lived. An informer had betrayed his whereabouts, having given a detailed report to Dublin Castle about his hiding-place. Sirr ordered the two Palmers out of the parlour and began questioning Emmet about his identity. Trapped, Emmet foolishly assumed a new alias and insisted his name was Cunningham. Sirr discovered the unfinished letter to the government on a chair and put it in his pocket. Then he left Emmet under the supervision of his officer and went to talk to Mrs Palmer. Here Emmet's bluff came unstuck. Mrs Palmer kept to the original story and said her lodger's name was Hewitt and that he was 'a very proper young man'.[59] When Sirr returned to the parlour he discovered Emmet lying on the ground, bleeding. The officer explained that he had tried to escape and that he had knocked him down with his pistol. Sirr asked Emmet how long he had been staying at the house, to which he replied that he had just arrived that morning. Growing in confidence, the town major went back to Mrs Palmer and discovered that Hewitt had in fact lodged there for a month.

The game was now up for Emmet. Sirr was convinced he had found 'some person of importance' and he went to the canal bridge to bring back reinforcements. He surrounded the house with sentries, put Emmet under guard and began to search for incriminating evidence against his suspect. Mrs Palmer was interrogated thoroughly and Sirr wrote down everything she said. Once more Emmet attempted to escape. Realising it was certain death if he was captured, he was willing to risk his life in a desperate break for freedom. He overpowered his guard and jumped out of the parlour window, closely following his original escape plan. Sirr heard the noise and, realising what was happening, cleverly anticipated that Emmet would head for the rear of the house. When he got outside he saw Emmet running into the fields and ordered a sentry to fire. Then he set off after Emmet himself and was fortunate not to have been caught in the line of fire; as it happened the musket misfired. Despite Emmet's head start he did not have Sirr's pace, probably because he was still feeling the effects of the blow he had received, and was quickly intercepted. The two men fell to the ground in a rough scuffle and Emmet was forced to surrender. Magnanimously, Sirr apologised for the violent treatment he had received. With a nonchalant smile, Emmet told him that 'All was fair in war.'[60] Searching Emmet's person, Sirr discovered the two most recent letters from Sarah Curran, which she had begged him to destroy. This guilt would weigh heavily on his mind in the weeks ahead. The prisoner was brought straight to Dublin Castle and it was later reported that he was identified by a man from Trinity College Dublin, possibly his old nemesis, Elrington.[61] In any case he had already accepted his fate and a few hours after his capture he confidently informed the authorities that his name was Robert Emmet.

9

CAPTIVITY AND CROSS-EXAMINATION

~

'Emmet = mad Raphael painting ideals of beauty on the walls of a cell
with human excrement.'
(Samuel Taylor Coleridge, Autumn 1803)

'I thought ten thousand swords must have leaped from their scabbards
to avenge even a look that threatened her with insult. But the age of
chivalry is gone . . . and the glory of Europe is extinguished for ever.'
(Edmund Burke on the treatment of Queen Marie Antoinette,
Reflections on the revolution in France, 1790)

Kilmainham Jail had opened in 1796 as a new prison to serve the county of Dublin. In theory it was run by Governor John Dunn, but the key figure in the jail was Dr Edward Trevor, the medical superintendent and chief supervisor. In 1804 allegations of cruelty and brutality were levelled against him by a delegation of prisoners including Anne Devlin, John Palmer, John Patten, James Tandy and Philip Long. They wrote to the earl of Hardwicke and revealed: 'The source of all our afflicting treatment is glaringly to be traced to . . . Dr Trevor, whose inhuman, hardened, and malignant disposition . . . has been forced on us.'[1] Trevor was said to have 'the zeal and ignorance of an inquisitor' and was accused of receiving 'complaints with contumelious laughter' and inviting anyone who challenged him to 'a pugilistic decision with him'. In addition, Tandy made shocking references to the 'suffocating vapour' of the 'fetid quagmire' and described wading 'up to my ankles through human excrement' on his daily trips to the dinner table. Not even the old Bastille in France, he claimed, had housed 'more wanton cruelty or more savage treatment'. Hardwicke was told that it was enough to lead 'a mind to madness'. Robert Emmet was committed to Kilmainham Jail on 26 August 1803. The prison register noted that this was on the authorisation of Secretary Wickham for the crime of high treason.

Within hours of Emmet's capture the government began constructing its case against him. William Wickham brought Ann Palmer and her son into Dublin Castle on 28 August and spent from midday until after 6 o'clock taking a lengthy deposition of their statements. The meeting was also attended by Standish O'Grady, the attorney general; Lord Redesdale, the lord chancellor; and Alexander Marsden, the under secretary. Wickham discovered that Emmet had mastered the art of disguising his handwriting and feared that the prosecution might fail because of this: 'Those who know his handwriting in better days cannot say that they believe the papers of which we are in possession to be written by him.'[2] There was worse news to report. Few people were willing to come forward and testify against Emmet. Wickham explained how 'He was very much beloved in private life, so that all the friends of his family, even those who abhorred his treasons, will be glad of any pretext to avoid appearing against him.' Thus the case for the prosecution might have to rest on the evidence of his captured accomplices, but Wickham suspected that they would give 'reluctant testimony against the man who was considered as the chief of the conspiracy'. It had been hoped that Patrick Farrell, the man who was held as a prisoner by the rebels, would give invaluable evidence. But it seems that Farrell remembered how Emmet had saved his life and refused to identify him.

Wickham's worst fear was that if Emmet denied having any involvement in the conspiracy he might go free and destroy the credibility of the government. Therefore it was crucial to find sufficient proof of his guilt to secure a conviction. Seven pieces of evidence linked Emmet to the rebellion. The first was an original draft of the proclamation of the provisional government in one version of Emmet's handwriting which was found in a bureau in the Marshal Lane depot, together with a letter addressed to him from his brother Thomas Addis. The second was an unfinished draft of a letter in the same handwriting as the proclamation from someone who was obviously a rebel. Next were letters in different handwriting '*evidently* written by him', but Wickham conceded that 'on account of the dissimilarity of the handwriting it will probably be thought most prudent not to produce them'. The fourth piece of evidence was a letter found on Emmet's person which 'clearly proves him to have been one of the party engaged in a conspiracy against the state'.[3] The next important point was 'the circumstances of his flight' from Dublin, his military dress and his attempted escape when captured. The sixth piece of evidence was the accounts of the two Palmers. And the final point was 'a material cypher' found in Emmet's desk, addressed to 'R.E.' The circumstantial nature of some of these exhibits made Wickham consider 'bringing forward secret information' — the confidential reports of Leonard MacNally, the barrister and informer who was completely in the confidence of Emmet and the other rebels. But after some reflection Wickham decided that 'there is but one opinion on the subject . . . it were a thousand times better that Emmet should escape than we should close for ever a most accurate source of information'. Wickham also lamented the 'melancholy thing' that the government was receiving 'no assistance whatever from the police'. After some reflection he remembered that there was a further material fact against Emmet: he had asked Mrs Palmer not to include his alias of Hewitt on the list of people staying at her house.

Locked in his cell, Emmet was consumed by feelings of guilt. Two letters from Sarah Curran had been discovered on his person. Although they were not signed, he was overwhelmed by the idea that he had incriminated her. He would have been greatly relieved if he had known that the government refused to believe they were love letters. Instead the paranoid ministers presumed that the letters had been sent by his sister, Robert Holmes's wife, and were written in a cypher which had not yet been cracked. They were confident that 'the language of a love-intrigue had been assumed as a means of misleading government'.[4] If Emmet had been aware of this he would have acted very differently in the days ahead, but instead he continued to suffer in the belief that his beloved Sarah was in danger. The loss of the lock of her hair, which had been taken from his stock, also affected him. His worst fear, although hardly a realistic one, was that the ministers might be able to make a shrewd guess about the identity of the woman from its colour and texture.[5]

An attempt was made to effect his escape. Shortly after his arrival in Kilmainham his first cousin, St John Mason, who was himself a prisoner in the jail, approached one of the turnkeys, George Dunn, and attempted to bribe him. He offered him £500 if he assisted in a rescue, with a further £500 if it was successful. Dunn told him that he would consider the proposal but immediately went to Dr Trevor and revealed everything. Instructed to have another meeting with Mason, Dunn agreed to help and was given a message to take to Emmet. Instead Dunn brought the note to Trevor, who sent it directly to Wickham at the Castle. The plan, which George Dunn pretended to go along with, was to steal the key from the governor, John Dunn (no relation), while at dinner and give it to Emmet. When Emmet was briefed about the plan he asked Mason to let him borrow some clothes 'for the purpose of disguise'. A copy of his letter was sent immediately to the chief secretary:

Ask G. [George Dunn] what time Mr D. [John Dunn] dines, and if he leaves anyone at the door then. Though it might be a little early, yet he is longer away then than at any other time, it would better enable us all to go out, and with the change of dress would not be noticed. If it cannot be done, then G. must watch the first opportunity after dinner that Mr D. goes down to the house, and let me out immediately. I will be ready at the moment.[6]

Clearly Emmet believed that success was possible, and had given the matter serious thought. He had calculated the best time for an attempt and believed that it should take place early in the evening before the guard was doubled. He wanted the plan to be implemented immediately, convinced that delay was fatal:

I am anxious not to defer it till tomorrow, as I heard the officers who came the rounds consulting with him [George Dunn] about placing the sentries for better security and I think I heard them mention me in the *hall*. D. also came in at one o'clock last night, under pretence that he thought he heard me calling. If it is delayed until tomorrow it must be done at dinner-time.[7]

Having considered all the possibilities, Emmet worked out the details of the escape. Afraid that sentries might be placed in the hall, his solution was for George Dunn to hide his clothes in the washroom, where he would go to change. As he explained to Mason:

If sentries are placed in the hall by day, the only way will be, whenever D. goes down let G. whistle *God save the king* in the passage, and I will immediately ask to go to the necessary, and will change my clothes there instantly; but in this case G. must previously convey them there. Send for a pair of spectacles (No. 5 fits my sight) which will facilitate the disguise. After I am gone, G. must convey the clothes I wore away.

The choice of signal revealed Emmet's quirky sense of humour. Despite the preparations, the treachery of the turnkey ensured there was no possibility of success. The note was shown to Governor Dunn, upon Trevor's instructions, and only then delivered to Mason.

On the morning of 30 August Emmet was taken from his cell for cross-examination. It was his first meeting with William Wickham, the chief secretary, whose reputation had made a deep impression. Also present for the interrogation were Lord Redesdale and Standish O'Grady, the attorney general. Emmet began the examination in an uncompromising mood. His early answers were defiant and sometimes ironic:

Attorney general: What is your name?
Emmet: Robert Emmet. Having now answered to my name, I must decline answering any further questions.[8]

He was then informed that he had been sent for so that he could have 'an opportunity of explaining what appeared suspicious in his late conduct'. Bemused, Emmet thanked them for the opportunity, for which he was 'much obliged', but insisted that he 'must still persist in declining'. Nevertheless he did not wish this to be taken as a sign that he was ashamed of his conduct and he wanted it to be understood that there 'was nothing which could come within the limits of this society to ask me which I would not answer with pride'. Then he explained his rule, the 'point of honour' which he had enforced on himself: 'It might be a breach of confidence unless the limit was laid down.' He realised that if he began answering it would be impossible to stop. Emmet would not incriminate others and he was convinced that 'If he answered one and not others he would draw an invidious distinction, which he did not wish to do.' Having stated this rule, as far as he was concerned the meeting was over.

The cross-examination resumed. A complete transcript of the meeting was taken by the government, although the name of the person who asked each question was not always recorded. In most cases it was the attorney general:

Attorney general: Have you been in France within these two years?
Emmet: I have already mentioned that I stop the examination.
Question: Where did you first hear of the insurrection?
Emmet: I decline answering any question.
Question: Had you any previous knowledge of it?
Emmet: Same observation.
Question: Were you in Dublin that night?
Emmet: Same answer.
Question: Have you corresponded with any persons in France?

The transcript is ambiguous. Either Emmet responded 'No answer' or else remained silent. The interrogation continued:

Question: It is unnecessary, then, to put any questions?
Emmet: Certainly.
Question: Why did you change your clothes?

The question was a subtle reference to the attempted escape. Emmet explained that he had asked Dr Trevor's permission to borrow clothes but that 'It would be infringing on the rule already laid down to go any further.' In any case the Castle already knew that the clothes had been taken from St John Mason.

Shrewdly moving to a different area, the attorney general attempted to tie Emmet to the various pieces of disguised handwriting. Again he had little luck:

Question: Are you acquainted with a person by the name of Howley?
Emmet: Same answer.
Question: Have you gone by the name of Hewitt, of Ellis, of Cunningham?
Emmet: Has only to mention what he has already said.
Question: Are you inclined to answer to your handwriting?
Emmet: No.
Question: Did you ever see a proclamation purporting to be a proclamation of the provisional government?
Emmet: I have only to make the same answer.
Question: Have you ever seen the same in manuscript?
Emmet: I have only to make the same answer.
Question: Have you seen the same in your own handwriting?
Emmet: Same answer.

The interrogation turned to the unsigned letters which had been discovered on his person. Emmet was shaken and became increasingly frantic in his attempts to shield Sarah Curran. For the first time he departed from his 'rule' by answering some questions and not others:

> *Question:* By whom are the letters written that were found on your person?
> *Emmet:* As to the letters taken out of my possession by Major Sirr, how can I avoid this being brought forward?

Emmet then vacillated and suggested that perhaps 'the letters were years in his custody' or even that 'a friend left those letters on a sudden'. Anxious to arrive at some arrangement to suppress the letters as evidence, he began asking the attorney general some questions of his own. He was desperate to learn if Sarah Curran had been identified, what was to be done about the letters, and how he might prevent them being read at his trial:

> *Emmet:* May I ask if the name of the writer might be mentioned to me? May I know by what means those letters may be prevented from coming forward? Has anything been done in consequence of those letters being taken? May I learn what means, or what has been done upon them?
> *Attorney general:* You cannot be answered as to this.
> *Emmet:* You must, gentlemen, be sensible how disagreeable it would be to one of yourselves to have a delicate and virtuous female brought into notice. What means would be necessary to bring the evidence in those letters forward without bringing the name forward? Might the passages in those letters be read to me?

But the attorney general still believed that the letters were a clever ruse and was unwilling to strike a deal. He rejected out of hand Emmet's suggestion for only quoting selectively from the documents at the trial.

> *Attorney general:* The expressions in those letters go far beyond a confidential communication between a gentleman and a lady. There are evidences of high treason, and therefore the production is necessary.
> *Emmet:* Might those be mentioned?
> *Attorney general:* Producing some parts and withholding others never was done.
> *Emmet:* May I not be told the utmost limits to go to prevent the exposure?

The attorney general shook his head.

> *Emmet:* Then nothing remains to be done. I would rather give up my own life than injure another person.

The final sentence made an impression on everyone in the room. The attorney general told Emmet: 'We knew before you came into the room that this would be the line you would take.' It was a gracious comment and Emmet thanked him for it. He then tried to shift his ground and move to take another line of conduct, one that might protect Sarah Curran better:

> *Emmet:* I am glad you have had that opinion of me. Have any proceedings been taken on those letters? I will mention as near as I can the line I mean to adopt. I will go so far as this: if I have assurances that nothing has been done, and nothing will be done, upon these letters, I will do everything consistent with honour to prevent their production.

In other words, Emmet would acquiesce in his conviction. He would plead guilty at his trial and allow the government to win its prosecution, provided the letters were not used as evidence against him. But first he was anxious to receive a guarantee that the author of the letters had not been arrested: 'May I know whether anything has been done? Might I, in the meantime, have assistance of counsel? Might I then make one request: that until my arraignment nothing has and nothing will be done?' The attorney general was still not inclined to make a deal:

> *Attorney general:* You are at liberty to make the request; but cannot receive an immediate answer.
> *Emmet:* I can only repeat what I have already said, that I would do anything to prevent the production of those letters. Personal safety I throw out of the question. With notions of honour in common, persons may have different principles, but all might be agreed as to what a person might owe a female. Personal safety would weigh nothing if the production of those letters could be prevented.
> *Question:* Are you aware that they form evidence against the person who wrote them?

Struck by this implication, Emmet searched for a way to extricate Sarah:

> *Emmet:* As to that, I do not know how far there can be proof as to who wrote them, however there may be opinions; and I am not aware how far similarity of handwriting might be evidence. But, if the person who is primarily concerned does all that in him lies, it is very unnecessary and very cruel to proceed against the writer. I feel the more acutely on this point, because it is the only act of my life, within these five months, of which I have to accuse myself.
> *Question:* Do you mean that the female who wrote these letters only had opinions?

The attorney general had misinterpreted the argument. Emmet had been suggesting that there could be no proof unless studies were done of the handwriting of the author of the letters, although he conceded that the government might have some *opinions* about the identity of the author. The attorney general however mistook him as saying that the views expressed in the letters were 'only' opinions. Emmet seized upon this confusion and attempted to turn it to his advantage by agreeing with the position:

> *Emmet:* I say it on my honour. I only say that a woman's sentiments are only opinions and they are not reality. When a man gives opinions it is supposed he has actions accordingly; but with a woman the utmost limit is only opinion. I declare on my honour as a man that the person had only opinions. I admit in the eye of the law it is otherwise, but they may have laid down the law where it is not necessary. The same sword cuts down a man as a babe, but it is the mind of the man which teaches him how to use it.

Seeking to profit from Emmet's strength of feeling on this point, the interrogation quickly shifted to another line of inquiry:

> *Question:* Do you know of any depot of arms or ammunition?
> *Emmet:* I have mentioned the only point on which I will speak.
> *Question:* Perhaps you consider the disclosure of names as inconsistent with your notions of honour?

But Emmet explained that he would not sacrifice his honour for personal safety. The attorney general then informed him that there could be no deal unless he was willing to tell them what they needed to know. But he emphasised that this would only earn protection for the writer of the letters; there could be no escape for Emmet:

> *Question:* You cannot expect to draw forth any compromise on the part of government. However, if you could render a service to government by making a disclosure which may entitle this person to some favour, it might be attended to as far as respects that person, although not extended to yourself. Is disclosing concealed arms dishonourable?
> *Emmet:* I must adhere to my former rule.
> *Question:* As a matter of curiosity I may put to you a question: why government should indulge you with consenting to a partial disclosure of these letters, when you decline on your part to make any satisfactory answer?
> *Emmet:* It is not an indulgence. I only ask it as if I was in a situation of power I would grant a like favour. I wish everyone in Ireland and England was as innocent as she is. I know when I say it is the only criminal act; that the young woman's affections were engaged without the knowledge of her friends, and in fact without her own. My resolution is taken. I have

mentioned that I will never save honour at the expense of what I think my duty. I wish I knew what is expected, that I might in my own mind consider what is my duty.

Question: Then I am to understand that nothing will induce you to make a full disclosure?

Emmet: No. I never will.

Question: You must draw the line and say how far you can go. I am not asking you where Mr Dowdall may be apprehended. I am not asking you who visited you two hours before you were taken.

Emmet refused to be drawn on these points. All he was concerned about was whether Sarah had been identified and if she had been arrested:

Emmet: May I not ask, although I am not told what I can do, or how far I am to go, whether those letters lie there to be used or not? Whether any disclosure has been made by them or any arrest has taken place?

Question: Would it answer your purpose to have the writer brought into the same room with you?

Emmet: It might perhaps answer yours better.

Unwittingly, the government had played its trump card. As far as the ministers were concerned, the writer of the letters was Mary Anne Holmes and this was the person they were threatening to bring forward. But Emmet could only think of Sarah in chains outside, and all because he had failed to destroy her letters. Suddenly his self-control began to desert him and the record noted that 'He rose from his chair in much agitation.' As he later admitted to Sarah, 'I was sure you were arrested, and I could not stand the idea of seeing you in that situation.'[9] He frantically attempted to change the subject:

Emmet: In respect of the person at whose house I was arrested, the lady was under personal obligations to a part of my family; her sentiments were not the same as mine. Their name might lead to a supposed connection with a person of the name of Palmer on the Coombe.

Question: The person who had the gunpowder or to Mr Patten?

Emmet: I do not mention the gunpowder; I do not mention who.

Question: Someone under obligations to you?

Emmet: Few people have obligations to me.

Question: If you come to any resolution you may have an opportunity for a further communication.

Emmet: In a case of this kind a person naturally wishes to have the opinion of someone beside himself.

Question: Who would you wish?

Emmet: It may be a very harmless person. To remove any doubt I name an Englishman whom I never saw but once and then not alone. May I ask to

know whether it will occasion any prejudice to him?
Question: Certainly not.
Emmet: Counsellor Burton is the person. May I ask another thing that from
the honour of every person here present — that no hint or suggestion will
be thrown out of what I have mentioned? There are things such as informers talked of. I hope that those things which go about may go without any
foundation. I wish I had been called up sooner. Might I know whether anything has been done to the person in whose house I was taken? I believe,
gentlemen, there are occasions in which you would not think it criminal in
me to shelter any of you.

The attorney general gently reminded him that in 1798 some of the United
Irishmen had made a deal with the government in return for saving the lives
of others. Emmet was amused by the hint:

Question: You are aware that the persons in '98, among whom was your
brother, made disclosures, concealing only the names of persons?
Emmet: I believe they of '98 were differently situated. The object for which
they spoke was to save the lives of others, their own never having been in
any danger. I know the comparison you are going to draw, and that it will
be taken down.

As Emmet said this he smiled. Further efforts were made on the same point:

Question: You are aware how far they went in '98. There was no minute
circumstance relating to the plot which they did not disclose.
Emmet: May I know when my arraignment will take place? Might I not be
permitted to see the gentleman I mentioned, previous to it?
Attorney general: It certainly is unusual to permit a person in your situation
such an indulgence.

By now Emmet's emotions were clearly exposed, and it was obvious he was
deeply upset. Lord Redesdale intervened and declared that the interrogation
was over:

Lord chancellor: Mr Emmet's feelings are a good deal affected.
Emmet: I wish they were at an end. I wish you good morning, gentlemen.

Emmet was taken back to his cell. Dr Trevor prepared a report for the Castle
and revealed that on his way, 'he expressed very considerable anxiety to prevent
any proceedings being taken against *a particular person*, and that to protect that
person he would sacrifice his own personal safety'.[10]
  There was a spyhole in Emmet's cell; its purpose was to allow witnesses to
identity prisoners without being identified. On 1 September John Doyle from

Ballynameece was brought to Kilmainham to see if he recognised Emmet. Much to the delight of the government he confirmed that the prisoner was the French general who had stayed with him on 26 July.[11]

The trials for the people captured in the wake of the rebellion began while Emmet was in prison. In each case the crown secured a conviction with ruthless efficiency. Edward Kearney was the first person to be tried, on 31 August, and he was found guilty in a matter of hours; he was executed the next day at Thomas Street. The next rebel to be prosecuted was Owen Kirwan. His defence lawyer, John Philpot Curran, destroyed the credibility of one crown eye-witness by revealing that Kirwan had seduced his wife, but did little to convince the jury of his client's innocence. Indeed the solicitor general, James McClelland, was astonished by Curran's bizarre behaviour in court. In an 'extraordinary' closing speech he began by praising the government, then proclaimed the loyalty of the majority of the people, professed his own loyalty, attacked Napoleon for causing the rebellion, and advised the mob '*as an old friend*, against their present folly'.[12] Then, suddenly, he changed direction and launched into an hour-long tirade suggesting that no rebellion had taken place and 'sat down, having totally forgotten his client in the transaction'. McClelland believed the speech was 'so extravagant' that he did not even bother answering it. Kirwan was found guilty and executed the next day outside his home on Plunket Street. Thomas Maxwell Roche, Walter Clare, James Byrne, John Begg, John Killen and John McCann, all minor figures who had been captured, were also prosecuted with great vigour and were hanged and beheaded for their involvement. Despite the best efforts of John Philpot Curran and the other defence lawyers, it proved impossible to counteract the overwhelming evidence which the crown had gathered. The trial for Felix Rourke was one of the longest. It began on the morning of 6 September and continued for three days. Again the relentless prosecution proved its case to the satisfaction of the jury and he was found guilty on 9 September. The next day he was executed at Rathcoole.

Denis Lambert Redmond was due to stand trial on 5 September. The day before, in a desperate attempt to strike a plea-bargain, he offered to 'make a full disclosure of all the sources from which money was advanced to the rebel chiefs; of all persons concerned; of the place and manner of procuring ammunition, and of everything done within his knowledge in France, England or Ireland'.[13] But his one proviso was that he could have an hour alone with Robert Emmet 'to settle with him the conditions of such explicit confession, and have his assistance therein'. Wickham rejected this offer. He would not allow any prisoner to meet with Emmet and warned Redmond that he 'must rely on the discretion of the government' with respect to any deal. Dejected, Redmond was visited by his aunt, a Mrs Hatshell, and his cousin on the morning of his trial. One of them smuggled a pistol in their clothes and surreptitiously passed it to Redmond. Just as he was about to be taken to Green Street Courthouse, he 'placed the pistol to his head, just above the ear' and fired.[14] Somehow he survived. The ball did not enter his skull, and by the evening he had recovered sufficiently to ask for some whey to eat. His trial was postponed for a month.

A suicide note was discovered on Redmond's body. It was addressed 'To the government' and began with a pathetic plea to end the executions: 'For God's sake stop your murder; that is, I mean, what you call executions.' Redmond was defiant at having, as he thought, cheated the hangman's noose and jeered the government for its conduct:

> Farewell, you tools of oppression. I will not give you that satisfaction you so wantonly expected in taking my life. I will be remembered when you are all forgot. Adieu, you poor wretches. You will shortly meet the fate of all tyrants.[15]

It was signed 'Citizen Denis Lambert Redmond'. There followed a lengthy post-cript in which Redmond asked for mercy for his soul and freedom for Emmet:

> May God forgive me, as you have drove me to it. O poor Emmet. He's deceived and betrayed into the hands of a lawless enemy . . . May God protect all the friends of liberty. May God deliver Mr Emmet from the hands of his enemies, so I say.

The note ended with a bitter denunciation of the behaviour of the prison guards towards the men who had been executed. They were despicable 'mis-creants of despotism', who had treated the prisoners like animals, 'grinning and laughing' whenever they were asked a question. Resigning himself to his death, Redmond concluded with a farewell to his fellow prisoners: 'May God protect you in the hour of danger. Adieu; adieu.' When the home secretary received a copy of this 'diabolical enclosure', he expressed a hope that Redmond's life would be saved so that he could stand trial and be executed for his 'atrocious crimes'.

Anne Devlin was admitted to Kilmainham Jail on 3 September. She was kept in solitary confinement and according to tradition was in a cell directly below Robert Emmet. Dr Trevor interrogated her regularly, but she denied any knowledge of the rebellion or of Emmet himself. One day the guards allowed her to exercise in the courtyard, a ruse to see if she would speak to Emmet who was also out walking. By her own account, when she saw 'Mr Robert' she was afraid she 'would have dropped'.[16] Terrified that Emmet would acknowledge her presence and speak to her, thus incriminating her before Dr Trevor who was watching the proceedings carefully, 'she kept her face away, and walked up and down on the other side'. The two prisoners crossed each other several times but finally walked into each other at the end. Anne Devlin took care 'when his eyes met hers, to have a frown on her face, and her fingers raised to her lips'. Emmet passed on as if he had never seen her before. But she was hugely comforted by 'the half smile that came over his face' and knew that he had recognised her. It was a subtle signal, and Anne Devlin later revealed that it 'could hardly have been observed, except by one who knew every turn of his countenance'. She was brought back to her cell and was not allowed to exercise outside again.

An alternative version of this story was recorded by Luke Cullen, who claimed to have been told it by Anne Devlin herself. Cullen was a Carmelite brother who taught at a school in Clondalkin and spent his spare time researching the events of 1798 and 1803. In the 1840s he interviewed Anne Devlin and left a detailed account of her life story. There are some major problems with his narrative, however. Occasionally his version contradicts established facts, and at other times reads like a fictionalised chronicle of events already known. In addition, on some important points it differs from the story Anne Devlin told R. R. Madden. Cullen was able to reproduce, verbatim, conversations that had taken place over forty years earlier, and it seems remarkable that the elderly Anne Devlin (who was then in her late sixties) was capable of providing such accurate transcripts. Certainly Cullen's manuscript is an interesting source, but should definitely be treated with great caution.[17]

According to Luke Cullen's account, when Anne Devlin was allowed out on Kilmainham yard she discovered Robert Emmet playing with a racquet and ball. He immediately recognised her, but she 'endeavoured by a stern countenance and a frown to silence him'.[18] A few minutes later he struck the ball in her direction to allow him an opportunity to talk to her. As he stooped to pick up the ball he wore a 'half-suppressed smile' and told her, 'Anne, dear, confess what you know of me and obtain your freedom and your family's release.' But Devlin refused to respond. To avoid attracting attention, Emmet went back to his game, but they soon met again in the centre of the yard. Devlin pretended to remove a stone from her shoe while Emmet collected his ball. She told him, 'I thought you would be the last man in the world that would encourage me to become an informer.' 'I don't mean that,' he replied, 'Tell of no one but me. I am a dead man, although here.' They continued on their separate ways. When they ran into each other for the third time, Devlin resorted to the ruse of stopping to fix her stockings. Emmet whispered to her, 'There will be enough to swear against me. I cannot die easy while you and your family are in such great danger through my means.' Upon hearing this, Anne Devlin swore that she would never give evidence against him, even to save the entire world. That conversation was, she supposedly claimed, her 'last word, and I may say, my last look at that generous soul, that noble-minded young man'.[19] The entire story is rich with scriptural resonances. Robert Emmet asked Anne Devlin to deny him three times, but on each occasion she remained faithful. It was a reworking of the gospel setting of the courtyard of Caiphas, with Anne Devlin cast as Peter, and Robert Emmet's life re-created in the image of Christ.

Becoming increasingly apprehensive in prison, Emmet agonised over how to protect Sarah Curran. Essentially he was a romantic idealist and his chivalrous instincts demanded that he do everything in his power to save the woman he loved. According to John Patten, Emmet had developed from his teens 'a sort of reverential deference' for women, believing that they 'preserved more traces of their original purity and excellence' than could be found in men.[20] For R. R. Madden, his attempts to save Sarah from prosecution in the final days of his life was unquestionable proof that his 'sentiment, with respect to the destiny and the noble qualities of women, was true and loyal in his chivalry, as every knight of old'.[21] Before his execution, Emmet admitted to Richard Curran that there had been 'moments in my imprisonment when my mind was so sunk by grief on her account, that death would have been a refuge'. On 3 September Robert decided to write directly to the chief secretary, William Wickham:

> Sir, I have heard of you as an honourable man, and as such I commit myself to you without reserve. I weighed well the proposal that was made to me when I was before the privy council. I know how much I owe to one whose peace of mind I have already too deeply injured, but every way that I turn I find obstacles almost insurmountable.[22]

He was torn between his public sense of duty and his private feelings of obligation towards Sarah. This was the crux for him and he rejected the suggestion that he could provide evidence like his brother had done in 1798. He insisted that there was 'no parallel' between that case and the present one: 'What was done then was neither done by one, nor for one, nor to spare their own personal feelings, nor to obtain an object of a private nature totally unconnected with the public act that was done.' But he was prepared to make a different offer to Wickham:

> Give me the same advantages. Let me have free communication with some friends; let the lives of others be spared; let the documents affecting another person be suppressed, and I will try how far in my conscience, and according to *my* notions of duty I ought to go.

Determined to act honourably, Emmet announced that he would not attempt to save his own live. He knew it was forfeit and was not interested in bargaining for it:

> I will stand my trial, for I will not purchase my own safety. If this proposal can be agreed to I request that the gentleman I mentioned [Burton] may be permitted to wait on me. I have the honour to be your very obedient humble servant, R. Emmet.

Three days later he received his response. The government would listen to any statement he wished to make, but would not consider itself bound to observe any of his conditions. On 7 September Emmet was brought to court and informed that a bill of indictment for high treason was found against him; his arraignment was set for the following week.[23] Asked to name his counsel, Emmet nominated John Philpot Curran, with Leonard MacNally Jr as his agent.

His escape attempt did not get very far. In early September Mason gave George Dunn 'several things to carry to Mr Emmet', but they were immediately examined by Trevor who removed some items which he thought 'were improper to be conveyed to him'. Emmet was convinced that Dunn should flee with him, and had to be dissuaded from this by his cousin. As Mason explained to him in a message which was immediately copied and sent to Dublin Castle, he must

> relinquish every idea of not going alone, or nothing can be done. I see no reason why G[eorge Dunn] should go; on the contrary consider it most imprudent and impolitic . . . Surely you would be less liable to discovery by being alone wherever you went for two nights . . . Prepare therefore to go alone.[24]

With typical concern for others, Emmet was afraid that the turnkey would suffer for having assisted in the escape, but Mason told him, 'It may be unpleasant to him at first, but he has nothing to do but to persist in his negligence, and brave it.' It was also another sign of Emmet's incurable optimism, that he believed he could break out of one of the most secure prisons in Ireland. Just as the plan was about to be implemented, George Dunn informed St John Mason that it had to be cancelled. His excuse was that the governor had become suspicious and had changed the security precautions.

Years later Mason was still filled with bitterness about Dunn's duplicity. In a letter to *The Times* in February 1842, replying to a previous correspondence, he stated that 'throughout the transaction . . . he [Dunn] practised the foulest perfidy'.[25] While pretending to be in a position to help, in reality he acted as the agent of 'the haunting spectre' of Kilmainham Jail, Dr Trevor, who was 'an incubus sojourning therein day and night, about sixteen hours of the twenty-four'. Mason accused Dunn of being nothing more than the pawn of Dr Trevor: he was 'merely his working instrument, the rope in the hands of the hangman'.[26] Writing as 'Verax', Mason also revealed that Dunn allowed Emmet to stop in the passage by his cell to allow them to converse and shake hands. But this was done,

> not from any congenial kindness of the inquisitor, but as a snare, not only for discovering whether any allusion would be made to the insurrection . . . but also to provoke in the presence of Dunn some proposition as to the escape which they could then wrest into a proof of a conspiracy and plot between the prisoners.

And while Mason insisted he viewed the rebellion 'with absolute and unquali-
fied condemnation', he admitted that he felt no moral guilt about the escape
attempt. His only regret was that it had failed. He revealed that his motives
were simple. Robert Emmet was his first cousin 'and the ties of nature are not
easily broken'. In addition he had enormous regard for Emmet and was even
a little in awe of him:

> He had a great and noble heart. He shared with the rest of his family those
> transcendent talents which have acquired for the name of Emmet an imper-
> ishable renown. But, above all, he was then upon the threshold of the grave
> — the finger of death was almost upon him; where lives the man having a
> human heart within him who would not under such circumstances have
> made a similar attempt?[27]

Mason's courageous efforts to free Emmet and later, it seems, Russell, convinced
the Castle of his involvement in the rebel conspiracy. In a parliamentary
inquiry into his case in 1812, Lord Castlereagh explained to the House of
Commons: 'The conduct of Mr Mason could be traced during his confinement
which greatly aggravated his guilt; for he had exerted himself to effect the
escape of Emmet and Russell, who were confined under the most serious
charge that could be brought against them, that of high treason.'[28]

In September, Henry Joseph Mason, Robert Emmet's uncle and St John's
father, was brought to Dublin Castle to make a statement about his knowledge
of the events. He revealed that he would not have 'the smallest hesitation in
giving evidence against Robert Emmet' and was determined to see justice
done against 'a man whose existence has been the cause of the death of so
many unfortunate men seduced' by his radical beliefs.[29] A few days later St
John was brought in to make his statement and he declared that he only knew
Robert Emmet in Trinity College when 'we were constant competitors during
all the examinations' and also at the meetings of the Historical Society. Apart
from those occasions, and despite being a first cousin, he claimed that he
'never even met him'.[30] This did not satisfy the authorities and Mason was left
in jail where he became increasingly embittered by his treatment at the hands
of Dr Trevor. He found Kilmainham Jail a 'loathsome den' and suffered from
the 'military violence' and 'rod of iron' of the ruthless superintendent.[31]

With the failure of his escape attempt, Emmet made the critical mistake of
writing to Sarah Curran. He was desperate to apologise to her and learn how she
was, naively believing that George Dunn would deliver the letter safely. It was being
examined by officials in Dublin Castle within the hour. Emmet had spent the day
of 8 September becoming increasingly frantic about Sarah's safety and had written to her father to visit. He was still hoping that John Philpot would defend him,
although he knew that if he discovered his relationship with Sarah this would be
impossible. As night fell he finally sat down to write to her, having spent the day
composing his thoughts. It began 'My dearest love' but continued bleakly:

I don't know how to write to you. I never felt so oppressed in my life as at the cruel injury I have done to you. I was seized and searched before I could destroy your letters. They have been compared with those found before. I was threatened with having them brought forward against me in court. I offered to plead guilty if they would suppress them. This was refused.[32]

He then summarised his cross-examination and his letter to Wickham, listing the attempts he had made to strike a deal that would save her from prosecution. Needless to say he did not mention his comments about women's 'opinions':

Information (without mentioning names) was required. I refused, but offered since, if I would be permitted to consult others, and that they would consent to enter into any accommodation of that nature to save the lives of those condemned, that I would require for my part of it to have those letters suppressed, and that I would stand my trial. It has been refused. My love, can you forgive me?

Returning to his cross-examination he explained that:

I wanted to know whether anything had been done respecting the person who wrote the letters, for I feared you might have been arrested. They refused to tell me for a long time. At length, when I said that it was but fair if they expected that I should enter into any accommodation that I should know for what I was to do it, then they asked me whether bringing you into the room to me would answer my purpose, upon which I got up and told them that it might answer theirs better. I was sure you were arrested, and I could not stand the idea of seeing you in that situation.

When no prisoner was produced, Emmet revealed that he gradually became convinced the Castle was bluffing. This was one of the reasons he wrote to Wickham, although with the rejection of the deal his old anxieties returned. He was torn between a belief that she might be prosecuted and a confidence that there was no proof to link her to the letters:

I began to think that they only meant to alarm me; but their refusal has only come this moment and my fears are renewed. Not that they can do anything to you even if they would be base enough to attempt it, for they can have no proof who wrote them, nor did I let your name escape me once, nor even to acknowledge that they were written directly to myself. But I fear they may suspect from the style, and from the hair, for they took the stock from me, and I have not been able to get it back from them, and that they may think of bringing you forward.

He explained that he had written to John Philpot Curran and asked him to call to the prison the next day. Until then Curran had no idea of his daughter's relationship, although Emmet was prepared to reveal everything at this meeting. Therefore he advised Sarah to pre-empt him and explain in advance: 'I have written to your father to come to me tomorrow. Had you not better speak to himself tonight?'

Not only concerned with how Sarah was feeling, Emmet was also worried about her physical safety. Therefore he pleaded with her to destroy all his letters, 'so that there may be nothing against yourself, and deny having any knowledge of me further than seeing me once or twice'. But, desperate to hear how she was, he added: 'For God's sake, write to me by the bearer one line to tell me how you are in spirits. I have no anxiety, no care, about myself; but I am terribly oppressed about you.' The very next line revealed the extent of his misery. 'My dearest love, I would with joy lay down my life, but ought I do more?' The letter ended with a poignant mixture of regret, affection and advice:

> Do not be alarmed; they may try to frighten you, but they cannot do more.
> God bless you, my dearest love. I must send this off at once; I have written
> it in the dark. My dearest Sarah, forgive me.'

The letter was addressed to 'Miss Sarah Curran'. After examining its contents, William Wickham authorised Major Sirr to search the Priory for incriminating documents at daybreak.

When Sirr arrived at the Curran residence in Rathfarnham on the Friday morning, Sarah was still in bed. Her father had not come home the night before, but the rest of the family were having breakfast in the dining room. The eldest daughter Amelia greeted the police when they arrived while her sister Jane and her brother Richard remained inside. Major Sirr presented his search warrant and then went straight to interrogate Sarah. When Wickham later read the report he regretted the fact that John Philpot had not been present, and felt genuine remorse about how the investigation had progressed. As he reported to Whitehall: 'The major entered the room where she was still in bed. This circumstance occasioned a scene of great confusion and distress.'[33] Upset at being confronted by strangers in her chamber and realising that her relationship with Emmet had been exposed, Sarah was 'thrown into violent convulsions'. Taking advantage of the chaos, Amelia raced to the secret alcove where her sister had stored her letters from Emmet and began burning the entire correspondence; the police attempted to stop her but only succeeded in saving a 'few scraps' which were 'all in Mr Emmet's handwriting'.

The attorney general visited the Priory later in the afternoon and was afterwards moved to report 'the most melancholy and affecting account of the state in which he left the whole family'. John Philpot Curran arrived home to discover his family in great distress; 'he was cruelly agitated at the visit' by the police.[34] Furious at Sarah's indiscretions, he discussed the matter thoroughly with Standish O'Grady and protested his own ignorance of the relationship. He did a good job convincing the government of his innocence and Wickham later confirmed that 'he was unquestionably ignorant of the connection between his daughter and Mr Emmet'. In turn, Curran noted that the government 'has acted throughout with great delicacy towards him', and was grateful for his treatment. The Irish administration was unwilling to make things even more difficult for the Curran family and immediately decided against prosecuting Sarah. Lord Hardwicke displayed an admirable spirit of generosity and 'particularly requests that Miss Curran's name may not be mentioned'. Wickham believed that it might be difficult to conceal her identity for long, but he did his best to ensure that it would not be mentioned publicly by either the British or Irish governments. The king, George III, later applauded 'the delicacy and management' which had been shown to the Curran family.[35] He read copies of the intercepted love letters with great interest and declared that 'Emmet's correspondence with the daughter of Mr Curran is certainly curious.' The home secretary believed that 'It is a sad affair' and made the interesting comment that 'Mademoiselle seems a true pupil of Mary Wollstonecraft.'

Thomas Russell was captured in Dublin that night. He had made his way to the capital after hearing of Emmet's arrest, in a quixotic attempt to liberate him. Arriving from Drogheda on 7 September, he rented a room at the home of Daniel Muley, the fifty-seven year old gunsmith who had made weapons for the conspiracy, at 28 Parliament Street.[36] This was taking a considerable risk, as he was right under the shadow of Dublin Castle, but it seems he was gambling that it would be the last place the government would look. Using the assumed name of Mr Harris, Russell only left the house at night-time. Soldiers patrolled the streets and on many occasions he was stopped, but he displayed his counterfeit pass and talked his way out of trouble.[37] Unfortunately for Russell there was a reward of £1,500 out for his capture and it became increasingly dangerous to remain in the city. Realising that there was little chance of rescuing Emmet, he decided to escape to the Isle of Man disguised as a clergyman.

Before he could finalise his plans, the house was raided by Major Sirr and a party of yeomanry on 9 September. Russell had left too much of a trail and his movements had come to the attention of John Swift Emerson, a member of the attorneys' yeomanry corps. Emerson had learned that 'a stranger of suspicious appearance' was staying with Muley and was being treated 'with mysterious respect and attention'. There is some uncertainty about how Emerson came to this information, although much suspicion has fallen on Walter Cox, a former newspaper editor and informer; he lived next door to Muley. When Major Sirr and Lieutenant Minchin entered Russell's room, he was so engrossed in his reading that he did not notice them. There was a long interrogation, but Russell refused to reveal his identity and insisted he was Mr Harris. Growing impatient, Sirr grabbed the ends of his neckcloth to see if it was marked with any initials. Angered by this affront to his honour, Russell declared that he would not be 'treated with indignity' and drew his pistol. Fatally, he hesitated for too long, and the two men disarmed him in the ensuing scuffle. Arrested and taken to Dublin Castle, Russell was recognised by his old friend, George Knox, who had been dining with William Wickham.[38]

It proved to be a particularly melancholy day for Emmet. Three disasters struck him on 9 September, although he never learned the unfortunate conjunction of events. His love Sarah Curran had a nervous breakdown after her house was raided; his friend and ally Thomas Russell was arrested; but there was also a final tragedy. His mother died at her home the same day. The death of her husband the previous year had taken its toll on her health, and the arrest of her youngest son only hastened her decline. She was buried on 13 September, although Robert only discovered her fate shortly before his execution.

After a lengthy meeting between William Wickham and John Philpot Curran it was decided that Robert would have to look elsewhere for representation. The lord lieutenant was adamant that Curran 'must decline being counsel for Emmet in a case in which his daughter may be implicated'. The whole affair was 'a very extraordinary story' but he believed it strengthened the case against Emmet.[39] On the morning of 10 September Curran met with Emmet's agent and informed him coldly that he could no longer defend him. Later in the day he sent Emmet a short letter explaining his position, urging him not to make any reference to Sarah at the trial. The icy tone was unmistakable:

> From the circumstances which you must suppose have come to my knowledge, you could not have been surprised at my intimation this morning to your agent that I could not act as your counsel. I write this merely to suggest to you that if those circumstances be not brought forward by crown, which from their humanity I hope will be suppressed, it cannot be of any advantage to you to disclose them to your agent or counsel.[40]

Counsellor Burton also refused to help Emmet 'from a motive of delicacy'; he was Curran's clerk. When Emmet received this news he took it 'with perfect calmness'.[41] It was the outcome he had expected and he sat down and wrote Curran a very long and detailed letter. Nevertheless some others predicted that 'Curran's refusing to act for Emmet will render him very unpopular; being assigned, the party say he is bound to act.'[42] As a result of these changes, Emmet's arraignment was delayed. He was due in court on 14 September to give his plea, but this was postponed for a day and on 12 September a motion was made to assign him new counsel. Thus Peter Burrowes, his brother's friend, took Curran's place to defend him, with Leonard MacNally assisting. It was a measure of just how distant Thomas Moore and Robert Emmet had become that it was only in September 1830 he discovered that Peter Burrowes had represented his friend. Burrowes informed him that after Sarah Curran's letter had been intercepted, Emmet was in such despair that he made 'the most earnest entreaties to the government' that if they suppressed it at his trial he would 'not say a word in his own defence but to go to his death in silence'.[43] He did this knowing 'how much it was an object with the authorities that he should not address the people'. The offer was peremptorily refused.

On Wednesday 15 September Emmet was brought before Green Street Court. The crown stated:

> Robert Emmet . . . not having the fear of God in his heart, nor weighing the duty of his allegiance, but being moved and seduced by the instigation of the devil, as a false traitor against our said lord the now king.[44]

There was a reading of the long indictment and he was accused repeatedly of being a 'false traitor'. After listening to the charges read against him, it was time for Emmet to make his plea: he declared he was not guilty. His trial was set for Monday 19 September. On Sunday, the day before, Richard Curran intervened to protect his sister. He had been torn between protecting her and helping one of his best friends, but in the end put family loyalty first. On 18 September he agreed to give the government samples of Emmet's handwriting, in return for the suppression of Sarah's letters and the screening of her identity. The attorney general was delighted by this and recognised that it would make the prosecution's task considerably easier.[45] But Richard had not turned his back on his old friend, and at the same time sent him a generous letter of support, affection and forgiveness; this helped to ease Robert's feelings of guilt and despondency in his final days, although he was tormented to learn that Sarah's mind was 'a prey to affliction'.[46]

Robert Emmet never learned the truth about how his letter to Sarah Curran had been discovered. To maintain George Dunn's trusted status, an elaborate explanation was prepared for his benefit. He was told that it had been sent too late and that the authorities had apprehended the messenger. In this version, when Dunn was caught he had attempted to throw the letter into the river, but it had only landed on the strand and was later intercepted.[47] When Emmet learned that Sarah was now incriminated and facing possible prosecution, he could no longer hide his feelings. His trusted counsel, Leonard MacNally, noticed that he was 'deeply affected on account of the young lady whose letters are in the possession of government'. Indeed he had given up any interest in saving his own life and now thought only about how he could protect her reputation. As MacNally recorded:

> On this subject his mind seems wholly bent, and cruelly afflicted. For his own personal safety he appears not to entertain an idea. He does not intend to call a single witness, nor to trouble any witness for the crown with a cross-examination, unless they misrepresent facts.

Since his arrest he had received several coded letters from his brother in Paris, but because he had lost his cypher he was unable to translate them. All this time he declared that 'it never was his intention that France should have a footing in Ireland'. Bemused, but feigning exasperation, MacNally wondered what use counsel could be, when Emmet would not 'controvert the charge by calling a single witness'.[48]

While Robert Emmet may have been a good leader, he was a terrible judge of men. Always too trusting, it was one of the main reasons why the rebellion failed: he had taken at face value the declarations of support and believed every promise that he received. In prison he allowed himself to be completely deceived by George Dunn, whose treachery implicated the very person he wanted to protect the most. But the greatest betrayal was still to come. Leonard MacNally, the trusted defender of the United Irishmen, reported everything he said back to Dublin Castle. With one of his barristers working against him all the time, Robert Emmet's defence never had a chance.

A dramatist as well as a lawyer, MacNally was an easily recognisable figure at the Four Courts in Dublin. He had a serious limp as one leg was shorter than the other, and when he was in a hurry 'he generally took two thumping steps with the short leg to bring up the space made by the long one'.[49] Jonah Barrington explained that 'his figure was ludicrous; he was very short, and nearly as broad as long . . . and he had a face which no washing could clean'. A noted duellist, MacNally lost his thumb in an affair of honour in 1797 but declined to wear a glove to conceal his deformity. Despite a shrill voice he was a brilliant cross-examiner, but because he was so dirty the circuit bar refused to allow him into its mess. He was also a composer of some note and had written the popular song 'The lass of Richmond Hill' for the woman he loved; she later became his wife.[50] Indeed at some of the state trials, MacNally took to quoting from his *Robin Hood*. For example, when he was defending John Macintosh, he reminded the court of the comment made by Little John to a friar: 'I have four reasons for hanging you, and one is, you have a damned hanging look.'[51]

The double life of Leonard MacNally would have astonished his contemporaries. It was only revealed long after his death by the historian W. J. Fitzpatrick. Charles Philips, the biographer of John Philpot Curran, refused to credit it and insisted that if he was 'called upon to point out, next to Curran, the man most obnoxious to the government — who most hated them, and was hated by them — it would have been Leonard MacNally'.[52] Nevertheless the evidence against him is overwhelming. As a reward for betraying his different clients, MacNally was given an annual secret service pension of £300 in 1800. He received an additional bonus of £100 on 14 September 1803 for keeping the government informed about Robert Emmet's private conversations. His son and namesake acted as Emmet's solicitor in his trial for treason. An aggressive character, he was once attacked by footpads near Rathcoole. When MacNally asked someone if they had heard of his son's robbery, the reply he received was, 'No, whom did he rob?'[53] On 13 February 1820 MacNally died after a long fever. On his deathbed he converted to Catholicism. His son's sarcastic comment was that he should 'go to the devil his own way'.

In his final letter to John Philpot Curran, written on 12 September, Robert Emmet made a brave attempt to apologise for his behaviour and protect Sarah.[54] It is an interesting though not always accurate account of their relationship; Emmet was primarily concerned with shielding Sarah from her father's anger and thus constantly downplayed her knowledge of his activities. He began by acknowledging that he had not really expected Curran to be his counsel: 'I nominated you because not to have done so might have appeared remarkable.' Then he apologised for the pain he had brought to the family and summarised the attempts he had made to prevent the letters being brought forward:

> I know that I have done you very severe injury, much greater than I can atone for with my life. That atonement I did offer to make before the privy council, by pleading guilty if those documents were suppressed. I offered more. I offered, if I was permitted to consult some persons, and if they would consent to an accommodation for saving the lives of others, that I would only require for my part of it the suppression of those documents, and that I would abide the event of my own trial.

He then explained that this too was rejected by the government. To guarantee that the letters would not have to be used as evidence, he revealed that he had even been willing to plead guilty and thus make their production unnecessary.

Embarking on a detailed but subjective account of his relationship with Sarah, Emmet insisted that he did not do this for his 'own justification', but rather to confirm her innocence. Again his modesty was much in evidence:

> When I first addressed your daughter I expected that in another week my own fate would be decided. I knew that in case of success many others might look on me differently from what they did at that moment, but I speak with sincerity when I say that I never was anxious for situation or distinction myself.

Nor, he insisted, did he seek to be married to someone who was important. He explained that he 'spoke to your daughter, neither expecting, nor, in fact, under those circumstances, wishing that there should be a return of attachment'. Rather he wanted to 'judge of her dispositions' and discover 'how far they might be not unfavourable or disengaged, and to know what foundation I might afterwards have to count on'. According to Emmet, he did not get far: 'I received no encouragement whatever.' Although Sarah told him that she 'had no attachment for any person', she did not think it possible that she could form any relationship that would make her want to leave her father. This was direct flattery but it was worth the effort.

Continuing with his narrative, Emmet explained that he 'stayed away till the time had elapsed when I found that the event to which I alluded was to be post-poned indefinitely'. It was as an insecure and nervous suitor that he later called to see her: 'I returned by a kind of infatuation, thinking that to myself only was I giving pleasure or pain. I perceived no progress of attachment on her part, nor anything in her conduct to distinguish me from a common acquaint-ance.' The first sign that Sarah had feelings for him, or so he claimed, was when it appeared that he was about to be arrested and was considering leaving the country: 'Afterwards I had reason to suppose that discoveries were made, and that I should be obliged to quit the kingdom immediately; and I came to make a renunciation of any approach to friendship that might have been formed.' It was at this meeting that 'she herself spoke to me to discontinue my visits'. When Emmet revealed that this was his intention, and gave the reason why, he discovered for the first time, 'when I was unfortunate, by the manner in which she was affected, that there was a return of affection, and also that it was too late to retreat'. He then explained: 'My own apprehensions, also, I afterwards found were without cause, and I remained.'

This romanticisation of his relationship with Sarah Curran was written to assuage her father's anger. There are far too many problems with the account, not least chronological distortions, for it to be accepted as a reliable narrative. The letter is deliberately vague for obvious reasons; otherwise it could have been used as evidence against him. Emmet claimed that he first addressed Sarah a week before he thought his own fate would be decided, in other words around 16 July. He said he received no encouragement. The next time he visited her was after the rebellion had been defeated (or rather 'postponed indefinitely'), and this could only have been around 1 August. Again there was no indication that she cared about him. The first occasion he discovered the extent of her feelings was 'afterwards' when he feared arrest and considered leaving the country. It was only then that he learned she loved him and, because he believed it was safe, he remained in Ireland. But since he was arrested on 25 August, the whole courtship, according to this version, could only have taken place over three weeks while he was in hiding. This time-frame was far too compressed for the relationship to have developed as far as it did. And undermining the entire account, apart from the skewered chronology, is the fact that a draft love letter from Robert to Sarah, written before 23 July, was discovered at the Marshal Lane depot.[55] In any case the account of the relationship which he sent to Richard Curran the night before his execution was substantially different. Emmet was a man of honour, but he was not above using deception to protect someone else's honour.

Emmet's letter to Curran developed into an extended apology for the pain he had caused and a defence of his relationship. He admitted that he bore much of the blame for what had happened: 'There has been much culpability on my part in all of this.' But with a touch of self-pity he suggested that there had also been 'a good deal of that misfortune which seems uniformly to have accompanied me'. Going on to explain his intercepted letter to Sarah, he conceded that it was 'an additional breach of propriety, for which I have suffered well'. Nevertheless he argued eloquently that it would have been a far greater insult not to have written, 'when an attachment was once formed between us, and a sincerer one never did exist'. He felt that 'to have left her uncertain of my situation would neither have weaned her affections nor lessened her anxiety'. In a tender portrayal of his imagined future with Sarah, he revealed that 'if I had lived, I hoped to have had my partner for life', with his only object 'the removing of her anxiety above every other consideration'. His love for Sarah was far greater than any personal ambition and he declared: 'I would rather have had the affections of your daughter in the back settlements of America, than the first situation this country could afford without them.' And he pledged that even if he was in an exalted position in charge of Ireland he would 'relinquish it to devote my life to her happiness'. All this he knew was unlikely to mitigate against his perceived offence or justify his actions. He was well aware that Curran was an ambitious man, and was attempting to appeal to every instinct. But he conceded he was unsure whether even great 'success would have blotted out the recollection of what I have done'.

Fighting back his despair, Emmet ended the letter on a melancholy note. In part it was a rebuke to John Philpot Curran for his ungracious behaviour: 'I know that a man with the coldness of death on him need not be made to feel any other coldness.' But it was also mingled with regret about the pain and suffering he had brought to the woman he loved. Therefore he made a desperate plea to 'be spared any addition to the misery he feels, not for himself, but for those to whom he has left nothing but sorrow'.

10

THE TRIAL OF ROBERT EMMET

~

'There is nothing like the courtroom to obliterate fellow-feeling.'
(Richard Ellmann on the trial of Oscar Wilde)

It seemed the only topic of conversation which people wanted to discuss in Dublin in the third week of September was the trial of Robert Emmet. As William Wickham informed Whitehall, 'It would be difficult for any stranger to form any idea of the degree of general interest and expectation' which the case 'begins to excite in this city.'[1] A number of rebels had already been convicted and executed, but this had only whetted the public's appetite and it eagerly awaited the biggest trial of them all. The judge entrusted with the case was Lord Norbury, the man who Jonah Barrington had once declared had 'a hand for every man, and a heart for nobody'. Always desperate to demonstrate his wit, without actually being funny, Norbury had a predilection for taking off his gown and turning his wig back to front when it became too hot in the courtroom.[2] He had a fat face and grey eyes, and his stern countenance once prompted a critic to note that he 'set dignity at defiance and put gravity to flight'. Assisting him on the special commission were Baron George and Baron Daly. After the brutal murder of their colleague, Lord Kilwarden, the three men were determined to see justice done on the morning of Monday 19 September.

Green Street Courthouse was filled with excited onlookers as Robert Emmet was led in chains under armed guard to stand at the dock. According to his cousin, St John Mason, when he left Kilmainham he passed by his cell and whispered '*Utrumque paratus*'.[3] This was a direct quotation from Virgil's *Aeneid*, the story of a hero from a fallen city who founds Rome. Emmet was drawing on his classical education to indicate that he was willing to accept whatever happened, and was equally prepared for life or death. The trial began at 9.30 a.m. The prosecution was taking no chances with securing a conviction and had assembled an extensive 'devil's brief' of all the evidence against Emmet.

Nineteen witnesses were brought forward throughout the day, introduced in an order best calculated to demonstrate the extent of his guilt. The crown was also prepared to call Pat McCabe, the rebel who had turned informer, to prove that the people were armed in the depot by Emmet personally. No witnesses were produced by the defence. The lord lieutenant was afterwards delighted to report that it was 'universally admitted that a more complete case of treason was never stated in a court of justice'.[4] The crown's job was made considerably easier by Emmet's refusal to defend himself; he rarely allowed his barristers to cross-examine and he forbade them from make a closing statement.

The twelve-man jury was sworn in: John Geale, John Dickson, Robert Turbett, Daniel Kinahan, Beaver Buchanan, William Davis, W. G. Galway, Charles Harte, Benjamin Holmes, John Lloyd, Walter Locke and Thomas Palmer.[5] As with all major trials a large panel of jurors had been selected in advance, but the prosecution dismissed twelve, while the defence challenged two for not living in the city, and rejected a further nineteen peremptorily. Standish O'Grady, the attorney general, was in charge of the case and he deposed the most important witnesses. The counsel for the crown also included the solicitor general James McClelland, William Plunket and four other barristers, Mayne, Townsend, Ridgeway and O'Grady.[6] Plunket was given the crucial responsibility for making the closing argument, but it was the attorney general who opened the trial for the prosecution. Two lawyers represented Emmet: Peter Burrowes was the leading barrister, assisted by Leonard MacNally.

In an exhaustive presentation of the evidence, Standish O'Grady addressed the court until midday. He began by acknowledging that 'Perhaps at former periods some allowances might be made for the heated imagination of enthusiasts,' but, he solemnly declared, 'sad experience has taught us that modern revolution is not the road to liberty.' Rather he insisted, it 'originates in anarchy, proceeds in bloodshed and ends in cruel and unrelenting despotism'. Directly addressing the jury, the attorney general accused Emmet of 'a crime of the blackest dye, and which under all existing circumstances does not admit of a momentary extenuation'. The indictment of Emmet was grounded on three clauses, all originating in the centuries-old treason statue of the 25 Edward III. O'Grady revealed that the prisoner had encompassed and imagined the death of the king, formed an alliance with the king's enemies, and had attempted to wage war against the crown. The final two of these charges were perfectly 'intelligible in themselves that they do not require any observation upon them', but O'Grady accepted that the 'first does admit of some technical consideration and may require upon my part a short explanation'. Defining the 'language of the law', the attorney general explained that 'compassing' the death of the king did not necessarily imply 'an immediate attack upon his person'. Any attack on the 'laws, constitution and government' of Ireland would create 'anarchy and general destruction' and therefore inevitably threaten the life of the king. Thus he revealed that any rebellious activity could be considered as 'compassing and imagining the death of the king'.

Moving on to a discussion of the 'overt' crimes which Emmet had committed, O'Grady made the melodramatic statement that he could disclose 'the traitorous imagination' of Emmet's heart.[7] It was the first of a number of lavish claims he would make in the course of his speech, as he habitually resorted to hyperbole to furnish his arguments. He informed the jury that it had only two questions to consider: first, 'Whether there has, or has not existed, some traitorous conspiracy and rebellion for the purpose of altering the law, the constitution and the government of the country by force?'; and second, 'Whether the prisoner has in any, and what degree participated in that conspiracy and rebellion?' Having laid down these points, O'Grady changed direction and launched into a speech thanking the public at large for remaining peaceful and aloof from the rebellion. He also took the opportunity to praise the government publicly for its 'vigilance and firmness' in dealing with the crisis.

Reflecting on the other prisoners who had been tried before the special commission, O'Grady acknowledged that some of them were possibly 'implicated in the rebellion' in 'inferior degrees'. But this was not the case with the prisoner, and he confidently asserted: 'We have now brought to the bar of justice, not a person who has been seduced by others, but a gentleman to whom the rebellion may be traced, as the origin, the life and the soul of it.' He then embarked on a brief résumé of Emmet's travels abroad and suggested that his 'continental tour, embracing France' filled him with 'mischievous designs'. France had already experienced the disastrous effects of revolution, so the attorney general insisted that Emmet had therefore embarked on his actions, 'with his eyes open, and with a previous knowledge of all its inevitable consequences'. He followed this with a remarkable attack on the nature of the rebellion, which he insisted was without comparison 'in any country, ancient or modern'. His reasoning was based on the fact that it had not been motivated by some recent injury, but rather by 'the memory of grievances which, if they ever existed, must have long since passed away'.[8] With a sweeping rhetorical flourish he declared that 'the provocations of 600 years have been ransacked, the sufferings of our ancestors have been exaggerated, our state in former ages, and at various remote times misrepresented' in order to legitimise the rising of 23 July.

This prompted O'Grady to conclude that there was no possible justification for what had happened. Emmet had plundered 'the ashes of our ancestors' to provoke a conflict and had wilfully ignored the fact that there 'is no motive for rebellion now'. Speaking for the entire nation he asserted: 'We live under a constitution which we love, free, affluent and happy'; therefore 'rebellion can have no incentive in our present condition.' The irresponsible actions of Emmet had launched a 'manifesto of treason' which threatened to wage 'eternal war against the British constitution'. He expressed no sympathy for the conspiracy and insisted that its leaders were rebels 'at heart' who had no valid reason for fighting against 'the mildest administration of our government'. Pausing for breath, he conceded that the warmth of his feelings might be 'giving a colour to the cause which it does not deserve'. If this was true, he insisted he was sorry, but he was adamant that the proclamation of the provisional government supported his claims.

Turning his speech to the role of Robert Emmet in all these events, O'Grady revealed that the source of the rebellion could be traced back to his return to Ireland at Christmas 1802. The only evidence which he presented for this claim was the line in the proclamation which referred to the preparations which had been made 'within the last eight months'. The use of aliases by Emmet was also commented on unfavourably. O'Grady discussed his suspicious behaviour in taking residence in an 'obscure house' in Harold's Cross using the name of Hewitt. The lease of a premises on Patrick Street was also mentioned, as well as the move to Butterfield Lane under the alias of Robert Ellis. After the explosion at Patrick Street on 16 July, O'Grady revealed that Emmet lived at the depot at Marshal Lane and acted as 'the master of the family, superintending the formation of pikes and ball cartridges, inspecting the ammunition, inspecting the arms, occasionally writing at his desk'.

O'Grady was a lawyer of limited ability who owed his rise more to his support of the government than to any legal accomplishments. His opening statement was filled with colourful flights of fancy and he could not resist resorting to hyperbole to press his arguments. When discussing the depot at Marshal Lane he embarked on an extraordinary commentary about Emmet's state of mind before the rebellion. His speculation centred on the mattress which had been discovered in the depot and which he suggested Emmet occasionally slept on, 'if indeed, under the circumstances, it is not going a little too far to suppose that any man could sleep, his mind must have been of more than ordinary temperature, if his slumbers were not a little disturbed'.[9] Becoming increasingly fevered in his analysis, O'Grady concluded that Emmet 'could not easily enjoy soft natural repose', because he was surrounded by the 'implements of death' while waiting to embark on a 'civil war for the destruction of his fellow citizens'. But he did not leave it at that. He then suggested an alternate analysis just in case it was revealed that Emmet had slept well before the rebellion. Then his sleep would have been 'produced by that wearing perturbation of mind, agitated by enthusiasm, which listens not to reason' but gives in to 'the phantoms of a disturbed brain' and forms 'the substance and stability of truth'. Having entangled himself in unnecessary knots on this subject, O'Grady then attempted to ascertain Emmet's religious principles by deducing that 'Under such circumstances, no man could lay his head upon his pillow, and call upon his God to lighten the darkness which surrounded him and to preserve him from the perils and dangers of the night.' And he asked solemnly how any mind 'could take refuge in the consolation of religion, when it was occupied in meditation how to drag our gracious monarch from his hereditary throne, and to immerse himself in the blood of his subjects'. But then, he said, 'the reflections of reason cannot be applied to the ravings of enthusiasm!'

As far as O'Grady was concerned, Emmet was an extremist and he quoted disapprovingly an extract from the paper discovered at the Marshal Lane depot which included the lines about 'the vision of happiness, that my fancy formed in the air'. This prompted him to conclude that Emmet was consumed by an 'ill-fated and delirious passion' and had long disguised his 'extravagance of vice' under 'the colour of virtue'. He informed the jury that Emmet's 'wild projects' had been nothing more than the product of a 'delicious dream' and his 'disturbed imagination'. Turning his attention to the proclamation of the provisional government, O'Grady revealed that a draft had been discovered in the main depot, the authorship of which he attributed to Emmet. There followed a long examination of this document, which the crown argued proved conclusively the treasonable design of the defendant. He also discussed the short proclamation and quoted selected sections to the court. The question of 'English oppression' was one he refuted, asking rhetorically, 'What is this oppression which is exercised over us?'[10] For, he explained, 'We live under the same king, we enjoy the same constitution, we are governed by the same laws, we speak the same language . . . in short we are united by every tie of interest, affinity and affection.'

Emmet's adventures in the Wicklow mountains were briefly summarised for the jury. O'Grady was scathing about the 'progress of the general, who escaped the memorable action which was intended to be fought'.[11] He explained how the rebels had sought refuge in John Doyle's house, with the leaders in the main bedroom, 'leaving their followers in the true spirit of equality to shift for themselves'. Then he traced Emmet's progress to Mrs Bagnall's farm, and from there back to Harold's Cross, where he resumed his identity of Hewitt. This prompted one of the most dramatic passages of the entire speech, as O'Grady imagined the 'distressing picture' of Emmet in this 'afflicting situation'. He described 'this young man' lying terrified in his room, 'trembling at every blast, and meditating plans, not of conquest but escape'. This, he felt, was a remarkable transformation for Emmet:

> he who was lately preparing arms and ammunition for the thousands he was to command, and laws and constitutions for the ten thousands he was to conquer, he who was to have been seated in his majesty's Castle, and to have shaken the British empire, is fallen from his fantastic dreams, reduced to becoming a voluntary prisoner, and to confine that ambition which embraced a nation, within the narrow limits of a cell.

He then discussed the capture of Robert Emmet and the 'activity and intrepidity' of Major Sirr in arresting him. Even his line, 'All was fair in war', was quoted as evidence of his treason.[12] Sarah Curran's final letter to Emmet was then presented to the court, but only extracts were read and O'Grady said that it appeared 'to have been written by a brother conspirator acquainted with his schemes and participating in his crimes'. Sarah's suspicions of French aid were seized upon as showing that every 'intelligent rebel' had concerns about 'his allies in France'. This prompted a brief digression about the French revolution and while O'Grady admitted that some grievances may have existed in the *ancien régime*, he argued that 'Having shaken off the sceptre of a lawful king, they were obliged to take refuge from their distractions in the power and authority of a military usurper.' Since then, he claimed, 'the turbulence of freedom has sunk into a tranquil tyranny'. The same would happen in Ireland, he insisted, and if the conspiracy had succeeded there would be 'an end of law, of justice and of religion' in Ireland.[13] Thus he argued that only a 'blind infatuation' could make a man desire to attempt 'the experiment'.

The letter to the government, which Emmet had been working on prior to his arrest, was quoted selectively to damage his reputation. This was seized upon as proof that Emmet had experienced, 'in the progress of guilt, some momentary compunction'. O'Grady claimed that the letter had been directed by a desire to stop the administration of justice and 'deter government from pursuing that temperate but inflexible course which it has adopted'. Significantly, Emmet's line about feeling, as an Irishman, an interest with 'the English part of the present administration' was studied in detail. By comparing it to the proclamation of the provisional government, O'Grady argued that it proved how men of Irish birth would be killed for supporting the administration. He said that British soldiers would be treated as prisoners of war, but yeomen and militia were 'to be tried by court martial and suffer death for their infidelity'. The fact that Emmet had assumed the 'language of an ambassador' in the letter astonished the attorney general. In addition, he was angered by the suggestion that the government knew 'comparatively speaking, nothing' about the conspiracy. In a powerful passage he argued that the

treason was dwarfed by the narrow limits within which vigilance restrained it. The moment it burst it evaporated. Within an hour, and with a force not amounting to one hundred men, this formidable rebellion was extinguished; and the mighty mass of eight months' preparation melted into nothing.[14]

O'Grady had missed the irony in Emmet's question, 'Is it only now we are to learn that entering into conspiracy exposes us to be hanged?' With complete seriousness he addressed this point and suggested that 'from the readiness with which some men enter into treasonable pursuits, it would appear as if this salutary lesson remained to be taught'. He dismissed Emmet's plea for mercy for captured rebels and called it 'a very feeling pathetic address'.

In his peroration, O'Grady called upon the jury to act impartially in the case. He acknowledged that some of the men who had already been brought to justice were 'comparatively speaking, insignificant persons'.[15] But he insisted that with Emmet they had 'the prime mover of this rebellion' before them. He was determined to cut the entire web of the conspiracy, and not just a few threads from the end, and for that reason 'The unhappy instruments, as well as their principals, must atone for the mischief they have committed.' Resorting to a truism, he insisted that 'there would be no rebellion if there were no conspirators' and 'there would be no conspirators if there were no instruments to be worked with'. Therefore, he insisted, both should be punished. Robert Emmet, he reminded the jury, was an innocent man until proven guilty and should be given the full benefit of the law. He hoped it would 'give the prisoner the full benefit of any defence, which he may make, and dispassionately consider the nature of his vindication'. But he also warned the jurors that they also had a duty to 'king and country' and must remember that 'many victims have fallen' in the rebellion. He intended to prove that Emmet was 'the spring which gave it life and activity', but if he was wrong he said he would 'heartily participate in the common joy that must result from the acquittal of an innocent man'.[16]

The first witness for the prosecution was Joseph Rawlins, the family attorney of the late Dr Emmet. He confirmed that Robert had arrived back in Ireland before December 1802 and said he had 'been to see his brother in Brussels'.[17] Peter Burrowes cross-examined, endeavouring to prove that Emmet had been highly critical of the French government. He wanted to know if Rawlins had any serious conversations with the prisoner. When he admitted that they discussed various matters before the death of his father, he asked:

> *Burrowes:* Did it turn upon continental politics?
> *Rawlins:* Yes. He said the inhabitants of the *Austrian Netherlands* execrated
>   *Buonaparte's* government.
> *Burrowes:* Did you not from the whole of the conversation collect that he
>   highly condemned that government?
> *Rawlins:* It certainly made that impression upon my mind.[18]

There were no further questions. Afterwards Robert Holmes was so disgusted with Rawlins's conduct in testifying against his brother-in-law that he never employed him in any legal matter again.

Next to be examined was another attorney, George Tyrrel, who had helped prepare the lease for 'Robert Ellis' at Butterfield Lane. He identified Robert Emmet to the satisfaction of the court as the person who had executed the lease and confirmed that he had used the alias Robert Ellis. Tyrrel who hailed from Mullingar, Co. Westmeath, recognised William Dowdall as one of Emmet's accomplices. The solicitor general attempted to ask the witness what he had heard of Dowdall, but Burrowes interjected that this was merely hearsay and Norbury ruled in his favour. The next witness was Michael Frayne, who lived next door to Emmet on Butterfield Lane. He testifed that the prisoner in the dock had taken the lease to the house and described how workmen had built fences for a fortnight before he took up residence.[19] He then revealed that the men who lived in the house were 'very quiet' and that there was neither 'noise nor drink; they lived in a sequestered manner, as if they did not wish to see any people'.[20] As far as Frayne was concerned the house was inhabited by 'an odd sort of people'. Burrowes cross-examined and asked him if he had ever heard of a man called Dowdall living at the house. Frayne admitted that he had only heard him mentioned the day the lease was taken. For the first time in the day, Robert Emmet spoke to the court. In a highly inappropriate intervention, he asked the witness, 'Did you ever see Mr Dowdall lie there?' Frayne admitted that he 'did not know whether he did or not' as he had never seen him in a bedroom. It may seem strange that Emmet was so preoccupied with attempting to show that Dowdall had not been present at Butterfield Lane. After all, Dowdall had indeed lived there, but Emmet was determined to suppress the truth about his accomplices so that any evidence given at his trial could not be used against them. As Burrowes later recounted, Emmet only prevented his defence from cross-examining 'on points bearing against himself, for whenever the testimony was likely to involve or incriminate others he showed the utmost anxiety that the truth should not appear'.[21] Rising to his feet, William Plunket asked Frayne if he could prove that Emmet had slept at Butterfield Lane. This was something he was able to answer a little better, and he told the court that when he called at the house one morning he was told by the maid that he was not up. But when Burrowes immediately followed up, Frayne was forced to concede that he had never seen 'any party there of any kind'.

An ostler who lived at the White Bull Inn on Thomas Street, John Fleming, was called to testify about the weapons and ammunition he had observed at the depot on Marshal Lane. Fleming was one of the rebels who had made a deal with the government after his arrest. He confirmed that he had witnessed the making of pikes and ball cartridges and the storage of 'blunderbusses, fire-locks and pistols'.[22] As one of the men who had fought on the night of the rebellion, he also testified to the uniforms the leaders had worn and the march on to Thomas Street. Burrowes performed a clever cross-examination of the witness, forcing him to admit that he only gave information to the government after his arrest on a charge of high treason about a month after the rebellion. He then asked him if his injuries had healed. Fleming insisted that he 'never got the least wound, but a little scratch upon the leg' on the night of 23 July.[23] In a clever move, Burrowes attempted to ascertain if Fleming had been offered immunity from prosecution in return for testifying against Emmet. Fleming denied this, but he was not convincing:

Burrowes: Upon your oath have you been promised any pardon in conse-
quence of making discoveries?
Fleming: I have not been promised anything. I gave myself up to government
to become a good subject.
Burrowes: Do you expect to be prosecuted?
Fleming: I cannot say.
Burrowes: What do you believe?
Fleming: To the best of my opinion, I cannot say.
Burrowes: On your oath, do you not think that you would be prosecuted, if
you did not give evidence?

> *Fleming:* If there would be evidence against me, surely I would be prosecuted.
> *Burrowes:* On your oath, did you give the information you did from a horror of the rebellion, or in hopes that it would be of service to yourself?
> *Fleming:* I gave it from a horror of the rebellion.
> *Burrowes:* And not from an expectation of being benefited thereby?
> *Fleming:* I never expected anything.

Burrowes then asked if Emmet had worn a greatcoat on the night of the rebellion. Fleming said that he had asked for one, but never got it.

The Lucan tailor, Terence Colgan, was the next crown witness and told an elaborate story of how he had ended up making uniforms for the rebels. It involved him drinking with a friend at the White Bull Inn, falling asleep and waking up in a dark out-house where he was forced to work for Emmet. Leonard MacNally was intrigued by Colgan's obviously invented story and questioned him at length about it. He asked him if he now lived in town. Colgan insisted that he did. But when MacNally asked him if he would swear to this, he hesitated and said, 'No, I am now upon the bench.' MacNally was bemused by his tale of late night drinking with a friend and asked him:

> *MacNally:* Do you not believe that your friend was a great rogue.
> *Colgan:* He was a great foe to me.
> *MacNally:* He was a great rebel?
> *Colgan:* I believe so.

But MacNally was curious about why Colgan hadn't reported this to the police after his release, which he would surely have done if he had been genuinely taken against his will. He learned that Colgan had been arrested after the rebellion when someone had informed on him. This prompted him to ask:

> *MacNally:* Would you have given information till the day of judgement if you had not been taken?
> *Colgan:* I believe not.
> *MacNally:* Was it for the sake of public justice that you gave information?
> *Colgan:* It was for the sake of my family.
> *MacNally:* How for the sake of your family?
> *Colgan:* To recover my liberty to earn bread for them.
> *MacNally:* But you would not have told anything of the matter if you had not been taken?
> *Colgan:* No.[24]

Colgan was a terrible liar. When a juror asked him if he had fallen asleep in the depot, or had been carried there while he was drunk, he contradicted his previous testimony completely. He told the man, 'Indeed, I believe I fell asleep there.'

A witness who had been genuinely held against his will by the rebels was Patrick Farrell, the man who had been captured on the night of 22 July. He was called to prove that Emmet was the leader of the conspiracy, but he also revealed how Emmet had saved his life. Farrell was asked specifically if Emmet had given the order that he was not to be killed and he insisted, 'I am positively sure.'[25] Robert Emmet was not satisfied with this testimony. At the end of the account he asked Leonard MacNally to put certain questions to the witness. MacNally stated that he had not intended to ask anything, 'but at the express desire of my client, I shall be excused in putting such questions as he suggests to me, and which will be considered as coming directly from him'. Emmet was anxious to prove three things: first, that Farrell had been treated well while in captivity; second, that French support was not depended upon by the rebels; and third, that some of the other rebels had questioned the merciful tone of the proclamation. The questions which Emmet asked through MacNally were intelligent and precise:

MacNally: You say you saw Quigley?
Farrell: I did.
MacNally: The prisoner wishes to know what business he is.
Farrell: I do not know what he is; but he was employed about Maynooth as a mason. I knew him and remember him well, and can not be mistaken.
MacNally: Did you see Dowdall there?
Farrell: If I did, I did not know him.
MacNally: How many people did you see there who appeared to be active men, having command in different situations?
Farrell: There were a good many, and every man very hearty in the business.
MacNally: Did many go in and out, who had no residence in the place?
Farrell: There did.
MacNally: What appearance had they?
Farrell: Some of them country people, and some like citizens, and some well dressed people.
MacNally: Were there any like esquires?
Farrell: I can't say.
MacNally: Were you not well fed while you were there and treated with lenity and humanity?
Farrell: Middling.
MacNally: You had the same allowance as the others?
Farrell: I had a little milk.
MacNally: Any meat?
Farrell: Not a bit.
MacNally: Any beer?
Farrell: No.
MacNally: Whiskey?
Farrell: No.

MacNally: Any bread?

Farrell: Yes.

MacNally: Was it cold?

Farrell: It was not very warm.

MacNally: Did you hear any printed paper read?

Farrell: I did, part of it only.

MacNally: What did it state?

Farrell: I cannot recollect it all now; but it appeared to me as if the man reading said that nineteen counties were ready to rise.

MacNally: Was anything said about the French?

Farrell: Not the smallest, as I heard. They said they had no idea as to French relief but to make it good themselves.

MacNally: Do you recollect that any person objected to the paper when it was read, or that any observation was made as to its being proper or improper?

Farrell: The observation I heard, listening like another, was that it was very good.

MacNally: Was there no observation of any other kind?

Farrell: No.

MacNally: Did you hear any person object that the paper was too merciful?

Farrell: No I did not hear it.[26]

Emmet had proved the first two of his points, but was foiled on the third. He ended the cross-examination at that point.

Sergeant Thomas Rice, who had discovered the printed proclamations at the Marshal Lane depot on 24 July, then gave evidence of his findings. He was followed by Colonel Spencer, Thomas Vassal, Alderman Frederick Darley, Captain Henry Evelyn and two soldiers, Robert Lindsay and Michael Clement Frayne, who were all called in succession to give evidence about what they had discovered at the depot in the aftermath of the rebellion. Darley had come across 'A treatise on the art of war', which was also referred to as 'Plan of the elements of war', and had handed it to Captain Evelyn. Frayne, the quartermaster sergeant of the 38th regiment, had found a letter from Thomas Addis Emmet addressed to 'Mrs Emmet, Milltown' but containing a letter which began 'My dearest Robert'.[27] None of these witnesses was cross-examined. Edward Wilson, the survivor of the skirmish on Marshal Lane, had much to contribute. He was a significant witness as he had also been the police officer called to investigate the explosion at the Patrick Street depot on 16 July. With much gusto, he described his adventures on the night of 23 July. Felix Brady of the 21st regiment then gave his account of the fighting in the streets and his capture of Edward Kearney.

Perhaps the most entertaining testimony was provided by John Doyle, the farmer at whose house the rebels had stayed on 26 July. He explained how he had been woken from his drunken sleep by a clamour at his door and had been forced to share a bed with the 'French general and French colonel'; he insisted that he 'gave them no assistance'.[28] One of the prosecutors asked him if he was able to identify Emmet as the leader of the group:

Mayne: Look at the prisoner.
Doyle: I see that young man, or boy, or whatever you call him.
Mayne: Was he in your bed?
Doyle: He was. He passed for a French officer.
Mayne: Did you hear him speak?
Doyle: I heard him striving to speak.
Mayne: What was it?
Doyle: I can't tell. I did not understand it.
Mayne: Was it Irish or English?
Doyle: It was neither.

Doyle revealed that he had discovered one of the small proclamations under the breakfast table the following morning and gave it to John Robinson, the barony constable. The defence lawyers, under instruction from Emmet, did not cross-examine. Burrowes was now discovering just how difficult it was to defend his client. When he attempted to destroy Doyle's credibility, he was prevented by Emmet who touched him gently on the shoulder and said, 'No, no, the man's speaking the truth.'[29] It was a warm afternoon in the courtroom and Emmet had been standing all day. A sympathetic onlooker decided to pass him a sprig of lavender for refreshment, but the vigilant soldiers, believing that it was an attempt to give him poison for a suicide attempt, confiscated it. Emmet gave them a disdainful glance to indicate that he had no intention of taking his own life.

Rose Bagnall was the next witness to be called. She summarised the visit of the rebel group to her farm, but claimed she had been 'so much frightened' that she had not been able to get a good look at any of their faces; therefore she 'cannot swear to any of them'. She was asked if she had been 'much alarmed' and she admitted that she 'was indeed', being 'a lone woman with some children'.[30] The defence did not cross-examine. The barony constable for Upper-Cross, John Robinson, then testified that he had received a copy of the small proclamation from Doyle. MacNally made a half-hearted attempt to cross-examine by asking who gave him the paper. He replied:

Robinson: Doyle, himself, out of his own hand.
MacNally: Why did you not say so at first?
Robinson: I did, sir.

Reluctantly obliged to testify was Joseph Palmer, who had struck up a friendship with Robert Emmet at Harold's Cross. He and his mother were guilty of harbouring someone they knew was a fugitive, but they knew they could avoid prosecution by giving evidence against Emmet. Palmer confirmed that Emmet had lived on two separate occasions at his mother's house and had used the alias of Hewitt. Hesitant and unhelpful, Palmer was forced to explain why the lodger's name had not been included on the list of people living in the house; he admitted that Emmet had said, 'He was afraid that government would take him up.'[31] Despite persistent questioning, he denied having any knowledge of Emmet's handwriting and could not confirm who had written the letter to the government discovered at his house. The attorney general conducted a skilful examination, questioning Palmer about whether anyone else had stayed at the house that summer or if any other person had been arrested there. To both questions Palmer stated that there had been no one else. All that remained to complete the deposition was for Palmer to identify the prisoner. O'Grady pointed at Emmet and asked Palmer if that was the man who had stayed at his mother's house. A reporter noted that the witness 'turned reluctantly' towards Emmet, who 'smiled and nodded his head'. Reassured by this signal of support, Palmer identified the prisoner.[32] The defence, under instructions from Emmet, did not cross-examine.

At this stage in the trial the attorney general decided to read selected extracts from the proclamation of the provisional government into evidence. These were deliberately chosen to emphasise the treasonable nature of the conspiracy, especially the vicious beliefs which the government believed underpinned it. After he was finished, Emmet asked his counsel to have a different extract read to the court. This was an attempt to vindicate the ideology of the insurrection and show the efforts he had made to prevent the rebellion degenerating into an excuse for cold-blooded murder. The attorney general did not wish to have anything further read and suggested that the defence should wait until it was stating its case. This was not good enough, as Emmet did not plan on defending himself, and Burrowes explained, 'It will be better to read it now, particularly as the prisoner desires it.'[33] The judge ruled in his favour and the sixth regulation of the proclamation was then read to the court: 'The generals are to assemble court-martials, who are to be sworn to administer justice, who are not to condemn without sufficient evidence, and before whom all military offenders are to be instantly sent for trial.' This was the wrong section, and Emmet asked for permission to look at the printed proclamation so that he could point to the correct passage. He indicated the seventh regulation, which was then read by the clerk of the crown:

No man is to suffer death by their sentence, except for mutiny; the sentences of such others as are judged worthy of death, shall not be put in execution until the provisional government declares its will; nor are court-martials on any pretext to sentence, nor is any offer to suffer the punishment of flogging, or any species of torture to be inflicted.

Burrowes attempted an unconvincing explanation about how his client was so familiar with the proclamation: he claimed that as it had been published in many newspapers it was perfectly conceivable that 'Mr Emmet might [have] learn[ed] its contents'. The short proclamation, addressed to the citizens of Dublin, was then read in full to the court.

The nineteenth and final crown witness was the man who had arrested Emmet, Major Henry Charles Sirr. He summarised the events which had taken place when he raided the house at Harold's Cross, including Emmet's attempted escape, and how he had intercepted him. According to his testimony, when Emmet was captured in the field he immediately said, 'I surrender.'[34] The attorney general then asked him if Emmet had said anything 'with regard to the wound he got'. Sirr revealed that when he expressed 'concern at being forced to treat him so roughly', Emmet had replied, 'All was fair in war.' O'Grady attempted to read into evidence extracts from the letter to the government which had been discovered in the back parlour. The defence had no objections, but Norbury refused permission insisting that 'the court has a duty to discharge, and nothing can be read but what is legally proved'. Attempting a brief cross-examination of Sirr, MacNally only asked one question about the letter to the provisional government, in an attempt to get it read into evidence. Upon hearing this, Norbury reluctantly agreed to allow it to be heard, but first he made it clear that he wanted to protect Emmet from the admission of any evidence 'which is not strictly legal'. After consulting with his fellow judges, he noted that 'it is our duty to give him the benefit of it, and we have been suggesting this matter to each other; we think the paper admissible'.[35] The letter was then read in full, followed by extracts from his correspondence with Sarah Curran and the paper beginning 'I have but little time to look.' This marked the close of the arguments for the crown.

It was now after 6 p.m. and it was the defence's turn to present its case. Peter Burrowes prepared to make his speech, and he later admitted that he was 'wearied to death with anxiety, and feeling both the painfulness and inutility of what he was about to do'. But Emmet checked him saying, 'Pray do not attempt to defend me — it is all in vain.'[36] It would have made little difference to the verdict. As one observer noted, 'The utmost subtlety of the subtlest lawyer' could have done 'nothing against the body of evidence which has been collected.'[37] Emmet was playing the soldier and was determined to take full responsibility for what had happened. He prohibited his lawyers from making any arguments or calling any witnesses. Therefore MacNally was forced to address the court:

My lord, Mr Emmet says he does not intend to call any witnesses, or to take up the time of the court by his counsel stating any case, or making observations upon the evidence; and, therefore, I presume the trial is now closed on both sides.[38]

Even though the defence had made no arguments, the prosecution decided to make a closing statement anyway. Plunket rose to his feet and announced that, 'with extreme reluctance', he could 'not feel himself at liberty to follow the example which has been set me by the counsel for the prisoner'. This infuri-ated the defence and immediately MacNally made an objection. He argued that since the defence had declined to make any arguments there could be nothing for the crown to answer. Begging the pardon of the court, MacNally called on Norbury to 'decide a matter of practice':

> No doubt, the crown is entitled to the last word, that is, a reply. But if I understand anything of the arrangement of criminal trials it is this: the counsel for the prosecution states the case; after the evidence given in sup-port of it, the prisoner is called upon to state his case; and if he does, the counsel for the prosecution has a right to reply. But I conceive that the word *reply*, according to its true meaning, is this: observing upon that which has been urged in answer to the charge.

Feigning astonishment, MacNally declared 'but if there has been no answer, there can be no reply'. However he admitted that he did 'not intend to press the objection' unless his 'learned friend' Burrowes had anything to add. Norbury overruled the defence. He declared that 'the counsel for the prisoner, cannot by their silence, preclude the crown' from the right of responding. He claimed that to do so would 'intrude a novel practice' and insisted there was no pre-cedent for the objection in any of the other state trials he had examined.

William Plunket had been a close friend of Thomas Addis from their time at university together until the 1790s, and his determination to speak angered Robert and disappointed those who remembered fondly his stand against the union. Shortly after Emmet's trial he was promoted to the position of solicitor general. For the cynical this confirmed that he had only spoken to ingratiate himself with the government. He was never forgiven by Thomas Addis for his personal attack on his brother. Three years later, in a letter to Peter Burrowes, he bitterly denounced the 'list of promotions' and admitted that there were certain 'men of whom I never wish to think; because I cannot think of them without the strongest emotions of aversion and disgust, strong and warm as was my former friendship'.[39] But Burrowes was not inclined to be too hard on Plunket and believed that it would have been impossible for him to refuse the brief of the government.[40] Plunket began his speech by informing the jury that he did not intend to take up much of its time 'by observing upon the evidence which has been given'.[41] But he revealed that as this was not an ordinary case but rather one 'of infinite importance indeed', he intended to 'bring home the evidence' of Emmet's guilt and prove that he was 'the centre, the life, blood and soul of this atrocious conspiracy'.

A brilliant orator, Plunket spoke for almost two hours as he recapitulated all the testimony that had been heard that day. For some reason he seemed nervous and spoke 'in a rapid manner'. However there was 'but one opinion' of the quality of his speech and William Wickham revealed that it was 'a most masterly performance'.[42] Plunket placed particular emphasis on the testimony of Fleming, which he believed proved conclusively that Emmet had played a major role in the rebellion. As this also tallied with the evidence of Colgan and Farrell, he argued that Emmet's guilt could not be doubted. Turning to the events of 23 July, or 'that night of horrors', he expressed a hope for the sake of Emmet's 'eternal welfare' that he was not 'a party to the barbarities which were committed'.[43] He then summarised how Emmet had abandoned the mob, 'whether from prudence, despair or disgust' and went into hiding. Tracing his path to Harold's Cross he mentioned the suspicious circumstances of his capture and the fact that he was 'a reluctant prisoner, twice attempting to escape, and only being brought within reach of the law by force and violence'. Plunket turned young Palmer's reluctance to incriminate Emmet to his advantage. He said that as the witness had not been 'carried away by any excess of over-zeal to say anything of injury to the prisoner, and therefore . . . you may with a safe conscience afford [it] a reasonable degree of credit'.

In a stunning rhetorical passage, Plunket then launched into a vehement attack on Emmet's plans. He began by discussing the letter to the government which had been discovered at Harold's Cross. He denounced the arrogance in telling the government, 'in diplomatic language, what conduct the under-signed will be compelled to adopt, if they shall presume to execute the law. He is the leader, whose nod is a fiat, and he warns them of the consequences.' The evidence of Emmet's guilt he believed was so overwhelming that he claimed, 'no man capable of putting together two ideas can have a doubt'. Why then, he asked, was he spending so much time on his closing remarks? It was because

> I feel this to be a case of great public expectation, of the very last national importance, and because I am prosecuting a man in whose veins the life's blood of this conspiracy flowed. I expose to the public eye the utter mean-ness and insufficiency of its resources.[44]

Upon hearing these criticisms Emmet, according to one yeoman present, looked with contempt at Plunket, and whenever 'the infatuation of his own conduct was alluded to he assumed an air of haughty and offended dignity'.[45] His countenance throughout the trial was 'expressive of stronger understand-ing' and he 'behaved throughout with manly firmness'.

Mocking the aims of the rebellion, Plunket laughed at its idea of establish-ing 'a free and independent republic in Ireland'.[46] 'High sounding name!' he said, but he wondered whether 'the man who used them understood what he meant.' Then Plunket explained the evils that would have been attached to it and how some 'free and independent republics' on the continent 'have seen the most abject slavery that ever groaned under iron despotism'. There was, he insisted, 'no magic in the name'. The speech had turned into a vitriolic attack on the character of the rebellion, and the figure of Emmet himself. Plunket spoke of the 'frantic desperation' of his plan in hoping to set Ireland adrift 'upon the turbulent ocean of revolution'. As far as he was concerned, Ireland would not survive 'as an independent country for a year' and he argued that 'God and nature have made the two countries essential to each other, let them cling to each other to the end of time, and their united affection and loyalty will be proof against the machinations of the world.' He accepted that revolutions were sometimes justified if they had the 'great call of the people', but he sneered at Emmet's rebellion which was nothing more than 'the voice of that pygmy authority, self-created and fearing to show itself'. The speech was electrifying, the invective against Emmet reverberating throughout the courtroom. He and his accomplices were dismissed contemptuously as 'a few, desperate, obscure, contemptible adventurers in the trade of revolution' who were attempting 'by force and violence to overthrow an ancient and venerable constitution and plunge a whole people into the horrors of civil war'. The question of French aid was then addressed. Plunket refused to accept the lines in the proclamation about the republic being achieved through independent means and accused Emmet of duplicity. All the other evidence, he insisted, pointed to an alliance with France in the war against Britain and that the rebels 'avowed in its naked deformity the abominable plan of an alliance with the usurper of the French throne, to overturn the ancient constitution of the land, and to substitute a new republic in its place'.[47]

Rejecting the proclamation's appeal to history, Plunket insisted that Ireland had been free from 'the slightest symptom of rebellion' for one hundred years until 'the infection of new-fangled French principles was introduced'.[48] In a dramatic development he then discussed the union, the measure which he had done so much to oppose. Referring to the rebel's desire 'for revenge on account of the removal of the parliament', he mentioned the irony that the very same people had risen up in 1798 to destroy it.[49] He commented on the divisions in the country during the passing of the union and explained that these were instantly forgotten when 'armed rebels appear against the laws and public peace'; then 'whatever may have been the difference of opinion heretofore among Irishmen upon some points . . . is annihilated in the paramount claim of duty to our king and country'.

The proclamation of the provisional government was roundly condemned. Plunket noted the distinction that was made in it between English and Irish soldiers captured by the rebels, and concluded that 'A sacred palladium is thrown over the rebel cause, while in the same breath undistinguishing vengeance is announced against those who stand up in defence of the existing and ancient laws of the country.' Addressing Emmet directly, he said he did not wish 'to say anything harsh of him — a young man of considerable talents, if used with precautions, and of respectable rank in society, if content to conform to its laws'. But he condemned the way Emmet had assumed the role of a legislator and had attempted in his proclamation to devise a new system for governing the country. In a passage rich in sarcasm, Plunket mocked the hierarchy of the rebellion. Near the top was William Dowdall, 'the vagrant politician', and its leaders stretched all the way 'to the bricklayer, to the baker, the old clothes man, the hodman, and the hostler'. This was a direct attack on the working-class character of the rebellion and Plunket was bemused by the fact that these men had the arrogance to tell the government 'not to be so mad as to oppose us'. They had been 'misled by those phantoms of revolutionary delusion' and he laughed at the way the rebels, 'disconcerted and alarmed, ran like hares when one hundred soldiers' charged them.

In the final section of his speech Plunket delivered a highly personal attack on the character of Emmet. He claimed that he 'did not wish to awaken any remorse, except such as may be salutary to himself and his country', but he then asked Emmet to reflect how he had 'stooped from the honourable situation in which his birth, talents and his education placed him, to debauch the minds of the lower orders of ignorant men with the phantoms of liberty and equality'. Contradicting his earlier comments, he predicted that Emmet must 'feel that it was an unworthy use of his talents' and that he should 'feel remorse for the consequences which ensued, grievous to humanity'. He called on him to recant his treason and 'make all the atonement he can' in the 'little time which remains for him'.[50] There was only one fact which Plunket said he could mention with satisfaction, the testimony that Emmet had intervened to save the life of Patrick Farrell, and he hoped 'the recollection of that one good action' might 'cheer him in his last moments'. But he refused to accept that Emmet was free from responsibility for how the rebellion had developed, and even though he 'may not have planned individual murders, there is no excuse to justify his embarking in treason'. He had chosen to 'let loose the rabble of the country' and was to blame for 'their barbarities': 'What claim then can the prisoner have upon the compassion of a jury, because in the general destruction, which his schemes necessarily produce, he did not meditate individual murder?' The speech ended with a sanctimonious call for Emmet to atone for his crimes. Plunket expressed the hope that,

> if this unfortunate young gentleman retains any of the seeds of humanity in his heart, or possess any of the qualities which a virtuous education in a liberal seminary must have planted in his bosom, he will make an atonement to God and his country, by employing whatever time remains to him in warning his deluded countrymen from persevering in his schemes.

The crimes Emmet had committed were 'atrocious, wicked and abominable' and Plunket attacked his 'blood-thirsty crew' for their violence. Plunket, who always had a natural gift with words, closed with a powerful dramatic image. He accused the rebels of attempting to dip their hands in 'the most sacred blood of the country' and he prayed that God would always 'confound and overwhelm' their schemes.

All that was left was for Lord Norbury to give his final speech to the jury. For almost an hour he explained that the charge for high treason comprised three separate branches of the statute of Edward III, and he summarised all of the written evidence along with his own observations. His last words to the jury were to remind it of the duty it had to perform:

> If you have a rational doubt, such as rational men may entertain upon the evidence, whether the prisoner was engaged in these transactions you should acquit him; if you believe the evidence, it is direct proof of all the treasons charged against him. But I say, if you have a doubt, you should acquit him. If you do not . . . you should find him guilty.[51]

The jury did not need to retire from the box. After a few minutes of deliberation the foreman addressed the court: 'My lord, I have consulted my brother jurors and we are all of opinion that the prisoner is guilty.' Upon hearing this, the attorney general made a motion for the judgment of the court to be delivered against the prisoner. The clerk of the crown asked the jailer to 'put Robert Emmet, esquire, to the bar'. At this Leonard MacNally made one final intervention, after some consultation with Emmet. He stated his client's request that the motion for judgment should not be made until the next day; this would give Emmet an extra day to sort his affairs before his inevitable execution. The attorney general however rejected any postponement and insisted that he had already made his motion. The clerk of the crown then read the indictment and 'stated the verdict found in the usual form'. He concluded by asking Emmet, 'What have you, therefore, now to say, why judgment of death and execution should not be awarded against you according to law?'

THE SPEECH FROM THE DOCK

No aspect of Emmet's life has received as much attention as his speech from the dock. It has also attracted the most controversy. There is no authoritative text of his speech which has been accepted throughout the years. The official version was prepared by William Ridgeway, one of the crown lawyers and a distinguished court reporter, who had been a member of the United Irishmen in the early 1790s. Ridgeway's account did not include the famous line about Ireland taking her place among the nations of the earth and was dismissed by some of Emmet's friends as government propaganda. Many different versions were later published by people sympathetic to Emmet, but they rewrote and reimagined the speech in such a way that it became overblown, verbose and far less impressive. The attacks on the French were expunged and several lyrical passages about 'the impurity of the judges' were included.[52] The contemporary newspaper reports by and large were taken from the Ridgeway account, and there are no real differences in the *State Trials* account published by Howell.[53] R. R. Madden, who spent much time sifting through the various versions and interviewing people who were present, finally produced a text that he believed was the most accurate account of Emmet's speech. However there remain some problems with his version and it is by no means a definitive text. Norman

Vance has identified that there are, 'broadly speaking, two strands of tradition to be considered, each with its special bias. These could be called the official and patriotic versions.'[54]

Emmet's speech from the dock can be divided neatly into two sections. The first half continues right up to Norbury's initial interruption and is 450 words longer in Ridgeway than in Madden. Despite all the controversy about which version is correct, the remarkable thing is that they differ so little in substance. Although there are some changes in the wording, the content is virtually identical. The only variances are in the style of how the arguments were presented. Both accounts stress Emmet's determination to vindicate his conduct and contain eloquent justifications of his struggle to secure Irish independence. Similarly, the two versions are clear that any French attempts to establish dominance in Ireland would be repelled by force. One major difference is that Emmet spends a large amount of time in the Ridgeway version defending his proclamation from the criticisms which had been levelled against it, and proving that it did not contain any references to handing Ireland over to France. A second more subtle difference concerns the reference to the agent negotiating with France. In Madden's version this is mentioned in the past tense and refers to an agent who was present in France at the time Emmet was there; however in Ridgeway's version this is in the present tense and refers to 'a new agent' who is currently there. As Thomas Addis Emmet was in France at that very time attempting to secure agreement on an invasion force, it seems clear that the Ridgeway version, on this point at least, is correct.

Ridgeway was an experienced court reporter and there is a strong argument to be made that the first half of his text is authentic. There was no reason for him to have lengthened Emmet's speech and add compelling arguments. In fact his version reads far better than the Madden account and is much more stirring and impressive. Certainly if the content differed from Madden's then a case could be made that it had been changed for propaganda reasons, but as there are no substantive differences there is little basis for such a claim. But while the first section of the Ridgeway version appears genuine, there are serious problems with the second half. In his version Norbury interrupts Emmet three times (it is twice this number in Madden), and delivers lengthy lectures on his conduct. Rather than respond in detail, Emmet only makes a few brief comments and then ends his speech rather abruptly with the lines, 'Let my character and my motives repose in obscurity and peace, till other times and other men can do them justice. Then shall my character be vindicated. Then may my epitaph be written.'[55] Vance has shrewdly noted that this was 'a less magniloquent, more staccato prose style, tinged with incipient panic, almost peevishly repetitive'.[56] Following the conclusion of his speech, Norbury makes a conciliatory speech about how he had hoped to have found Emmet in 'a more composed state of mind'. In response, Emmet begs the pardon of the court and insists that he had not come from France and had not created the conspiracy. It was a highly unimpressive ending for the speech. His final words were, 'I was told expressly that it was no matter whether I did join it or not, it would go on. I then, finding my principles in accord with the measure, did join it, and under the same circumstances would do so again.'[57] The Madden version however was substantially longer and contained Emmet's rebuttal of Norbury's comments about betraying his father's memory, and a more impassioned denunciation of his treatment by the court and the mistreatment of Ireland.

It is worth examining the government's own report of the oration. The chief secretary, William Wickham, wrote to Whitehall that the speech had been 'long and most inflammatory' and 'very eloquent'.[58] This cuts to the heart of the difference between the second half of the Ridgeway and Madden versions. Not only is the peroration in Ridgeway not particularly eloquent, it contains virtually nothing that is inflammatory. In fact the entire speech appears to have been expunged of any criticisms of British rule in Ireland, while the hostile references to France were left unaltered. Therefore there is a case to be made that Ridgeway or someone at the Castle deliberately censored any comments which might encourage or incite rebellion. Another possible explanation for the divergence between the two versions is that as the speech degenerated into a bitter debate between Emmet and Norbury, and the tone became increasingly emotional, Ridgeway began to synopsise the speech rather than transcribe it in its entirety. This helps explain why it is notably shorter than other contemporary versions. Thus there is a case to be made that the first half of Ridgeway's speech and the second part of Madden's speech should be combined to produce an accurate text of Emmet's final oration. To further complicate matters, there are also three sections in the Madden version which read as authentic but which do not appear in the first half of Ridgeway; these were anti-French comments and are marked in italics in the text below.

Stung by the harsh invective of William Plunket, Emmet's speech was in part a rebuttal of the previous arguments, but it was also directed at a wider audience. He was determined to vindicate his actions and rescue his vision of what the rebellion should have been, from both the harsh reality and government propaganda. This speech was his final opportunity to explain his actions, and there were a number of themes he wished to address. The question of Ireland becoming a victim of the French was one which infuriated him, and a major section of his speech refuted that allegation. However the vindication did not proceed as Emmet would have liked; he was interrupted by Lord Norbury on a number of occasions and was forced to cut short his speech. One issue which he had intended to address at the end was the sympathetic treatment he had received in prison, and he wanted to thank the Dublin Castle administration for its kindness.[59] Throughout his oration, whenever Emmet was 'enforcing his arguments against his accusers, his hand was stretched forward, and the two forefingers of the right hand were slowly laid on the open palm of the other'.[60] Rhythmically he tapped his fingers on his palm, as his body gently swayed from side to side, and the effect was 'as if his body, as well as his mind, were swelling beyond the measure of their chains'.[61] No one was more impressed with the speech than Peter Burrowes and he always spoke of the 'wonderful strength and resolution of Emmet in standing so long, twelve hours, I think, through all the fatigue and anxiety of the trial and then delivering that noble speech with such energy before the pronouncing of the sentence'.[62]

My lords, as to why judgement of death and execution should not be passed upon me I have nothing to say; why the sentence which in the public mind is usually attached to that of the law, ought to be reversed, I have much to say. I stand here a conspirator, as one engaged in a conspiracy for the over-throw of the British government in Ireland. For the fact of which I am to suffer by the law; for the motives of which I am to answer before God. I am ready to do both. Was it only the fact of treason, was it that naked fact alone with which I stood charged, was I to suffer no other punishment, than the death of the body, I would not obtrude on your attention, but having received the sentence, I would bow my neck in silence to the stroke. But, my lords, I well know, that when a man enters into a conspiracy, he not only has to combat against the difficulties of fortune, but to contend against the still more insurmountable obstacles of prejudice. And that if, in the end, for-tune abandons him and delivers him over bound into the hands of the law, his character is previously loaded with calumny and misrepresentation. For what purpose, I know not, except, that the prisoner, thus weighed down in mind and body, may be delivered over a more unresisting victim to con-demnation. It is well. But the victim being once obtained and firmly in your power, let him now unmanacle his reputation. Not, my lords, that I have much to demand from you. It is a claim on your memory, rather than on your candour, that I am making. I do not ask you to believe implicitly what I say. I do not hope that you will let my vindication ride at anchor in your breasts. I only ask you, to let it float upon the surface of your recollection, till it comes to some more friendly port to receive it, and give it shelter against the heavy storms with which it is buffeted.

I am charged with being an emissary of France, for the purpose of incit-ing insurrection in the country and then delivering it over to a foreign enemy. It is false! I did not wish to join this country with France. I did join, I did not create the rebellion, not for France, but for its liberty. *Small indeed would be our claim to patriotism and to sense, and palpable our affection of the love of liberty, if we were to sell our country to a people who are not only slaves themselves, but the unprincipled and abandoned instruments of imposing slavery on others. And, my lords, let me here observe that I am not the head and life's blood of this rebellion. When I came to Ireland I found the business ripe for execution. I was asked to join in it. I took time to consider, and after mature deliberation I became one of the pro-visional government.* It is true, there were communications between the United Irishmen and France; it is true, that by that, the war was no surprise upon us. There is a new agent in Paris, at this moment, negotiating with the

French government to obtain from them an aid sufficient to accomplish the separation of Ireland from England, and before any expedition sails, it is intended to have a treaty signed, as a guarantee, similar to that which Franklin obtained for America. Whether they will do that now, England, you may judge. But the only question with the members of the provisional government was: whether France should come to this country as an enemy? Whether she should have any pretext for doing so? Whether the people should look to France, as their only deliverer, or through the medium and control of the provisional government attain their object? It is not now, that I discovered, or that the rest of the provisional government of Ireland feel what it is that binds states together. They well know, my lords, that such a dis-position exists only in proportion to its mutuality of interest; and wherever that mutuality does not exist, no written articles can secure the inferior state, nor supply the means of protecting its independence.

In this view, it never was the intention of the provisional government of Ireland to form a permanent alliance with France; well knowing, that if there is between states a permanent mutual interest, more or less, though treaties may be made, yet for the most part, it is not the treaty which binds them together, but a sense of common interest, and where that interest does not exist, treaties are soon represented as unjust. They are qualified and interpreted at pleasure, and violated under any pretext. Under these views, it never was the intention to form a permanent treaty with France, and in the treaty which they did make, they had the same guarantee which America had, that an independent government should be established in the country, before the French should come. God forbid that I should ever see my coun-try under the hands of a foreign power. On the contrary, it is evident from the introductory paragraph of the address of the provisional government of Ireland that every hazard attending an independent effort was deemed preferable to the more fatal risk of introducing a French army into the country. For what? When it has liberty to maintain and independence to keep, may no consideration induce it to submit. *Connexion with France was indeed intended, but only as far as mutual interest would sanction or require. Were they to assume any authority inconsistent with the purest independence it would be the signal for their destruction. We sought aid and we sought it, as we had assurance we should obtain it, as auxiliaries in war and allies in peace.* If the French come as a foreign enemy, oh my countrymen, meet them on the shore with a torch in one hand — a sword in the other — receive them with all the destruction of war. Immolate them in their boats, before our native soil shall be polluted by a foreign foe. If they succeed in landing, fight them on the strand, burn every blade of grass before them, as they advance; raze every house. And if you are driven to the centre of your country, collect your pro-visions, your property, your wives and your daughters, form a circle around them, fight while two men are left, and when but one remains, let that man set fire to the pile, and release himself and the families of his fallen countrymen from the tyranny of France.

Deliver my country into the hands of France! Look at the proclamation. Where is it stated? Is it in that part where the people of Ireland are called upon to show the world that they are competent to take their place among nations? That they have a right to claim acknowledgement as an independent country, by the satisfactory proof of their capability of maintaining their independence, by wresting it from England, with their own hands? Is it in that part, where it is stated that the system has been organised within the last eight months, without the hope of foreign assistance, and which the renewal of hostilities has not accelerated? Is it in that part, which desires England not to create a deadly national antipathy between the two countries? Look then to another part of the proclamation — look at the military regulations — is there a word introduced from the French nomenclature? Are not all the terms English, all the appellations of the intended constituted authorities English? Why then say the system was from France? Yes, there was one argument urged, one quotation from the proclamation relied upon, to prove that we must have meant to resort to France: 'You are to show to us, that you have something in reserve wherewith to crush hereafter, not only a greater exertion on the part of the people; but a greater exertion, rendered still greater by foreign assistance.' From which an inference is drawn, that foreign assistance is the support of the present system. Because you are called upon to show, that your strength is such, that you can put down the present attempt without bringing out all your force — to show, that you have something in reserve, wherewith to crush hereafter. Therefore, the conclusion drawn is, because a further exertion may be rendered greater by foreign assistance, that foreign assistance is the foundation of the present exertion.

But it is said, we must have had it in view to deliver up the country to France, and this is not attempted to be proved on any ground, but that of assertion. It is not proved upon any ground, but that of assertion. It is not proved from our declarations or actions; because every circumstance attending the attempt which took place shows, that our object was to anticipate France. How could we speak of freedom to our countrymen, how assume such an exalted motive and meditate the introduction of a power, which has been the enemy of freedom wherever she appears. See how she has behaved to other countries, how she has behaved to Switzerland, to Holland, and to Italy. Could we expect better conduct towards us? No! Let not then any man calumniate my memory, by believing that I could have hoped for freedom from the government of France, or that I would have betrayed the sacred cause of the liberty of this country, by committing it to the power of her most determined foe.

Had I done so I had not deserved to live — and dying with such a weight upon my character, I had merited the honest execration of that country which gave me birth, and to which I would give freedom. What has been the conduct of France towards

other countries? They promised them liberty, and when they got them into their power
they enslaved them.

With regard to this, I have one observation to make. It has been stated
that I came from abroad. If I had been in Switzerland I would have fought
against the French; for I believe the Swiss are hostile to the French. In the
dignity of freedom, I would have expired on the frontiers of that country,
and they should have entered it only by passing over my lifeless corpse.[63] But
if I thought the people were favourable to the French, I have seen so much
what the consequences of the failure of revolutions are, the oppressions of
the higher upon the lower orders of the people, I say, if I saw them disposed
to admit the French, I would not join them, but I would put myself between
the French and the people, not as a victim, but to protect them from sub-
jugation, and endeavour to gain their confidence, by sharing in their danger.

So would I have done with the people of Ireland, and so would I do, if I was
called upon tomorrow. Our object was to effect a separation from England.

At this point Lord Norbury interrupted for the first time and warned Emmet
that he was making 'an avowal of dreadful treason, and of a determined purpose
to have persevered in them; which I do believe has astonished your audience'.[64]
He claimed that the court was anxious to give him 'the utmost latitude of
indulgence' to speak, but would not allow him to abuse the privilege by vindicating 'the most criminal measures and principles, through the dangerous
medium of eloquent but perverted talents'. Pleading with him to 'compose his
mind', Norbury told him he should 'make some better atonement to expiate
your own crimes, and to alleviate the misfortunes you have brought upon your
country'. Answering these charges, Emmet informed the judge:

When my spirit shall have joined those bands of martyred heroes who have
shed their blood on the scaffold and in the field in defence of their country,
this is my hope, that my memory and name may serve to animate those who
survive me.

While the destruction of that government which upholds its dominion by
impiety against the most high, which displays its power over man as over the
beasts of the field, which sets man upon his brother, and lifts his hands in
religion's name against the throat of his fellow who believes a little more or
less than the government standard, which reigns amidst the cries of the
orphans and of the widows it has made . . .

Again Norbury interrupted, and Emmet informed him:

What I have spoken was not intended for your lordships, whose situation I
commiserate rather than envy; my expressions were for my countrymen. If
there be a true Irishman present, let my last words cheer him in the hour of
his affliction.

Once more Norbury interjected and this drew a cutting aside from Emmet:

I have always understood it to be the duty of a judge, when a prisoner has been convicted, to pronounce the sentence of the law. I have also understood that judges sometimes think it their duty to hear with patience and to speak with humanity — to exhort the victims of the laws, and to offer with tender benignity his opinions of the motives by which he was actuated in the crime of which he was adjudged guilty. That a judge has thought it his duty so to have done I have no doubt; but where is the boasted freedom of your institutions — where is the vaunted impartiality, clemency, and mildness of your courts of justice, if an unfortunate prisoner whom your policy, and *not justice*, is about to deliver into the hands of the executioner, is not suffered to explain his motives sincerely and truly, and to vindicate the principles by which he was actuated?

My lords, it may be a part of the system of angry justice to bow a man's mind by humiliation to the purposed ignominy of the scaffold. But worse to me than the purposed shame of the scaffold's terrors would be the tame endurance of such foul and unfounded imputations as have been laid against me in this court. You, my lord, are a judge. I am the supposed culprit. I am a man — you are a man also. By a revolution of power we might change places, though we could never change characters. If I stand at the bar of this court and dare not vindicate my character, *what a farce is your justice!* If I stand at this bar and dare not vindicate my character, *how dare you calumniate it?* Does the sentence of death which your unhallowed policy inflicts on my body condemn my tongue to silence, and my reputation to reproach? Your executioner may abridge the period of my existence, but while I exist I shall not forbear to vindicate my character and motives from your aspersions; and as a man to whom fame is dearer than life, I will make the last use of that life in doing justice to that reputation which is to live after me, and which is the only legacy I can leave to those I honour and love, and for whom I am proud to perish. As men, my lords, we must appear on the great day at one common tribunal, and it will then remain for the searcher of all hearts to show a collective universe, who was engaged in the most virtuous actions, or actuated by the purest motives: my country's oppressors or . . .

Becoming exasperated, Norbury explained, 'If you have anything to urge in point of law, you will be heard; but what you have hitherto said, confirms and justifies the verdict of the jury.' In response Emmet asked,

My lords, will a dying man be denied the legal privilege of exculpating himself in the eyes of the community from a reproach thrown upon him during his trial, by charging him with ambition, and attempting to cast away for a paltry consideration the liberties of his country? Why then insult me, or rather why insult justice, in demanding why sentence of death should not be pronounced against me? I know, my lords, that the form prescribes that you should put the question; the form also confers a right of answering. This, no doubt, may be dispensed with, and so might the whole ceremony of the trial, since sentence was already pronounced at the Castle before your jury was empanelled. Your lordships are but the priests of the oracle, and I submit, but I insist on the whole of the forms.

Here, as Madden notes, 'Emmet paused, and the court desired him to proceed.'

I have been charged with that importance in the efforts to emancipate my country as to considered the keystone of the combination of Irishmen, or, as it has been expressed, 'the life and blood of the conspiracy'. You do me honour overmuch. You have given to the subaltern all the credit of the superior. There are men concerned in this conspiracy who are not only superior to me, but even to your own conceptions of yourself, my lord. Men, before the splendour of whose genius and virtues I should bow with respectful deference, and who would not deign to call you friend; who would not disgrace themselves by shaking your bloodstained hand.

Again Norbury intervened. The lord lieutenant later reported that Emmet was 'more than once interrupted by the judge and was prevented from proceeding to the conclusion of his speech which appeared rather calculated to excite the indignation than the pity of those who were present'.[65] Emmet continued:

What, my lord, shall you tell me on my passage to the scaffold — which that tyranny, of which you are only the intermediate minister, has erected for my death — that I am accountable for all the blood that has and will be shed in this struggle of the oppressed against the oppressor? Shall you tell me this, and must I be so very a slave as not to repel it?

I do not fear to approach the omnipotent judge to answer for the conduct of my short life; and am I to stand appalled here before a mere remnant of mortality? Let no man dare, when I am dead, to charge me with dishonour; let no man attaint my memory by believing that I could have engaged in any cause but of my country's liberty and independence. The proclamation of the provisional government speaks my views: no inference can be tortured from it to countenance barbarity or debasement. I would not have submitted to a foreign oppression for the same reason that I would have resisted tyranny at home.

Then, reminding Emmet of the distinguished family he had come from, Norbury accused him of having betrayed his inheritance:

You, sir, had the honour to be a gentleman by birth, and your father filled a respectable station under the government. You had an eldest brother whom death snatched away, and who when living was one of the greatest ornaments of the bar. The laws of this country were the study of his youth, and the study of his maturer life was to cultivate and support them. He left you a proud example to follow, and if he had lived he would have given your talents the same virtuous direction as his own, and have taught you to admire and preserve that constitution, for the destruction of which you have conspired with the most profligate and abandoned, and associated yourself with hostlers, bakers, butchers, and such persons whom you invited to councils, when you created your provisional government. When you sallied forth at midnight with such a band of assassins, and found yourself implicated in their atrocities, your heart must have lost all recollection of what you were. You had been educated at a most virtuous and enlightened seminary of learning, and amidst the ingenuous youth of your country, many of whom now surround you with the conscious pride of having taken up arms to save their country against the attacks upon it; and amongst them there may be a throb of indignant sorrow, which would say, 'Had it been an open enemy, I could have borne it; but that it should have been my companion and friend.'

Angered by this reference to his family, Emmet made an impassioned appeal to the memory of his dead father. He asked,

If the spirits of the illustrious dead participate in the concerns of those who were dear to them in this transitory scene, dear shade of my venerated father look down on your suffering son and see has he for one moment deviated from those moral and patriotic principles which you so early instilled into his youthful mind, and for which he now has to offer up his life.

In time, Emmet's oration would be considered one of the greatest speeches from the dock in history. This reputation owed much to the brilliance of his impassioned closing statement:

My lords, you are impatient for the sacrifice. The blood which you seek is not congealed by the artificial terrors which surround your victim. It circulates warmly and unruffled through its channels, and in a short time it will cry to heaven. Be yet patient! I have but a few words to say: my ministry is now ended. I am going to my cold and silent grave; my lamp of life is nearly extinguished. I have parted with everything that was dear to me in this life for my country's cause, and abandoned another idol I adored in my heart, the object of my affections. My race is run. The grave opens to receive me, and I sink into its bosom. I am ready to die. I have not been allowed to vindicate my character. I have but one request to ask at my departure from this world: it is *the charity of its silence.* Let no man write my epitaph; for as no man who knows my motives dares now vindicate them, let not prejudice or ignorance asperse them. Let them rest in obscurity and peace: my memory be left in oblivion and my tomb remain uninscribed, until other times and other men can do justice to my character. When my country takes her place among the nations of the earth, then, and not till then, let my epitaph be written. I have done.

Stunned by this dramatic finale, Lord Norbury made some bland closing remarks and exhorted Emmet 'not to depart this life with such rooted hostility to your country as those which you have expressed'. He ended by calling upon him to seek 'forgiveness and mercy in that which is to come — as well as to give you fortitude to bear that dreadful sentence which at this awful moment I must pronounce'. The sentence of death was then delivered and Emmet bowed his head. According to one tradition, Norbury was so moved by the pathos of the scene and Emmet's final remarks, that he burst into tears.[66] As if caught up in the emotion of the moment, Leonard MacNally flung his arms around Emmet and kissed him on the forehead. Emmet was led away by the guards to Newgate Prison. He was to be executed the next day on Thomas Street, opposite St Catherine's Church, and only a short distance away from his depot on Marshal Lane.

11

THE APPOINTED TIME:
DEATH AND REINVENTION

~

'I am just going to do my last duty to my country. It can be done as well on
the scaffold as on the field.'
(The opening lines of Robert Emmet's letter to his brother,
20 September 1803)

At midnight Emmet was removed from Newgate Prison and brought
to spend his final night at Kilmainham Jail. It was a kindness for
which he was extremely grateful and he remembered to thank the
authorities before his death.[1] Before he left Newgate he had a long
conversation with the Rev. Gamble, the clergyman who attended to the prisoners, who promised to visit him the next day.[2] Apparently while Emmet was
in his cell he was asked if he favoured a French invasion, to which he replied
with much vehemence, 'I execrate the French, they are only actuated by a
thirst for carnage and spoil, and I consider Bonaparte as the most savage tyrant
by whom the word was ever disgraced.'[3] Once back at Kilmainham Emmet
appears to have slept little, for he wrote an extraordinary amount in his final
hours. One of the first things he prepared was a detailed account of his military
plans for the rebellion which he wanted to send to his brother in Paris. This
was a sophisticated document showing intelligence and military ability and
which contained the original plan for the rising on 23 July; it was marked
'points of attack', 'points of check' and 'lines of defence'.[4] Because of all the
calamities which had beset his project, Emmet acknowledged that he had been
forced to abandon 'the whole of this plan . . . for the want of means, except
the Castle and lines of defence'. Then he catalogued all the disasters, before
admitting, 'Had I another week — had I one thousand pounds — had I one
thousand men, I would have feared nothing . . . but there was failure in all —
plan, preparation and men'.

Reflecting on the collapse of his ambitious project to liberate Ireland, Robert was concerned that people would insist they had predicted it and claim defeat was inevitable. But in a carefully worded rebuttal, he suggested that his critics would ignore 'the circumstances that occasioned it' and would not care whether 'its failure was caused by chance, or by any of the grounds on which they made their prediction . . . they will make no distinction between a prediction fulfilled and justified'. He made an impassioned defence of his strategy, arguing that he had at least succeeded in proving the doubters wrong who had confidently asserted that 'no system could be formed, that no secrecy nor confidence could be restored, that no preparations could be made, that no plan could be arranged, [and] that no day could be fixed, without being instantly known at the Castle'. Somewhat bitterly he predicted that 'the very same men' would have praised the rebellion if it had succeeded and would have 'made an offering of unlimited sagacity at the shrine of victory'. Now they would 'calumniate' and 'violate the sanctuary of misfortune, and strip her of that covering that candour would have left her'. It was an emphatic plea for respect, signed simply 'RE' at the end.

Waiting patiently in his cell, Robert wrote his final letter to his brother Thomas Addis and his sister-in-law Jane. The first half was a brave attempt to rally their spirits and he urged them, 'not to give way to any weak feelings on my account, but rather encourage proud ones that I have possessed fortitude and tranquillity of mind to the last'.[5] His thoughts were with his young nephews and nieces. 'God bless you and the young hopes that are growing up about you', and he prayed that they might 'be more fortunate than their uncle'. To this he added the melancholy desire that they might 'preserve as pure and ardent an attachment to their country' as he had done. His only bequest was his watch which he passed on to his nephew and namesake, 'little Robert', and hoped that 'he will not prize it the less for having been in the possession of two Roberts before him'.

The second half of the letter was about Sarah Curran. It began solemnly, 'I have one dying request to make to you.' For the first time, Robert told his brother that he

> was attached to Sarah Curran, the youngest daughter of your friend. I did hope to have had her my companion for life. I did hope that she would not only have constituted my happiness, but that her heart and understanding would have made her one of Jane's dearest friends.

The pain was barely concealed beneath the surface as he added, 'I know that Jane would have loved her on my account, and I feel also that had they been acquainted she must have loved her on her own.' Explaining the secrecy which had enshrouded the romance, he revealed that 'No one knew of the attachment till now, nor is it generally known'; therefore he pleaded with them not to speak of it to others. The letter ended with a posthumous request for his relatives:

She is now with her father and brother, but if those protectors should fall off and that no other should replace them, take her as my wife and love her as a sister. God almighty bless and preserve you all. Give my love to all my friends. [Signed] Robert Emmet.

So many of Emmet's final thoughts seemed to return to Sarah Curran. He had been moved by Richard Curran's message forgiving him, but still could not help feeling responsible for everything that had happened. In a letter to Richard he took the opportunity to again seek redemption for the pain he had caused. It began, 'My dearest Richard', and continued:

I find I have but a few hours to live; but if it was the last moment, and that the power of utterance was leaving me, I would thank you from the bottom of my heart for your generous expressions of affection and forgiveness to me. If there was anyone in the world in whose breast my death might be supposed not to stifle every spark of resentment, it might be you.[6]

He begged forgiveness for having 'deeply injured' him, and worse, for injuring 'the happiness of a sister that you love, and who was formed to give happiness to everyone about her, instead of having her own mind a prey to affliction'. Well aware that there was little he could say to make things better, he attempted an emotional exposition of his feelings:

Oh Richard! I have no excuse to offer, but that I meant the reverse; I intended as much happiness for Sarah as the most ardent love could have given her. I never did tell you how much I idolised her. It was not with a wild or unfounded passion, but it was an attachment increasing every hour, from an admiration of the purity of her mind and respect for her talents.

He also admitted that he had dreamt of their marriage:

I did dwell in secret upon the prospect of our union. I did hope that success, while it afforded the opportunity of our union, might be a means of confirming an attachment which misfortune had called forth. I did not look to honours for myself, praise I would have asked from the lips of no man. But I would have wished to read in the glow of Sarah's countenance that her husband was respected.

Overcome with feeling, Robert addressed the penultimate paragraph to Sarah directly. It was mingled with sorrow and regret:

My love, Sarah! It was not thus that I thought to have requited your affection. I did hope to be a prop round which your affections might have clung, and which would never have been shaken; but a rude blast has snapped it, and they have fallen over a grave.

In the final section Emmet attempted to recover his self-control, insisting that 'This is no time for affliction.' It was the second time he used the word 'affliction' in the letter; the first referred to Sarah. Ending the letter on a resilient note, he revealed the extent of torment he had suffered on her behalf:

> I have had public motives to sustain my mind, and I have not suffered it to sink; but there have been moments in my imprisonment when my mind was so sunk by grief on her account that death would have been a refuge. God bless you, my dearest Richard. I am obliged to leave off immediately. [Signed] Robert Emmet.

Allowed few visitors in his final hours except those approved by the Castle, Emmet was permitted to see one member of his defence team, Leonard MacNally. Within a few hours MacNally was giving a full account of their conversation to the government, and on 25 September William Wickham had a 'long conference' with him about the matters which had been discussed.[7] However, while the accounts were detailed, they were by no means accurate. MacNally was desperate to prove his worth to the Castle and justify the secret service money he regularly received, so he deliberately exaggerated and in some cases invented stories which the government readily accepted. The most imaginative part of his statement concerned the attack on Edward Wilson on the night of 23 July. Wilson had been seriously wounded with a pike in the belly, but had managed to shoot his assailant with a pistol. According to MacNally, it was 'Emmet himself who engaged Mr Wilson'. The story is incredible and it seems remarkable that Wickham gave it any credence. While he recognised that the 'account differs materially from Wilson's', he explained this away by the fact 'that the night was uncommonly dark' and he believed that 'the two stories may be reconciled'. In MacNally's version, when Emmet saw

> Wilson coming on very gallantly he stepped forward himself, being then muffled in his great-coat (exactly as Wilson described the man who wounded him), and ordered the pikemen to fall off to the right and left and make way for the firearms, at the same time he struck with Wilson at his sword, which was mistaken for a pike, and wounded him in the belly. Wilson immediately fired at him, but missed him. The watchmen fired some other shots, which were returned by Emmet's people, of whom he does not believe that one was materially hurt, nor did any of them throw down their pikes.

The story is riddled with holes. First, as the defence established at the trial, Emmet asked for a greatcoat on the night of the rebellion, but did not receive one.[8] Second, it seems astonishing that Wilson, no matter how dark it was in the lane, was unable to distinguish between being impaled by a pike and a sword. Not only that, when he fired his pistol at point-blank range, not only did he miss but he convinced himself that he had killed his man. Wilson gave evidence at Emmet's trial, and it is surprising that he did not recognise him as the tall, well-dressed man who was only 'muffled up . . . to his chin'.[9] It would certainly have made the crown's case substantially easier if they could have tied Emmet to the attack on the police officers. Instead we are led to believe that despite all of Wilson's experience, he was so confused by the 'fog of war' that he mistakenly thought he had killed a tall man in a greatcoat with a pike, when actually he had fired on and missed a man of average height, without a great-coat, who carried a sword.

MacNally's account of his final conversation with Emmet should be treated with great caution. Some parts seem genuine, but most of it reads like nothing more than self-aggrandising fantasy aimed at increasing his own status and value. He was well aware when he made these statements that he had complete freedom to say whatever he wanted, as there was no one alive to contradict him. One example of his inventiveness is when he said Emmet expected the French to land in ten days, and regretted that he had not been able to post-pone the trial until their arrival:

> He said the plan recommended to Bonaparte by the Irish in Paris was to land in Galway Bay but, instead of pushing for Dublin, to march to the north and secure Londonderry, taking a position with the county of Donegal behind them, and waiting there till they should receive, by small detach-ments such a force as would enable them to threaten not only Ireland but Scotland. In this situation they trusted that the south would rise in the rear of the British army.

If Emmet genuinely said any such thing then he must have been delirious; the French were by no means ready to invade Ireland within ten weeks, never mind ten days. But this information was useful in increasing MacNally's importance and made him appear an indispensable agent. Apparently Emmet also 'persisted in saying that he only had the command of the Dublin district' and was ignorant of the names of the generals in the other districts. But even the government recognised this could not have been true as he was 'in direct communication with Russell'.

Some parts of the conversation have an air of authenticity. For example, Emmet kept insisting that the 300 men from Wexford had arrived at Coal Quay, as Miles Byrne had assured him. But MacNally informed him the pikes had not been distributed and 'the Wexford leaders had all left Dublin to avoid having anything to do with the business'. When reminded that he 'had been grossly imposed on in many other instances', Emmet became dejected and admitted that there were many times when he had been 'most cruelly deceived'. Nevertheless he refused to accept the truth and deluded himself 'that the Wexford men were all there, ready to join him'. Towards the end of the conversation he declared, in the most solemn manner, and as a dying man, that not more than ten persons knew that the rising was fixed for the 23rd before the 21st or 22nd. He says that most of those who came up to town did not know of the day of the rising until the afternoon of the 23rd.

The conversation turned to personal matters, and MacNally mentioned Emmet's mother. Overcome with excitement, Emmet exclaimed, 'Oh, what I would not give to see her!'[10] He still did not know she had died. Feigning a pious sensitivity, MacNally pointed upwards and said, 'Take courage, Robert, you will see her this night.' The truth hit Emmet hard, and he bowed his head and murmured, 'It is better so.' Before their conversation ended, Emmet reminisced about his childhood and reflected that 'he had from infancy been bred with principles of refined liberty, which had increased with his years' and that he had wanted to establish in Ireland 'as free a government as Washington had done in America, but failing was contented, having done his utmost'.[11] This prompted one government observer to blame Dr Emmet for Robert's actions and conclude, 'the son was mad like the father'; as evidence he told a story about Dr Emmet in Paris when he had suggested a radical surgical procedure and was 'opposed by the whole faculty and sunk into disrepute'.[12] In his conversation with MacNally, Emmet also admitted that he had been 'the principal instigator and conductor' of the rebellion and had furnished the great depot at his own expense. The conversation turned to the conduct of William Plunket at the trial. Emmet allegedly denounced him bitterly as 'that viper whom my father nourished! He it was from whose lips I first imbibed those principles and doctrines which now, by their effects, drag me to my grave.'[13] However, again this comment cannot be verified, and the bitter tone seems at odds with everything else Emmet said and wrote in his final hours.

Reflecting on Emmet's talents and abilities, the Romantic poet, Samuel Taylor Coleridge, expressed his disappointment that he had not been exiled and rehabilitated rather than executed. In a flourishing rhetorical passage he exclaimed:

> Oh if our ministers had saved him and taken his oath and word of honour to have remained in America or some of our other colonies for the next ten years of his life, we *might* have had in him a sublimely great man, we assuredly should have had in him a good man, and heart and soul an Englishman![14]

This sympathetic view of Emmet's qualities was shared by Lord Hardwicke, the viceroy, who believed he was 'a perfect enthusiast' who 'possessed talents, though his judgement was weak'.[15] Hardwicke was a devout Protestant and was anxious that Emmet should 'have a fair chance of being brought to a proper temper of mind before his death'.[16] Therefore he gave permission for two clergyman, Mr Gamble and Mr Grant, to visit him in his cell and accompany him to the gallows.

Gamble had already tended to Emmet the night before and was impressed by his composure on the morning of his execution. The conversation turned to the rebellion and both clergymen attempted to make Emmet admit 'the guilt of the crime for which he suffered'. He refused to do this, but he was willing to profess a 'sense of religion' and ask for 'a general repentance' of all his sins. He revealed that although some of his accomplices had been deists, he himself was

> a Christian in the true sense of the word, that he had received the sacrament, though not regularly and habitually, and that he wished to receive it then; that what he felt he felt sincerely, and would avow his principles in his last moments; that he was conscious of sins and wished to receive the sacrament.

Impressed by this declaration of faith, Gamble prayed with him and 'felt himself justified in administering the sacrament'. He considered Emmet 'a visionary enthusiast' and wanted 'to bring his mind to a proper temper and sense of religion'.

Emmet had a few surprises for the clergymen. He took the opportunity to thank the government for his treatment which he said was considerably better than he had expected; he also 'admitted the lenity and moderation of the government' in general. The apparent irony of this position was not lost on Emmet, and he recognised that it might appear strange, coming from the leader of a conspiracy aimed at overthrowing that very same government, but he insisted there was no contradiction. Emmet was hostile to the principle of British government in Ireland, not the practice, and he was not blind to the good points of the administration. He was careful to distinguish between the British government which he opposed and the administration in Ireland which he respected. The atrocities which had been committed on the night of the rebellion weighed on his mind. He 'solemnly declared' to the clergyman that he had left Dublin before Kilwarden's murder and 'was anxious to disclaim any knowledge of the murders and assassinations on 23 July'.

At about 1 o'clock Emmet was taken from his cell, to be brought by carriage to Thomas Street. A large cavalry and infantry contingent waited outside Kilmainham to escort him and prevent any last-minute attempts at a rescue. As he was being led away by the sheriff, Emmet remembered one final duty which he had left undone. He begged for permission to return to his room and asked for a pen, ink and some paper, so 'that he might perform an essential duty which he had omitted'.[17] The sheriff, not wishing to deny the last request of a condemned man, led him back to his cell and supplied him with what was needed. Emmet sat down at his desk and wrote his final letter in a 'strong, firm hand, without blot, correction or erasure'. It was addressed to the chief secretary, William Wickham, the man who by his own admission had been 'the principal means of bringing the writer to the fate which at that moment awaited him'.[18] It was a remarkable letter and deserves to be quoted in full:

Sir,
Had I been permitted to proceed with my vindication it was my intention
not only to have acknowledged the delicacy with which I feel with gratitude
that I have been personally treated, but also to have done the most public
justice to the mildness of the present administration of this country, and at
the same time to have acquitted them, as far as rested with me, of any charge
of remissness in not having previously detected a conspiracy which from its
closeness I know it was impossible to have done. I confess that I should have
preferred this mode had it been permitted, as it would thereby have
enabled me to clear myself from an imputation under which I might in consequence lie, and to have stated why such an *administration* did not prevent,
but under the peculiar situation of this country, perhaps rather accelerated
my determination, to make an effort for the overthrow of a *government* of
which I do not think equally highly. However as I have been deprived of that
opportunity I think it right now to make an acknowledgement which justice
requires of me as a man, and which I do not feel in the least derogatory
from my decided principles as an Irishman.

I have the honour to be, sir, with the greatest respect, your most obedient,
humble servant, Robert Emmet.[19]

Finishing the letter, he closed and sealed it, and then said, 'I am now quite
prepared.' Emmet had accepted his martyrdom and was either deliberately or
subconsciously copying 'the brave death of legend'.[20] It was perhaps no
wonder that Patrick Pearse, who was so inspired by Emmet's example, called
his death 'a sacrifice Christ-like in its perfection'. Emmet was led to the carriage and brought under armed guard to his place of execution. It was a slow
and careful procession. Almost two hours later William Wickham received the
letter, by which time Emmet was dead, and he was immediately moved by 'the
truly Christian spirits which it breathes'.[21] It would change his life for ever.

On the way to Thomas Street, Emmet discussed various matters with the two
clergymen. Once more they attempted to get him to renounce his treason, but
he refused to disavow the justice of his cause. At one stage they asked him
'whether if he had foreseen the blood that had been spilt in consequence of his
attempt' he would still have 'persisted in his design to overthrow the government'.[22] He did not accept the logic of the argument and 'observed that no
one went to battle without being prepared for similar events'. He resolutely
believed that his attempt to achieve Irish independence was 'free from moral
reproach, in consequence of what he conceived to be the goodness of the
motive which produced it'.

A temporary scaffold had been erected where Bridgewater Street met
Thomas Street, with two posts about fifteen feet high making the gallows. The
platform was five or six feet from the ground and a ladder rested against it.[23]
Mrs Fox, the wife of the commander-of-the-forces, passed by the street and was
horrified by the sight of sentries guarding the gibbet which was 'now in daily

use'. As she afterwards noted in her journal with genuine regret, 'What a horrible state for a country to be in!'[24] It was now about 2 p.m. The Castle had confidently predicted that Emmet would 'wince' when about to experience the 'terror of execution'. This was not so much a slur on Emmet's character as a recognition that few people in the eighteenth or nineteenth century avoided succumbing to 'the terror of death' when faced with the gallows.[25] V. A. C. Gatrell has noted from contemporary accounts that 'Most people would mount the scaffold trembling in a very extraordinary manner, their whole frame . . . violently convulsed, their minds bordering on stupefaction, having to be supported by officials.'[26] Even highwaymen were unable to maintain their composure and McLean, Wilkinson and Hetrington all 'wept despairingly in their cells' before execution.[27] On many occasions the prisoners were so overwhelmed with fear that they had to be supported to the drop; one pirate in 1865 had to be hanged seated from a chair as he was too faint to stand. It was therefore no surprise that many people found courage in alcohol before their execution, and in the eighteenth century Bernard Mandeville concluded that even the strongest character would lose his nerve if he did not take 'refuge in strong liquors'.[28] Other prisoners chose to mock the hangman, in a final desperate attempt 'to anaesthetise mortal fear'. Gatrell recognised that 'It could hardly be otherwise' when 'most of these people had no chance of sustaining the equilibrium which would equip them for the brave legend of death.'[29] Political prisoners at least had some higher cause to sustain them, and this enabled many to maintain a greater composure at the moment of death.

Contributing to the sense of terror was an understanding of how the sentence of death was executed: 'The gallows was the site of physical pain.'[30] It was a slow, painful and unreliable method of killing. In 1774 Dr Alexander Munro, professor of anatomy at Edinburgh, gave James Boswell a detailed account of the procedure. He revealed that,

> the man who is hanged suffers a great deal; that he is not at once stupefied by the shock . . . a man is suffocated by hanging in a rope just as by having his respiration stopped by having a pillow pressed on the face. For some time after a man is thrown over he is sensible, and is conscious that he is *hanging*.

Even after the introduction of the long drop in the 1880s, hanging still took a long time to kill; consciousness was only lost after a couple of minutes, the heart kept beating for several minutes more, and finally muscular convulsions set in. In a medical analysis of the effects of hanging on the body, it was noted that the corpse always revealed evidence of what had happened from the

> lividity and swelling of the face, especially of the ears and lips, which appear distorted; the eyelids swollen, and of a blueish colour; the eyes red, projecting forwards; and sometimes partially forced out of their cavities . . . the

fingers are generally much contracted or firmly clenched . . . the urine and faeces are sometimes involuntarily expelled at the moment of death.[31]

It was therefore only to be expected that men and women usually had to be dragged to the gallows, as *The Daily Telegraph* noted in 1868, 'sometimes struggling fiercely with the executioner, to plunge, and shriek, and kick, until the lumbering drop falls'.[32] Or as Gatrell concludes, 'the law killed people who were powerless to prevent that outcome and whose bodies were dissolving in terror'.[33]

When Emmet reached the gallows, one government observer was disappointed to observe that he 'appeared perfectly devout and composed'.[34] He asked for permission to address the crowd, but this was refused. The clergyman explained to him that any speech might 'produce tumult and bloodshed'; apparently he wanted to say that he had never taken any oath but that of the United Irishmen, and by that oath he meant to abide.[35] Emmet betrayed no hint of being disappointed and acquiesced in the decision 'without appearing to be disturbed or agitated'. He 'boldly mounted the ladder', and even though his hands were tied he needed no assistance. When William Wickham learned of Emmet's composure he was impressed by just how 'stout hearted' he had been.[36] At the top of the platform Emmet made a brief statement to the assembled crowd, 'My friends, I die in peace and with sentiments of universal love and kindness towards all men.'[37] Untied, he shook hands with the men beside him, said his farewells and gave some money to the executioner. The reporter for *The London Chronicle* noted with grudging respect:

he behaved without the least symptom of fear, and with all the effrontery and nonchalance which so much distinguished his conduct on his trial yesterday. He seemed to scoff at the dreadful circumstances attendant on him; at the same time, with all the coolness and complacency that can be possibly imagined.[38]

The reporter could not help admitting: 'Even as it was, I never saw a man die like him; and God forbid I should see many with his principles.' Displaying a fearless composure, Emmet helped the executioner put the noose around his neck.

A large crowd had gathered for the execution. It is impossible to know whether they were sympathetic or hostile to Emmet's fate, but they were most likely a mixed collection of the curious and the interested. Scaffold crowds usually had the characteristics of any other crowd, with elements that were 'cohesive, custom-defensive, celebratory, carnivalesque, parodic, oppositional, [and] insurrectionary'.[39] Historically, more women attended executions than men; Boswell noted in 1778 that 'the greatest proportion of spectators is composed of women', and other people at different times made the same observation. There was a tradition that touching the dead man's hand could cure cancer, and relics of the crime, such as pieces of the hangman's rope, were sold afterwards to those eager for a souvenir.[40] Emmet's death has been compared to one of Foucault's examples in *Discipline and punish*. It certainly had all the elements of the 'scaffold as spectacle'.[41]

Determined to betray no sign of fear on the scaffold, Emmet 'behaved with dignified firmness to the last'.[42] It was now time for the sentence to be executed, and he continued to play the hero as if indifferent to his fate. A black night-cap was put over his head and a handkerchief placed in his hands. When this was dropped it would be the signal for the executioner to remove the single plank beneath the cross-beam and send him to his death. Three times Emmet was asked if he was ready. But he was lost in his thoughts and wavered, each time replying in the negative. In his speech from the dock he had guessed correctly that the authorities were impatient for the sacrifice. Now on the gallows, the hangman was not prepared to give him the time he required to compose his final thoughts. The plank was kicked from under his feet and, to use the newspaper euphemism of the day, he was 'launched into eternity'. As Emmet swung in the air the noose tightened around his neck and cut off his air supply. He died bravely without a struggle or a cry.[43] Because of the 'lightness of his frame' the life drained out of him slowly and he remained alive for longer than usual. He hung on the scaffold for thirty minutes.[44] Then his corpse was taken down and the executioner cut his head from his body, before presenting it to the crowd with the sinister words, 'This is the head of a traitor, Robert Emmet. This is the head of a traitor.' As W. B. Yeats would later write of the 1916 leaders, 'sleep at last has come/ On limbs that had run wild . . . What is it but nightfall?'[45]

Emmet's body was put in a cart and brought back to Kilmainham Jail. The artist, James Petrie, visited the prison and took a plaster cast of the face to make into a death-mask.[46] No one came forward to claim the body and it was buried in Bully's Acre at the hospital fields, where paupers and criminals were interred. But it seems a short time later his remains were removed by his friends and buried in a secret location. Gatrell noted:

> Since the body's integrity mattered for its resurrection, people worried how it was treated after hanging — anatomised, decapitated, gibbeted as might be. Surgeons were hated, grave-diggers execrated. Felons wanted to be buried *decently*, preferably in the home churchyard; 'decently' was always the word used.[47]

For example, when James Wilson was hanged and decapitated in 1820 he was buried in unhallowed ground, but his daughter and niece dug him up by night and took him to his local churchyard.

The final resting place of Robert Emmet has never been satisfactorily proved. The debate has generated its own industry and every few years a new theory is produced, only to be discarded after investigation. There are a number of possibilities, including St Peter's churchyard, Aungier Street, where his father was buried and which was the family graveyard, but the question will only be resolved when the body is exhumed and conclusively identified. In many ways, the failure to find Emmet's body has contributed to his deification. It provided a point of controversy to encourage two centuries of debate, and added an extra layer of mystery to the circumstances of his death. The fact that Emmet died, and then his body disappeared, only facilitated his resurrection into a nationalist icon. Once again the details of his life were being shrouded in quasi-Christian iconography. To borrow the Yeatsian description, 'He died, and immediately became an image.'

THE RESURRECTION OF ROBERT EMMET

After Emmet's request that his epitaph should not be written, his 'uninscribed tomb' contributed to the myth-making that followed his death. It was this subject which inspired Thomas Moore to write his famous verses on the death of his friend:

> Oh breathe not his name — let it sleep in the shade,
> Where cold and unhonoured his relics are laid;
> Sad, silent, and dark, be the tears that we shed,
> As the night-dew that falls on the grass o'er his head.

> But the night-dew that falls, though in silence it weeps,
> Shall brighten with verdure the grave where he sleeps;
> And the tear that we shed, though in secret in rolls,
> Shall long keep his memory green in our souls.[48]

W. B. Yeats noted the irony that the British authorities had unintentionally helped grant Emmet's request for his epitaph to remain unwritten. In an address in New York in 1904, Yeats spoke about how his 'enemies seemed to have wished that his dust might mingle with the earth obscurely; that no pilgrimages might come to his tomb and keep living the cause he served'. And he offered a perceptive and poetic interpretation that, 'by doing so, they have unwittingly made all Ireland his tomb'.[49]

A number of the Romantic poets were profoundly moved by Emmet's fate. Reflecting from Keswick in England, Robert Southey, the future poet laureate, rushed into print with a poem entitled 'Written immediately after reading the speech of Robert Emmet'. Inspired by Emmet's sacrifice, he wrote of how the blow

> Hath fallen, the indiscriminating blow,
> That for its portion to the grave consign'd
> Youth, genius, generous virtue. Oh, grief, grief!
> Oh, sorrow and reproach![50]

Emmet's injunction that no man should write his epitaph was disputed by Southey, who insisted that he should not be allowed to die

> Without thy funeral strain! O young and good
> And wise, though erring here, thou shalt not go
> Unhonour'd nor unsung.

Towards the end of the poem Southey reflected that it was better for Emmet to have failed and died, than to have lived to see Ireland under the control of the French.

> And better thus
> Beneath that undiscriminating stroke,
> Better to fall, than to have lived to mourn,
> As sure thou wouldst, in misery and remorse,
> Thine own disastrous triumph.

However the poem ended with an acknowledgment that Emmet's 'heroic mood' had triumphed over 'the sting of death' and that his sacrifice would be,

> By all the good, and all the wise forgiven,
> Yea, in all ages by the wise and good
> To be remember'd, mourn'd, and honour'd still.

Tom Paulin has criticised Southey for being concerned 'on a deeper level' with vindicating England of any blame for what had happened. He argues that the poem is 'less of a tribute than a vulnerable and revealing piece of self-exculpation which serves finally to vindicate political necessity and colonial rule'.[51] To a certain extent this is true, but Southey had to protect himself from appearing to support treason and sedition, and was far less restrained in his private writings. On 28 September 1803, eight days after Emmet's death, he wrote a letter which criticised the government for its response to the rebellion and argued somewhat naively that:

> To have spared the young man's life would have indeed strengthened the government. Had they said to him, 'Promise to plot no more and you shall be free', such a man would have been as safe under such a promise as in the grave. But so it is; the king has no heart for pardon: he wants goodness, and his counsellors want understanding.[52]

With an ominous final warning, Southey suggested that if the government really wanted 'to extirpate disaffection in Ireland by the gallows, they must sow the whole island with hemp'. It was a far cry from his unsympathetic treatment of Ireland two years earlier, when he wrote to Coleridge from Dublin suggesting that a journey to the country had 'the great advantage of enabling us to study savage life'.[53]

Southey's great friend, Samuel Taylor Coleridge, was also moved by Emmet's example. But like Southey, he was determined to put a conservative interpretation on events and was restrained in his criticisms of the government. On 1 October he reflected on his own flirtations with radical activity when he was Emmet's age, and was by no means modest in his claims:

> Like him, I was very young, very enthusiastic, distinguished by talents and acquirements and a sort of turbid eloquence; like him, I was a zealous partisan of Christianity, a despiser and abhorrer of French philosophy and French morals; like him, I would have given my body to be burnt inch by inch, rather than that a French army should have insulted my native shores.[54]

Sharing some of the same radical beliefs as Southey, he concluded that Emmet should have been exiled rather than executed. His curious analysis of Emmet's life has prompted Paulin to conclude that he used this letter to his aristocratic patrons to turn his 'intellectual autobiography' into a 'mixture of flattery, self-pity, pathological bigotry and hypochondria'.[55]

A third Romantic poet inspired by Emmet was Percy Bysshe Shelley who wrote a poem in his honour in 1812 shortly after his twentieth birthday. Entitled 'On Robert Emmet's tomb', it was a simple and elegiac tribute to the dead patriot:

> May the tempests of winter that sweep o'er thy tomb
> Disturb not a slumber so sacred as thine!
> May the breezes of summer that breathe of perfume
> Waft their balmiest dews to so hallowed a shrine!
>
> . . .
>
> When the storm-cloud that lowers o'er the daybeam is gone,
> Unchanged, unextinguished its life-spring will shine;
> When Erin has ceased with their memory to groan,
> She will smile through the tears of revival on thine.

Thomas Russell, only eleven years older than Emmet but in so many ways representing a different generation, was tried and executed in October 1803. In his speech from the dock he paid a poignant tribute to the 'youthful hero' who had 'just died for his country' and had become 'a martyr in the cause of liberty'.[56] The influence which Emmet exerted over Russell is an impressive testimony to his dynamic personality. Sentenced to death, Russell pleaded for three extra days to complete his commentary on the Book of Revelations, but the judge, Baron George, dismissed the request with gleeful mockery. Russell was hanged and beheaded the next day.

'The youthful hero' was a fertile source of inspiration for playwrights as well as poets in the years ahead. For the fiftieth anniversary of his death, a play was produced in New York entitled, *Robert Emmet: a martyr of Irish liberty*, which included songs like the 'Lament of the Irish emigrant'. It was written by James Pilgrim, who made a cameo appearance on stage as Darby O'Gaff, 'a sprig of the Emerald Isle'.[57] Intended primarily for an Irish-American audience, the play included a love interest for Emmet who was not Sarah Curran, but rather 'his wife' Maria. This idea of Emmet as a married man proved popular and it was continued in Gerard O'Sullivan's *Robert Emmet, the Irish martyr* (1863), which ran for several seasons in Dublin. An attempt to revive it at the Queen's Theatre, Dublin, in the 1880s did not get far. The government threatened to withdraw the theatre's patent if it was ever performed. There was further trouble with Frank A. Marshall's *Robert Emmet* which was written in 1881 for Sir Henry Irving. Scheduled to be performed at the Lyceum Theatre in London, it was cancelled because of the Land League agitation in Ireland, with the lord chamberlain advising that the subject matter was inappropriate. This play was later 'reworked' by Dion Boucicault, who produced his plagiarised version in Chicago on 4 November 1884.[58]

As the centenary of Emmet's death approached there was a renewed interest in his story. Brandon Tynan wrote *Robert Emmet, or, The days of 1803* for the Fourteenth Street Theatre in New York in 1902, which was performed in a theatrical extravaganza with a cast of over 150 actors. Further plays were written and performed in New York and Dublin in 1903 and 1904, but all were more concerned with dramatic effect and patriotic sentiment than any historical regard. The speech from the dock was also performed regularly in theatres, making its earliest appearance at the New York Theatre on 26 May 1806 when it was delivered by a Mrs Hamilton from Dublin.

The cinematic quality of Emmet's life was not lost on film directors in the early days of the movie industry. In 1914 Walter MacNamara returned to Dublin from America to shoot *Ireland a nation*, a five-reel silent film which took quite spectacular liberties with the narrative of Irish history. The story began with the passing of the Act of Union in 1800 by Lord Castlereagh, who was depicted as the epitome of male ugliness. This prompted the outbreak of the 1798 Rebellion and a desperate attempt by Robert Emmet to free his country. The film was released in the United States in 1914, in Ireland in 1917, and was re-released in America three years later when footage of Eamon de Valera and the 1920 Cork hunger strikes was included. Emmet also made an appearance in *Michael Dwyer, the Irish outlaw* which was filmed in 1912. However the first print bound for Ireland was sunk on board the *Lusitania* in 1915 and it was only screened in Dublin on 8 January 1917. The government quickly intervened to ban it because of public enthusiasm for the nationalist sentiments expressed, which included shouts of 'Up the rebels' at screenings.[58]

It was not the first film featuring Emmet to run foul of the authorities. The talented director Sidney Olcott came to Dublin in 1915 to make *Bold Emmett, Ireland's martyr*, which contained more serious errors than the repeated mis-pelling of the central character's name. Emmet was portrayed as a brilliant guerrilla leader and action hero, who escaped from his enemies by climbing up a chimney and outwitting the British soldiers after playing the tin whistle. It was shown in Dublin's largest theatre, the Rotunda, in late 1915 but was withdrawn after the government complained that it was interfering with its recruitment campaign in Ireland.[60] From beyond the grave it seems that once again Robert Emmet was damaging the British empire's attempt to fight a major military conflict. During the Irish War of Independence the image of Robert Emmet was employed in the revolutionary struggle. In 1919 a short documentary film was made to raise funds in the United States; it featured Michael Collins signing loan bonds on the block which supposedly was where Emmet had been beheaded. Mrs Pearse, the mother of Patrick, was one of the many people filmed honouring at this shrine.

THE FINAL LETTER OF ROBERT EMMET

Waiting in Dublin Castle on 20 September 1803 for news that the execution had taken place without incident was William Wickham. The messenger arrived after 3 o'clock with a full report and carried with him the final letter of Robert Emmet. The chief secretary read it carefully over and over again and it soon became engrained on his memory. It seems strange that a man who had been the head of British intelligence on the continent, and one of the most ruthless spymasters, should have been so affected by a message from beyond the grave. In 1835 Wickham was still copying the letter to show to people and unashamedly admitted that 'for the long space of thirty-two years it has been my constant companion'.[61] Not only did he interpret it as 'a full, free and gratuitous expression of forgiveness of his enemies', but he also believed that Emmet had done him 'a direct and important service' by sending it.

Soon Wickham was 'painfully affected' by Emmet's 'melancholy fate' and could not forget the remarkable gesture, 'honourable to his memory', which had been 'the last act of his life'. Beginning to doubt the justice of his own side, he had a crisis of conscience and confidence, and by the end of 1803 had lost faith with British rule in Ireland. He suffered an accident during the winter, damaging his knee, and he used this as an excuse to resign as chief secretary.[62] His official letter of resignation only mentioned the knee injury, but in a private letter to his friends in January 1804 he gave different grounds for his determination to leave. The first was that he could not support the establishment of the Protestant Church in Ireland, which he believed was 'a mistaken policy' reflecting the 'deep rooted prejudices of the legislature and people of Ireland'.[63] He confessed that this had become such a 'firm belief' that he was no longer 'a fit person to hold my present office'. The second reason was the fact that the Addington ministry had been formed in 1801 on anti-Catholic lines, and in his present state of mind he could no longer in conscience support it. The third and decisive reason was the courageous example of Robert Emmet. His noble-hearted gesture of forgiveness haunted him and he was constantly reminded of the lines in the Gospel of St Matthew 6: 44–5. 'But I say unto you, love your enemies, bless them that injure you, *do good to them that hate you*, and pray for them that despise and persecute you.'[64] His mind was tormented by the knowledge that a young and talented man had felt obliged to sacrifice his life to help his country, and he decided he could no longer remain in office and enforce laws which he had come to believe were 'unjust, oppressive and unchristian'.

This effectively marked the end of William Wickham's political career. By sending such a detailed justification to his friends, he knew that the government would learn of his real motives and decide that he was no longer sound on questions of empire. As he later reflected, the real cause of his resignation was 'more than suspected in higher quarters, and amounted in its very nature to absolute exclusion'.[65] He had gone native, and was prepared to accept the punishment of being cast into the wilderness. More importantly, he realised that his resignation would 'place an almost insuperable barrier to my future advancement and condemn myself to a life of retirement, without a chance of any provision for my family, probably for the remainder of my days'.[66] During the pro-Catholic ministry of his friend, Lord Grenville, in 1806–07 he served as a finance minister, but after its collapse he never held office again.

Years later, Wickham revealed that only his wife had been aware of the 'almost intolerable burden' on his mind and conscience when he had been 'compelled by the duty of my office to pursue to the death such men as Emmet and Russell'.[67] Yet he retained enough of his old cynicism to recognise that 'the manner in which I have suffered myself to be afflicted by this letter' would be 'attributed to a sort of morbid sensibility, rather than to its real cause'.[68] Overcome with guilt at having been 'condemned by his official duty to dip his hands in the blood of his fellow countrymen', in late 1803 Wickham concluded that the administration of British rule in Ireland was something 'which, in his conscience he cannot approve'. With an almost evangelical zeal, he decided that the only solution to the problems in the Anglo-Irish relationship was to change the entire system of government which he believed was unjust and sectarian. Wickham had now become the 'visionary enthusiast', and while he recognised that 'many will have strong opinions and prejudices to overcome', he drew inspiration from the example of Robert Emmet. He wrote of 'how light the strongest of such feelings must appear when compared with those which Emmet so nobly overcame even at his last hour, on his very march to the scaffold'.[69] In his speech from the dock, Robert Emmet had asked for his epitaph not to be written. But perhaps he would have been satisfied with the elegiac tribute of William Wickham, when he reflected on Emmet's attempt to free Ireland from 'a state of depression and humiliation'. Wickham revealed that 'had I been an Irishman, I should most unquestionably have joined him'.[70]

APPENDIX A
THE TEMPLE AND EMMET GENEALOGY

~

The dynamic Temple political dynasty began with Thomas Temple (1566–1637), who in 1611 was created the 1st baronet of Stowe. He married Hester Sandys of Latimer in Buckinghamshire in the 1590s and they had thirteen children. This progeny increased quickly and exponentially, and it was said that Lady Temple lived to see 700 of her own descendants.[1] They had four sons and the eldest, Peter, succeeded his father as the 2nd baronet of Stowe in 1637. Sir Peter was MP for Buckingham in the final two parliaments of King Charles I and in 1614 married Anne Throckmorton; they had one daughter, Anne. His wife died in 1620 and he remarried Christiana Leveson on 20 May 1630; they had one son, Richard, and two daughters. Sir Peter died in 1653 and was succeeded by his only son as the 3rd baronet of Stowe. Sir Richard married Mary Knapp of Oxford in 1675 and they had three sons and four daughters. His eldest son, Richard, succeeded him as 4th baronet in 1697 and was later created 1st Viscount Cobham, but died without issue in 1749. His sister, Hester, succeeded him as Countess Temple, Viscountess Cobham and Baroness Cobham. She married Richard Grenville of Wooton, Buckinghamshire, in 1710, and they had five sons and one daughter. Her only daughter was also named Hester, and on 16 October 1754 she married William Pitt the elder, who was later prime minister of Britain. Their youngest son, William, followed his father into politics and was the dominant figure in the House of Commons in the final part of the eighteenth century.[2]

Sir Thomas Temple (1st baronet)
|
Sir Peter Temple (2nd baronet)
|
Sir Richard Temple (3rd baronet)
|
Hester Temple = Richard Grenville
|
Hester Grenville = William Pitt the elder
|
William Pitt the younger (b. 1759)

The second son of Sir Thomas Temple, 1st baronet, was Sir John Temple and he married Dorothy Lee of Stanton, Bury; they had four sons and three daughters. Their eldest son, Sir Peter, married Eleanor Tyrrell and had five sons. Only the youngest, William, had any children, and he named his two sons William (later the 5th baronet) and Peter (later the 6th baronet). With the death of Sir Richard Temple, 4th baronet, in 1749 his title passed to his male heir, William Temple, the grandson of Sir Peter Temple. Sir William, the 5th baronet, married Elizabeth Paxton; they had two daughters. He remarried Elizabeth Ethersey in 1731 and had one daughter, Anna Sophia Temple. Upon Sir William's death in 1760 the baronetcy passed to his only brother, Peter Temple. Sir Peter, the 6th baronet, married Elizabeth Broughton of London and they had one son and one daughter, both of whom died unmarried. He remarried Elizabeth Mold in 1729 and they had one son, Richard. Upon his death in 1761 his son from his second marriage succeeded as 7th baronet. Sir Richard married his first cousin, Anna Sophia Temple, on 24 June 1758 but they had no children. Upon Sir Richard's death on 15 November 1786 the baronetcy became dormant while the family investigated who was next in line to the title.

Given the responsibility for deciding who should inherit the baronetcy was the marquess of Buckingham, the acknowledged head of the Temple family. Born George Grenville, he was the eldest son of George Grenville (1712–70), later prime minister of Britain, and his wife Elizabeth Grenville (née Wyndham). His brother was William Wyndham Grenville, who was created Lord Grenville in 1790, and who became foreign secretary in the administration of their first cousin, William Pitt the younger. George Grenville succeeded his uncle as 3rd Earl Temple in 1779 and was lord lieutenant for Ireland on two occasions. The first time was 1782–3, when he was accompanied by his brother William as chief secretary.[3] On 4 December 1784 he was created marquess of Buckingham, and it was under this name that he returned to Ireland in 1787 when he was again appointed lord lieutenant for Ireland; he remained for two years. As senior heir-general, Buckingham wrote to John Temple in New York in 1786 informing him that he had inherited the title and was now the 8th baronet of Stowe.[4]

Buckingham and John Temple knew each other well, and had been friends for a number of years. John Temple was another descendent of the 1st baronet, although his lineage is not as detailed, and was later disputed. He traced his ancestors back to the Rev. Dr Thomas Temple, a clergyman, who was the third son of Sir Thomas Temple, 1st baronet, and his wife, Lady Temple. Born in 1604, Dr Thomas was rector of Burton-in-the-Water, Co. Gloucester (1622–49), and married a daughter of the Rev. Dr Green; they left a number of children, including at least three sons, Thomas, John and Sandys.[5] Temple Prime, in his history of the Temple family, states that the eldest son Thomas was the father of the Thomas Temple who married Agnes White after settling in Ireland.[6] This union produced one son, Robert, and one daughter, Rebecca. A captain in the army, Robert Temple emigrated to America where he married his third cousin, Mehitable Nelson. Mehitable was the daughter of the merchant adventurer John Nelson[7] and his wife Elizabeth Nelson (née Tailer), and was the granddaughter of Robert Nelson and Mary Temple, Mary Temple being the youngest daughter of Sir John Temple and his wife Dorothy Temple (née Lee). Robert and Mehitable Temple's eldest son was John Temple (1732–98) who was born at their home at Ten Hills, Boston, in Massachusetts. John spent his early adulthood in London where he benefited from his family connections to the influential Grenville family. In 1761 he was named surveyor-general of customs for the northern district of America, an unpaid position that was specially created, as he himself admitted, 'purposely to give me rank in that country'.[8] In January 1767 he married Elizabeth Bowdoin, the daughter of the American patriot leader James Bowdoin; they had five children. The same year he was appointed a customs commissioner but he was dismissed during the controversy over the Townshend Acts. He returned to England in 1771 and remained there during the outbreak of the American War of Independence. Stripped of all his offices he was 'shunned by loyalist exiles, unemployed, and dependent on friends and relatives'.[9] With the threat of an American-French alliance in 1778 Temple was sent back to Boston by the Lord North ministry to help negotiate a peace. His mission was not a success and he returned to England in 1779. With the victory of the colonists at Yorktown in 1781, the British government was forced to acknowledge American independence. Family influence rescued Temple from obscurity. On 24 November 1785 he arrived in New York where he served as the first British consul-general to the United States. He was delighted to become the 8th baronet of Stowe in 1786 especially as the British government had reneged upon an earlier promise to give him a baronetcy. He continued to live in New York, serving as consul-general, and kept Buckingham regularly informed about the state of affairs in America. As Buckingham noted with bemusment his letters were filled with details about 'American misery, discontent and anarchy'.[10]

The Emmet family was connected directly with the Temple family in America: Sir John Temple and Dr Robert Emmet were first cousins.

Sir Thomas Temple (1st baronet)
|
Rev. Thomas Temple
|
Thomas Temple
|
Thomas Temple = Agnes White
|
Rebecca Temple = Christopher Emett
|
Robert Emmet the elder = Elizabeth Mason
|
Robert Emmet the younger (d. 1803)

Unhappily for Sir John Temple his descendents were unable to inherit his title. His eldest son Grenville Temple (1768–1829) succeeded him as 9th baronet on 17 November 1798 but afterwards his family's claim was challenged. It seems there had been closer living relatives in England who should have inherited the title, and that Buckingham either deliberately or accidentally chose to ignore them. The title became extinct in 1914.[11] But it is not particularly relevant that John Temple should not have inherited the baronetcy. Whether he was next in line or not, the fact remained that he was a descendent of the original Temple family of Stowe at Buckinghamshire and this connection was never disputed.

APPENDIX B
THE EARLY POETRY OF ROBERT EMMET

~

ERIN'S CALL
Brothers arise! Our country calls —
Let us gain her rights or die;
In her cause who nobly falls,
Decked with brightest wreaths shall lie;
And freedom's genius o'er his bier
Shall place the wreath and drop a tear.

Long by England's power opprest,
Groaning long beneath her chain,
England's ill-used power detest;
Burst her yoke; your rights regain;
The standard raise to liberty —
Ireland, you shall be free!

Brothers, march, march on to glory —
In your country's cause unite;
Freedom's blessing see before you —
Erin's sons, for freedom fight:
England's legions we defy
We swear to conquer or to die.

THE LONDON PRIDE AND SHAMROCK
A FABLE

Full many a year, close side by side,
A shamrock grew and London pride:
Together how they came to grow
I do not care, nor do I know;
But this I know, that overhead
A laurel cast a wholesome shade.
The shamrock was of lovely green
In early days as e'er was seen;
And she had many a hardy son
In days of old, but they are gone —
For soon the other's creeping shoots
Did steal themselves around Shamrock's roots.
Then, thief-like, fastened in her soil,
And sucked the sap of poor Trefoil;
Until in time pert London pride
Got up so high as quite to hide
Poor shamrock, who could seldom see
The sun's bright face, nor seen was she,
Save when an adverse blast did blow,
And laid her neighbour's honours low.
Then, in the angry lady's spite,
She drank the show'r, she saw the light,
She bath'd her sicklied charms in dew,
And gathered health and strength anew.
She saw those joys had come from heaven
And ne'er were by her neighbour given;
Yet, her good nature aye to prove,
She paid her jealous hate with love.
But when once more kind zephyrs came,
And raised the o'ergrown, storm-bent dame,
The ingrate strove her all to take,
And forced poor shamrock thus to speak:
'Neighbour, we're born with equal right
To feel yon sun and see his light,
T'enjoy the blessings of this earth
Or if right follows prior birth,
In this still stronger is my claim —
Long was I known and great my fame,
Before the world e'er heard thy name.
But letting all these strong claims lie,
Pray tell me, is it policy,
To thwart my offspring as they rise,

To break my heart, to blind their eyes?
Sure if they spread the earth along,
Grow handsome, healthy, stout and strong,
They will as usual happy be
To lend that useful strength to thee:
Thus would we keep each other warm,
And guard us from all coming harm;
We'd steady stand when wild winds blow,
And laugh in spite of frost and snow,
And guard the roots of our loved laurel,
Grown sick and pale to see us quarrel.'
'No more!' the vex'd virago cries,
Wild fury flashing from her eyes,
'I'll hear no more — your bounds I'll mark,
And keep you ever in the dark;
Here is a circle — look you here —
One step beyond it if you dare!
And if I hear you more complain
I'll tear thy rising heart in twain;
I've made thy sons kill one another,
And soon they shall destroy their mother.
I'll thus' — a flash of heavenly fire,
Full fraught with Jove's most deadly ire,
Scatter'd the London pride around;
The black clouds roar'd with horrid sound;
The vivid lightning flashed again,
And laid the laurel on the plain.
But soon succeeds a heavenly calm —
Soft dews descend and show'rs of balm —
The sun shoots forth its kindest ray,
And shamrock strengthens every day,
And, raise'd by heaven's assistance bland,
Bids fair to spread o'er all the land;
She guards the blasted laurel's roots,
The nurtur'd laurel upward shoots,
And grateful wreaths its dark green boughs
To grace great shamrock's aged brows.

MORAL

Take heed, learn wisdom hence, weak man,
And keep a good friend while you can;
If to your friend you are unkind,
E'en love will be against you join'd;
Reflect that every act you do
To strengthen him doth strengthen you;
To serve you he is willing — able —
Two twists will make the strongest cable,
To bind a friend and keep him steady,
To have him e'er in reach and ready.

THE TWO SHIPS

A FABLE

Et ergo malim audire tales fabulas
Quam experiri — Naufrag. Eras.
A ship that weathered many a gale,
With oft-fished mast and tattered sail,
And many a shot, and many a scar,
That she received in deadly war;
Afraid of ev'ry angry cloud
Of breeze that whistled thro' a shroud;
O'erburdened, lab'ring, heaving, creaking,
In danger every wave of wrecking.
Thus to a vessel stout and tight
That constant had kept close in sight;
And ev'ry gale had lent assistance,
Or when the foe kept not his distance.
'Your crew, good ship, you can't deny,
Is tainted strong with mutiny;
Now mine is loyal, if you mix 'em
We'll make to honest crews betwixt 'em.
And that we may keep close together,
And stoutly face all sorts of weather,
We'll tow you by the strongest cable
That to devise my crew is able.
And if you leave it to my master,
We both shall sail more safe and faster.
As to our burden, though you'll share it
His skill will give you strength to bear it.
My solemn faith shall plighted be,
Your share I'll just apportioned see —
And to your strength your load I'll square,
Nor stow a pound you cannot bear.

A common fate we then shall have,
Together mount the boisterous wave;
Or down the wat'ry vale so low
Together we shall cheerful go.
The storm, dear ship, that injures you
Shall sink thy constant comrade too.'
The trim-built vessel thus replied,
As proud she wrote upon the tide:
'I know I have on board some men,
That seem rebellious now and then,
But what's the cause? You know full well —
Allowance short — makes men rebel;
And you have many a hand of mine
That on my crew's provision dine;
Each day on biscuit we must work,
Forsooth to send you beef and pork.
Send me my men, their pay and stores,
Cease to rip up our healing sores,
In honour and in wisdom's name,
Help me, some prudent plan to frame,
To gain a happy crew's affection; —
Blow it, 'twill be thy own protection,
Our ship we'll work, its deck we'll clear,
Nor wind, nor wave, nor both we'll fear.
As to the tow-rope I am loath
To try it, for 'twill hurt us both;
A course for you's no course for me,
Our trims are diff'rent as can be;
But I shall, as I'm wont to do,
Keep constant company with you,
And overboard the traitor-hearted
Shall go — that wish to see us parted;
But I perceive 'tis my crew's mind
By ropes we never should be joined.'
'Twas all in vain — a scoundrel few
About the helm, betrayed the crew;
And for a bounty, basely gotten,
Lash'd the sound vessel to the rotten.
No sooner was this fouled deed done
Then slap on board comes ton on ton
Of cargo — a most grievous burden,
Ten times as much as she'd her name on;
A storm comes on — a dreadful blast,
Now goes a sail! now groans a mast!

The silvery waves in mountains curled
Now wrap them in the wat'ry world!
Shot on the billow, now they rise,
And seem to penetrate the skies.
Their heaving sides with frightful crash
The rolling ships together dash;
The tight-built ship now 'gan to think
That thus united both must sink;
And better 'twas that they should part
For ever, than a plank should start.
To save herself, nought else was left,
She cut the rope, and sent adrift
The crazy ship, to live at sea
Well as she could and bore away.

HELP FROM HEAVEN

'The right hand of the lord bringeth mighty things to pass — the Lord has chastened and corrected me; but he hath not given me over to death.' (118th Psalm)

'Twas as the solemn midnight hour,
When minds at ease are sunk in sleep,
But sorrow's sons their wailings pour,
Teaching the woods and wilds to weep;

Beside a lake whose waters black
The pale-eyed moon doth dimly spy,
Scarce peeping o'er a mountain back,
That rudely lifts its head on high;

Where the wild willows green and dank
Their weeping heads wave to and fro;
And bending reeds upon its bank
Oft kiss the stream that runs below —

There, on a long-fall'n mould'ring mass
An ancient castle's crumbling wall,
That, now grown o'er with weeds and grass,
Was once gay mirth's and beauty's hall,

Ierne, lonely, pale, and sad,
All hapless sighing, sat her down,
And sorrowing mused, till almost mad,
She snatched her harp her cares to drown.

Now wildly waved her auburn hair
In the unheeded blast that blew;
Fixed were her eyes in deep despair,
Whilst o'er the strings her fingers flew.

The sounds, at first so loud and wild,
Now slowly softened on the ear;
And e'en the savage blast grew mild,
Such soothing sounds well pleased to hear.

Her druids' ghosts around her throng —
For ling'ring still, tho' seldom seen,
They fondly flit the oaks among,
And haunt the grove for ever green;

And list'ning fairies troop around,
Whilst high upon the ivied tow'r,
The long-haired banshees catch the sound,
And rapt, forget their crying hour.

For, in the saddest, softest strain,
She wail'd the woes of Erin's land —
Ah! wretched Erin, rent in twain
By some curs'd demon's hellish hand,

That aye inflames with deadly rage
Sons against sons in foulest fight
And youth to murder hoary age,
In nature's and in reason's spite.

The cottage now she sings in flames,
Now the injur'd maiden dying,
And now the burning baby's screams
To its mother's bosom flying;

Ah! luckless mother, vain you shed
Thy tears or blood thy babe to save,
For lo! poor soul, thy baby's dead,
And now thy breast must be its grave!

Thy breast of life, where, as it slept,
Thy song-sooth'd cherub oft would start;
Then heav'd its little sighs, and wept —
Sad sighs that rack'd thy boding heart.

The thought too deep Ierne stung —
She started frantic from her seat,
Her silver harp deep thrilling rung,
Neglected, falling at her feet.

Nor silver harp Ierne cheers,
Nor the bright starry-studded skies;
The light of heaven's unseen through tears —
The sweetest sound's unheard through sighs.

The withered shamrock from her breast,
Scorch'd with her burning sighs, she threw,
And the dark, deadly dew she pressed,
Cold dripping with unhallowed dew.

'Here, here,' she cries, 'unseen I'll dwell,
Here hopeless lay my tearful head,
And fairies nightly in this cell
Shall strew my dew-cold leafy bed.'

Then down she sinks with grief oppress'd
Her saffron sleeve thrown o'er her face,
And soft-winged sleep lights on her breast,
And soothes its heavings into peace.

But ah! too soon, fell Discord's cries,
Borne on an eastern breeze's wings,
Rude sweep her harp, that downward lies,
And moan amongst its trembling strings.

Scared with a sound he did not know,
Peace-loving sleep dared not to stay,
But, sighing for Ierne's woe,
He bent his noiseless flight away.

Ierne, starting, paused a while:
'Too true,' she cries, 'ye powers above!
Dread Discord comes from that fair isle
Where still I looked for peace and love.'

Thought-rapt she stood in dumb amaze,
When on the western mountain's height,
To sounds seraphic, rose a blaze
Of mildly-beaming heavenly light.

There in the midst, loose rob'd was seen
Sweet Hope, that soothes our ev'ry ill,
Beck'ning with calm and smiling mien
Poor, sad Ierne up the hill.

The woe-begone thus Hope address'd:
'Lift up thy looks, Ierne, cheer!
For know we come at heaven's behest
To soothe thy sorrow, check thy fear.

'Thy cares, thy dangers soon shall cease,
Thy days of tears and sighs are gone,
Thou foulest feuds shall turn to peace —
Thus shall the will of heav'n be done.

'Pluck from thy breast that yew away —
Be steady, cool, collected, calm;
So shalt thou soon a wreath display
Of shamrock woven with the palm.'

Words so bland, as dew descending
Lifts the drooping lily's head,
Rais'd the fair Ierne bending,
Fairest flow'r in nature's bed.

'My fervent thanks, high heav'n,' she cries,
'Be ever, ever given to thee;
Thou'st chas'd my sorrow, tears and sigh —
Thou'st sent me Hope and Liberty.'

GENIUS OF ERIN
Genius of Erin, tune thy harp
To freedom, let its sound awake
Thy prostrate sons, and nerve their hearts
Oppression's iron bonds to break.

Long and strong then strike the lyre —
Strike it with prophetic lays,
Bid it rouse the slumbering fire,
Bid the fire of freedom blaze.

Tell them glory waits their efforts —
Strongly wooed, she will be won;
Freedom, show, by peace attended,
Waits to crown each gallant son.

Greatly daring, bid them gain her;
Conquerors, bid them live or die;
Erin in her children triumphs,
Even where her martyrs lie.

But if her sons, too long opprest,
No spark of freedom's fire retain,
And with sad and servile breast,
Basely wear the galling chain;

Vainly then you'd call to glory,
Vainly freedom's blessing praise —
Man debased to willing thraldom
Freedom's blessing cannot raise.

Check thy hand, and change thy strain,
Check it to a sound of woe, —
Ireland's blasted hopes proclaim,
Ireland's endless sufferings show.

Show her fields with blood ensanguined,
With her children's blood bedewed —
Show her desolated plains,
With their murdered bodies strewed.

Mark that hamlet — how it blazes!
Hear the shrieks of horror rise —
See! the fiends prepare their tortures —
See! a tortured victim dies.

Ruin stalks his haggard round,
O'er the plains his banner waves,
Sweeping from her wasted land
All but tyrants and their slaves.

All but tyrants and their slaves!
Shall they live in Erin's isle?
O'er her martyred patriot's graves
Shall oppression's minions smile?

Erin's sons, awake! — awake!
Oh! too long, too long, you sleep;
Awake! arise! your fetters break,
Nor let your country bleed and weep.

ARBOUR HILL

No rising column marks this spot
Where many a victim lies,
But oh! the blood which here has streamed
To heaven for justice cries.

It claims it on the oppressor's head
Who joys in human woe,
Who drinks the tears by misery shed,
And mocks them as they flow.

It claims it on the callous judge
Whose hands in blood are dyed,
Who arms injustice with the sword,
The balance thrown aside.

It claims it for this ruined isle —
Her wretched children's grave —
Where withered Freedom droops her head,
And man exists — a slave.

O sacred Justice! free this land
From tyranny abhorred;
Resume thy balance and thy seat,
Resume, but sheath thy sword.

No retribution should we seek —
Too long has horror reigned;
By mercy marked may freedom rise,
By cruelty unstained.

Nor shall a tyrant's ashes mix
With those our martyred dead;
This is the place where Erin's sons
In Erin's cause have bled.

And those who here are laid at rest,
Oh! hallowed be each name;
Their memories are for ever blest —
Consigned to endless fame.

Unconsecrated is this ground,
Unblessed by holy hands —
No bell here tolls its solemn sound —
No monument here stands.

But here the patriot's tears are shed,
The poor man's blessing given —
These consecrate the virtuous dead,
These waft their way to heaven.

APPENDIX C
MANIFESTO OF THE
PROVISIONAL GOVERNMENT

~

THE PROVISIONAL GOVERNMENT TO THE PEOPLE OF IRELAND.
You are now called upon to show the world that you are competent to take your place among nations; that you have a right to claim their recognizance of you, as an independent country; by the only satisfactory proof you can furnish of your capability of maintaining your independence, your wresting it from England with your own hands.

In the development of this system, which has been organized within the last eight months; at the close of internal defeat, and without the hope of foreign assistance, which has been conducted with a tranquillity mistaken for obedience, which neither the failure of a similar attempt in England has retarded, nor the renewal of hostilities has accelerated; in the development of this system you will show the people of England, that there is a spirit of perseverance in this country beyond their power to calculate or repress; you will show to them that as long as they think to hold unjust dominion over Ireland, under no change of circumstances can they count on its obedience, under no aspect of affairs can they judge of its intentions; you will show to them that the question which it now behooves them to take into serious consideration, is not whether they will resist a separation, which it is our fixed determination to effect, but whether or not they will drive us beyond separation, whether they will by a sanguinary resistance create a deadly national antipathy between the two countries, or whether they take the only means still left of driving such a sentiment from our minds, by a prompt, manly, and sagacious acquiescence in our just and reasonable determination. If the secrecy with which the present effort has been conducted shall have led our enemies to suppose that its extent must have been partial, a few days will undeceive them. That confidence which was once lost by trusting to external support, and suffering our own means to be gradually undermined, has been again restored. We have been mutually pledged to each other to look only to our own strength, and that the first introduction of a system of terror, the first attempt to execute an individual in one county, should be the signal of insurrection in all. We have now, without the loss of a man, with our means of communication untouched, brought our plans to the moment when they are ripe for execution, and, in the promptitude with which nineteen counties will come forward at once to execute them, it will be found that neither confidence nor communication are wanting to the people of Ireland.

In calling on our countrymen to come forward, we feel ourselves bound, at the same time, to justify our claim to their confidence by a precise declaration of our views. We therefore solemnly declare that our object is to establish a free and independent republic in Ireland; that the pursuit of this object we will relinquish only with our lives; that we will never, unless at the express call of our country, abandon our posts until the acknowledgment of its independence is obtained from England, and that we will enter into no negociation (but for exchange of prisoners) with the government of that country while a British army remains in Ireland. Such is the declaration on which we call first on that part of Ireland which was once paralysed by the want of intelligence, to show that to that cause only was its inaction to be attributed; on that part of Ireland which was once foremost in its fortitude in suffering; on that part of Ireland which once offered to take the salvation of the country on itself; on that part of Ireland where the flame of liberty first glowed; we call upon the North to stand up and shake off their slumber and their oppression.

Men of Leinster! stand to your arms; to the courage which you have already displayed is your country indebted for the confidence which truth feels in its own strength, and for the dismay with which our enemies will be overcome, when they find this effort to be universal. But, men of Leinster, you owe more to your country than the having animated it by your past example, you owe more to your own courage than the having obtained protection by it. If six years ago you rose without arms, without plan, without co-operation, with more troops against you alone, than are now in the country at large, you were able to remain six weeks in open defiance of the government, and within a few miles of the capital, what will you now effect, with that capital, and every other part of Ireland, ready to support you? But it is not on this head we have need to address you. No! we now speak to you, and, through you, to the rest of Ireland, on a subject dear to us, even as the success of our country — its honour. You are accused by your enemies of having violated that honour by excesses, which they themselves had in their fullest extent provoked, but which they have grossly exaggerated, and which have been attributed to you. The opportunity for vindicating yourselves by actions is now, for the first time, in your power, and we call upon you to give the lie to such assertions, by carefully avoiding all appearance of intoxication, plunder, or revenge, recollecting that you lost Ireland before, not from want of courage, but from not having that courage rightly directed by discipline. But we trust that your past sufferings have taught you experience, and that you will respect the declaration we now make, which we are determined by every means in our power to enforce. The nation alone has the right, and alone possesses the power of punishing individuals, and whosoever shall put another to death, except in battle, without a fair trial by his country, is guilty of murder. The intention of the Provisional Government of Ireland, is to claim from the English government such Irishmen as have been sold or transported by it for their attachment to freedom, and, for this purpose, it will retain as hostages, for their safe return, such adherents for that government as shall fall into its hands. It therefore calls upon the people to respect such hostages, and to recollect that, in spilling their blood, they would leave their own countrymen in the hands of their enemies.

The intentions of the Provisional Government is to resign its functions as soon as the nation shall have chosen its delegates, but, in the mean time, it is determined to enforce the regulations hereunto subjoined; it, in consequence, takes the property of the country under its protection, and will punish with the utmost rigour any person who shall violate that property, and thereby injure the resources and future prosperity of Ireland.

Whosoever refuses to march to any part of the country he is ordered, is guilty of disobedience to the government, which alone is competent to decide in what place his service is necessary, and which desires him to recollect that in whatever part of Ireland he is fighting, he is still fighting for its freedom. Whoever presumes, by acts or otherwise, to give countenance to the calumny propagated by our enemies, that this is a religious contest, is guilty of the grievous crime, that of belying the motives of the country. Religious disqualifications are but one of the many grievances of which Ireland has to complain. Our intention is to remove not that only, but every other oppression under which we labour. We fight that all of us may have our country, and, that done, each of us shall have our religion.

We are aware of the apprehensions which you have expressed, that, in quitting your own counties, you leave your wives and your children in the hands of your enemies, but on this head have no uneasiness; if there are still men base enough to persecute those who are unable to resist, show them by your victories that you have the power to punish, and, by your obedience, that you have the power to protect, and we pledge ourselves to you, that these men shall be made to feel that the safety of every thing they hold dear depends on the conduct they observe to you. Go forth then with confidence, conquer the foreign enemies of your country, and leave to us the care of preserving its internal tranquillity; recollect that not only the victory, but also the honour of your country is placed in your hands: give up your private resentments, and show to the world that the Irish are not only a brave, but also a generous and forgiving people.

Men of Munster and Connaught, you have your instructions, you will execute them. The example of the rest of your countrymen is now before you, your own strength is unbroken; five months ago you were eager to act without any other assistance, we now call upon you to show what you then declared you only wanted, the opportunity of proving that you possess the same love of liberty, and the same courage with which the rest of your countrymen are animated.

We turn now to that portion of our countrymen whose prejudices we had rather overcome by a frank declaration of our intentions, than conquer in the field; and, in making this declaration, we do not wish to dwell on events, which, however they may bring ten-fold odium on their authors, must still tend to keep alive in the minds, both of the instruments and victims of them, a spirit of animosity, which it is our wish to destroy. We will enter into no detail of the atrocities and oppressions which Ireland has laboured under, during its connection with England; but we justify our determination to separate from that country, on the broad historical statement, that, during six hundred years, she has been unable to conciliate the affections of the people of Ireland; that, during that time, five rebellions were entered into, to shake off the yoke; that she has been obliged to enter into a system of unprecedented torture in her defence; that she has broken every tie of voluntary connection, by taking even the name of independence from Ireland, through the intervention of a parliament notoriously bribed, and not representing the will of the people; that in vindication of this measure, she has herself given the justification of the views of the United Irishmen, by declaring, in the words of her ministers, 'That Ireland never had, and never could enjoy, under the then circumstances, the benefits of British connection; that it necessarily must happen, when one country is connected with another, that the interests of the lesser will be borne down by the greater. That England had supported, and encouraged the English Colonist in their oppression towards the natives of Ireland; that Ireland had been left in a state of ignorance, rudeness, and barbarism, worse in its effects, and more degrading in its nature, than that in which it was found six centuries before.' [Lord Castlereagh's speech] Now to what cause are these things to be attributed? Did the curse of the Almighty keep alive a spirit of obstinacy in the minds of the Irish people for six hundred years? Did the doctrines of the French revolution produce five rebellions? Could the misrepresentations of ambitious designing men drive from the mind of a whole people the recollection of defeat, and raise the infant from the cradle, with the same feelings with which its father sank to the grave? Will this gross avowal, which our enemies have made of their own views, remove none of the calumny that has been thrown upon ours? Will none of the credit, which has been lavished on them, be transferred to the solemn declaration which we now make in the face of God, and our country?

We war not against property, — we war against no religious sect, — we war not against past opinions or prejudices, — we war against English dominion. We will not, however, deny that there are some men, who, not because they have supported the government of our oppressors, but because they have violated the common laws of morality, which exist alike under all, or under no government, have put it beyond our power to give to them the protection of a government. We will not hazard the influence we may have with the people, and the power it may give us of preventing the excesses of revolution, by undertaking to place in tranquillity the man who has been guilty of torture, free-quarter, rape, and murder, by the side of the sufferer, or their relations; but in the frankness with which we warn those men of their danger, let those who do not feel that they have passed this boundary of mediation count on their safety.

We had hoped, for the sake of our enemies, to have taken them by surprise, and to have committed the cause of our country before they could have time to commit themselves against it: but, though we have not altogether been able to succeed, we are yet rejoiced to find that they have not come forward with promptitude on the side of those who have deceived them; and we now call upon them, before it is yet too late, not to commit themselves against a people which they are unable to resist, and in support of a government, which, by their own declaration, had forfeited its claim to their allegiance. To that government, in whose hands, though not the issue, at least the features with which the present contest is marked, or placed, we now turn. How is it to be decided? Is open and honourable force alone to be resorted to? or is it your intention to employ those laws which custom has placed in your hands, and to force us to employ the law of retaliation in our defence?

Of the inefficacy of a system of terror, in preventing the people of Ireland from coming forward to assert their freedom, you have already had experience. Of the effect which such a system will have on our minds, in case of success, we have already forewarned you. We now address to you another consideration: if in the question which is now to receive a solemn and we trust final decision; if we have been deceived, reflection would point out that conduct should be resorted to which was best calculated to produce conviction on our minds.

What would that conduct be?

It would be to show us that the difference of strength between the two countries is such as to render it unnecessary for you to bring out all your forces; to show that you have something in reserve to crush hereafter, not only a greater exertion of the people, but one rendered still greater by foreign assistance. It would be to show us, that what we vainly supposed to be a prosperity growing beyond your grasp, is only a partial exuberance, requiring but the pressure of your hand to reduce to form.

But for your own sakes, do not resort to a system which, while it increased the acrimony of our minds, would leave us under the melancholy delusion, that we had been forced to yield, not to the sound and temperate exertions of your superior strength, but to the frantic struggles of weakness, concealing itself under desperation. Consider that the distinction of rebel and enemy, is of a very fluctuating nature; that during the course of your own experience, you have already been obliged to lay it aside: that should you be obliged to abandon it towards Ireland, you cannot hope to do so as tranquilly as you have done towards America: for in the exasperated state to which you have roused the minds of the Irish people — a people whom you profess to have left in a state of barbarism and ignorance, with what confidence can you say to that people, 'While the advantage of cruelty lay upon our side, we slaughtered you without mercy, but the measure of your own blood is beginning to preponderate.' It is no longer our interest that this bloody system should continue, show us then that forbearance which we never taught you by precept or example, lay aside your resentment; give quarter to us, and let us mutually forget we never gave quarter to you. Cease then, we entreat you, uselessly to violate humanity, by resorting to a system inefficacious as a mode of defence; inefficacious as a mode of conviction; ruinous to the future relations of the two countries in case of our success; and destructive of those instruments of defence which you will then find it doubly necessary to have preserved unimpaired. But if your determination be otherwise, hear ours. We will not imitate you in cruelty; we will put no man to death in cold blood; the prisoners which first fall into our hands shall be treated with the respect due to the unfortunate, but if the life of a single unfortunate Irish soldier is taken after the battle is over, the orders thenceforth to be delivered to the Irish army is, neither to give nor to take quarter. Countrymen, if a cruel necessity force us to retaliate, we will bury our resentment in the field of battle; if we fall, we will fall where we fight for our country. Fully impressed with this determination, of the necessity of adhering to which past experience has but too fatally convinced us; fully impressed with the justice of our cause, which we now put to issue, we make our last and solemn appeal to the sword, and to heaven; and, as the cause of Ireland deserves to prosper, may God give us the victory.

Conformably to the above Proclamation, the Provisional Government of Ireland — decree that as follows:-

1. From the date, and promulgation hereof, tithes are forever abolished, and church lands are the property of the nation.
2. From the same date, all transfers of landed property are prohibited, each person paying his rent until the National Government is established; the national will declared, and the courts of justice be organized.
3. From the same date, all transfer of bonds, debentures, and all public securities, are in like manner forbidden, and declared void for the same time, and for the same reason.
4. The Irish generals, commanding districts, shall seize such of the partisans of England as may serve as hostages, and shall apprise the English commanders, opposed to them, that a strict retaliation shall take place, if any outrages contrary to the laws of war shall be committed by the troops under command of each; or by the partisans of England in the district which he occupies.
5. That the Irish generals are to treat, (except where retaliation makes it necessary), the English troops who may fall into their hands, or such Irish as serve in the regular forces of England, and who shall have acted conformably to the laws of war, shall be treated as prisoners of war; but all Irish militia, yeomen, or volunteer corps, or bodies of Irish, or individuals,

who fourteen days after the promulgation and date hereof shall be found in arms, shall be considered as rebels, committed for trial, and their properties confiscated.

6. The generals are to assemble court-martials, who are to be sworn to administer justice: who are not to condemn without sufficient evidence, and before whom all military offenders are to be sent instantly for trial.

7. No man is to suffer death by their sentence but for mutiny; the sentence of such others are as judged worthy of death, shall not be put into execution until the Provisional Government declares its will; nor are court-martials on any pretence or sentence, nor is any officer to suffer the punishment of flogging, or any species of torture to be inflicted.

8. The generals are to enforce the strictest discipline, and to send offenders immediately to the court-martial; and are enjoined to chase away from the Irish armies, all such as shall disgrace themselves by being drunk in the presence of the enemy.

9. The generals are to apprize their respective armies that all military stores and ammunition, belonging to the English government, be the property of the captors, and the value equally divided, without respect of rank, between them, except that the widows, orphans, parents, or other heirs of those who gloriously fall in the attack, shall be entitled to a double share.

10. As the English nation has made war on Ireland, all English property in ships or otherwise, is subjected to the same rule, and all transfer of them forbidden, and declared void in like manner as is expressed in No. 2, and 3.

11. The generals of the different districts are hereby empowered to confer rank up to colonels inclusive, on such as they conceive merit it from the nation, but are not to make more colonels than one for fifteen hundred men, nor more lieutenant colonels than one for every thousand men.

12 The general shall seize on all sums of public money in the custom houses, in their districts, or in the hands of the different collectors, county treasurers, or other revenue officers, whom they shall render responsible for the sums in their hands. The generals shall pass receipts for the amount, and account to the Provisional Government for the same.

13. When the people elect their officers up to the colonels, the general is bound to confirm it, no officer can be broke but by sentence of a court-martial.

14. The generals shall correspond with the Provisional Government, to whom they shall give details of all their operations; they are to correspond with the neighbouring generals, to whom they are to transmit all necessary intelligence and to co-operate with them.

15. The general commanding in each county shall as soon as it is cleared of the enemy, assemble the county committee, who shall be elected conformably to the constitution of United Irishmen. All the requisitions necessary for the army shall be made in writing, by the generals, to the

committee, who are hereby empowered, and enjoined, to pass receipts for each article to the owners, to the end that they may receive their full value from the nation.

16. The county committee is charged with the civil direction of the county, the care of the national property, and the preservation of order and justice in the county, for which purpose the county committee are to appoint a high sheriff, and one or more sub-sheriffs, to execute their orders; a sufficient number of justices of the peace for the county; a high and a sufficient number of petty constables in each barony, who are respectively charged with the duties now performed by those magistrates.

17. The county of Cork, on account of its extent is to be divided, conformably to the boundaries for raising militia, into the counties of north and south Cork; for each of which a county constable, high sheriff, and all magistrates above directed are to be appointed.

18. The county committee are hereby empowered and enjoined to issue warrants to apprehend such persons as it shall appear, on sufficient evidence, perpetrated murder, torture, and other breaches of the acknowledged articles of war and morality on the people, to the end that they may be tried for these offences so soon as the competent courts of justice are established by the nation.

19. The county committee shall cause the sheriff, or his officers, to seize on all the personal property of such, to put seals on their effects, to appoint proper persons to preserve all such property until the national courts of justice shall have decided on the fate of the proprietors.

20. The county committee shall act in like manner with all state and church lands, parochial estates, and all public lands and edifices.

21. The county committee shall, in the interim, receive all the rents and debts of such persons, and estates, and give receipts for the same; shall transmit to the government an exact account of their value, extent, and amount, and receive the directions of the provisional government thereon.

22. They shall appoint some proper house in the counties where the sheriff is permanently to reside, and where the county committee shall assemble; they shall cause all the records and papers of the county to be there transmitted, arranged, and kept, and the orders of the government to be there transmitted and received.

23. The county committee is hereby empowered to pay out of these effects, or by assessment, reasonable salaries for themselves, the sheriffs, justices, and other magistrates, whom they shall appoint.

24. They shall keep a written journal of all their proceedings, signed each day by members of the committee, or a sufficient number of them, for the inspection of government.

25. The county committee shall correspond with government on all subjects with which they are charged, and transmit to the general of the district such information as they shall conceive useful to the public.

26. The county committee shall take care that all state prisoners, however great their offences, shall be treated with humanity, and allow them sufficient support, to the end that all the world may know that the Irish nation is not actuated by a spirit of revenge, but of justice.

27. The Provisional Government wishing to commit, as soon as possible, the sovereign authority to the people, direct that each county and city shall elect, agreeably to the constitution of United Irishmen, representatives to meet in Dublin, to whom, the moment they assemble, the Provisional Government will resign its functions, and, without presuming to dictate to the people, they beg leave to suggest, that for the important purpose to which these electors are called, integrity of character should be the first object.

28. The number of representatives being arbitrary, the provisional government have adopted that of the late House of Commons, 300, and, according to the best returns of the population of the cities and counties, the following number are to be returned from each:- Antrim, 13; Armagh, 9; Belfast Town, 1; Carlow, 3; Cavan, 7; Clare, 8; Cork County, north, 14; Cork county, south, 14; Cork city, 6; Donegal, 10; Down, 16; Drogheda, 1; Dublin county, 4; Dublin city, 14; Fermanagh, 5; Galway, 10; Kerry, 9; Kildare, 14; Kilkenny, 7; King's county, 6; Leitrim, 5; Limerick county, 10; Limerick city, 3; Londonderry, 9; Longford, 4; Louth, 4; Mayo, 12; Meath, 9; Monaghan, 9; Queen's county, 6; Roscommon, 8; Sligo, 6; Tipperary, 13; Tyrone, 14; Waterford county, 6; Waterford city, 2; Westmeath, 5; Wicklow, 5.

29. In the cities the same regulations as in the counties shall be adopted; the city committees shall appoint one or more sheriffs, as they think proper, and shall take possession of all the public and corporation properties in their jurisdiction, in like manner as is directed in counties.

30. The provisional government strictly exhort and enjoin all magistrates, officers, civil and military, and the whole of the nation, to cause the law of morality to be enforced and respected, and to execute, as far as in them lies, justice with mercy, by which liberty alone can be established, and the blessings of divine providence secured.

ABBREVIATIONS

A.N.P.	Archives Nationales, Paris
B.L.	British Library
C.U.L.	Cambridge University Library
Emmet, *Memoirs*	Thomas Addis Emmet, *Memoir of Thomas Addis and Robert Emmet*, 2 vols, New York 1915.
G.E.C., *Peerage*	George Edward Cokayne, *The complete peerage*, 8 vols, London 1887–98.
Grattan, *Life*	*Memoirs of the life and times of the Rt Hon. Henry Grattan*, ed. Henry Grattan Jr, 5 vols, London, 1839–4.
HO	Home Office, London.
Madden, *United Irishmen*	Richard R. Madden, *The United Irishmen, their lives and times*, third series, second edition, London 1860.
M.H.S.	Massachusetts Historical Society
N.A.I.	National Archives of Ireland
N.L.I.	National Library of Ireland
N.Y.H.S.	New York Historical Society
N.Y.P.L.	New York Public Library
PH	*Parliamentary History*
P.R.O.	Public Record Office, London
P.R.O.N.I.	Public Record Office Northern Ireland
R.I.A.	Royal Irish Academy
T.C.D.	Trinity College Dublin
Trial of Robert Emmet	William Ridgeway, *A report of the proceedings in cases of high treason at a court of oyer and terminer*, Dublin, 1803.

References

Preface (pp ix–xiii)

1. W. B. Yeats, 'Emmet the apostle of Irish liberty' in J. P. Frayne and Colton Johnson (eds) *Uncollected prose of W. B. Yeats* (2 vols, London 1975) ii, 315.
2. Joseph Campbell, *The hero with a thousand faces* (New York 1949).
3. Ibid. 356.
4. Ibid. 391.
5. Thomas Addis Emmet to Peter Burrowes, 19 November 1806 (R.I.A., MS. 23.K.53/5).
6. Madden, *United Irishmen*, 257.
7. Yeats, 'Emmet the apostle of Irish liberty', 318.
8. Madden, *United Irishmen*, 258–9.
9. Norman Vance, *Irish literature: a social history* (Oxford 1990) 110.
10. Quoted in Sean Ryder, 'Young Ireland and the 1798 rebellion' in L. M. Geary (ed.) *Rebellion and remembrance in modern Ireland* (Dublin 2001) 144.
11. John Kelly (ed.) *The collected letters of W. B. Yeats* (3 vols, Oxford 1986–94) iii, 538.
12. R. F. Foster, *W. B. Yeats: a life* (Oxford 1997) i, 312–14.
13. Yeats, 'Emmet the apostle of Irish liberty', 315.
14. Ibid. 318–19.
15. P. H. Pearse, *How does she stand? Three addresses* (Dublin 1915) 7.
16. Ibid. 8.
17. R. F. Foster, *The Irish story* (London 2001) 62.
18. Pearse, *How does she stand*, 9.
19. Ibid. 10.

Chapter 1 Sacrifice and catharsis (pp 3–22)

1. Account of R. Rainey, 19 September 1803 (N.L.I., MS. 4597); it was also the opinion of some journalists present.
2. Recounted by Burrowes to Thomas Moore (Wilfred S. Dowden (ed.) *The journal of Thomas Moore* (4 vols, London 1983–7) iii, 1318).
3. Hardwicke to Charles Yorke, 20 September 1803 (B.L., Add. MS. 35742, f. 192).
4. Emmet, *Memoirs*, ii, 213.
5. Account of R. Rainey, 19 September 1803 (N.L.I., MS. 4597).
6. Account of Thomas Moore in Lord John Russell (ed.) *Memoirs, journals and correspondence of Thomas Moore* (8 vols, London 1853–6) i, 51–2.

7. *Walker's Hibernian Magazine*, October 1803, 610.
8. Madden, *United Irishmen*, 471.
9. Ibid.
10. *Trial of Robert Emmet*, 96. The historical controversy over Robert Emmet's speech from the dock will be dealt with in Chapter 10, and will include a discussion of the version used here.
11. Emmet, *Memoirs*, ii, 220.
12. Madden, *United Irishmen*, Appendix.
13. [Henry Brereton Code] *The insurrection of 23 July 1803* (Dublin 1803) vii–viii.
14. Madden, *United Irishmen*, 456.
15. Ibid. 456–7.
16. The recollection of a future judge (quoted in Madden, *United Irishmen*, 457).
17. Madden, *United Irishmen*, 453. The emphasis is that used by Madden.
18. In Madden's version the line reads 'no interference can be tortured' but this is obviously incorrect and should read 'inference'.
19. Madden, *United Irishmen*, 457.
20. Most notably Norman Vance whose arguments were followed by Marianne Elliott.
21. Michael MacDonagh, *The viceroy's post-bag* (London 1904) 306–7.
22. B.L., Add. MS. 35742, f. 197.
23. Madden, *United Irishmen*, 518.
24. N.A.I., Reb. Papers 620/11/133.
25. Hardwicke to Yorke, 20 September 1803 (B.L., Add. MS. 35742, f. 193).
26. W. H. Maxwell, *History of the Irish rebellion in 1798, with memoirs of the union, and Emmet's insurrection in 1803* (London 1845) 432.
27. *The London Chronicle*, 24-7 September 1803 (quoted in Madden, *United Irishmen*, 466).
28. Hardwicke to Yorke, 20 September 1803 (B.L., Add. MS. 35742, f. 193).
29. Ibid. f. 192.
30. Madden, *United Irishmen*, 461.
31. Charles Phillips, *Curran and his contemporaries* (London 1818) 437.
32. Jonah Barrington, *Personal sketches* (3 vols, Dublin 1827–32) (chapter on 'Duelling Extraordinary').
33. *The London Chronicle*, 24-7 September 1803 (both accounts are in Madden, *United Irishmen*, 461–3).
34. Madden, *United Irishmen*, 463.
35. Ibid. 461.
36. Quoted by William Wickham in his account of the scene (P.R.O.N.I., T.2627/5/2/18).
37. Ibid.
38. Another account by William Wickham written in 1835 (P.R.O.N.I., T.2627/5/2/13).
39. P.R.O.N.I., T.2627/5/2/18.
40. Hardwicke to Yorke, 20 September 1803 (B.L., Add. MS. 35742, f. 193).
41. Report of the clergymen (Hardwicke to Yorke, 20 September 1803 (B.L., Add. MS. 35742, f. 193)).
42. Comtesse d'Haussonville, *Robert Emmet* (Belfast 1858) 130.
43. Madden, *United Irishmen*, 467.
44. B.L., Add. MS. 33112, f. 14.
45. Hardwicke to Yorke, 20 September 1803 (B.L., Add. MS. 35742, f. 193).
46. Ibid.
47. Madden, *United Irishmen*, 467.

48. Ibid. 466.
49. G. Hume to Lord Pelham, 20 September 1803 (B.L., Add. MS. 33112, f. 44).
50. Madden, *United Irishmen*, 467.
51. *Dublin Evening Post* (22 September 1803); account of R. Rainey, 20 September 1803 (N.L.I., MS. 4597).
52. Hume to Pelham, 20 September 1803 (B.L., Add. MS. 33112, f. 44).
53. Madden, *United Irishmen*, 468.
54. Ibid.

Chapter 2 Romance revisited (pp 23–37)
1. George Petrie's account is quoted in William Stokes, *The life and labours in art and archaeology of George Petrie* (London 1868) 389.
2. J. W. Glover (ed.) *Irish melodies* (Dublin 1859) 208–9.
3. Anonymous, *The life of Robert Emmet: Ireland's greatest patriot* (Nottingham n.d.).
4. Leslie Hale, *John Philpot Curran: his life and times* (London 1958) 233.
5. Ibid.
6. John Philpot Curran to William Wickham, 21 September 1803 (B.L., Add. MS. 35703, f. 188).
7. Emmet to Richard Curran (Emmet, *Memoirs*, ii, 232).
8. Robert Emmet to T. A. Emmet and Jane Emmet, 20 September 1803 (B.L., Add. MS. 35742, f. 197).
9. H. T. MacMullan, *The voice of Sarah Curran* (Dublin 1955) 68.
10. Hale, *Curran*, 134.
11. Ibid. 138.
12. Ibid. 139.
13. See letter from Sicily.
14. MacMullan, *Voice*, 68.
15. Sarah Curran to Anne Penrose, 29 September 1809 (MacMullan, *Voice*, 68).
16. Sarah Curran to Robert Emmet [August 1803] (P.R.O., HO 100/113, f. 82).
17. N.L.I., MS. 8327/1.
18. Sarah Curran to Robert Emmet [August 1803] (P.R.O., HO 100/113, f. 81).
19. A description of Sarah Curran at eighteen that was given to R. R. Madden, *United Irishmen*, 520.
20. MacMullan, *Voice*, 9.
21. Madden, *United Irishmen*, 506.
22. Emmet to Richard Curran (Madden, *United Irishmen*, 518).
23. As Robert Emmet's final letter to Richard Curran from prison makes clear.
24. Emmet, *Memoirs*, ii, 232.
25. Sarah Curran to Robert Emmet [August 1803] (P.R.O., HO 100/113, f. 80).
26. Ibid. f. 78.
27. Ibid.
28. Ibid. Emphasis as in original.
29. Emmet, *Memoirs*, ii, 124.
30. Sarah Curran to Robert Emmet [August 1803] (P.R.O., HO 100/113, f. 78).
31. Ibid. f. 77.
32. Robert Emmet to Sarah Curran, 8 September 1803 (P.R.O., HO 100/113, f. 74).
33. Wickham to Sirr, September 1803 (Madden, *United Irishmen*, 510).
34. Thomas Bartlett (ed.) *Life of Theobald Wolfe Tone* (Dublin 1998) 879.

35. Emmet to Richard Curran (Madden, *United Irishmen*, 518).
36. Sarah Curran to Anne Penrose, 29 September 1807 (N.L.I., MS. 8326/1).
37. Sarah Curran to Anne Penrose, 29 September 1807 (N.L.I., MS. 8326/1); same to same, 1 July 1807 (N.L.I., MS. 8326/1).
38. John Curran to John Crawford, May 1808 (N.L.I., MS. 8905).
39. Account of J. D. Penrose (N.L.I., MS. 8362/2).
40. *Gentleman's Magazine* (1805) ii, 1170.
41. Sarah Curran to Anne Penrose, 1 July 1807 (N.L.I., MS. 8326/1).
42. Quoted in Madden, *United Irishmen*, 503.
43. Penrose tradition quoted in MacMullan, *Voice*, 38.
44. Sarah Curran to Anne and Bess Penrose, 24 October 1806 (N.L.I., MS. 8326/1).
45. Sarah Curran to Anne and Bess Penrose, 24 October 1806 (N.L.I., MS. 8327/2).
46. Sarah Curran to Anne and Bess Penrose, 13 December 1806 (N.L.I., MS. 8326/1).
47. Ibid.
48. Ibid.
49. Sarah Curran to Anne and Bess Penrose, 24 October 1806 (N.L.I., MS. 8327/2).
50. Ibid.
51. Sarah Curran to Anne Penrose, 31 October 1806 (N.L.I., MS. 8327/2).
52. Sarah Curran to Anne Penrose, 28 December 1806 (N.L.I., MS. 8327/4).
53. Sarah Curran to Anne Penrose, 25 July 1807 (N.L.I., MS. 8327/6).
54. Sarah Curran to Anne Penrose, 28 December 1806 (N.L.I., MS. 8327/4).
55. Ibid.
56. Sarah Curran to Anne Penrose, 1 July 1807 (N.L.I., MS. 8327/5).
57. Sarah Curran to Anne Penrose, 1 July 1807 (N.L.I., MS. 8326/1).
58. MacDonagh, *Viceroy's post-bag*, 392.
59. Sarah Curran to Anne Penrose, 25 July 1807 (N.L.I., MS. 8327/6).
60. Sarah Curran to Anne Penrose, 29 September 1807 (N.L.I., MS. 8327/7).
61. Sarah Curran to Bess Penrose, 25 July 1807 (N.L.I., MS. 8326/1).
62. Sarah Curran to Anne Penrose, 7 January 1808 (N.L.I., MS. 8326/1).
63. Letter from Sarah Curran to unknown, 17 April 1808 (quoted in Madden, *United Irishmen*, 532).
64. Sarah Curran to Anne Penrose, 7 January 1808 (N.L.I., MS. 8326/1).
65. Sarah Curran to Anne Penrose, 7 January 1808 (N.L.I., MS. 8327/8).
66. Sarah Curran to Anne Penrose, 10 January 1808 (N.L.I., MS. 8327/9).
67. Sarah Curran to unknown, 17 April 1808 (quoted in Madden, *United Irishmen*, 532).
68. Sarah Curran to Anne Penrose, 10 January 1808 (N.L.I., MS. 8327/9).
69. Sarah Curran to unknown, 17 April 1808 (quoted in Madden, *United Irishmen*, 532).
70. Sarah Curran to Anne Penrose, 10 January 1808 (N.L.I., MS. 8327/9).
71. Sarah Curran to Anne Penrose, January 1808 (N.L.I., MS. 8326/1).
72. Sarah Curran to Anne Penrose, 13 January 1808 (N.L.I., MS. 8327/10).
73. Sarah Curran to Anne Penrose, 20 March 1808 (MacMullan, *Voice*, 74).
74. William Napier (ed.) *The life and opinions of General Sir Charles Napier* (4 vols, London 1857) i, 85.
75. Sarah Curran to Anne Penrose, 20 March 1808 (MacMullan, *Voice*, 74).
76. Madden, *United Irishmen*, 509.
77. John Curran to John Crawford, May 1808 (N.L.I., MS. 8905).
78. Napier (ed.) *Sir Charles Napier*, i, 85.
79. John A. Hall, *A history of the Peninsular war: the biographical dictionary of British officers*

killed and wounded, 1808–14 (London 1998) 543.

80. Ibid.
81. *Gentleman's Magazine* (1814) i, 416.
82. Madden, *United Irishmen*, 515.

Chapter 3 Conspiracies and connections (pp 38–48)

1. Madame Campan, *Memoirs of the private life of Marie Antoinette* (2 vols, London 1823) ii, 188.
2. John Ehrman, *The younger Pitt* (3 vols, 1969–96) iii, 543.
3. Ibid. See also Duchess of Cleveland, *The life and letters of Lady Hester Stanhope* (London 1914) 67.
4. Ehrman, *Pitt*, iii, 542.
5. Ibid. 543.
6. Thomas Addis Emmet, *The Emmet family* (New York 1898); J. J. Reynolds, *Footprints of Emmet* (Dublin 1903); Helen Landreth, *The pursuit of Robert Emmet* (London 1949).
7. Emmet, *Emmet family*, 143.
8. Emmet, *Memoirs*, i, 214.
9. Landreth, *Pursuit*, ix.
10. Reynolds, *Footprints*, 44.
11. 'The truth about Robert Emmet' in *The Dublin Magazine* (July–September 1950) 44.
12. Emmet, *Memoirs*, ii, 42–3.
13. T.C.D., MS. 7253/1, f. 3.
14. See P. M. Geoghegan, *The Irish Act of Union* (Dublin 1999) Chapter 7.
15. Landreth, *Pursuit*, x.
16. Ibid. x–xi; my italics.
17. Ibid. vii.
18. Ibid. vii and xi; again my italics.
19. See Appendix A for a detailed account of their respective genealogies.
20. Emmet, *Emmet family*, 11.
21. Ibid. Appendices.
22. Dr Emmet to John Temple, 7 June 1785 (M.H.S., Winthrop papers).
23. Elizabeth Emmet to Thomas Addis Emmet, 15 October 1801 (T.C.D., MS. 873/582, f. 5).
24. Elizabeth Emmet to Mrs John Temple, 27 August 1773 (M.H.S., Winthrop papers).
25. Thomas Addis Emmet to Rufus King, 9 April 1807 (quoted in R. R. Madden, *The life and times of Robert Emmet* (New York n.d.) 313).
26. William Drennan to Martha McTier, 15 January 1805 (Jean Agnew (ed.) *The Drennan-McTier letters* (3 vols, 1998–9) iii, 306).
27. Erich Eyck, *Pitt versus Fox: father and son, 1735-1806* (London 1950) 219.
28. Ehrman, *Pitt*, i, 65, fn 2.
29. Mentioned by Dr Emmet in a letter to John Temple, 23 October 1784 (M.H.S., Winthrop papers); (quoted in Thomas P. Robinson, 'The life of Thomas Addis Emmet' (Ph.D. thesis, New York University 1955) 15).
30. Robinson, 'Thomas Addis Emmet', 16.
31. Ibid.
32. See Lewis Namier and John Brooke (eds) *The Commons, 1754–90* (3 vols, London 1985) [see entries on Pitt and Shelburne (sub Petty)]; Stanley Ayling, *The elder Pitt: earl of Chatham* (London 1976) 368.
33. Namier and Brooke (eds) *The Commons*.

34. Ibid.
35. Ehrman, *Pitt*, i, 137.
36. Namier and Brooke (eds) *The Commons*.
37. Lord Edmond Fitzmaurice, *Life of William, earl of Shelburne* (3 vols, London 1875) iii, 324.
38. Ehrman, *Pitt*, i, 100.
39. Namier and Brooke (eds) *The Commons*.
40. The recollection of Wraxall (quoted in Ehrman, *Pitt*, i, 231).
41. John Barrell, *Imagining the king's death* (Oxford 2000) 30.
42. Ibid. 35.
43. Ibid. 522.
44. Ibid. 524.
45. Ibid. 573–4.
46. Elizabeth Sparrow, 'The alien office' in *The Historical Journal*, no. 33, 2 (1990) 366.
47. Earl Stanhope, *Notes of conversations with the duke of Wellington*, 1831–51 (London 1998) 85.
48. George III to Pitt, 18 February 1801 (C.U.L., Add. MS. 6958, f. 2849).
49. See entry in G.E.C., *Peerage*.
50. Ibid.
51. Namier and Brooke (eds) *The Commons*.
52. R. G. Thorne (ed.) *The Commons, 1790–1820* (5 vols, London 1986) iv, 789.
53. G.E.C., *Peerage*.
54. Thomas Pakenham, *The year of liberty* (London 1969) 102.
55. G.E.C., *Peerage*.
56. Thorne (ed.) *The Commons*, iv, 788.
57. Ibid. 789.
58. Report of 17 August 1803 (P.R.O., 100/112, f. 299).
59. Madden, *United Irishmen*, 358–9; William Wickham to Earl Wycombe, 27 December 1803 (B.L., Add. MS. 35704, f. 243); Wycombe had enquired on 10 December if a warrant of arrest had been issued in his name.
60. Thorne (ed.) *The Commons*, iv, 789.
61. See ibid. 783.
62. Stella Tillyard, *Aristocrats* (London 1995) 92.
63. Fitzmaurice, *Shelburne*, i, 78.
64. John Derry, *Charles James Fox* (Gateshead 1972) 11–12.
65. Fitzmaurice, *Shelburne*, i, 78.
66. *Dictionary of National Biography*.
67. Tillyard, *Aristocrats*, 335.

Chapter 4 'An Irish Washington' (pp 51–85)

1. See Emmet, *Emmet family*, 7. The first Robert Emmet died between 1772 and 1774. On 3 September 1772 another son was born and was christened John; the second Robert was born in 1774.
2. *Dublin Directory* (1777) 89. Madden, *United Irishmen*, and Emmet, *Memoirs*, both make separate mistakes about the location of Robert Emmet's birthplace.
3. Emmet, *Emmet family*, 7.
4. David A. Quaid, *Robert Emmet: his birth-place and burial* (Dublin 1902) 2; Emmet, *Memoirs*, ii, 3.
5. Emmet, *Memoirs*, ii, 3.

6. Samuel Whyte, *The art of speaking* (Dublin 1763) Introduction.
7. Ibid. This followed the definition of Thomas Sheridan.
8. Ibid. 9.
9. Ibid. 48.
10. Ibid. 27; see also Samuel Whyte, *The shamrock, or Hibernian cresses* (Dublin 1772); same, *The theatre: a didactic essay* (Dublin 1790); Patrick Fagan, *A Georgian celebration: Irish poets in the eighteenth century* (Dublin 1989).
11. Quoted in Whyte, *The shamrock*, 50.
12. Dr Robert Emmet to Sir John Temple, 29 August 1787 (M.H.S., Winthrop papers).
13. Thomas Addis Emmet to Jeannette (Jane Erin) Emmet, 26 January 1816 (N.Y.H.S., Uncatalogued Thomas Addis Emmet papers).
14. Madden, *United Irishmen*, 264.
15. Anecdote from Madden, *United Irishmen*, 340.
16. William Drennan to Sam McTier, 3 May 1790 (*Drennan-McTier letters*, i, 349).
17. The story was recounted by John Patten to R. R. Madden (Madden, *United Irishmen*, 265). Haussonville also recounts the same story with some minor modifications, but her account appears to be derived from Madden.
18. Madden, *United Irishmen*, 265.
19. T.C.D., MS. 873/576; Grattan, *Life*, iv, 356.
20. T.C.D., MS. 873/576 and T.C.D., MS. 873/578.
21. For example, see Thomas Addis Emmet to John Patten, 29 July 1820 (Emmet, *Memoirs*, i, 437).
22. Thomas Addis Emmet to Jeannette (Jane Erin) Emmet, 26 January 1826 (N.Y.H.S., Uncatalogued Thomas Addis Emmet papers).
23. Sir Edward Newenham to Franklin, 12 January 1786 (American Philosophical Society, *Franklin Papers*, xxxiv/4). I would like to thank Dr James Kelly for kindly sending me a copy of this letter.
24. Elizabeth Emmet to the wife of John Temple, 29 November 1773 (M.H.S., Winthrop papers).
25. Ibid., original emphasis.
26. William Drennan to Sam McTier, 3 May 1790 (*Drennan-McTier letters*, i, 349).
27. Ibid. 348–9.
28. Grattan, *Life*, iv, 360.
29. Ibid. 356.
30. Ibid. 357.
31. Hardwicke to Pelham, 20 September 1803 (B.L., Add. MS. 33112, f. 44).
32. Ibid.
33. Grattan, *Life*, iv, 356. It should be noted that Dr Emmet always referred to his son as Tom and never as Addis.
34. Ibid.
35. Madden, *United Irishmen*, 12.
36. 'Dr Emmet's Cork residence' in *Cork HASJ*, li (1946) 190–1.
37. Taken from the Emmet family records (Emmet, *Emmet family*, 7).
38. William Drennan to Martha McTier, 15 January 1805 (*Drennan-McTier letters*, iii, 306).
39. Madden, *United Irishmen*, 4 and 10.
40. William Drennan to Martha McTier, 15 January 1805 (*Drennan-McTier letters*, iii, 306); William Drennan to Martha McTier, 14 December 1802 (*Drennan-McTier letters*, iii, 87); Dr Emmet to John Temple, 17 April 1785 (M.H.S., Winthrop papers).

41. Dr Emmet to John Temple, 28 October 1784 (M.H.S., Winthrop papers). He revealed that his salary was £200 per annum, and wanted this doubled or at least raised to a pound a day.
42. Ibid.
43. F. G. Hall, *The Bank of Ireland, 1783–1946* (Dublin 1949) 509.
44. As explained by William Wickham in a letter to the earl of Hardwicke, 9 December 1803 (P.R.O.N.I., T.2627/5/E/284).
45. Dr Emmet to John Temple, 28 October 1784 (M.H.S., Winthrop papers).
46. *Dublin Directory*, 74; William Wickham to Hardwicke, 9 December 1803 (P.R.O.N.I., T.2627/5/E/284).
47. T.C.D., MS. 873/562.
48. *Dublin University Calendar* (Dublin 1833) 63.
49. T.C.D., MUN/V/27/3.
50. T.C.D., MS. 873/562.
51. Grattan, *Life*, iv, 357.
52. Ibid.
53. Ibid. 358.
54. Ibid. 357.
55. Dr Emmet to John Temple, 28 October 1784 (M.H.S., Winthrop papers).
56. Emmet, *Memoirs*, i, 197.
57. Mrs Emmet to the wife of John Temple, 29 November 1773 (M.H.S., Winthrop papers).
58. Dr Emmet to John Temple, 17 April 1785 (M.H.S., Winthrop papers).
59. Dr Emmet to Sir John Temple, 29 August 1787 (M.H.S., Winthrop papers).
60. Ibid.
61. Ibid.
62. Dr Emmet to John Temple, 17 April 1785 (M.H.S., Winthrop papers).
63. T.C.D., MS. 873/562.
64. Newenham to Franklin, 12 January 1786 (American Philosophical Society, *Franklin Papers*, xxxiv/4). Again I would like to thank Dr James Kelly for sending me this information.
65. Ibid.
66. Dr Emmet to John Temple, 17 April 1785 (M.H.S., Winthrop papers).
67. T.C.D., MS. 873/582, f. 7.
68. T.C.D., MUN/V/27/3.
69. Ibid. Plunket was in his junior sophister year. For evidence of his friendship with Emmet, see Madden, *United Irishmen*, 76.
70. Thomas Addis Emmet to Jeannette (Jane Erin) Emmet, 25 February 1820 (N.Y.H.S., Uncatalogued Thomas Addis Emmet papers).
71. T.C.D., MS. 873/578.
72. Thomas Addis Emmet to Jeannette (Jane Erin) Emmet, 20 February 1817 (N.Y.H.S., Uncatalogued Thomas Addis Emmet papers).
73. Dr Emmet to John Temple, 29 August 1787 (M.H.S., Winthrop papers).
74. Edward Keane *et al*, *King's Inns admission papers* (Dublin 1986) 153.
75. Thomas Addis Emmet to Jeannette (Jane Erin) Emmet, 20 February 1817 (N.Y.H.S., Uncatalogued Thomas Addis Emmet papers).
76. Ibid.
77. Madden, *United Irishmen*, 11–12.
78. Grattan, *Life*, iv, 358.
79. Ibid. 360–1.

80. Thomas Addis Emmet to Jeannette (Jane Erin) Emmet, 25 February 1820 (N.Y.H.S., Uncatalogued Thomas Addis Emmet papers).
81. Thomas Addis Emmet to Jeannette (Jane Erin) Emmet, 23 January 1820 (N.Y.H.S., Uncatalogued Thomas Addis Emmet papers).
82. Ibid.
83. Ibid.
84. T.C.D., MS. 873/578.
85. Madden, *United Irishmen*, 37.
86. Ibid. 42.
87. Thomas Addis Emmet to 'F' (quoted in Robinson, 'Thomas Addis Emmet', 68).
88. Drennan to Martha McTier, 1 August 1797 (*Drennan-McTier letters*, ii, 329).
89. Charles Gildden Haines, *Memoir of Thomas Addis Emmet* (New York 1829) 119.
90. Madden, *United Irishmen*, 12.
91. MacDonagh, *Viceroy's post-bag*, 344.
92. Dr Emmet to Sir John Temple, 29 August 1787 (M.H.S., Winthrop papers).
93. William Drennan to Ann Drennan, 13 June 1791 (*Drennan-McTier letters*, i, 359).
94. Madden, *United Irishmen*, 259, 263.
95. Quoted in Madden, *United Irishmen*, 339.
96. Madden says he took this account 'word for word' from John Patten (Madden, *United Irishmen*, 339).
97. Madden, *United Irishmen*, 340.
98. Ibid.
99. Dr Emmet to John Temple, 17 April 1785 (M.H.S., Winthrop papers).
100. Dr Emmet to Sir John Temple, 29 August 1787 (M.H.S., Winthrop papers).
101. William Drennan to Sam McTier, 3 May 1790 (*Drennan-McTier letters*, i, 349).
102. Madden, *Robert Emmet* (New York n.d.) 242.
103. Apparently the poem was preserved by the Emmet family in America (Emmet, *Memoirs*, ii, 6); it was also one of the poems given to Madden by Mary McCracken but with slight changes. For example, the first sentence is 'Brothers, rise! Your country calls' (Madden, *United Irishmen*, 497). Robert Emmet's poetry is contained in Appendix B.
104. Emmet, *Memoirs*, ii, 4.
105. See Marianne Elliott, *Wolfe Tone* (Yale 1990) 14.
106. Madden, *United Irishmen*, 6.
107. Lord John Russell (ed.) *Memoirs, journals and correspondence of Thomas Moore* (8 vols, London 1853–6) i, 58.
108. Ibid. vii, 253.
109. T.C.D., MUN/V/27/3.
110. Wolfe Tone entered the Middle Temple in London on 3 February 1787, which gave him formal admission to the King's Inns on the same date because of a 1783 statute (*King's Inns admission papers*, viii–ix).
111. *King's Inns admission papers*, ix.
112. For a discussion of this, see Luke Gibbons, in Jim Smith (ed.) *Revolution, counter-revolution and union* (Cambridge 2000) 225.
113. Russell, *Moore*, i, 58.
114. See Seamus Deane (ed.) *The Field Day anthology of Irish writing* (3 vols, Derry 1991) i, 1061.
115. Russell, *Moore*, i, 57.
116. Ibid. iii, 1161.
117. *The Press*, 2 December 1797.

118. Russell, *Moore*, i, 56–7.
119. Ibid. 57.
120. Quoted in Madden, *United Irishmen*, 269.
121. Ibid. 266.
122. Ibid. 280.
123. John William Stubbs, *The history of the University of Dublin* (Dublin 1889) 296.
124. For a reproduction of the seal, see Emmet, *Memoirs*, ii, 22–3.
125. Robert Emmet's height is given by Thomas Elrington who gave a report to the government in 1803 (Madden, *United Irishmen*, 336).
126. Roderick Floud, Kenneth Wachter, Annabel Gregory (eds) *Height, health and history: nutritional status in the United Kingdom, 1750–1980* (Cambridge 1990) 23.
127. Ibid. 30 and 142.
128. Ibid. 136–7.
129. Ibid. 114. The height requirement for the heavy cavalry between 1802 and 1806 was five feet eight inches or usually above. Emmet in 1803 was barely five feet eight inches tall.
130. Quoted in Madden, *United Irishmen*, 336–7.
131. d'Haussonville, *Robert Emmet*, 34.
132. Quoted in Madden, *United Irishmen*, 267.
133. A variation of this motion was later discussed at the Historical Society on 25 April 1798, but Emmet was not present as it was shortly after his expulsion (T.C.D., MUN/SOC/HIST/12).
134. Russell, *Moore*, i, 47.
135. Ibid.
136. Jane Austen to Cassandra Austen, 9 January 1796, Deirdre Le Faye (ed.) *Jane Austen's letters* (Oxford 1995) 1.
137. Ibid.
138. Recollection of Rev. Dr Macartney (Madden, *United Irishmen*, 266). Macartney claimed that Lefroy answered Emmet's début speech at the Historical Society, but this is impossible as Lefroy was not present, nor was his speech recorded in the minutes of the society (T.C.D., MUN/SOC/HIST/12).
139. Declan Budd and Ross Hinds (eds) *The Hist and Edmund Burke's club* (Dublin 1997) 36.
140. T.C.D., MUN/SOC/HIST/12.
141. Ibid.
142. The description is in Madden, *United Irishmen*, 16. Madden is incorrect that the meetings took place on a Monday. As the records of the Historical Society show, they took place on Wednesdays (T.C.D., MUN/SOC/HIST/12).
143. For details about the Historical Society, see Stubbs, *University of Dublin*, and especially 'The Historical Society: first era' and 'The Historical Society: second era' in *Irish Quarterly Review*, iv (1845) 305–28 and 502–20. Despite much to admire, there are some regrettable errors in the recent study by Budd and Hinds, *The Hist*.
144. See David Brion Davis and Steven Mintz, *The boisterous sea of liberty* (New York 1999); after the 500th anniversary of the discovery of America the historian Arthur M. Schlesinger wrote an essay on this subject asking 'Was America a mistake?' He argued persuasively that it was not. Coincidentally, Schlesinger is married to a descendant of Thomas Addis Emmet.
145. The Rev. Dr Macartney, later vicar of Antrim, remembered that he had attended to hear Emmet (Madden, *United Irishmen*, 265); but as Emmet only spoke because others had not shown up this cannot be correct.

146. Madden, *United Irishmen*, 265. See also Budd and Hinds, *The Hist*, 36. Moore remembered the motion as: 'Is a complete freedom of discussion essential to the well-being of a good and virtuous government?'
147. Madden, *United Irishmen*, 265–6.
148. Ibid. 266.
149. T.C.D., MUN/SOC/HIST/12.
150. Ibid. Moore claimed that Lefroy anwered Emmet at this debate but his name does not appear in the minutes of the society. He probably confused this with a different debate.
151. Ibid.
152. Moore quoted in Madden, *United Irishmen*, 266.
153. Ibid. 267.
154. 'The Historical Society', 506.
155. Moore remembered the motion as 'Whether a soldier was bound on all occasions to obey the orders of his commanding officer?' He also claimed that this and another motion were discussed the same evening, but he was mistaken on this point and incorrect about the choice of motion (Russell, *Moore*, i, 46–7).
156. T.C.D., MS. 873/272.
157. Russell, *Moore*, i, 47.
158. Ibid. 283.
159. Account of Russell, *Moore*, i, 51–2.
160. Quoted in Madden, *United Irishmen*, 266.
161. T.C.D., MUN/SOC/HIST/12. This followed his expulsion after the visitation of 19–21 April.
162. T.C.D., MUN/V/5/5.
163. T.C.D., MS. 1203, f. 29.
164. Walsh quoted in Madden, *United Irishmen*, 275.
165. T.C.D., MS. 3363.
166. T.C.D., MS. 3373.
167. Budd and Hinds, *The Hist*, 15.
168. Quoted in Madden, *United Irishmen*, 278.
169. Quoted in A. C. Kavanaugh, *John FitzGibbon, earl of Clare* (Dublin 1997) 342.
170. Madden, *United Irishmen*, 280.
171. Ibid.
172. Quoted in ibid. 285.
173. Ibid.
174. Ibid. 284.
175. Ibid.
176. Ibid.
177. Ibid. 285.
178. Ibid. 286.
179. Ibid.
180. T.C.D., MS. 1203.
181. T.C.D., MS. 1203 and MS. 3363.
182. Madden, *United Irishmen*, 281.
183. Drennan to Martha McTier, 23 April 1798 (*Drennan-McTier letters*, ii, 392).
184. Examination of 11 January 1804 (P.R.O.N.I., T.3030/12/1).
185. Recollection of Curran (quoted in Madden, *United Irishmen*, 287).
186. Ibid.

Chapter 5 Warfare and technology (pp 86–115)

1. B.L., Add. MS. 71593, f. 134. I would like to thank Eoin Keehan for his advice on this chapter, and also his suggestions for the title.

2. See Robert Fulton, *On submarine navigation and attack* (London 1806), bound manuscript in the New York Public Library; and same, *Torpedo war and submarine explosions* (New York 1810); see also the entry on Robert Fulton in the *American National Biography* (New York 1999); and Wallace Hutcheon Jr, *Robert Fulton: pioneer of undersea warfare* (Annapolis 1981). For Fulton's own drawings and designs for his submarines and torpedoes, see the four boxes of Robert Fulton papers in the New York Public Library.

3. Hutcheon, *Robert Fulton*, 18. The *Nautilus* was also the name given to Captain Nemo's submarine in Jules Verne's, *Twenty thousand leagues under the sea* (1879).

4. John Keegan, *Battle at sea: from man-of-war to submarine* (London 1988) 214. Keegan mistakenly states that the mission was a success, but see Bushnell's entry in the *American National Biography*.

5. Quoted in H. W. Dickinson, *Robert Fulton: engineer and artist* (London 1913) Chapter 6.

6. Fulton to French government, 5 October 1799 (quoted in Dickinson, *Robert Fulton*, Chapter 6).

7. Quoted in Alice Crary Sutcliffe, *Robert Fulton and the 'Clermont'* (New York 1909) 71.

8. Fulton to Stanhope, 14 April 1798 (N.Y.P.L., The William Barclay Parsons 'Robert Fulton' collection, box one).

9. Robert H. Thurston, *Robert Fulton: his life and its results* (New York 1891) Chapter 5.

10. Dickinson, *Robert Fulton*, Chapter 6.

11. Hutcheon, *Robert Fulton*, 53.

12. Evan Nepean to the admiralty, 19 June 1803 (N.Y.P.L., The William Barclay Parsons 'Robert Fulton' collection, box one).

13. Ibid.

14. Robert Fulton's account of his defection, 'Motives for inventing submarine navigation and attack; statement of the causes which brought me to England', 10 August 1806 (N.Y.P.L., The William Barclay Parsons 'Robert Fulton' collection, box one).

15. Fulton to Grenville [no date but must be the 'Ministry of the talents' (1806-7)] B.L., Add. MS. 71593, f. 135.

16. Thurston, *Robert Fulton*, Chapter 5.

17. Robert Fulton, *Torpedo war and submarine explosions* (New York 1810) 7.

18. Fulton to Grenville, 2 September 1806 (quoted in Robert Fulton (ed.) *Letters principally to the right honourable Lord Grenville on submarine navigation and attack* (London 1806) 11).

19. The incident is ignored in most studies of the future Duke of Wellington; for an account see Denys Forrest, *Tiger of Mysore: the life and death of Tipu Sultan* (London 1970) 283.

20. Robin Wigington, *The firearms of Tipu Sultan, 1783-99* (Hatfield 1992) 13.

21. Walter Wood (ed.) *The despatches of field-marshal, the Duke of Wellington* (London 1902) 10.

22. Forrest, *Tiger of Mysore*, 291.

23. These are now on display in the Royal Artillery Museum at Woolwich Arsenal where William Congreve worked.

24. Information on the history of rockets provided by the NASA Spacelink System.

25. P.R.O., 30/8/158, f. 1.

26. Meares to Pitt, report dated 10 October 1803 (P.R.O., 30/8/158, f. 4).
27. Ibid. ff 4–5.
28. There is some confusion among historians about whether a warrant was issued for his arrest on 3 April 1799; certainly his name appears on one written by Castlereagh and given to Major Sirr (T.C.D., MS. 869/6, ff 10–11) but it does not appear to have been acted upon and Wickham's denial seems to confirm this.
29. See Tom Paulin, 'English political writers on Ireland' in Michael Allen and Angela Wilcox (eds) *Critical approaches to Anglo-Irish literature* (Buckinghamshire 1989) 134–5.
30. Robert Southey to John King, 28 September 1803 (John Wood Warter (ed.) *Selections from the letters of Robert Southey* (London 1856) i, 236).
31. Ibid. i, 237.
32. See Reynolds, *Footprints*, 49–51.
33. Donal Kerr (ed.) *Emmet's Casino and the Marists at Milltown* (Dublin 1970) 5.
34. Madden, *United Irishmen*, 287.
35. Quoted in Elliott, *Wolfe Tone*, 392.
36. Ibid.
37. Thomas Bartlett (ed.) *Life of Theobald Wolfe Tone* (Dublin 1998) xxxvii. For the controversy over the exact text of his speech from the dock, see Elliott, *Wolfe Tone*, 392–5.
38. Elliott, *Wolfe Tone*, 393.
39. Bartlett, *Life of Theobald Wolfe Tone*, 37.
40. Account of Matilda Tone (1826) in ibid. 923.
41. Wickham to Rufus King, 16 September 1798 (quoted in Robinson, 'Thomas Addis Emmet', 146).
42. Castlereagh to Wickham, 29 October 1798 (quoted in Robinson, 'Thomas Addis Emmet', 152).
43. Thomas Addis Emmet to Rufus King, 9 April 1807 (quoted in Emmet, *Emmet family*, 192).
44. For example, on 3 January 1799 (N.A.I., Reb. Papers, 620/7/74/2).
45. Report of 15 February 1799 (N.A.I., Reb. Papers, 620/7/74/11).
46. N.A.I., Reb. Papers, 620/7/74/22.
47. N.A.I., Reb. Papers, 620/7/74/26. Quoted in Ruán O'Donnell, *Aftermath: Post-rebellion insurgency in Wicklow, 1799-1803* (Dublin 2000) 110.
48. N.A.I. Reb. Papers, 620/8/72/2.
49. MacDonagh, *Viceroy's post-bag*, 277.
50. 13 February 1799 (N.A.I., Reb. Papers, 620/8/85/4).
51. See P. M. Geoghegan, *The Irish Act of Union* (Dublin 1999).
52. 22–3 January 1799 (quoted in J. C. Hoey (ed.) *Speeches of Lord Plunket*, (Dublin 1873) 30).
53. Emmet, *Memoirs*, ii, 13–15. I would like to thank Eoin Keehan for his assistance on some of the poetry points.
54. 9 March 1799 (Emmet, *Memoirs*, ii, 17–20).
55. Emmet, *Memoirs*, ii, 16–17.
56. Ibid. 15–16.
57. Quoted in Emmet, *Memoirs*, ii, 24.
58. Report of 31 August 1803 (N.A.I., Reb. Papers, 620/11/130/26).
59. Madden, *United Irishmen*, 288; there is some confusion about when this visit took place. Madden claims it happened in early 1800, while Robinson is sceptical about whether it ever took place ('Thomas Addis Emmet', 187). As the conflict with Arthur

O'Connor only flared in June 1800, and Jane Emmet visited a few months later, it must have taken place in this period, with mid-June the most likely date.

60. Madden, *United Irishmen*, 288.
61. Robinson, 'Thomas Addis Emmet', 172.
62. Madden, *United Irishmen*, 108.
63. T.C.D., MS. 873/582, f. 1.
64. Elizabeth to Thomas Addis Emmet, 8 October 1801 (Emmet, *Emmet family*, 95).
65. T.C.D., MS. 873/582, f. 5.
66. Ibid. f. 6.
67. Ibid. f. 8.
68. Thomas Addis Emmet to Jeannette (Jane Erin) Emmet, 26 January 1816 (N.Y.H.S., Uncatalogued Thomas Addis Emmet papers).
69. Thomas Addis Emmet to Jeannette (Jane Erin) Emmet, 2 March 1818 (N.Y.H.S., Uncatalogued Thomas Addis Emmet papers).
70. Thomas Addis Emmet to Jeannette (Jane Erin) Emmet, 25 February 1820 (N.Y.H.S., Uncatalogued Thomas Addis Emmet papers).
71. Hunter to Pelham, 5 November 1801 (quoted in MacDonagh, *Viceroy's post-bag*, 259).
72. See Madden, *United Irishmen*, 102–8.
73. Statement of John Chambers, 8 July 1802 (quoted in Madden, *United Irishmen*, 105).
74. Ibid., 106.
75. Report of 31 August 1803 (N.A.I., Reb. Papers, 620/11/130/26).
76. William Wickham to John King, 24 October 1803 (P.R.O., HO 100/114, f. 113).
77. Report of 20 August 1803 (N.A.I., Reb. Papers, 620/11/130/18).
78. William Wickham's account of Robert Emmet's movements prior to the rebellion, December 1803 (B.L., Add. MS. 35740, f. 202).
79. R.I.A., MS. 12 L 32, 77.
80. William Wickham's account of Robert Emmet's movements prior to the rebellion, December 1803 (B.L., Add. MS. 35740, f. 203).
81. P.R.O., HO 100/114/123.
82. 4 March 1801 (N.A.I., Reb. Papers, 620/10/118/9).
83. Emmet to Madame la marquise de Fontenay, 6 October 1801 (quoted in Emmet, *Memoirs*, ii, 26-7).
84. See Miles Byrne, *Memoirs of Miles Byrne* (3 vols, Paris 1863) i, 334.
85. Madden, *United Irishmen*, 38.
86. Emmet to Madame la marquise de Fontenay, 19 December 1801 (N.A.I., Reb. Papers, 620/18/14).
87. Ibid.
88. Quoted in James Quinn, 'In pursuit of the millennium' (Ph.D. thesis, University College Dublin 1995) 158.
89. Ibid. 159.
90. *An appeal to the public by James Tandy* (Dublin 1807) 13–14.
91. R.I.A., MS. 12 L 32, f. 86; see also Thomas U. Sadleir (ed.) *An Irish peer on the continent, 1801-03* (London 1924).
92. See Emmet, *Memoirs*, ii, 28.
93. Bartlett (ed.) *Life of Theobald Wolfe Tone*, 906.
94. R.I.A., MS. 12 L 32, f. 87. Emphasis as in original.
95. Bartlett (ed.) *Life of Theobald Wolfe Tone*, 906.
96. R.I.A., MS. 12 L 32, f. 87.

97. Bartlett (ed.) *Life of Theobald Wolfe Tone*, 906.
98. R.I.A., MS. 12 L 32, f. 87.
99. Bartlett (ed.) *Life of Theobald Wolfe Tone*, 924.
100. R.I.A., MS. 12 L 32, f. 77.
101. Ibid. ff 105–6.
102. Ibid. f. 106.
103. Ibid.
104. See Emmet, *Memoirs*, ii, 28.
105. R.I.A., MS. 12 L 32, f. 86.
106. N.A.I., Reb. Papers, 620/11/130/43.
107. William Wickham to Reginald Pole-Carew, 8 October 1803 (P.R.O., HO 100/114, f. 20).
108. Robert Emmet's opinion is stated by Thomas Addis Emmet in a letter to W. J. Macneven, n.d. (quoted in Madden, *United Irishmen*, 119).
109. Colin Lindsay (ed.) *Extracts from Colonel Templehoff's history of the seven years' war* (2 vols, London 1793) i, xxxi.
110. Ibid. i, 22 and also i, 154–5.
111. Ibid. i, 25.
112. Ibid. i, 38.
113. Ibid. i, 81.
114. Ibid. i, 82.
115. Ibid. i, 84.
116. Ibid. i, 92.
117. Ibid. i, 106.
118. Ibid. i, 205.
119. See MacDonagh, *Viceroy's post-bag*, 357.
120. Lindsay, *Extracts*, i, 127.
121. Ibid. ii, 272.
122. Ibid. ii, 272–82.
123. Ibid. ii, 433.
124. B.L., Add. MS. 35740, f. 209.
125. See Mitchell R. Sharpe, 'Robert Emmet and the development of the war rocket' in *Éire-Ireland*, 5: 4 (1970) 3–8; and Leon O'Broin, *The unfortunate Mr Emmet*, 49, for statements about Emmet and Fulton in France.
126. Emmet, *Memoirs*, i, 427 fn.
127. See Emmet, *Memoirs*, ii, Appendix.
128. Thomas Addis Emmet to Henry Baldwin, 23 March 1815 (N.Y.P.L., The Gilbert H. Montague collection of Robert Fulton manuscripts, box two); see also Robert Fulton's request for help from Thomas Addis Emmet, 25 August 1812 (N.Y.H.S., Robert R. Livingston papers). Emmet explains the circumstances of his first meeting with Fulton in these letters.
129. William Congreve, *A concise account of the origin and progress of the rocket system* (London 1810) 1.
130. Quoted in Sharpe, 'Robert Emmet and the development of the war rocket', 5; Sharpe emphasises the crucial similarity of both men using iron for their cases. See also Mitchell R. Sharpe, 'Robert Emmet's rockets' in *The Irish Sword*, ix, 136 (1970) 161–4.
131. Madden, *United Irishmen*, 363.
132. Ibid.
133. Robert Emmet's plan for the insurrection (B.L., Add. MS. 38103, f. 19).

134. Ibid.
135. See Sharpe, 'Robert Emmet and the development of the war rocket', 7.
136. Statement of James Hope (Madden, *United Irishmen*, 357).
137. Robert Emmet to Madame la marquise de Fontenay, 24 April 1802 (quoted in Emmet, *Memoirs*, ii, 28).
138. Ibid.
139. See Marianne Elliott, 'The "Despard conspiracy" reconsidered' in *Past and Present*, 75 (1977) 46–61; Roger Wells, *Insurrection* (Gloucester 1986).
140. Elliott, 'The "Despard conspiracy" reconsidered', 47.
141. V. A. C. Gatrell, *The hanging tree: execution and the English people* (Oxford 1994) 50–1.
142. Ibid. 88.
143. Elliott, 'The "Despard conspiracy" reconsidered', 249.
144. Wells, *Insurrection*, 242.
145. N.A.I., Reb. Papers, 620/10/121/2.
146. N.A.I., Reb. Papers, 620/3/32/20.
147. Quinn, 'In pursuit of the millennium', 165.
148. William Wickham to John King, 13 October 1803 (P.R.O., HO 100/114, f. 56).
149. Report of William Wickham [24 October 1803] (P.R.O., HO 100/114, f. 123).
150. Evidence of Thomas Frayne, 3 October 1803 (N.A.I., Reb. Papers, 620/11/130/44).
151. William Wickham to Pole-Carew, 28 August 1803 (quoted in MacDonagh, *Viceroy's post-bag*, 339).
152. This is one of the poems given to Madden by Mary McCracken (Madden, *United Irishmen*, 497).
153. For details of Cloncurry in Paris, see A.N.P., F⁷ 2232, f. 73.
154. Madden, *United Irishmen*, 137.
155. As W. J. Macneven's undated memorandum makes clear (quoted in Madden, *United Irishmen*, 316–17).
156. Robinson, 'Thomas Addis Emmet', 192.
157. N.A.I., Reb. Papers, 620/11/130/18.
158. Madden, *United Irishmen*, 328.
159. Ibid.
160. Byrne, *Memoirs*, i, 340-1.
161. Alexander Marsden to Charles Flint, 14 March 1803 (P.R.O.N.I., T.2627/5/K/75).
162. Marsden to Wickham, 29 March 1803 (P.R.O.N.I., T.2627/5/K/96).
163. B.L., Add. MS. 35740, f. 203.
164. Robert Emmet to Madame la marquise de Fontenay, 24 April 1802 (quoted in Emmet, *Memoirs*, ii, 28).

Chapter 6 Return to Ireland (pp 116–153)
1. Byrne, *Memoirs*, i, 349.
2. T.C.D., MS. 873/583.
3. Madden, *United Irishmen*, 345.
4. Report of Wickham (quoted in Emmet, *Memoirs*, ii, 42, who gives the tanner's name as 'Noms'; it is more likely to have been the Mr Norris mentioned in Byrne's *Memoirs*, i, 332).
5. Byrne, *Memoirs*, i, 349.
6. Madden, *United Irishmen*, 370.
7. Examination of Long, 18 August 1803 (N.A.I., Reb. Papers, 620/11/138/4).

8. Madden, *United Irishmen*, 370.
9. Ibid. 343.
10. Mrs Emmet to Thomas Addis Emmet, 7 January 1803 (quoted in Emmet, *Memoirs*, i, 186).
11. Ibid.
12. Ibid. 187.
13. William Drennan to Martha McTier, 14 December 1802 (*Drennan-McTier letters*, iii, 87).
14. N.A.I., Reb. Papers, 620/11/129/2.
15. Roger Wells, *Insurrection* (Gloucester 1986) 251.
16. Madden states that this dinner took place shortly after his return, but from the content it can be dated to early 1803 when Emmet had joined the conspiracy (Madden, *United Irishmen*, 330).
17. Ibid.
18. Emmet to Richard Curran [August 1803] (Madden, *United Irishmen*, 518).
19. See Chapter 9.
20. As Robert Emmet's final letter to Richard Curran from prison reveals.
21. Byrne, *Memoirs*, i, 347.
22. N.A.I., Reb. Papers, 620/14/194.
23. Ibid.
24. N.A.I., Reb. Papers, 620/14/195.
25. Madden, *United Irishmen*, 361.
26. *Trial of Thomas Keenan* (Dublin 1803) 6.
27. Madden, *United Irishmen*, 360.
28. Byrne, *Memoirs*, i, 334. Whether Miles Byrne's transcript of Emmet's speech can be trusted is debatable. He may have taken notes at the time, but even then it is unlikely that the conversation would have made such a deep impression that he could have recollected it word for word.
29. N.A.I., Reb. Papers, 620/13/178/48.
30. Byrne, *Memoirs*, i, 336–7.
31. Madden, *United Irishmen*, 360.
32. Testimony of Edward Wilson.
33. Byrne, *Memoirs*, i, 337.
34. Ibid. 338.
35. N.A.I., Reb. Papers, 620/14/194.
36. Byrne, *Memoirs*, i, 339.
37. N.A.I., Reb. Papers, 620/14/194.
38. Byrne, *Memoirs*, i, 340.
39. Ibid.
40. *Trial of John Macintosh* (Dublin 1803) 8.
41. Byrne, *Memoirs*, i, 341.
42. Madden, *United Irishmen*, 360.
43. MacDonagh, *Viceroy's post-bag*, 283.
44. Byrne, *Memoirs*, i, 342.
45. Testimony of John Fleming (quoted in Emmet, *Memoirs*, ii, 178).
46. Byrne, *Memoirs*, i, 343.
47. O'Donnell, *Aftermath*, 118.
48. Byrne, *Memoirs*, i, 344.
49. Byrne mentions 'a scientific work', but it was more than likely a book that contained notes of his own research, and Fulton's, taken in Paris.

50. Byrne, *Memoirs*, i, 345.
51. Madden, *United Irishmen*, 362.
52. Ibid. 355.
53. Byrne, *Memoirs*, i, 346.
54. Madden, *United Irishmen*, 356.
55. Ibid. 357.
56. Ibid. 359.
57. Hardwicke to Pelham, 7 August 1803 (P.R.O., HO 100/112, ff 158–62); the cypher had been captured by the government.
58. Testimony of Ross McCann, 11 August 1803 (N.A.I., Reb. Papers, 620/11/138/3).
59. Ibid.
60. Byrne, *Memoirs*, i, 347.
61. O'Donnell, *Aftermath*, 118.
62. A.N.P., F^7 6338, dos. 7123.
63. Byrne, *Memoirs*, i, 349.
64. Ibid. 350.
65. Ibid. 351.
66. Ibid. 352.
67. The best account of Thomas Russell's life is James Quinn's 'In pursuit of the millennium: the career of Thomas Russell, 1790–1803' (Ph.D. thesis, University College Dublin 1995) published by Irish Academic Press in 2002. The flattering description of his appearance is from Mary Ann McCracken (quoted in Quinn, 16).
68. Quinn, 'In pursuit of the millennium', 9.
69. Elliott, *Wolfe Tone*, 96.
70. Quinn, 'In pursuit of the millennium', 13.
71. Ibid. 22.
72. Ibid. 136–7.
73. Quoted in ibid. 157.
74. Evidence of James Farrell, 24 October 1803 (P.R.O., HO 100/114/123).
75. Byrne, *Memoirs*, i, 353.
76. Ibid. 355.
77. Madden, *United Irishmen*, 356.
78. Wickham to Pole-Carew, 28 August 1803 (P.R.O., HO 100/112, f. 381).
79. Wickham to Pole-Carew, 9 September 1803 (P.R.O., 100/113, f. 53).
80. *Trial of Robert Emmet*, 30.
81. N.A.I., Reb. Papers, 620/3/32/20.
82. Byrne, *Memoirs*, i, 353. This was around 7 May.
83. See the work of Ruán O'Donnell on Dwyer.
84. Report of Dwyer to Dublin Castle, 11 January 1804 (P.R.O.N.I., T.3030/12/1).
85. Ibid.
86. Quoted in O'Donnell, *Aftermath*, 121.
87. N.A.I., Reb. papers 620/67/81.
88. Madden, *United Irishmen*, 407, 417; P.R.O., HO 100/118.
89. N.L.I., MS. 9761, f. 1.
90. Madden, *United Irishmen*, 415.
91. Byrne, *Memoirs*, i, 356.
92. Ibid. 357.
93. Madden, *United Irishmen*, 364.

94. Ibid. 358.
95. Ibid. 370.
96. Quinn, 'In pursuit of the millennium', 172.
97. A.N.P., F^7 2231–2.
98. *Trial of Robert Emmet*, 97.
99. Emmet, *Memoirs*, i, 342.
100. See the trials of Robert Emmet and John Macintosh. I would like to thank Dr James Livesey for his help on the writings of Volney.
101. Wells, *Insurrection*, 251.
102. N.A.I., Reb. papers, 620/11/138/4.
103. N.A.I., Reb. papers, 620/11/1138/3.
104. Madden, *United Irishmen*, 378.
105. Ehrman, *Pitt*, iii, 604.
106. Ibid. 605.
107. Ibid. 606.
108. Wickham account (Geraldine Hume and Anthony Malcomson (eds) *Robert Emmet: the insurrection of 1803*, P.R.O.N.I., Education facsimiles 181–200, n.d. (hereafter cited as P.R.O.N.I. booklet on Emmet) 9).
109. For details of Wickham's career, see Harvey Mitchell, *The underground war against revolutionary France: William Wickham's missions, 1794–1800* (Oxford 1965); Elizabeth Sparrow, *Secret service in France: British agents in France, 1792–1815* (Woodbridge 1999).
110. Elizabeth Sparrow, 'The alien office, 1792–1806' in *Historical Journal*, 33, 2 (1990) 365.
111. Ibid., 367.
112. Wickham to Portland, 3 January 1801 (B.L., Add. MS. 33107, ff 1–2).
113. Wells, *Insurrection*, 31.
114. Wells, *Wretched faces* (Gloucester 1988) 285.
115. Quoted in Wells, *Insurrection*, 30.
116. Wickham to Grenville, 7 March 1801 (H.M.C., *Dropmore papers*, vi, 467).
117. Ibid. 466–7.
118. Sparrow, *Secret service*, 307.
119. 8 April 1803, N.A.I., Reb. Papers, 620/67/33.
120. N.A.I., Reb. Papers, 620/66/166.
121. Burrowes to Knox, 28 May 1803 (quoted in MacDonagh, *Viceroy's post-bag*, 450).
122. MacDonagh, *Viceroy's post-bag*, 450–1.
123. Quoted in MacDonagh, *Viceroy's post-bag*, 279.
124. Emmet's plan for the rebellion written 19 September 1803 (quoted fully in Madden, *United Irishmen*, 398–401).
125. Ibid. 400.
126. Ibid. 401.
127. Ibid. 402.
128. The letter is not dated, addressed or signed, but is in Emmet's handwriting (N.A.I., Reb. Papers, 620/12/155/6).
129. N.A.I., Reb. Papers, 620/12/155/8.
130. Byrne, *Memoirs*, i, 357.
131. Ibid. 355.
132. Ibid. 358.
133. Madden, *United Irishmen*, 357–8.
134. Byrne, *Memoirs*, i, 361.

135. Some reports stated that it was at 10 o'clock, but at the state trials witnesses said it occurred between 6 and 7.
136. *Trial of Macintosh*, 6.
137. Report of Marsden to Hardwicke, August 1803 (N.A.I., Reb. Papers, 620/11/131/1).
138. Madden, *United Irishmen*, 360, 363. Hope incorrectly called him Michael McDaniel, but see N.A.I., Reb. Papers, 620/14/194.
139. According to James Hope a man called Michael McDaniel made the rockets and was responsible for the explosion (Madden, *United Irishmen*, 360).
140. Ibid. 373.
141. Ibid.
142. Report of Marsden to Hardwicke, August 1803 (N.A.I., Reb. Papers, 620/11/131/1).
143. P.R.O.N.I. booklet on Emmet, 9.
144. Ibid. 11.
145. N.A.I., Reb. Papers, 620/14/194.
146. *Freeman's Journal*, 21 July 1803.
147. *Trial of Macintosh*, 6.
148. P.R.O.N.I. booklet on Emmet, 11.
149. *Dublin Evening Post*, 19 July 1803.
150. Report of Marsden to Hardwicke, August 1803 (N.A.I., Reb. Papers, 620/11/131/1).
151. Byrne, *Memoirs*, i, 362.
152. Robert Emmet's account of the rebellion (in P.R.O.N.I. booklet, 415).
153. MacDonagh, *Viceroy's post-bag*, 403.
154. Emmet, *Memoirs*, ii, 180.
155. Ibid. 181.
156. Examination of Stafford, 4 November 1803 (N.A.I., Reb. Papers, 620/11/138/45).
157. Byrne, *Memoirs*, i, 364.
158. Madden, *United Irishmen*, 365.
159. *An appeal to the public by James Tandy* (Dublin 1807) 139.
160. Ibid.
161. Madden, *United Irishmen*, 364–5.
162. N.A.I., Reb. Papers, 620/13/177/13.
163. Madden, *United Irishmen*, 365.
164. Ibid. 359.
165. Report given to Wickham, 17 August 1803 (P.R.O., H.O. 100/112, f. 299).
166. *Burke's Irish family records* (2 vols, London 1976) i, 419.
167. *Freeman's Journal*, 23 July 1803.
168. Emmet, *Memoirs*, ii, 176.
169. Madden, *United Irishmen*, 357.
170. Robert Emmet's account of the insurrection.
171. Emmet, *Memoirs*, ii, 182.
172. Ibid. 97.
173. Byrne, *Memoirs*, i, 376 (incorrectly paginated as 380).
174. Ibid. 390.
175. Ibid. 391.
176. Trial of Robert Emmet (quoted in Emmet, *Memoirs*, ii, 161).
177. Quoted in Robinson, 'Thomas Addis Emmet', 204.
178. Thomas Addis Emmet to Jeannette (Jane Erin) Emmet, 23 January 1820 (N.Y.H.S., Uncatalogued Thomas Addis Emmet papers).

179. Quoted in Emmet, *Memoirs*, ii, 161; N.L.I., MS. 4597.

Chapter 7 *Coup d'état* and bloody protest (pp 154–182)

1. P.R.O.N.I., T/2627/5/D/64.
2. P.R.O.N.I., T/3465/121.
3. Hardwicke to Yorke, 11 August 1803 (B.L., Add. MS. 35702, f. 317).
4. Wickham to Marsden, 13 July 1803 (P.R.O.N.I., T/2627/5/K/164).
5. Wickham to Addington, 9 August 1803 (P.R.O.N.I., T/2627/5/D/64).
6. Byrne, *Memoirs*, i, 368.
7. Marsden report (quoted in Emmet, *Memoirs*, ii, 99).
8. N.A.I., Reb. Papers, 620/12/155/3.
9. Hardwicke to Yorke, 11 August 1803 (B.L., Add. MS. 35702, f. 317).
10. MacDonagh, *Viceroy's post-bag*, 339.
11. Testimony of Patrick Farrell at the trial of Robert Emmet (quoted in Emmet, *Memoirs*, ii, 184).
12. Opening speech of Standish O'Grady at the trial of Robert Emmet (quoted in Emmet, *Memoirs*, ii, 161).
13. As Robert Emmet revealed at his trial; for transcript, see Chapter 10. These were questions which MacNally asked Patrick Farrell, but which he said 'could be considered as coming directly' from his client.
14. N.A.I., Reb. Papers, 620/11/130/44.
15. MacDonagh, *Viceroy's post-bag*, 442.
16. Most of these proclamations were destroyed by the government. A draft survives in the National Archives of Ireland Rebellion Papers (620/12/155/3) and a full text was preserved by the P.R.O.N.I. Conservation Section and is included in their booklet on the 1803 rebellion.
17. In the original draft this reads 'every man shall have his religion' (N.A.I., Reb. Papers, 620/12/155/3).
18. N.A.I., Reb. Papers, 620/12/155/3.
19. There is one on display in Kilmainham Jail.
20. Emmet, *Memoirs*, ii, 197.
21. N.A.I., Reb. Papers, 620/12/155/5.
22. Madden, *United Irishmen*, 349.
23. Wickham account, 1803 (B.L., Add. MS. 35740, f. 210).
24. Ibid. f. 211.
25. MacDonagh, *Viceroy's post-bag*, 285.
26. Marsden to Hardwicke, 23 July 1803 (B.L., Add. MS. 35740, f. 160).
27. Marsden to Hardwicke (N.A.I., Reb. Papers, 620/11/131/2).
28. Wickham report (B.L., Add. MS. 35740, f. 176).
29. Marsden to Hardwicke (N.A.I., Reb. Papers, 620/11/131/2).
30. P.R.O.N.I. booklet on Emmet, 13. Duggan is not named, but from the description and account it could only be him.
31. Hardwicke to Yorke, 28 August 1803 (B.L., Add. MS. 35703, f. 38).
32. Madden, *United Irishmen*, 388.
33. Hardwicke to Yorke, 23 August 1803 (B.L., Add. MS. 35703, f. 12).
34. B.L., Add. MS. 35740, f. 261; Wickham to Addington, 9 August 1803 (P.R.O.N.I., T/2627/5/D/64).
35. Ibid. f. 264.

36. P.R.O.N.I. booklet on Emmet, 16.
37. Emmet, *Memoirs*, ii, 183.
38. Madden, *United Irishmen*, 372.
39. N.A.I., Reb. Papers, 620/14/194. See also P.R.O., HO 100/118.
40. Emmet's account of the rebellion.
41. Wickham report (B.L., Add. MS. 35740, f. 212).
42. Testimony of Terence Colgan at the trial of Robert Emmet (quoted in Emmet, *Memoirs*, ii, 180).
43. Sarah Curran to Robert Emmet [August 1803] (P.R.O., HO 100/113, f. 78).
44. Quoted in Bernard Bass (ed.) *Stogdhill's handbook of leadership* (New York 1981) 9.
45. Madden, *United Irishmen*, 367–8.
46. Ibid. 368.
47. Wickham report (B.L., Add. MS. 35740, f. 211).
48. Marsden to Hardwicke (N.A.I., Reb. Papers, 620/11/131/2).
49. Allan Blackstock, *An Ascendancy army* (Dublin 1998) 192.
50. Ibid.
51. Madden, *United Irishmen*, 366; statement of Duggan.
52. Ibid. 366–7.
53. Account of Miles Byrne (quoted in Emmet, *Memoirs*, ii, 75).
54. MacDonagh, *Viceroy's post-bag*, 402–3.
55. *Trial of Felix Rourke* (Dublin 1803) 24.
56. N.A.I., Reb. Papers, 620/11/130/44.
57. Madden, *United Irishmen*, 349.
58. The account is Wilson's description from the trial (quoted in Emmet, *Memoirs* ii, 188–9).
59. P.R.O.N.I. booklet on Emmet, Education facsimile no. 185.
60. See *Trial of Felix Rourke*, 19.
61. P.R.O.N.I., D/207/5/69.
62. The account is compiled from various sources. Wilson testified at all the state trials and gave a number of descriptions of his adventures.
63. Taken from Emmet's conversation with MacNally on 19 September 1803 (MacDonagh, *Viceroy's post-bag*, 403). MacNally claimed that Emmet said he was the man who attacked Wilson, but as will be shown in Chapter 11, this was highly unlikely.
64. P.R.O.N.I., D/207/5/69.
65. N.A.I., Reb. Papers, 620/11/138/13.
66. As John Fleming revealed under cross-examination (*Trial of Robert Emmet*, 49).
67. Some accounts say that one rocket was fired, but Emmet insisted that they were not used in a subsequent conversation with Miles Byrne (Emmet, *Memoirs*, ii, 79).
68. Report of Wickham, 10 September 1803 (P.R.O., HO 100/113, f. 91).
69. Emmet, *Memoirs*, ii, 178.
70. Hardwicke to Fox, 23 July 1803 (B.L., Add. MS. 35740, f. 176).
71. Clarke to the attorney general, 12 March 1805 (N.A.I., Reb. Papers, 620/14/188/10).
72. Testimony of Richard Wilcocks (N.A.I., Reb. Papers, 620/11/129/11).
73. *Trial of Felix Rourke*, 61.
74. Madden, *United Irishmen*, 366. Duggan after his capture denied having fired on Clarke but all the witnesses recognised him.
75. *Trial of Felix Rourke*, 63.
76. Madden, *United Irishmen*, 350.

77. Quoted in Emmet, *Memoirs*, ii, 79.
78. Ibid.
79. *Trial of Owen Kirwan* (Dublin 1803) 8.
80. Report of Wickham (B.L., Add. MS. 35740, f. 212).
81. Statement of Duggan (quoted in Madden, *United Irishmen*, 366). A different but unreliable account by Miles Byrne is in Emmet, *Memoirs*, ii, 79.
82. MacDonagh, *Viceroy's post-bag*, 288.
83. B.L., Add. MS. 35740, f. 264; Redesdale to Perceval, 16 August 1803 (P.R.O.N.I., T/3030/7/7).
84. Hardwicke to Yorke, 23 August 1803 (B.L., Add. MS. 35703, f. 13).
85. Description of Richard Wornall, 30 August 1803 (N.A.I., Reb. Papers, 620/11/129/14). He described the man as being between thirty or forty years old, but there is little doubt that it was Emmet and not Stafford. For one thing, he was wearing more than one epaulette. John Fisher recognised Emmet saying, 'Come on my boys, we'll take the Castle', earlier in the evening on Francis Street (Madden, *United Irishmen*, 354).
86. Madden, *United Irishmen*, 403.
87. Description of Richard Wornall, 30 August 1803 (N.A.I., Reb. Papers, 620/11/129/14).
88. Description of Wickham (B.L., Add. MS. 35740, f. 210).
89. Ibid. f. 212.
90. Madden, *United Irishmen*, 350. Madden gives his name as Leech, but see N.A.I., Reb. Papers, 620/11/131/2.
91. Testimony of Thomas Moorehead (*Trial of Edward Kearney* (Dublin 1803) 61).
92. Madden, *United Irishmen*, 351.
93. This account is in B.L., Add. MS. 33119, f. 312.
94. MacDonagh, *Viceroy's post-bag*, 44 and pp 296–7.
95. *Trial of Felix Rourke*, 22.
96. *Trial of John Hayes* (Dublin 1803) 72.
97. *Trial of John Killen and John McCann* (Dublin 1803) 8.
98. *Trial of Felix Rourke*, 26.
99. Ibid. 36.
100. *Trial of John Hayes*, 68.
101. Wickham to Pole-Carew, 1 September 1803 (MacDonagh, *Viceroy's post-bag*, 370).
102. Hardwicke to Yorke, 23 July 1803 (P.R.O., HO 100/112, f. 131).
103. Trial of Kearney (quoted in Emmet, *Memoirs*, ii, 192).
104. *Trial of John Hayes*, 82.
105. Examination of John Cox (N.A.I., Reb. Papers, 620/11/129/9).
106. Marsden to Pelham, 23 July 1803 (P.R.O., HO 100/112, f. 127).
107. Hardwicke to Yorke, 24 September 1803 (B.L., Add. MS. 35703, f. 2 and ff 185–6).
108. Wickham to Addington, 9 August 1803 (P.R.O.N.I., T/2627/5/D/64).
109. Wickham to Addington, 12 August 1803 (P.R.O.N.I., T/2627/5/D/65).
110. Wickham to Addington, 9 August 1803 (P.R.O.N.I., T/2627/5/D/64).
111. Wickham to Addington, 29 January 1803 (P.R.O.N.I., T/2627/5/D/67).
112. Madden, *United Irishmen*, 408.
113. Pearse, *How does she stand*, 9.

Chapter 8 The pursuit of Robert Emmet (pp 183–200)
1. Information of John Doyle, 31 August 1803 (N.A.I., Reb. Papers, 620/11/129/16).
2. Emmet, *Memoirs*, ii, 193.
3. N.A.I., Reb. Papers, 620/11/129/20.
4. O'Donnell, *Aftermath*, 146.
5. Information of John Doyle, 31 August 1803 (N.A.I., Reb. Papers, 620/11/129/16).
6. Testimony of John Robinson at the trial of Robert Emmet (quoted in Emmet, *Memoirs*, ii, 194).
7. N.A.I., Reb. Papers, 620/11/129/18.
8. N.A.I., Reb. Papers, 620/11/129/19 and 20.
9. N.A.I., Reb. Papers, 620/11/129/19.
10. Madden, *United Irishmen*, 409.
11. d'Haussonville, *Robert Emmet*, 84–5.
12. William Downes to Lord Sheffield, 15 August 1803 (P.R.O.N.I., T/3465/137).
13. Quinn, 'In pursuit of the millennium', 174.
14. Ibid. 179.
15. McClelland to Wickham, 9 August 1803 (B.L., Add. MS. 35741, f. 196).
16. Quinn, 'In pursuit of the millennium', 205.
17. *Journal of the House of Commons*, 28 July 1803.
18. Yeats, 'The apostle of liberty', 319.
19. *Trial of John Mitchel with a correct report of the speech of Robert Holmes* (Dublin 1848) 21.
20. Ibid. 23.
21. Ibid. 26.
22. Ibid. 28.
23. John Mitchel, *The history of Ireland* (2 vols, London 1869) ii, 88.
24. Emmet, *Memoirs*, ii, 77.
25. Madden, *United Irishmen*, 431.
26. N.A.I., Reb. Papers, 620/11/130/7.
27. A.N.P., F[7] 6338, dos. 7123.
28. Ibid.
29. Hardwicke to Yorke, 29 July 1803 (B.L., Add. MS. 35702, f. 267).
30. Hardwicke to Yorke, 30 July 1803 (B.L., Add. MS. 35702, f. 272).
31. Wickham to Addington, 9 August 1803 (P.R.O.N.I., T/2627/5/D/64); Hardwicke to Yorke, 24 September 1803 (B.L., Add. MS. 35703, f. 186).
32. Wickham to Addington, 12 August 1803 (P.R.O.N.I., T/2627/5/D/65).
33. Hardwicke to Yorke, 11 August 1803 (B.L., Add. MS. 35702, f. 313).
34. Beckwith to Wickham, 17 August 1803 (B.L., Add. MS. 35702, f. 338).
35. Wickham to Pole-Carew, 9 October 1803 (B.L., Add. MS. 35742, f. 314).
36. Foster to Sheffield, July 1803 (P.R.O.N.I., T/3465/21).
37. Perceval to Redesdale, 14 August 1803 (P.R.O.N.I., T/3030/7/6).
38. Redesdale to Perceval, 29 August 1803 (P.R.O.N.I., T/3030/7/8).
39. Emmet, *Memoirs*, ii, 79.
40. Sarah Curran to Robert Emmet [August 1803] (P.R.O., HO 100/113, f. 81).
41. See P.R.O., HO 100/113, ff 77–82.
42. Sarah Curran to Robert Emmet [August 1803] (P.R.O., HO 100/113, f. 81).
43. Ibid. f. 82.
44. N.A.I., Reb. Papers, 620/11/138/4.
45. N.A.I., Reb. Papers, 620/11/130/59.

46. Sarah Curran to Robert Emmet [August 1803] (P.R.O., HO 100/113, f. 78).
47. Madden, *United Irishmen*, 409.
48. Ibid. 410.
49. Sarah Curran to Robert Emmet [August 1803] (P.R.O., HO 100/113, f. 78).
50. Madden, *United Irishmen*, 410.
51. The letter was read at his trial (*Trial of Robert Emmet*, 76–7). In it he referred to 'the intention of the undersigned', showing his confidence by attaching his own name.
52. *Trial of Robert Emmet*, 76–7.
53. Testimony of Joseph Palmer at the trial of Robert Emmet (quoted in Emmet, *Memoirs*, ii, 195).
54. Ibid. 196.
55. Ibid. 195.
56. Wickham to John King, 13 October 1803 (P.R.O., HO 100/114, f. 56).
57. Sarah Curran to Robert Emmet [August 1803] (P.R.O., HO 100/113, f. 78). This letter was listed as No. 1, with the other letter discovered on Emmet labelled No. 2. But from internal evidence it seems likely that the order should be reversed.
58. Emmet, *Memoirs*, ii, 166.
59. Trial of Robert Emmet (quoted in Emmet, *Memoirs*, ii, 166).
60. Emmet, *Memoirs*, ii, 198.
61. Madden, *United Irishmen*, 419–20.

Chapter 9 Captivity and cross-examination (pp 201–225)

1. 12 August 1804 (*Kilmainham Gaol registers*).
2. Wickham to Pole-Carew, 28 August 1803 (P.R.O., HO 100/112, f. 383).
3. Ibid. f. 384.
4. P.R.O., HO 100/113, f. 19.
5. Robert Emmet to Sarah Curran, 8 September 1803 (MacDonagh, *Viceroy's post-bag*, 358).
6. MacDonagh, *Viceroy's post-bag*, 356. MacDonagh believed the plan was hatched on 5 September, but from the details about the change of clothes it clearly took place before 30 August.
7. Ibid. 357.
8. P.R.O., HO 100/113, ff 15–20.
9. Robert Emmet to Sarah Curran, 8 September 1803 (MacDonagh, *Viceroy's post-bag*, 358).
10. MacDonagh, *Viceroy's post-bag*, 354.
11. N.A.I., Reb. Papers, 620/11/129/16.
12. MacDonagh, *Viceroy's post-bag*, 372.
13. Ibid.
14. Ibid. 373.
15. B.L., Add. MS. 35703, f. 89.
16. Madden, *United Irishmen*, 411.
17. This has been published by John Finegan as *Anne Devlin: patriot and heroine* (Dublin 1992). The account of Emmet's escape to the mountains contains many errors. According to the Cullen version Anne Devlin was tortured on 26 July, a couple of days after she returned from meeting Emmet in the Wicklow mountains. But she was not arrested until a few weeks later. Not only is this version chronologically impossible, but it also differs from the version Anne Devlin told Madden.

18. Finegan, *Anne Devlin*, 87.
19. Ibid. 88.
20. Madden, *United Irishmen*, 515–16.
21. Ibid. 515.
22. Emmet to Wickham, 3 September 1803 (P.R.O., HO 100/113, f. 25).
23. Ridgeway, *Trial of Robert Emmet*, 1.
24. Emmet, *Memoirs*, ii, 144.
25. Ibid. 139.
26. Ibid. 141.
27. Ibid. 140.
28. *Parliamentary Debates*, xxiii (1812) col. 1052.
29. N.A.I., Reb. Papers, 620/12/141/20.
30. Ibid.
31. St John Mason to Evan Nepean, 19 September 1804 (N.A.I., Reb. Papers, 620/12/170/6).
32. Robert Emmet to Sarah Curran, 8 September 1803 (P.R.O., HO 100/113, f. 73).
33. Wickham to Pole-Carew, 9 September 1803 (P.R.O., HO 100/113, f. 53).
34. P.R.O., HO 100/113, f. 127.
35. MacDonagh, *Viceroy's post-bag*, 361.
36. P.R.O., HO 100/118.
37. Quinn, 'In pursuit of the millennium', 192–3.
38. Ibid. 193.
39. Ibid. 388.
40. Curran to Emmet, 10 September 1803 (P.R.O., HO 100/113, f. 69).
41. P.R.O., HO 100/113, f. 125.
42. Ibid. f. 127.
43. Dowden, *Moore*, iii, 1318.
44. Ridgeway, *Trial of Robert Emmet*, 2.
45. Standish O'Grady to William Wickham, 18 September 1803 (P.R.O.N.I., T/2627/5/Y/18).
46. Robert Emmet to Richard Curran, 20 September 1803 (MacDonagh, *Viceroy's post-bag*, 400).
47. P.R.O., HO 100/113, ff 127–8.
48. Ibid.
49. Jonah Barrington, *Personal sketches*, 206.
50. See Chapter 1.
51. *Trial of Macintosh*, 32–3.
52. W. J. Fitzpatrick, *Secret service under Pitt* (Dublin 1892) 177.
53. Ibid. 209–10.
54. MacDonagh, *Viceroy's post-bag*, 391–3. Some have suggested that this letter was written on 19 September but from MacNally's account it was obviously written a week earlier.
55. See Chapter 6.

Chapter 10 The trial of Robert Emmet (pp 226–254)
1. Quoted in Landreth, *Pursuit*, 323.
2. Eveline Bertha Mitford, *Life of Lord Redesdale* (London 1939) 59.
3. Madden, *United Irishmen*, 466.
4. Hardwicke to Yorke, 20 September 1803 (B.L., Add. MS. 35742, f. 192).

5. Emmet, *Memoirs*, ii, 157.
6. *Trial of Robert Emmet*, 103.
7. Emmet, *Memoirs*, ii, 158.
8. Ibid. 159.
9. Ibid. 161.
10. Ibid. 164.
11. Ibid. 165.
12. Ibid. 166.
13. Ibid. 167.
14. Ibid. 168.
15. Ibid. 169.
16. Ibid. 170.
17. Ibid. 171.
18. Ibid. 172.
19. Ibid. 173.
20. Ibid. 174.
21. Dowden, *Moore*, iii, 1318.
22. Emmet, *Memoirs*, ii, 175.
23. *Trial of Robert Emmet*, 48.
24. Emmet, *Memoirs*, ii, 181.
25. Ibid. 182.
26. Ibid. 184.
27. Madden, *United Irishmen*, 442.
28. Emmet, *Memoirs*, ii, 193.
29. See Chapter 1 of this book and also Madden, *United Irishmen*, 440.
30. Emmet, *Memoirs*, ii, 194.
31. Ibid. 195.
32. Ibid. 196.
33. Ibid. 197.
34. Ibid. 198.
35. Ibid. 199.
36. Recounted by Burrowes to Thomas Moore (Dowden, *Moore*, iii, 1318).
37. Letter of R. Rainey, 19–20 September 1803 (N.L.I., MS. 4597).
38. Emmet, *Memoirs*, ii, 201.
39. Thomas Addis Emmet to Peter Burrowes, 19 November 1806 (R.I.A., MS. 23/K.53/51).
40. Dowden, *Moore*, iii, 1382.
41. Emmet, *Memoirs*, ii, 202.
42. Wickham to Pole-Carew, 19 September 1803 (P.R.O., HO 100/113, f. 167).
43. Emmet, *Memoirs*, ii, 204.
44. Ibid. 205.
45. Letter of R. Rainey, 19–20 September 1803 (N.L.I., MS. 4597).
46. Emmet, *Memoirs*, ii, 205.
47. Ibid.
48. Ibid. 206.
49. Ibid. 207.
50. Ibid. 208.
51. Ibid. 213.

52. See N.L.I., Joly pamphlets, 637 (in P.R.O.N.I. booklet on Emmet, Education facsimile no. 192). See also Anonymous, *The trial of Robert Emmet for high treason* (Dublin 1803).
53. T. B. Howell and T. J. Howell (eds) *State Trials* (London 1820) xxviii, 1171–7. For a brief analysis of the controversy, see Seamus Deane (ed.) *The Field Day anthology of Irish literature*, 3 vols (Derry 1991) i, 933–9.
54. Norman Vance, 'Text and tradition: Robert Emmet's speech from the dock' in *Studies* 71 (1982) 186.
55. *Trial of Robert Emmet*, 102.
56. Vance, 'Text and tradition', 188.
57. *Trial of Robert Emmet*, 103.
58. Wickham to Pole-Carew, 19 September 1803 (P.R.O., HO 100/113, f. 167).
59. See his letter to William Wickham, discussed in the next chapter.
60. The recollection of a future judge (quoted in Madden, *United Irishmen*, 457).
61. Madden, *United Irishmen*, 457.
62. Dowden, *Moore*, iii, 1383.
63. In the Ridgeway version this is 'corse', an archaic word for corpse.
64. *Trial of Robert Emmet*, 99.
65. Hardwicke to Yorke, 20 September 1803 (B.L., Add. MS. 35742, f. 192).
66. MacDonagh, *Viceroy's post-bag*, 396.

Chapter 11 The appointed time (pp 255–271)
1. Hardwicke to Yorke, 20 September 1803 (B.L., Add. MS. 35742, f. 193).
2. Ibid. f. 192.
3. N.A.I., Reb. Papers, 620/11/133.
4. P.R.O., HO 100/113, ff 203–5; this was discussed in Chapter 6.
5. Robert Emmet to Thomas Addis Emmet, 20 September 1803 (B.L., Add. MS. 35742, f. 197).
6. Robert Emmet to Richard Curran, 20 September 1803 (N.L.I., MS. 8079).
7. Hardwicke to Pelham, 20 September 1803 (B.L., Add. MS. 33112, f. 44); Wickham to Reginald Pole-Carew, 25 September 1803 (P.R.O., HO 100/113, f. 199).
8. See Peter Burrowes' cross-examination of John Fleming in Chapter 10.
9. See Wilson's testimony at the various state trials in Chapter 7.
10. MacDonagh, *Viceroy's post-bag*, 401; Madden, *United Irishmen*, 461.
11. Gustavus Hume to Pelham, 20 September 1803 (B.L., Add. MS. 33112, f. 44).
12. Ibid.
13. Dowden, *Moore*, iii, 1382; Madden, *United Irishmen*, 570.
14. Quoted in Timothy Webb, 'Coleridge and Robert Emmet: reading the text of Irish revolution' in *Irish Studies Review*, vol. 8, no. 3 (2000) 320.
15. Hardwicke to Yorke, 20 September 1803 (B.L., Add. MS. 35742, ff 192–3).
16. Ibid.
17. P.R.O.N.I., T/2627/5/Z/18.
18. P.R.O.N.I., T/2627/5/Z/13.
19. Robert Emmet to Wickham, 20 September 1803 (B.L., Add. MS. 35742, f. 196). The emphasis is Emmet's.
20. Gatrell, *The hanging tree*, 40.
21. P.R.O.N.I., T/2627/5/Z/18.
22. Hardwicke to Yorke, 20 September 1803 (B.L., Add. MS. 35742, f. 193).
23. Madden, *United Irishmen*, 467.

24. Napier (ed.) *Sir Charles Napier*, i, 31.
25. Government report, 10 September 1803 (B.L., Add. MS. 33112, f. 14); Gatrell, *The hanging tree*, 38.
26. Gatrell, *The hanging tree*, 39. Part of this description was from a contemporary account.
27. Ibid. 38–9.
28. Ibid. 38.
29. Ibid. 40.
30. Ibid. 45.
31. Ibid. 46.
32. Ibid. 39.
33. Ibid. 40.
34. Hume to Pelham, 20 September 1803 (B.L., Add. MS. 33112, f. 44).
35. Hardwicke to Yorke, 20 September 1803 (B.L., Add. MS. 35742, f. 193).
36. Wickham to Pole-Carew, 2 October 1803 (P.R.O., 100/114, f. 6).
37. Madden, *United Irishmen*, 467.
38. Ibid. 466.
39. Gatrell, *The hanging tree*, 61.
40. Ibid. 68–9.
41. John Rocco, 'Beckett and the politics of nothing' in *Modernity: critiques of visual culture*, vol. i (1999); Michel Foucault, *Discipline and punish* (London 1977).
42. N.L.I., MS. 4597.
43. To borrow a vivid phrase from Richard Ellmann, *Oscar Wilde*, 473.
44. Hume to Pelham, 20 September 1803 (B.L., Add. MS. 33112, f. 44).
45. See R. F. Foster's excellent Prothero lecture, 'Yeats at war' in *Transactions of the Royal Historical Society*, sixth series, xi (2001) 132.
46. Madden, *United Irishmen*, 472–3. This death mask is now in Kilmainham Jail museum.
47. Gatrell, *The hanging tree*, 87.
48. Madden, *United Irishmen*, 475.
49. W. B. Yeats, 'Emmet the apostle of Irish liberty', ii, 319. For details of Yeats's private views on the subject, see R. F. Foster, *W. B. Yeats: a life* (Oxford 1997) i, 312–14.
50. M. H. Fitzgerald (ed.) *Poems of Robert Southey* (Oxford 1909) 396.
51. Tom Paulin, 'English political writers on Ireland' in Michael Allen and Angela Wilcox (eds) *Critical approaches to Anglo-Irish literature* (Buckinghamshire 1989) 136.
52. Robert Southey to John King, 28 September 1803 (John Wood Warter (ed.) *Selections from the letters of Robert Southey* (London 1856) i, 236).
53. Quoted in Paulin, 'English political writers', 181, fn 7.
54. Coleridge to Sir George and Lady Beaumont, 1 October 1803, in Earl Leslie Griggs (ed.) *Collected letters of Samuel Taylor Coleridge* (Oxford 1956) ii, 1002.
55. Paulin, 'English political writers', 140.
56. T.C.D., MS. 873/700.
57. Micheál O hAodha, 'A list of plays about Robert Emmet' in *The Irish Book*, ii, no. 2 (1963) 53.
58. Ibid. 54.
59. Kevin Rockett, *The Irish filmography* (Dublin 1996) 271; Kevin Rockett *et al*, *Cinema and Ireland* (London 1987) 15.
60. Rockett *et al*, *Cinema and Ireland*, 9.
61. Wickham to Armstrong, 20 November 1835 (P.R.O.N.I., T/2627/5/Z/12).
62. Abbot to Wickham, 12 December 1803 (P.R.O.N.I., T/2627/5/F/30).

63. P.R.O.N.I., T/2627/5/Z/18. Wickham was reflecting on his resignation in 1835.
64. P.R.O.N.I., T/2627/5/Z/13. The emphasis is Wickham's.
65. Wickham to the earl of Leitrim, 10 June 1839 (N.L.I., MS. 36053, f. 15). I would like to express my sincerest thanks to Dr A. P. W. Malcomson for drawing my attention to this letter.
66. P.R.O.N.I., T/2627/5/Z/25.
67. P.R.O.N.I., T/2627/5/Z/25.
68. P.R.O.N.I., T/2627/5/Z/18.
69. Wickham to Armstrong, 20 November 1835 (P.R.O.N.I., T/2627/5/Z/12).
70. P.R.O.N.I., T/2627/5/Z/25.

Appendix A (pp 272–275)

1. George Lipscomb, *The history and antiquities of the county of Buckingham* (4 vols, London 1847) iii, 86; see also Burke's *Peerage, baronetage and knightage* (1912) 1837–8 for the Temple genealogy, and G.E.C., *Peerage*.
2. See Burke, *Peerage, baronetage and knightage* (1912) 1837–8.
3. T. W. Moody *et al* (eds) *A new history of Ireland* (Oxford 1984) ix, 495.
4. See also *Gentleman's Magazine* (1786) 1003, where the change is announced.
5. Temple Prime, *Some account of the Temple family* (New York 1899) 53.
6. Ibid.
7. For further information about him, see R. R. Johnson, *John Nelson: merchant adventurer* (Oxford 1991).
8. *ANB* (1999).
9. Ibid.
10. Buckingham to Lord Grenville, 8 December 1786 (H.M.C., *Dropmore papers*, i, 275).
11. John Alexander Temple, *The Temple memoirs* (London 1925) 83.

BIBLIOGRAPHY

~

Primary Sources

A. *Manuscript Sources*

National Library of Ireland (Dublin)
MS. 4597 Account of trial and execution.
MS. 8077 Burial of Robert Emmet
MS. 8079 Speech from dock
MS. 8325 Speech from dock
MS. 8326 Transcript of Sarah Curran letters
MS. 8327 Sarah Curran material
MS. 8905 Sarah Curran letters
MSS 9760-2, 8339 Luke Cullen papers
MS. 10650 Fly-leaves of a music book with drawings by Sarah Curran
MS. 10752 Pedigree of Emmet family
MS. 10425 Cuttings (1803–50)

Trinity College Dublin
MS. 1469 (S.3), 1472 Cullen papers
MS. 869 Sirr papers
MS. 873 Madden papers
MS. 1203 Visitation of Trinity College, April 1798
MSS 7255–6 Madden research materials on Emmet and Hope
MS. 3363 Thomas Prior's notes of the College visitation
MS. 3373 Thomas Prior's notes of the College visitation
MUN/V/5/4–5 Trinity College Dublin registers
MUN/V/27/3 Exam results for Trinity College Dublin, 1771–97
MUN/V/27/4 Exam results for Trinity College Dublin, 1797–1809
MUN/V/43/1 Entry records for Trinity College Dublin in 1790s
MUN/SOC/HIST 12–13 Records of the College Historical Society, 1796–1801
MUN/SOC/HIST 52–54 Membership lists of the College Historical Society

Royal Irish Academy (Dublin)
MS. 12 M 8 Papers relating to the Emmet rebellion
MS. 23 K 53/5 Burrowes' papers
MS. 12 G 14 Emmet family bible
Templehoff's *History of the seven years' war* (with Robert Emmet's own annotations)
MS. 12 L 22–34 Wilmot papers
MS. 12 M 18 Wilmot portfolio of papers

National Archives of Ireland (Dublin)
MS. 620 Rebellion papers (1798–1803)

Kilmainham Jail (Dublin)
Prison registers for 1803

Public Record Office of Northern Ireland (Belfast)
T.2626–7 Wickham papers
T.3030 Emmet transcripts
T.3048 Emmet transcripts
D.3030 Castlereagh papers
D.754/9 Map of Dublin, 1 June 1798

British Library (London)
MSS 35728–44 Hardwicke papers
MSS 35703 Hardwicke papers
MSS 35711–2 Hardwicke papers
MSS 35729–44 Hardwicke papers
MS. 34216 Trial of Robert Emmet
MS. 38103 Letter of Robert Emmet to his brother

Cambridge University Library
Add. MS. 6958 William Pitt correspondence (17 boxes)

New York Public Library
The Gilbert H. Montague collection of Robert Fulton manuscripts
The William Barclay Parsons 'Robert Fulton' collection

New York Historical Society
Uncatalogued folder of Thomas Addis Emmet papers
Robert Fulton papers
Robert R. Livingston papers

University of Notre Dame (Indiana)
Robert Emmet's copy of John Locke's *Two treatises of government* (Reel IND 98–6012)

Archives Nationales (Paris)
F^7 2231–2 Police générale. Étrangers de passage á Paris. An X–1814.
F^7 6338 Police générale. Affaires politiques. An V–1830.

Ministère des Affairs Étrangères, Quai d'Orsay (Paris)
Correspondance Politique. Angleterre. vols 594–602.
Mémoires et Documents. Angleterre. vol 19.

B. *Printed Sources*

I. Parliamentary Records

Journal of the House of Commons (1803)
Parliamentary Debates (1812)
Speeches at the bar and in the senate by the Rt Hon. William Conyngham, Lord Plunket, ed. J. C. Hoey, Dublin, 1873.
Speeches of the Rt Hon. Henry Grattan, ed. D. O. Madden, London, 1874.
Speeches of the Rt Hon. William Pitt, ed. W. S. Hataway, 4 vols, London, 1806.

II. Newspapers and Periodicals

Annual Register
Dublin Directory
Dublin Evening Post
Dublin University Calendar (1833)
Freeman's Journal
Gaelic American
Gentleman's Magazine
London Chronicle
The Dublin Magazine
The Nation
The Press, 1797–8
The Times
Walker's Hibernian Magazine

III. Diaries, Memoirs, Poetry and Correspondence

Castlereagh, *Memoirs and correspondence of Viscount Castlereagh*, ed. Marquis of Londonderry, 12 vols, London, 1848–53.
Coleridge, *Collected letters of Samuel Taylor Coleridge*, ed. Earl Leslie Griggs, vol ii, Oxford, 1956.
Cornwallis, *The correspondence of Charles, 1st Marquis Cornwallis*, ed. Charles Ross, 3 vols, London, 1859.
Drennan, *The Drennan-McTier Letters*, ed. Jean Agnew, 3 vols, Dublin, 1998–99.
Elliot, *Life and letters of Sir Gilbert Elliot, first earl of Minto*, ed. Countess of Minto, 2 vols, London, 1874.
George III, *The later correspondence of George III*, ed. Arthur Aspinall, vol iii, Cambridge, 1967.
Grattan, *Memoirs of the life and times of the Rt Hon. Henry Grattan*, ed. Henry Grattan Jr, 5 vols, London, 1839–44.
Grenville, *The manuscripts of J. B. Fortescue, esq., preserved at Dropmore*, 10 vols, H.M.C., London, 1892–1927.
McCracken, *The life and times of Mary Ann McCracken*, ed. Mary McNeill, Dublin, 1960.

Moore, *Memoirs, journals and correspondence of Thomas Moore*, ed. Lord John Russell, 8 vols, London, 1853–6.
—— *The journal of Thomas Moore*, ed. Wilfred S. Dowden, 4 vols, London, 1983–7.
Southey, *Poems of Robert Southey*, ed. M. H. Fitzgerald, Oxford, 1909.
—— *Selections from the letters of Robert Southey*, ed. John Wood Warter, 2 vols, London, 1856.
Tone, *The writings of Theobald Wolfe Tone, 1763–98*, eds T. W. Moody, R. B. McDowell and C. J. Woods, vol i, Oxford, 1998.
Wickham, *The correspondence of the Rt Hon. William Wickham*, ed. William Wickham Jr, 2 vols, London, 1870.
Yeats, *The collected letters of W. B. Yeats*, ed. John Kelly, vol iii, Oxford, 1994.

IV. Collections of Documents

Aspinall, A. & Smith, E. A. (eds) *English Historical Documents, 1783–1832*, London, 1959.
Curtis, Edmund & McDowell, R. B. (eds) *Irish Historical Documents, 1172–1922*, London, 1977.

V. Contemporary and Near Contemporary Works and Descriptions

Anonymous, *Memoirs of nine illustrious characters*, Dublin, 1799.
—— *Public characters*, Baltimore, 1803.
—— *A correct report of the trial of Robert Emmet, esquire, for high treason on Monday, 29 September 1803*, 3 parts, Dublin, 1803.
—— *An appeal to the public by James Tandy*, Dublin, 1807.
—— *Trial of John Mitchel with a correct report of the speech of Robert Holmes*, Dublin, 1848.
Barrington, Jonah, *The rise and fall of the Irish nation*, Dublin, 1853.
—— *Historic memoirs of Ireland*, 2 vols, London, 1833.
—— *Personal sketches of his own times*, 3 vols, London, 1827–32.
Brougham, Henry Lord, *Historical sketches of statesmen who flourished in the time of George III*, 6 vols, London, 1845.
Byrne, Miles, *Memoirs of Miles Byrne*, 3 vols, Paris, 1863.
Campan, Madame, *Memoirs of the private life of Marie Antoinette*, 2 vols, London, 1823.
Campbell, John Lord, *The lives of the lord chancellors*, 7 vols, London, 1847.
Cleveland, Duchess of, *The life and letters of Lady Hester Stanhope*, London, 1914.
Cloncurry, Valentine Lord, *Personal recollections of the life and times of Valentine Lord Cloncurry*, Dublin, 1849.
Code, H. B., *The insurrection of the 23rd of July 1803*, Dublin, 1803.
Emmet, Thomas Addis, *The Emmet family*, New York, 1898.
—— *Memoir of Thomas Addis and Robert Emmet*, 2 vols, New York, 1915.
Finegan, J. J. (ed.) *The Anne Devlin gaol journal, faithfully written down by Luke Cullen*, Cork, 1968.
Fulton, Robert, *Letters principally to the right honourable Lord Grenville on submarine navigation and attack*, London, 1806.
—— *Torpedo war and submarine explosions*, New York, 1810.
Howell, T. B. and Howell, T. J. (eds) *A complete collection of state trials*, 34 vols, London, 1811–26.
Le Faye, Deirdre (ed.) *Jane Austen's letters*, Oxford, 1995.
Lindsay, Colin (ed.) *Extracts from Colonel Templehoff's history of the seven years' war*, 2 vols, London, 1793.

MacDonagh, Michael (ed.) *The viceroy's post-bag*, London, 1904.
Madden, R. R., *The life and times of Robert Emmet*, Dublin, 1847.
—— *The life and times of Robert Emmet*, New York, n.d.
—— *The United Irishmen, their lives and times*, 3rd series, 3 vols, Dublin, 1846.
—— *The United Irishmen, their lives and times*, 2nd edition, series 1–4, in 4 vols, Dublin, 1858.
—— *The United Irishmen, their lives and times*, 4th series, 2nd edition, Dublin, 1860.
Maxwell, W. H., *History of the Irish rebellion in 1798, with memoirs of the union, and Emmet's insurrection in 1803*, London, 1845.
Mitchel, John, *The history of Ireland*, 2 vols, London, 1869.
Napier, William (ed.) *The life and opinions of General Sir Charles Napier*, 4 vols, London, 1857.
Ridgeway, William, *A report of the proceedings in cases of high treason at a court of oyer and terminer*, Dublin, 1803.
Sadleir, T. U. (ed.) *An Irish peer on the continent, 1801–03*, London, 1924.
Stanhope, Earl, *Notes of conversations with the duke of Wellington, 1831–51*, London, 1998.
Whyte, Samuel, *The art of speaking*, Dublin, 1763.
—— *The shamrock, or Hibernian cresses*, Dublin, 1772.
—— *The theatre: a didactic essay*, Dublin, 1790.
Wood, Walter (ed.) *The despatches of field-marshal, the duke of Wellington*, London, 1902.
Woods, C. J. (ed.) *Journals and memoirs of Thomas Russell*, Dublin, 1991.

Secondary Sources

Anonymous, *The life of Robert Emmet: Ireland's greatest patriot*, Nottingham, n.d.
—— 'Dr Emmet's Cork residence' in *Journal of the Cork Historical and Archaeological Society*, li (1946) 190–1.
Atkinson, Eleanor, *A loyal love*, Boston, 1912.
Ayling, Stanley, *The elder Pitt: earl of Chatham*, London, 1976.
—— *George the third*, London, 1972.
Barrell, John, *Imagining the king's death: figurative treason, fantasies of regicide, 1793-6*, Oxford, 2000.
Barry, M., *The mystery of Robert Emmet's grave: a fascinating story of deception, intrigue and misunderstanding*, Fermoy, 1991.
Bartlett, Thomas, *The fall and rise of the Irish nation: the catholic question, 1690–1830*, Dublin, 1992.
—— *Theobald Wolfe Tone*, Dundalk, 1997.
—— *Life of Theobald Wolfe Tone*, Dublin, 1998.
Bartlett, Thomas and Jeffrey, Keith (eds) *A military history of Ireland*, Cambridge, 1996.
Bass, Bernard (ed.) *Stogdhill's handbook of leadership*, New York, 1981.
Beckett, J. C., *The Anglo-Irish tradition*, London, 1976.
Blackstock, Allan, *An Ascendancy army, the Irish yeomanry, 1796–1834*, Dublin, 1998.
Bourke, F. S., *The rebellion of 1803: an essay in bibliography*, Dublin, 1933.
Brooke, John, *King George III*, London, 1972.
Budd, Declan and Hinds, Ross (eds) *The Hist and Edmund Burke's club*, Dublin, 1997.
Buttimer, Cornelius G., 'A Gaelic reaction to Robert Emmet's rebellion' in *Journal of the Cork Historical and Archaeological Society*, 97 (1992) 36–53.
Carroll, Denis, *The man from God knows where: Thomas Russell, 1767–1803* (Dublin 1995).
Chambers, Liam, *Rebellion in Kildare, 1790–1803*, Dublin, 1998.
Collins, John T., 'The Emmet family connections with Munster' in *Journal of the Cork Historical and Archaeological Society*, lviii (1953) 77–93.

Coughlan, Rupert J., *Napper Tandy*, Dublin, 1976.

Curtin, Nancy, *The United Irishmen*, Oxford, 1994.

Davis, David Brion and Mintz, Steven, *The boisterous sea of liberty*, New York, 1999.

Deane, Seamus (ed.) *The Field Day anthology of Irish literature*, 3 vols, Derry, 1991.

Derry, John, *William Pitt*, London, 1962.

—— *Charles James Fox*, Gateshead, 1972.

—— *Castlereagh*, London, 1976.

Dickinson, H. W., *Robert Fulton: engineer and artist*, London, 1913.

Dickson, Charles, *The life of Michael Dwyer*, Dublin, 1944.

Durey, Michael, 'Thomas Paine's apostles: radical émigrés and the triumph of Jeffersonian republicanism' in *William and Mary Quarterly*, 3rd series, 44, no. 4 (1987) 661–88.

—— *Transatlantic radicals*, Kansas, 1997.

Edwards, Ruth Dudley, *Patrick Pearse: the triumph of failure*, London, 1977.

Ehrman, John, *The younger Pitt*, 3 vols, London, 1969–96.

Elliott, Marianne, 'The "Despard conspiracy" reconsidered' in *Past and Present*, 75 (1977) 46–61.

—— *Partners in revolution: the United Irishmen and France*, New Haven, 1982.

—— *Wolfe Tone: prophet of Irish independence*, Yale, 1990.

Eyck, Erich, *Pitt versus Fox: father and son, 1735–1806*, London, 1950.

Fagan, Patrick, *A Georgian celebration: Irish poets in the eighteenth century*, Dublin, 1989.

Ferrar, Harold, 'Robert Emmet in Irish drama' in *Éire-Ireland*, vol. i, 2 (1966) 19–28.

Finegan, Fancis, 'Was John Keogh an informer?' in *Studies*, 39 (1950) 75–86.

Finegan, John, *Anne Devlin: patriot and heroine*, Dublin, 1992.

Fitzmaurice, Lord Edmond, *Life of William, earl of Shelburne*, 3 vols, London, 1875.

Fitzpatrick, W. J., *The life, times, and contemporaries of Lord Cloncurry*, Dublin, 1855.

—— *The sham squire*, Dublin, 1866.

—— *Secret service under Pitt*, Dublin, 1892.

Floud, Roderick, Wachter, Kenneth and Gregory, Annabel (eds) *Height, health and history: nutritional status in the United Kingdom, 1750–1980*, Cambridge, 1990.

Forrest, Denys, *Tiger of Mysore: the life and death of Tipu Sultan*, London, 1970.

Foster, R. F., *Modern Ireland, 1600–1972*, London, 1988.

—— *W. B. Yeats: a life*, vol i, Oxford, 1997.

—— *The Irish story*, London, 2001.

—— 'Yeats at war: poetic strategies and political reconstruction from the Easter rising to the Free State' in *Transactions of the Royal Historical Society*, 6th series, xi (2001) 125–45.

Foucault, Michel, *Discipline and punish*, London, 1977.

Furber, Holden, 'Fulton and Napoleon in 1800: new light on the submarine *Nautilus*' in *The American Historical Review*, 39, no. 3 (1934) 489–94.

Gatrell, V. A. C., *The hanging tree: execution and the English people*, Oxford, 1994.

Geoghegan, P. M., *The Irish Act of Union*, Dublin, 1998.

—— 'An act of power and corruption? The union debate' in *History Ireland*, viii, no. 2 (summer 2000) 22–6.

—— 'The Catholics and the union' in *Transactions of the Royal Historical Society*, 6th series, x (2000) 243–58.

—— *Lord Castlereagh*, Dundalk, 2002.

Gilbert, John (ed.) *Documents relating to Ireland 1795–1804*, Shannon, 1970.

Glover, J. W. (ed.) *Irish melodies*, Dublin, 1859.

Gray, John, 'Millennial vision . . . Thomas Russell re-assessed' in *The Linen Hall Review*, 6, no. 1 (1989) 5–9.

Guiney, Louise Imogen, *Robert Emmet: a survey of his rebellion and of his romance*, London, 1904.

Gwynn, Stephen, *Robert Emmet: a historical romance*, London, 1909.

Haines, Charles Glidden, *Memoir of Thomas Addis Emmet*, New York, 1829.

Hale, Leslie, *John Philpot Curran*, London, 1958.

Hall, F. G., *The Bank of Ireland, 1783–1946*, Dublin, 1949.

Hall, J. A., *A history of the Peninsular war: the biographical dictionary of British officers killed and wounded, 1808–14*, London, 1998.

Hammond, Joseph W., 'Behind the scenes of the Emmet insurrection' in *Dublin Historical Record*, vi, 4 (1944) 91–106.

—— 'The Rev Thomas Gamble and Robert Emmet' in *Dublin Historical Record*, xiv, 4 (1956) 98–101.

Harlow, Barbara, 'Speaking from the dock' in *Callaloo*, 16, no. 4 (1993) 874–90.

d'Haussonville, Louise Comtesse, *Robert Emmet*, Belfast, 1858.

Hawkins, Maureen S. G., 'Heroic kings and romantic rebels: the dramatic treatment of Brian Boru and Robert Emmet as Irish national heroes', Ph.D. thesis, University of Toronto, 1992.

Hay, Douglas *et al Albion's fatal tree: crime and society in eighteenth century England*, London, 1975.

Hayes, Richard, *Biographical dictionary of Irishmen in France*, Dublin, 1949.

Herold, J. Christopher, *Mistress to an age: a life of Madame de Staël*, London, 1959.

Hibbert, Christopher, *Wellington: a personal history*, London, 1997.

Hinde, Wendy, *George Canning*, London, 1973.

—— *Castlereagh*, London, 1981.

Hoffman R. J. S., *The marquis: a study of Lord Rockingham, 1730–82*, New York, 1973.

Hume, Geraldine and Malcomson, Anthony, *Robert Emmet: the insurrection of 1803*, P.R.O.N.I. Education facsimiles 181–200, n.d.

Hutcheon Jr, Wallace, *Robert Fulton: pioneer of undersea warfare*, Annapolis, 1981.

Hyde, H. M., *The rise of Castlereagh*, London, 1933.

—— *The strange death of Lord Castlereagh*, London, 1959.

Irving, Washington, *The sketch book*, New York, 1962.

Johnson, R. R., *John Nelson: merchant adventurer*, Oxford, 1991.

Johnston, E. M., *Great Britain and Ireland, 1760–1800*, Edinburgh, 1963.

Joyce, John, *General Thomas Cloney: a Wexford rebel of 1798*, Dublin, 1988.

Jupp, Peter, *Lord Grenville, 1759–1834*, Oxford, 1985.

Kavanaugh, A. C., *John FitzGibbon, earl of Clare*, Dublin, 1997.

Keegan, John, *Battle at sea: from man-of-war to submarine*, London, 1988.

Kerr, Donal (ed.) *Emmet's Casino and the Marists at Milltown*, Dublin, 1970.

Kiberd, Declan, *Inventing Ireland*, London, 1995.

Landreth, Helen, *The pursuit of Robert Emmet*, Dublin, 1949.

Lascelles, Edward, *The life of Charles James Fox*, New York, 1970.

Lecky, W. E. H., *Ireland in the eighteenth century*, 5 vols, London, 1898.

Lipscomb, George, *The history and antiquities of the county of Buckingham*, 4 vols, London, 1847.

Longford, Elizabeth, *Wellington: the years of the sword*, London, 1971.

MacDermott, Frank, *Theobald Wolfe Tone*, London, 1939.

—— 'Arthur O'Connor' in *Irish Historical Studies*, xv (1966–7) 48–69.

MacDonagh, Oliver, *Ireland: the union and its aftermath*, London, 1977.

—— *States of mind: two centuries of Anglo-Irish conflict, 1780–1980*, London, 1983.

Malcomson, A. P. W., *John Foster: the politics of the Anglo-Irish ascendancy*, Oxford, 1978.

McBride, Ian, *Scripture politics: Ulster Presbyterians and Irish radicalism in the late eighteenth century*, Oxford, 1998.

McCabe, A. M. E., 'The medical connections of Robert Emmet' in *Irish Journal of Medical Science*, 6th series, no. 448 (1963).

McCormack, John, 'Robert Emmet: portrait of an Irish patriot' in *British History Illustrated*, 6:3 (1979) 6–15.

McGuffie, T. H., 'Robert Emmet's insurrection' in *The Irish Sword*, i, 4 (1952–3) 322–3.

McMahon, Seán, *The minstrel boy: Thomas Moore and his melodies*, Cork, 2001.

MacMullen, H. T., *The voice of Sarah Curran*, Dublin, 1955.

McNally, V. J., *Reform, revolution and reaction: Archbishop John Thomas Troy and the catholic church in Ireland, 1787–1817*, Dublin, 1995.

McSkimmin, Samuel, 'Secret history of the Irish insurrection of 1803' in *Frazer's Magazine*, xiv (1936) 546–67.

Mitchel, John, *The history of Ireland*, 2 vols, London, 1969.

Mitchell, Harvey, *The underground war against revolutionary France*, Oxford, 1965.

Mitford, Eveline Bertha, *Life of Lord Redesdale*, London, 1939.

Moody, T. W. and Vaughan, W. E. (eds) *A new history of Ireland, 1691–1800*, Oxford, 1986.

Moore, G. M., 'The story of Sarah Curran' in *Journal of the Cork Historical and Archaeological Society*, xxvii (1919) 60–4.

Murphy, Helen, '"What stood in the post office/With Pearse and Connolly?": the case for Robert Emmet' in *Éire-Ireland*, xiv, no. 3 (1979) 141–3.

Ó Broin, Leon, *The unfortunate Mr Robert Emmet*, Dublin, 1958.

O'Donnell, Ruan, *Insurgent Wicklow 1798: the story as written by Luke Cullen, O.D.C.* (Bray 1998).

—— *Aftermath: post-rebellion insurgency in Wicklow, 1799–1803*, Dublin, 2000.

O hAodha, Micheál, 'A list of plays about Robert Emmet' in *The Irish Book*, ii, no. 2 (1963) 53–7.

Pakenham, Thomas, *The year of liberty*, London, 1969.

Parks, E. Taylor, 'Robert Fulton and submarine warfare' in *Military Affairs*, 25, no. 4 (1961–2) 177–82.

Paulin, Tom, 'English political writers on Ireland' in Allen, Michael and Wilcox, Angela (eds) *Critical approaches to Anglo-Irish literature*, Buckinghamshire, 1989.

—— *The day-star of liberty: William Hazlitt's radical style*, London, 1998.

Pearse, P. H., *How does she stand? Three addresses*, Dublin, 1915.

Platt, Hester, 'Anne Devlin: an outline of her story' in *The Catholic Bulletin*, vii (1917) 498–503.

Pocock, J. G. A., *The Machiavellian moment: Florentine political thought and the Atlantic republican tradition*, Princeton, 1975.

Post, R. M., 'Pathos in Robert Emmet's speech from the dock' in *Western Speech*, 30:1 (1966) 19–25.

Postgate, R. W., *Robert Emmet*, London, 1931.

Prime, Temple, *Some account of the Temple family*, New York, 1899.

Quaid, David A., *Robert Emmet: his birth-place and burial*, Dublin, 1902.

Quinn, James, 'In pursuit of the millennium: the career of Thomas Russell, 1790–1803', Ph.D. thesis, University College Dublin, 1995.

—— 'The United Irishmen and social reform' in *Irish Historical Studies*, 31 (1998) 188–201.

Reynolds, J. J., *Footprints of Emmet*, Dublin, 1903.

Robinson, Thomas P., 'The life of Thomas Addis Emmet', Ph.D. thesis, New York University, 1955.

Rocco, John, 'Beckett and the politics of nothing' in *Modernity: critiques of visual culture*, i (1999).

Rockett, Kevin, Gibbons, Luke and Hill, John, *Cinema and Ireland*, London, 1987.

Rockett, Kevin, *Still Irish: a century of the Irish in film*, Dublin, 1995.

—— *The Irish filmography: fiction films, 1896–1996*, Dublin, 1996.

Ryder, Sean, 'Young Ireland and the 1798 rebellion' in L. M. Geary, (ed.) *Rebellion and remembrance in modern Ireland* (Dublin 2001).

Sharpe, Mitchell R., 'Robert Emmet's rockets' in *The Irish Sword*, ix, no. 36 (1970) 161–5.

—— 'Robert Emmet and the development of the war rocket' in *Éire-Ireland*, 5:4 (1970) 3–8.

Sirr, Harry, *Sarah Curran's and Robert Emmet's letters*, Dublin, 1910.

Smith, Jim (ed.) *Revolution, counter-revolution and union*, Cambridge, 2000.

Sparrow, Elizabeth, 'The alien office, 1792–1806' in *The Historical Journal*, 33, 2 (1990) 361–84.

—— *Secret service in France: British agents in France, 1792–1815*, Woodbridge, 1999.

de Staël-Holstein, Baroness, *Ten years' exile*, Sussex, 1968.

Stanhope, Lord, *Life of the Right Honourable William Pitt*, 4 vols, London, 1861–2.

Stokes, William, *The life and labours in art and archaeology of George Petrie*, London, 1868.

Storey, Mark, *Robert Southey: a life*, Oxford, 1997.

Stubbs, John Williams, *The history of the University of Dublin*, Dublin, 1889.

Sutcliffe, Alice Crary, *Robert Fulton and the 'Clermont'*, New York, 1909.

Tappert, Tara Leigh, *The Emmets: a generation of gifted women*, New York, 1993.

Temple, John Alexander, *The Temple memoirs*, London, 1925.

Thomson, David Whittet, 'Robert Fulton and the French invasion of England' in *Military Affairs*, 18, no. 2 (1954) 57–63.

Thurston, Robert H., *Robert Fulton: his life and its results*, New York, 1891.

Tillyard, Stella, *Aristocrats*, London, 1995.

Tuite, T. P., 'The Emmet portrait of Robert Fulton' in *The Journal of the American Irish Historical Society*, xiii (1914) 261–77.

Vance, Norman, 'Text and tradition: Robert Emmet's speech from the dock' in *Studies*, 71 (1982) 185–91.

—— *Irish literature: a social history*, Oxford, 1990.

Webb, Timothy, 'Coleridge and Robert Emmet: reading the text of Irish revolution' in *Irish Studies Review*, 8, no. 3 (2000) 303–324.

Weber, Paul, *On the road to rebellion: the United Irishmen and Hamburg*, Dublin, 1997.

Wells, Roger, *Insurrection: the British experience, 1795–1803*, Gloucester, 1986.

—— *Wretched faces: famine in wartime England, 1793–1801*, Gloucester, 1988.

Wigington, Robin, *The firearms of Tipu Sultan, 1783–99*, Hatfield, 1992.

[Whitty, Michael James] *Robert Emmet*, Dublin, 1870.

Wood, C. J., 'The place of Thomas Russell in the United Irish movement' in Hugh Gough and David Dickson (eds) *Ireland and the French revolution*, Dublin, 1990.

Yeats, W. B., 'Emmet the apostle of Irish liberty' in John P. Frayne and Colton Johnson (eds) *Uncollected prose of W. B. Yeats*, 2 vols, vol. ii, London, 1975.

Ziegler, Philip, *Addington*, London, 1965.

Reviews •

Laprande, William Thomas, Review of Thomas Addis Emmet, *Memoir of Thomas Addis and Robert Emmet* in *The American Historical Review*, vol. 21 (1915) 147–8.

McDowell, R. B., Review of Helen Landreth, *The pursuit of Robert Emmet* in *Irish Historical Studies*, vol. vii (1951) 303–5.

Moore, D. F., Review of Leon Ó Broin, *The unfortunate Mr Robert Emmet* in *Dublin Historical Record*, vol. xv (1959) 64.

O'Hegarty, P. S., Review of Helen Landreth, *The pursuit of Robert Emmet* in *The Dublin Magazine* (July–September 1950) 40–5 (includes response by Landreth to the criticisms).

Palmer, Norman D., Review of Helen Landreth, *The pursuit of Robert Emmet* in *The Journal of Modern History*, vol. 21 (1949) 247–8.

Porritt, Edward, Review of Thomas Addis Emmet, *Memoir of Thomas Addis and Robert Emmet* in *Political Science Quarterly*, vol. 30 (1915) 699–700.

Dictionaries and Reference Works

American National Biography, 24 vols, New York, 1999.
Dictionary of American Biography, 22 vols, London, 1928–58.
Dictionary of National Biography, 22 vols, Rev. ed., London, 1908–9.
Burke's Irish family records, 2 vols, 5th ed., London, 1976.
Cokayne, George Edward, *The complete peerage*, 8 vols, London, 1887–98.
Keane, Edward *et al* (eds) *King's Inns admission papers*, Dublin, 1986.
Moody, T. W. *et al* (eds) *A new history of Ireland*, vol. ix, Oxford, 1984.
Namier, Lewis and Brooke, John (eds) *The Commons, 1754–90*, 3 vols, London, 1985.
Thorne, R. G. (ed.) *The Commons, 1790–1820*, 5 vols, London, 1986.

INDEX

~